Remedial Bark

MW01119543

DEVELOPMENT ECONOMICS RESEARCH TRENDS

DEVELOPMENT ECONOMICS RESEARCH TRENDS

GUSTAVO T. ROCHA
EDITOR

Nova Science Publishers, Inc.
New York

For permission to use material from this book please contact us:
Telephone 631-231-7269; Fax 631-231-8175
Web Site: http://www.novapublishers.com

NOTICE TO THE READER

LIBRARY OF CONGRESS CATALOGING-IN-PUBLICATION DATA
Development economics research trends / Gustavo T. Rocha (editor).
    p. cm.
  ISBN 978-1-60456-172-2 (hardcover)
  1. Development economics--Research. I. Rocha, Gustavo T.
HD77.D44   2008
338.9--dc22   2007052753

Published by Nova Science Publishers, Inc. ✦ New York

CONTENTS

PREFACE

Development economics is a branch of economics which largely deals with the economic aspects of the development process in developing countries with a focus on methods of promoting economic growth while also dealing "with the economic, social, political and institutional mechanisms, both public and private, necessary to bring about rapid…and large-scale improvemenents in levels of living for the peoples" living in developing countries. This new book presents the latest research in this growing field.

Chapter 1 – This study is a review of the recent trends in development economics research. The focus is on the development in the recent decades as a result of increased globalization of knowledge, technologies and economies. In particular I look at the development in a number of areas where similar trends are observed. The areas studied include globalization, in-sourcing and outsourcing activities, the increased flow of direct foreign investment and its heterogeneous regional distribution, increased public investment in information and communication technologies as infrastructure for development, the importance of commercialization and transfer of technologies, and increased income inequality and concentration of severe poverty in certain regions. In addition I briefly elaborate on the role of education, research, and training to enhance development capability and capacity, the increased strategic importance of natural resources and the increased interregional trade flow. I also investigate the development in the Federal Region of Kurdistan since its gained self-governance in 1991 as a case study by referring to the above developments.

Chapter 2 - This paper attempts to examine the socioeconomic structure of Nepal based on social accounting matrices (SAM) that utilizes some available macroeconomic information. Nepal is struggling to meet basic human needs such as an adequate supply of food, water, health care, shelter, and minimum education to majority of population. At least one fourth of households deprived of basic endowments like land, or skills (education). As the SAM coefficients reveal, investment in household sectors have high multipliers, and it is imperative to intervene at the household level to enrich human capital in order to alleviate poverty particularly at the socio-economically deprived households. Poverty alleviation through a trickle down approach has been a major planning theme since few decades, but it is yet to reach to the needy households. Planners and policy makers should realize that least developed country like Nepal does not need to follow an exact economic growth model adopted by the developed countries; they would rather focus on indigenous needs, skills, and resources and build a sustainable system.

Chapter 3 - In recent years, the dilemma of weak, failing and fragile states has been at the center of global development research and policy development on issues concerning the small, less developed and poor countries. Regarded as one of the greatest economic and social challenges to humankind, questions on the conception of state fragility within the framework of global development and security are complex and analytically difficult, but are too important to ignore, hence the need to place the fragile states in the spotlight as problematic development spaces on Earth. This Chapter reviews the notion of state fragility as another concept used to describe the world's poorest countries and raises the economic security question in the study of development economics and geography. Fragile states are invariably referred to as weak and potentially failing states, places that are highly vulnerable to internal and external shocks, and pressures, and areas at risk and at the brink of further decline- or even failure. Here, the less examined but vital aspect of economic security as a pragmatic, down-to-earth approach for protecting the fragile states and fragile peoples of the world is discussed to understand their functioning in many respects. It reviews the changing landscape of global development vis-à-vis state fragility in terms of emerging frameworks on country classification. Its central task is to provide an understanding of the directions and nature of growth and development of the poor developing states from the standpoint of state fragility and economic security. Broadly, the purpose is to explore and stimulate thought and discussion on the economics of development with respect to fragility and the relevance of economic security as the critical missing link in tackling poverty in developing economies.

Chapter 4 - This chapter reviews the theoretical foundations of the Prebisch Singer Hypothesis and the evolution of the associated empirical discussion. The review of the theory is set against the background of balance of payments constrained growth theory. The secular decline in the net barter terms of trade predicted by the Prebisch Singer Hypothesis implies a tightening of the balance of payments constraint. It has therefore historically been expected to counteract the convergence of per capita income levels between developed and developing economies and to limit the prospects of trade based development strategies.

The empirical validity of the Prebisch Singer Hypothesis has been assessed through the measurement of negative trends in the real price of primary commodities. At the onset, this discussion centred on the quality characteristics of the data series employed. At a later stage, the focus of the applied literature shifted towards the consideration of stationarity characteristics and the stability of the data series over time.

In so far as a consensus has been established in the empirical literature it tends to point towards a high degree of volatility as the main characteristic of commodity prices. Any trends that can be detected tend to be small by comparison. This conclusion has implications for the balance of payments constraint of commodity dependent developing countries. In addition to diversification out of the agri-sector, it now appears that in some cases diversification within the primary sector may be a useful intermediate step in the evolution of trade based development strategies.

From the post World War II era onwards, the growth performance of developing countries has attracted the attention of numerous economists, so much so that development economics emerged as a distinct field of enquiry during the 1950s. One of the hypotheses which emerged during this time and has been widely discussed until the present is the Prebisch Singer Hypothesis. This chapter will address the available evidence on this hypothesis and its predicted implications for developing economy growth. In doing so reference will be made to the original discussion as well as the more recent balance of payments constrained approach to modelling emerging market growth.

Chapter 5 - The competitiveness of a country is an issue of particular importance to the managers of both firms and national economies. In this study, the authors investigate the factors that influence two of the main drivers of competitiveness, namely account balance and GDP growth. They also suggest an alternative methodology, namely PROMETHEE II, for assessing the competitiveness of EU countries in terms of their economic performance, government efficiency, business efficiency, and infrastructure. The results indicate differences in the determinants of GDP growth and account balance. As for the ranking of the countries, Luxembourg, Ireland and UK are included in top five in most of the cases, while the Southeuropean countries are ranked in the last positions.

Chapter 6 - Pacific Island countries (PICs) are a very diverse group with varied culture, traditions and language. In addition, the diversity in the size of their economies presents special challenges for their development. Niue with a population of 1,700 is the smallest and Papua New Guinea with a population of about 5 million is the biggest and with the largest amount of natural resources. Almost all the PICs have in the last decade faced serious economic problems characterized by low levels of economic growth. Unemployment, poverty and other social problems have been increasing in all these countries. The economic performance of the PICs has generally been weak despite high investment ratios recorded). The weak performance is attributed to both lower external demand due to global economic slowdown, and domestic structural problems relating to the small size of the economies, remoteness from the main markets, narrow resources base, political instability, civil unrest, market rigidities, depletion of already limited resources and dominance of the public sector. Over the last six years up to 2004, the PICs have experienced variable but generally low growth rates. From a weighted average growth rate in GDP of 6 per cent in 1999, the GDP growth rate fell to -1 per cent in 2000 and -0.8 per cent in 2001. With a recorded GDP growth rate of 1 per cent in 2002, performance improved in 2003 and 2004 with average growth rates in GDP of 2.6 per cent and 2.7 per cent respectively. In the context of a predicted weaker international economic environment, it is expected that economic growth in the Pacific Region will decline to 2.3 per cent in 2005.

Chapter 7 - Korea began the process of industrialisation in the late 1960s, followed by Thailand and Indonesia in the mid-1970s. Despite variations in resource endowments, all three countries had recorded such impressive records of industrialization that international society loudly applauded their economic successes. In the late 1990s, however, the Asian economic crisis had entered a totally new phase, spawned by the July 1997 foreign currency crisis in Thailand. 'Currency crisis,' defined as a large drop in the value of currency in a short period of time, had spread to Southeast Asia, and eventually reached Korea. Among the victims, Thailand, Indonesia and South Korea (hereafter Korea) asked the International Monetary Fund (IMF) for rescue loans, but Malaysia, which also had been hard hit by the crisis, closed its foreign exchange market instead of requesting the IMF for help.

The three Greater East Asian countries had several characteristics in common when they encountered economic crisis: they relied on trade in the process of economic development; enjoyed high levels of liquidity; had recently introduced financial liberalization; and had opaque corporate and banking systems. After they accepted the IMF stabilization programs, they also faced such problems together as the precipitate decline of currency value, the instability of financial sectors, market contractions, decreases in investment, and increases in unemployment. As of early 2001, the economic crisis appears to be contained in Korea, but it still scratches Indonesia with its fingernails, and Thailand is located somewhere between the two.

Although there has been much research on the Asian economic crises, many issues still remain unclear and unanswered. Were the crises unavoidable? What was the decisive cause(s) of the foreign exchange crises? Were the IMF interventions adequate? What were the political and economic consequences of the crises? Should and can Asian countries reform their political and economic management styles? Which international political economy approach, for example, the interdependence school, neomercantilism, or structuralism, more adequately explains the crises?

This analysis examines the economic crises of Indonesia, Thailand and Korea in order to understand better their causes, processes and consequences. A comparative study has an advantage in that it clarifies the issue by contrasting similarities and differences. In the next section, the pre-crisis political and economic developments is compared. The following section explores the causes of the three countries' economic crises. Then, IMF programs and each country's reform efforts, and the consequences of the economic crises, are surveyed. The last section critically assesses the nature of the Asian economic crises based on the discussions of the previous parts, and presents theoretical and policy implications.

Chapter 8 - The objective of this chapter is to review the transmission mechanisms uniting equity market development and economic growth in developing countries. Overall, conclusions suggest that domestic development and international integration of equity markets have dissociated effects on economic welfare. At the domestic level, equity markets foster the mobilization and allocation of financial resources, and improve corporate governance subject to a satisfactory level of informational efficiency. However, equity market integration lowers the cost of capital, but increases financial vulnerability and exerts a non linear impact on capital flows. The authors summarize these ambiguous mechanisms in an 'equity market development triangle' and suggest a few directions for future research.

Chapter 9 - As the number of newly independent countries continues to rise, the need for the World Community to assist the leaders of these countries with finance, technology and other goods and services to enable them to implement development programs to eliminate poverty and to achieve better quality of life for their citizens continues to rise in the world. This kind of help is provided by individual governments and by multilateral agencies. But during the last few decades, the countries, which gained independence, and received substantial amount of international finance and other assistance, have not been able to improve the economic and social conditions of the population. The economic and social condition of the people living in newly independent former breakaway provinces of some sovereign states has become worse than when they were citizens of their former states, although the leaders of these newly independent states immediately sought and received international aid to help rebuild their countries. So where has all the aid money gone? One can then argue that the real reasons for the leaders of a community to seek independence from their former rulers is, perhaps to obtain aid money, a large part of which disappears into their pockets as their personal wealth and to capture the state powers to further their own benefit at the expense of the benefits of the country as a whole.

Many former Soviet Union Republics, Russia, Papua New Guinea, East Timor and many African states are examples of countries in which economic and social conditions of the people at large have significantly worsened after these countries became independent, although these countries received significant amounts of international aid.

If the aid money is misused in this way, then one may legitimately argue that it should be channeled to the newly independent countries only on the condition that this assistance is used productively.

Amongst the developing countries, the more developed ones have achieved progress in economic and human development. While the gap between the potential and actual achievements in growth and development outcomes in these countries is narrowing, the gap still persists and for some of these countries, it is quite large. In terms of economic theory, the authors can say, that the persistence of a gap between a country's potential output and actual output means that the country is currently at a point inside its production possibility frontier (PPP) and not on the PPP. The reasons are misallocation of resources resulting from inappropriate policy formulation and ineffective policy implementation. These in turn result from inefficient governance of the economy.

Governance failure which results from institutional failure can be blamed for hunger, starvation and poverty malnutrition which contribute to deaths of thousands of adults and children in several African countries, such as Sierra Leone, Rwanda and Ethiopia every year. International organizations (World Bank 2002 and donor governments), accordingly, in recent years have been insisting on the need to improve governance in the economic and political sphere as a pre-condition for the granting and eventual disbursement of any financial assistance to the developing countries. With these comments the authors now turn to the discussion of the crucial role that "governance" plays in growth and development outcomes of any country.

In: Development Economics Research Trends
Editor: Gustavo T. Rocha, pp. 1-63

ISBN 978-1-60456-172-2
© 2008 Nova Science Publishers, Inc

Chapter 1

REVIEW OF THE RECENT TRENDS IN DEVELOPMENT ECONOMICS RESEARCH: WITH EXPERIENCE FROM THE FEDERAL REGION OF KURDISTAN

Almas Heshmati [1]

University of Kurdistan Hawler and Hawler Institute
for Economic and Policy Research, 30 Metri Zaniary, Hawler,
Federal Region of Kurdistan, Iraq

ABSTRACT

This study is a review of the recent trends in development economics research. The focus is on the development in the recent decades as a result of increased globalization of knowledge, technologies and economies. In particular I look at the development in a number of areas where similar trends are observed. The areas studied include globalization, in-sourcing and outsourcing activities, the increased flow of direct foreign investment and its heterogeneous regional distribution, increased public investment in information and communication technologies as infrastructure for development, the importance of commercialization and transfer of technologies, and increased income inequality and concentration of severe poverty in certain regions. In addition I briefly elaborate on the role of education, research, and training to enhance development capability and capacity, the increased strategic importance of natural resources and the increased interregional trade flow. I also investigate the development in the Federal Region of Kurdistan since its gained self-governance in 1991 as a case study by referring to the above developments.

Keywords: *development economics, information and communication technology, foreign direct investment, globalization, outsourcing, technology, capability, energy, trade flows, inequality and poverty, technology transfer.*

---

1 E-mail: almas.heshmati@ukh.ac and heshmati@snu.ac.kr.

1. INTRODUCTION

In recent decades the global economy has gone through major changes and in particular within the area of development economics. An example of major changes in this area is the rapid development in several newly industrialized economies mainly in the South and East Asia region. Here I find systematic patterns in the development process where the development of East Asian economies has proceeded in a number of waves, starting from Japan as a leading country, followed by the first tier of new industrialized economies (South Korea, Taiwan, Singapore, Hong Kong), then by the second tier (Thailand, Malaysia, Philippines), and, finally, by the third tier (China and Indochina as well as India in selected areas). The common development patterns in many of the countries have been a gradual shift in their specialization from labor-intensive industries such as textiles and footwear toward higher-technology sectors like electrical machinery and telecommunications equipment.

The newly industrialized economies, in addition to being competitors of the old industrialized countries through their successful development and despite their different initial conditions, policies and efforts, serve as a model for development to the developing countries. There has been a flow of investment, technology and management to these countries in their search for low cost, disciplined and skilled labor, rich natural resources and market access. The textile, shipbuilding, steel, mining, and electronics industries are among those that have migrated from industrialized to newly industrialized and developing countries. The process has generated research suggesting a number of trends in development economics research. There are several areas of development, including information and telecommunications technology (ICT), globalization, economic growth, inequality, poverty and their linkages, direct foreign investment (FDI), in and outsourcing, spillover and transfer of technology and management, investment in education, training and research, increased strategic importance of natural resources, increased interregional trade and more.

This chapter is aimed at reviewing recent trends in economic development and development economics research which has a great impact on welfare. First, information and telecommunications technology is one area where both old and newly industrialized economies have contributed equally to the industries' development. Several countries see this new sector as a major contributor with significant infrastructure and as an enabler for countries to catch up with the development in the newly industrialized economies. A second area for consideration is the recent wave of globalization with great implications for free flow of labor, capital, goods, processes and services across borders. Third, economic growth is not equality distributed across industrial sectors, regions and the sub-groups of population. There is evidence that growth reduces poverty but it increases income inequality. This section investigates economic growth, inequality, poverty and their linkages. Fourth, direct foreign investment is analyzed with respect to changes in views about its effects and contributions to economics development. Fifth, in and outsourcing is a new phenomenon in making operation of businesses effective and less costly. Sixth, spillover and transfer of technology and management is a positive outcome of relocation of production, contracting out activities, direct investments and joint ventures. Seventh, development in the Federal Region of Kurdistan in light of the above developments shows potential and pitfalls in taking full advantages of the above factors in a small open economy with the minimum of restrictions and in the presence of many incentives to attract direct foreign investment and production activities.

The rest of the chapter is organized as follows. In Section 2 I provide an introduction to ICT, investment in ICT and its diffusion, and its effects on economic growth. Section 3 introduces the globalization and its recent waves. I present a composite measure of globalization and suggest improvements in the index to quantify globalization. I also present results and variations in the impacts of globalization on economic development. The issues of openness, economic growth, inequality, poverty, their relationships and redistribution policies together with recent empirical evidence are discussed in Section 4. Section 5 is on the global and regional development of FDI and the focus is in particular on the South-South perspective on investment and I discuss the success of the Chinese FDI policy and review empirical research. In Section 6 I review measurement and causal relationship among key determinants of outsourcing and their impacts on economic growth. The issues of capability, incentives and technology transfer with emphasis on university-industry relationships, knowledge diffusion and technology transfer, technology valuation in the new era of globalization are discussed in Section 7. The development in the Federal Region of Kurdistan as an illustration of the development in a small open economy subjected to intensive changes is investigated in Chapter 8. The final Section 9 concludes this chapter.

2. INFORMATION AND COMMUNICATIONS TECHNOLOGY

2.1. An Introduction to the ICT

Information and communications technology (ICT) combines all technologies and devices that are used in managing and processing information systems. In contrast to the manufacturing industries that create values directly, ICT, in the form of computers, software, the internet, multimedia, and management of information services, creates value indirectly through provision of related services. Thus, ICT includes data for business use, voice communication, images, multimedia and other types of technologies for development and exchange of information.[2] The continuously increasing processing power of hardware together with the rapid development of software and telecommunications infrastructure have enhanced the ability to store, retrieve, analyze and communicate data and information within and between suppliers, organizations, their partners and the consumers. In general, an increasing use of capital and labor as important elements in the production and growth of an economy lead to decreasing returns to scale. Therefore, even though the factors of production may increase, the growth of an economy over a certain level cannot be expected. However, information and associated technologies may produce increasing returns to scale and become an important factor for sustainable economic growth.

In the literature, ICT is considered as one of the three—and the most recent—major technological breakthroughs (Edquist and Henrekson, 2007). The other two being steam power and electricity. ICT includes some of the wider innovations and applications, and its commercialization and transfer to the most remote areas in this world has been more rapid than ever seen previously. In addition to communication between individuals, ICT enhances

---

2 For definitions of the ICT sector applied by the USA and OECD see Lee and Heshmati (2007).

the communication of value-added information to workers, managers, planners and consumers, and thus reduces uncertainty and time use in conducting many types of communication, research, business and production activities. It is an important technology and production factor which has the potential to contribute to more rapid economic growth and productivity gains in the years to come.

There has been great interest among researchers to investigate how some old and newly industrialized countries were able to take advantage of ICT to accelerate their rates of economic growth and productivity. The focus in these studies has been on examining the contribution of ICT investment on economic growth. In particular, in recent years, ICT is considered not only as a development infrastructure variable but also as an input in the production of goods and services and a factor that affects total factor productivity growth (Shiu and Heshmati, 2006). Studies on the contribution of ICT to economic growth find that the returns on IT investment are positive while the studies also find evidence of underinvestment towards telecommunications infrastructure in many transitional countries. The result suggests that improving investment conditions may ultimately improve the channel between aggregate investment and growth, economy-wide. (See also Zhu, 1996; Madden and Savage, 1998).

2.2. Investment in ICT and its Diffusion

Existing limited evidence suggest that return on IT and non-IT capital inputs differs by the country's level of development. Results from inter-country studies suggest that for the developed countries returns from IT investments to GDP are positive, while returns from non-IT capital investments are lower than their relative shares. The situation is reversed for the developing countries, where returns from non-IT capital investments are quite substantial, but those from IT capital are not significant. Dewan and Kraemer (2000) and Pohjola (2001) in studies of the impacts of IT investment on economic growth show that the relative contribution of IT to GDP growth in developing counties between 1980 and 1995 was less than 2 percent compared to more than 10 percent in the developed countries.

The limited evidence on the role of ICT investment indicates that ICT has been a very dynamic area of investment. The steep decline in ICT prices has encouraged investment in ICT and expansion of production and at the same time it has shifted investment opportunities making ICT an important driver of economic growth especially in newly industrialized economies. Thus, ICT as infrastructure and its role as an investment factor are of considerable interest in examining growth performance in many countries. The pace of investment in ICT differs widely by country and their level of development. The lowest levels of the share of investment in ICT are found in low income countries, while the highest is in the high income industrialized nations. Part of the difference is explained by the fact that, generally, products like telephones, e-mail, the Internet, computer hardware and software have distinct features like network effect, critical mass, and path dependency which affect their diffusion rate. A positive direct network effect means a positive utility gain for consumers when the number of users increases. Since the introduction of e-mail in 1969, internet traffic has doubled every year.

The diffusion of key ICT services such as the Internet, mobile phones, fixed phones and personal computers are shown in Figures 1.A to 1.D. The graphs show that countries with a high income show a high level of diffusion.

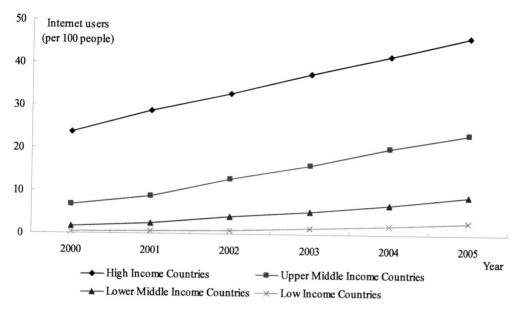

Figure 1.A. The diffusion of Internet to countries grouped by level of income.

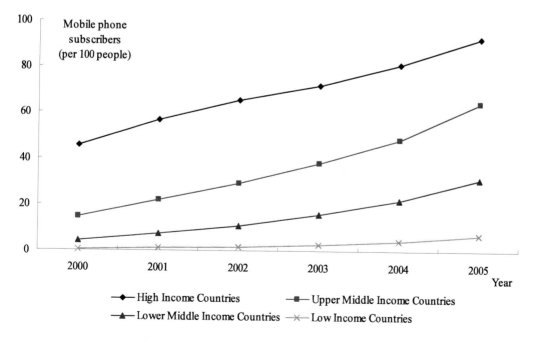

Figure 1.B. The diffusion of mobile phones to countries grouped by level of income.

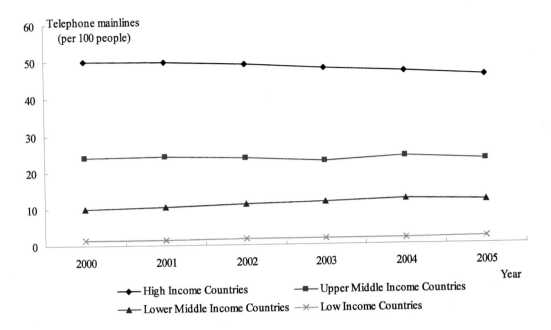

Figure 1.C. The diffusion of fixed telephones to countries grouped by level of income.

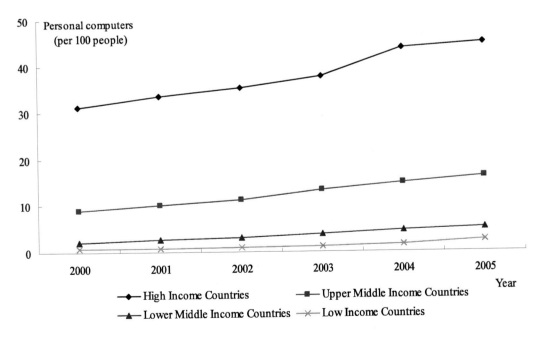

Figure 1.D. The diffusion of personal computers to countries grouped by level of income.

The gap between high-income and low-income countries, measured in the share of internet users, increases over time. The gap which is labelled as "digital divide" measures the socioeconomic difference associated with access to computers and the internet between communities. At the micro level, it refers to the gap between individuals, households and business with regard to their opportunities and abilities to access and to use ICT services. The gap is often due to differing literacy and technical skills and in the availability of digital content. At the international level the digital divide, the gap between the developed and the developing nations, is discussed concerning the access and the use of digital communication technologies. The developed countries are far better equipped than developing countries to take advantage of internet technology. The rapid rate of internet technology development and diffusion increases the quality-of-life differences between developed and developing countries. Given the productivity, connectivity and other positive effects associated with ICT, a widening international digital divide has become a serious issue of concern. See Table 1 on diffusion of different telecommunication technologies.

2.3. The Effects of ICT on Economic Growth

Jorgenson (2001) in his research pays much attention to how much IT affects the growth of an economy.

Table 1. Internet users, Phones and Computers connectivity per 100 people by the countries level of income

Year	2000	2001	2002	2003	2004	2005
A. Internet users:						
High Income	23.67	28.76	32.91	37.47	41.82	46.39
Upper Middle Income	6.66	8.75	12.83	16.09	20.14	23.39
Lower Middle Income Low	1.61	2.45	4.04	5.28	6.85	8.93
Income	0.38	0.58	0.92	1.51	2.10	2.80
B. Mobile phone subscribers:						
High Income	45.41	56.78	65.46	72.07	81.36	92.91
Upper Middle Income	14.54	21.97	29.01	38.10	48.34	64.28
Lower Middle Income	4.12	7.28	10.85	15.55	21.69	30.86
Low Income	0.57	1.03	1.70	2.76	4.30	6.91
C. Telephone mainlines:						
High Income	50.09	49.70	49.11	47.81	47.03	45.86
Upper Middle Income	23.86	24.17	23.78	22.65	24.04	23.03
Lower Middle Income	9.87	10.49	11.08	11.67	12.33	11.90
Low Income	1.37	1.49	1.61	1.74	1.74	1.95
D. Personal computers:						
High Income	31.10	33.53	35.13	37.71	43.81	44.84
Upper Middle Income	8.94	9.99	11.23	13.27	14.90	16.24
Lower Middle Income	2.18	2.61	3.00	3.82	4.57	5.06
Law income	0.70	0.79	1.00	1.22	1.48	2.56

Sources of data: OECD, UNCTAD, US Department of Commerce and World Bank .

The focus is on the role of IT in the transformation of our economic system by increasing productivity and provoking economic growth. At the firm level, there are four mechanisms or channels recognized through which IT investment affects the growth of an economy.

The first channel is that the IT industry itself grows dramatically, and the industrialized nations where the IT industry occupies a leading technology position may have more than one leading growth sector. For example, in China, with 8% annual growth rate during the last decade, the growth of IT sectors has been faster than the overall economic growth. Accordingly, the expansion of IT sectors affects the growth of the overall economy positively. As the second channel, IT can facilitate the catch-up process by enhancing the diffusion process of non-IT related technologies. According to Antonelli (1990), developing countries can take advantage of the opportunity by overcoming disequilibrium of information. The third relation between IT and economic growth is the market integration effect in which IT affects the integration and efficiency of markets. In the final mechanism, IT improves the management and decision making process of corporations. At the firm level the effects of IT include to gain market share, to raise overall productivity, to expand a firm's product range, to customize the services offered, to respond better to client demand and to reduce production and management inefficiency.

A successful implementation of ICT investment might have enabled economies to overcome barriers that have held them back in their participation in the rapidly developing global trade. The recent decades of rapid spread of the internet has opened up the possibility of accessing commercial and political information that was previously not possible. In particular, ICT has reduced the transaction costs of participating in sub-contracting and it is facilitating the operations of suppliers of IT services based in developing countries with low cost skilled labor. Thus, IT increases the total production through the decreasing cost of information and reduced transaction costs. Due to insufficient infrastructure and capability, the cost of information is higher and the market efficiency is lower in the less developing countries. Different complementary policies for IT investment must be introduced to enhance the conditions for development. Provision of necessary infrastructure, prohibition of monopoly power, elimination of entry barriers, efficient laws, regulations and education systems correspond to complementary policies for ICT investments. Edquist and Henrekson (2007) examined productivity growth following the major technological breakthroughs. In distinguishing between sectors producing and sectors using the new technology, they found the highest productivity growth rates and declining prices in the ICT-producing industries.

The US economy experienced an extraordinary performance in the late 1990s which is referred to as the 'new economy'. It was labeled as a new economy because it was unlike the mainstream economists' theoretical models; while inflation and unemployment were low at the same time, sustained growth and a booming stock market prevailed. Several factors are used to explain the emergence of the new economy phenomenon. Firstly, increased efficiency in firms' management by ICT adoption affected productivity growth at the firm level and connected productivity growth in each industry through spillover effects which led to increased aggregate productivity in the economy. Secondly, productivity gains led to a low inflation rate, a low interest rate and an increased investment rate. Thus, productivity growth and sustained economic growth are linked in an interconnected cycle of investment, productivity improvement and economic growth. Thirdly, the wide-ranging and rapid diffusion of IT and internet use made it possible for the new economy to evolve. The spread of IT and the internet, due to price reductions, affected the network effect and it induced sustained economic growth by utilizing increasing returns to scale in the economy.

In disagreement with the widespread view about productivity gain by ICT adoption, Robert Solow commented on the IT productivity paradox, which means that the productivity of the workforce due to office automation has not risen as IT has extended through industrial countries. The causes of the productivity paradox are found to be the following. Firstly, a portion of the benefit from a high rate of investment in ICT in service sectors like the financial sector, insurance, business and health services is not included in productivity statistics. Secondly, there may be a lag in productivity improvements, because computers did not show their productivity until things like software and the internet became prevalent. It takes a long time for a new technology to be accommodated by companies. Thirdly, previously much of the research with the purpose of identifying the effect of ICT at the company level was based on small samples. Thus, research in the early stage will not properly capture the contribution of ICT. In the search for explanations of the productivity paradox, Oliner and Sichel (2000) deny the significance of the IT-sector by arguing that IT accounted for no more than two percent of the capital stock in most countries.

2.4. Concluding Summary of the Impact of ICT on the Economy

The OECD (2004) report on the impact of ICT provides two important messages. First, ICT continues to have strong impacts on performance. Productivity growth in the US, the main example of ICT-led growth and productivity improvements, has continued to be strong. The release of increasingly powerful microprocessors is projected to continue and it will encourage ICT investment and support further productivity growth. Second, the diffusion and impacts of ICT differ markedly across OECD economies. It is expected that the largest economic benefits of ICT will be observed in countries with high levels of ICT diffusion. However, having the equipment or network is not sufficient to derive the full economic benefits. Other factors, such as the regulatory environment, skills, ability to change organizational set-ups as well as the strength of innovations in ICT applications, affect the ability of firms to seize the benefits of ICT technology. Consequently, countries with equal ICT diffusion will have heterogeneous impacts on their economic growth and performance.

IT has a positive although small contribution to economic growth, but its impact is positively related to the level of development. Studies of the relationships between IT and economic performance suggest that the impacts of IT diffusion can differ even among developed countries with a similar level of development. The limited existing empirical evidence shows that developing counties which did not adopt complementary policies have gained less effect from IT investment. In general, for the developing countries, it is rather difficult to catch any systematic evidence about such relationships. While the evidence suggests that IT contributes to the growth of developed countries, this relationship is rather weak in the case of developing countries. In order to link IT investment to economic growth and to establish causal relationship between the two a longer time period is required. In particular, for IT to be effective, it should be spread such that it reaches the critical point. For developing countries to obtain high returns from IT investment, active complementary policies must be employed. These polices are to fulfil conditions for economic development including building up the basic infrastructure, competitive telecommunications market,

market opening, introduction of effective laws, regulations, law enforcement and the educational system.

3. GLOBALIZATION

3.1. An Introduction to Globalization

Globalization is defined by economists as the free movement of goods, services, labour and capital across borders. However, the free movement is often restricted for various political and economic reasons both over time and across national borders. Globalization is a process and it is viewed as a means of integration of markets, economies and technologies in a way that is enabling individuals and corporations to reach around the world faster, deeper and more economically than ever before. Despite its advantages, some groups view globalization as an ideological project of economic liberalization which subjects states and individuals to more intense market forces. As a result, the anti-globalization movement has been growing both in size and in their opposition. Globalization causes rapid changes in trade relations, financial flows and labor mobility. It has brought the developed economies closer together. However, there is a large heterogeneity in the degree of the process of globalization over time and across countries and regions. This heterogeneity causes or is a basis for disparity in development among countries. See Heshmati (2006b).

The process of globalization during the period 1870-1913 is classified as the first wave of globalization: the years 1913-50 are called the de-globalization period; the period 1950-73 is called the golden age of globalization; and the period after 1973 is called the second wave of globalization (see O'Rourke and Williamson, 2000; O'Rourke, 2001; Maddison, 2001; and Williamson, 2002). In recent years, research on the link between globalization and world inequality and poverty has been intensive (Cornia and Court, 2001; Lindert and Williamson, 2001; Talbot, 2002; Babones, 2002; Beer and Boswell, 2002; Bornschier, 2002; Bergesen and Bata, 2002; and Heshmati, 2006b). Globalization has other dimensions and can be looked at from different perspectives. For instance, James (2002) analyses the causes of globalization in terms of transaction costs. Bhagwati (2000) focuses on trade and FDI and suggests appropriate governance to manage globalization. Milanovic (2002) finds that the effect of openness on income distribution depends on a country's initial income level. Seshanna and Decornez (2003) focus on the inequality and polarization of the world economy. Mahler (2001) finds little evidence of a systematic relationship between the main modes of economic globalization and the distribution of household income in developed countries.

3.2. The Recent Wave of Globalization

The literature on various aspects of the recent wave of globalization is developing. Several special issues of journals have been published. Editorial introductions to these special issues are provided by Woods (1998), Manning (1999), Bata and Bergesen (2002a, 2002b) and Bevan and Fosu (2003). In addition, a number of books on the issue have been published. For instance, Nissanke and Thorbecke (2006) present a collection of studies evaluating the impact of globalization on the world's poor. Dollar and Collier (2001) and the World Bank (2002) explore the relationships between globalization, growth and poverty; James (2002) analyses technology, globalization and poverty; Aghion and Williamson (1998) examine the relationships between globalization, growth and inequality; and Khan and Riskin (2001) study the development in China and focus on the effects of history and policies. Tausch and Herrmann (2002) analyse globalization and European integration. Agénor (2003) examines the extent to which globalization affects the poor in developing countries. Collier and Dollar (2001) estimate the decline in poverty in developing countries. Collier and Dollar (2002) find that the level of poverty and the quality of policies do matter. Yusuf (2003) lists a number of factors that are relevant as a source of growth to both poor and rich countries. Mussa (2003) gives an overview of the challenges faced by the international community because of globalization. Heshmati and Tausch (2006) discuss the EU's Lisbon development strategy, globalization and the structures of global inequality.

Despite the great importance placed on the globalization process, its sources and consequences still remain poorly understood. Thus the construction of an index of globalization is an important tool to enable quantification of its sources and impacts. Kearney (2002, 2003) computed a simple composite globalization index. The index is composed of economic, personal contact, technology and political components. Using a smaller set of countries, Lockwood (2004) finds the ranking of countries to be sensitive to the way the indicators of an index are measured, normalized and weighted. There are two alternative approaches to the Kearney index for computing an index of globalization: using principal component analysis (Heshmati, 2006b) or factor analysis (Andersen and Herbertsson, 2003). Agénor (2003) used trade and financial openness to compute a simple economic globalization index. Recently Lockwood and Redoano (2005) presented an index of globalization that measures the economic, social and political dimensions. Heshmati (2006b) investigates the usefulness of the Kearney database in the development of a multidimensional index of globalization. The index has a number of features. First, it is comparable to the one introduced by Kearney. Second, an alternative but less restrictive and decomposable index is obtained using principal component analysis. Third, countries are compared by their integration in the world economy. Fourth, the indices are used to study the development over time. Finally, Heshmati provides guidelines for the creation of a globalization database and the computation of a modified index that incorporates more relevant determinant factors.

3.3. A Composite Index of Globalization

Kearney (2002, 2003) is the first to attempt to construct a database and to compute a composite globalization index. The index is a simple combination of several forces driving the worldwide integration of ideas, people, technology and economies. It is composed of four major components: economic integration, personal contact, internet technology, and political engagement, each being generated from a number of determinants. The data contains information from 62 countries—each observed during the years 1995-2000. The total number of variables is 13. Heshmati (2006b) used the same data to compute the following composite indices of globalization:

$$GINDEX_{it} = \sum_{j=1}^{J} \omega_j \left(\sum_{m=1}^{M} \omega_m \left(\frac{X_{jmit} - X_{jmt}^{\min}}{X_{jmt}^{\max} - X_{jmt}^{\min}} \right) \right) \tag{1}$$

where i and t indicate country and time periods; m and j are within and between major component variables; ω_m are the weights attached to each contributing X-variable within a component; ω_j are weights attached to each of the four components; and *min* and *max* are minimum and maximum values of respective variables across countries in a given year. The index quantifies economic integration by combining data on trade, foreign direct investment, portfolio capital flows, and income payments and receipts. It gauges technological connection by accounting for Internet users, Internet hosts, and a number of secure servers. The index assesses political engagement by using the number of international organizations and UN Security Council missions in which each country participates and the number of foreign embassies that each country hosts. Finally, personal contact is computed by looking at international travel and tourism, international telephone traffic, and cross-border money transfers.

The Kearney index is a non-parametric index. In calculating the index, the component's weights were chosen on an ad hoc basis. In Heshmati (2006b) this index is considered as a benchmark index where each of the 13 determinants of the index are given equal weights. In an alternative case, a number of variables are given double weights. In the parametric approach the principal component (PC) is used for examining relationships among the variables. The two globalization indices that were computed, Kearney and PC Analysis, indicate which countries have become most globalised, and they quantify the state of inequality in globalization among countries. They show how globalization has developed for different countries and regions over time. A breakdown of the index into four major components provides possibilities to identify sources of globalization. This information can be associated with economic policy measures to bring about desirable changes in relations. The indices can also be used to study the causal relationship between different dimensions of globalization, inequality, poverty, growth, openness and wages.

There is a growing literature on the link between globalization and a number of indicators such as income inequality, poverty and growth. However, with a few exceptions like Mahler (2001), Agénor (2003) and Heshmati (2006a) who looked at the relationship between inequality, poverty and globalization, the lack of a properly defined globalization index has not allowed statistical estimation and testing of the relationship. The globalization index is so far defined as the unweighted and weighted Kearney-based indices and the PC index. These indices serve as a major first step forward to measure a composite index of globalization. There exist similar indices introduced by Andersen and Herbertsson (2003), Dreher (2005) and Lockwood and Redoano (2005). Andersen and Herbertsson use factor analysis to measure a globalization index based on trade for OECD countries. The index is based on nine indicators related to exchange, FDI, trade and capital flows. The Dreher and the Lockwood and Redoano indices cover economic, social and political integration. Dreher's results suggest that globalization promotes growth. Lockwood and Redoano obtained results that suggest the ranking of the countries is sensitive to the way the indicators are measured, normalized, and weighted. The composite index in Heshmati (2006a) is based on a large number of indicators and it conducted sensitivity analysis.

3.4. Improvements in the Measurement of Globalization

Despite progress made in construction of a simple but composite globalization index, several essential improvements are still necessary and have been suggested by Heshmati (2006a). It is desired that the index takes an axiomatic approach that sets out its desirable properties. Other improvements should involve identification of the key dimensions of globalization. In its current form it is just a partial index, but a better index should fully quantify globalization. In addition to the four components listed above it should incorporate several other relevant components. These additional components could include some measure of cost-benefit analysis of integration, separation of micro and macro aspects of globalization effects, its impacts on standards of living, the environment, wage inequality, skill biased technological change, foreign trade volume and its direction, democracy and conflict, financial markets, access to information and flows of information, the direction of movement of skilled labor, female labor participation, issues of child labour, business concentration, power of multinational corporations, and finally a shift in power and cultural uniformity.

Investment in technology along with education, management and planning capacity are strong determinants of capability and participation in the globalization process. In the Kearney's index there is a complete reliance on Internet technology. It does not reflect technology in a broad meaning. Technology is an important component and a complement to economic integration. Non-internet technology factors such as the role of inward foreign investment, fees on foreign-owned patents, numbers of engineers and scientists, investment in Rand D, innovations, patents registered, technological capability and spillover effects should be accounted for in the measurement of the technology component. Among other relevant factors are the capital intensity per worker, population growth and skill requirements. The latter makes the efficiency of the educational system very important to development. A pooling of the data and application of regression analysis require the grouping of countries by globalization levels. Industrialized countries dominate the existing sample. The over-weighting of the industrialized countries may result in biased inferences about the development of globalization. One should perform various sensitivity analyses of the composite index. These are important issues in the understanding of how globalization functions and also serve as a guide to policy formulation and evaluation.

The identification of major determinants of globalization and how these affect the ranking of countries are key issues forming the basis on which policy options can be provided. Since rich countries benefit most from globalization, developing countries need advantageous and non-protectionist policies to be able to compete effectively in the international markets. Analysis will help in identifying ways for a fair treatment of products, services and people that enable poor countries to benefit from globalization to a greater extent than they do currently. To reduce the negative effects of inequality and on the poor from increased openness and globalization, these ways need to be accompanied by effective redistributive policies and an improvement in social protection in developing countries. The World Bank and the UN should create a comprehensive database. It could serve as a source for researchers conducting empirical research on globalization and its relation with other macro variables. The composite globalization index based on such a database would differ from the one above by incorporating more components like financial markets, institutions, the environment, democracy, conflict, the labor market, public policy and cultural differences and would be modeled more flexibly.

3.5. Variations in the Impacts of Globalization

Variations in the globalization indices and their components presented in Heshmati (2006a) can be reported in the form of differences among counties and changes over time (see Figure 2). The information is used in an analysis of country heterogeneity in globalization and its development over time. The results, based on an index with same weight given to each indicator, showed that Iran, Taiwan, Peru, Ukraine, Colombia and Uganda are ranked as the least globalized countries, compared with Ireland, Singapore, Switzerland, Sweden and Canada, ranked as the most globalized countries. The low rank is due to political and personal factors with limited possibilities that can be affected by the country , while the high ranked countries share similar patterns in the distributions of the various components. Several exceptions are found where some countries enjoy a high or low rank in a certain factor which affects their position such as low political factor in the case of Singapore and Taiwan and a high political factor in the case of Russia and France. The rank of countries by degree of globalization and their transition in position over time differ somewhat depending on the method of measurement or the weighting system applied.

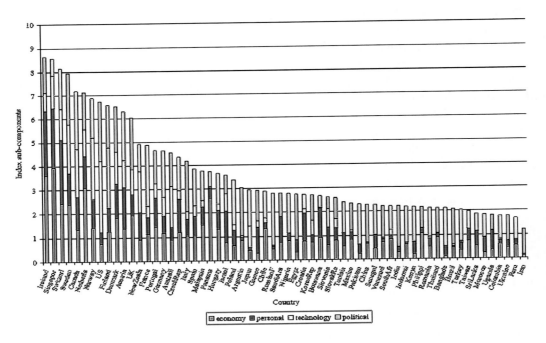

Figure 2. Weighted globalization index and its decomposition by sub-components, 1995-2000.

The mean globalization index by regions shows that the South Asian region is the least globalized region. The position is very much determined by the low level of the technology factor. The regions of East Europe, Middle East and North Africa, and Latin America, are ranked as at a medium level of globalization, but they differ by individual index components. For instance, Latin America is advantageous in economic integration, while the Middle East, North Africa and sub-Saharan Africa enjoy better personal contacts. The East Asian region shows relatively higher technology diffusion. The East European region is showing progress in all four components, but the countries have failed to benefit from the relocation of West European plants or from increased production that could be a result of their low wages despite their relatively highly educated labor force. As expected, the West European and North American regions take the positions of the highest globalized economic and geographic regions. The technology and political components are higher for North America, while Western Europe enjoys a higher economic integration and personal contacts. The Southeast Asian countries differ by the degree of globalization. The index for Singapore is four times that of Thailand. A similar large dispersion is found among countries in the Western European region, where Ireland's score is 10 times higher than that of Greece.

Ideally, the mean overall index and its components for each year should be weighted by the countries' share of aggregate GDP or population of the world to provide a more accurate picture of the temporal changes in the globalization process. Despite the weighting limitation, the study provides a partial picture of the development and distribution of the globalization process. In terms of total GDP produced, size of population and total trade, the countries included provide a satisfactory coverage of globalization. Major economies and highly populated countries are included in the data. The time pattern of the index is largely influenced by economic integration. The economic integration component has increased during 1995 to 1997 but it declined in 1998 and remained constant until 2000. The economic integration consists of variables that are largely defined by trade and capital flows. The decline is a consequence of the East Asian financial crisis of 1997/98 and crisis in the emerging Russian and Brazilian markets in 1998. These crises resulted in a major decline in the capital flows to the emerging markets and they caused high volatility in the East Asian financial markets.

3.6. Concluding Summary of Globalization and its Development and Impacts

There are a few studies that attempt to quantify the level and development of globalization with the purpose of ranking countries. The indices are in general composed of four main components: economic integration, personal contact, internet technology diffusion, and political engagements, each developing differently over time. Some of the indices are nonparametric while others parametric. In the former, weights are assigned on an ad hoc basis to each indicator, while in the latter they are estimated. The results in Heshmati (2006b) show that internal and external conflicts seem to effectively reduce the globalization prospects of the developing countries. The low rank of countries is often associated with political and technology factors that several developing countries are unable to address. The high-ranked countries share similar patterns in various index components distribution. The mean value of the globalization index by region shows that economic and technology factors play an important role in the ranking of the geographic and economic regions of the world.

Although the current version of the index quantifies the level of globalization relatively well, it has certain limitations and it should be considered as a partial measure. Heshmati addresses a number of extensions to overcome the shortcomings. These concerns are the use of an axiomatic approach to set out the desirable properties of the index, identification and incorporation of more relevant dimensions or components and the use of alternative estimation methods to avoid an ad hoc choice of components weights. A decomposition of the total variation in globalization into between and within country components is important. For data limitation reasons, the existing studies have mainly focused on only the between country variation. The within-country factors might explain much of the variance and, in particular, it can provide useful information about the distributional shifts within different population groups, sectors and regions. Globalization is considered a possible source and driving force of inequality differences across countries and over time. Identification and quantification of its effects will benefit the allocation of resources and redistribution policies. Thus, research on the measurement of globalization gives guidelines on how empirically to link globalization to inequality, poverty and economic growth.

4. THE LINK BETWEEN GROWTH, INEQUALITY AND POVERTY

4.1. Introduction to the Inequality and Poverty Reduction Impacts of Growth

The world economy is growing constantly but the growth pattern and its distribution differs over time and among countries and regions. This growth is due to technological change, increased efficiency, productivity and capacity in the use of resource and creation of wealth. Economic growth can also be negative as a result of mismanagement, economic downturn and crisis. There is comprehensive literature investigating the relationship between openness, growth, inequality and poverty (Dollar and Kraay, 2001a; Deininger and Squire, 1998; Goudie and Ladd, 1999; van der Hoeven and Shorrocks, 2003). In general they find a positive relationship between openness and growth but the impacts of growth on the poor can be different. Therefore, in recent years the research and debate in the area has focused on the extent to which the poor benefit from economic growth (Ravallion, 1998 and 2001; Ravallion and Chen, 2003; Ravallion and Datt, 2000; Quah, 2001). Empirical results suggest that the outcomes of policy measures are heterogeneous in their impacts and effective redistribution policies are needed to make economic growth pro-poor. There are disagreements about the impacts of growth. One extreme of the debate argues that the potential benefits of economic growth to the poor are undermined or offset by the inadequate redistributive policies and by increases in inequality that accompany economic growth. The second extreme argues that despite increased inequality, growth raise incomes of everyone in the society inclusive of the poor which reduces the incidence of poverty.

A significant portion of the previous work in the growth area has used econometric methods to test the hypothesis of income per capita convergence across countries. Convergence can be absolute or conditional (Barro and Sala-i-Martin, 1995; Quah, 1996c; Barro, 1997; Dowrick and DeLong, 2003; and Jones, 2002). When the absolute convergence holding a negative relationship between GDP levels and growth rates is observed, it implies that the poorer economies are growing faster than the richer countries. Conditional convergence refers to the convergence after differences in the steady state across countries are controlled. Here in addition to the GDP (initial income) level one control for other determinants of growth including population growth, education and investment (Mankiew et al., 1992). However, there are still disagreements about the concepts, modeling and estimation of growth and convergence models. The proponents of conditional convergence (Mankiew et al., 1992; Barro, 1997) find evidence of convergence at the annual 2-5 percent rates. To overcome the problems of losing the year-to-year growth rate variations, Islam (1995) uses a dynamic panel data approach and different estimators for studying growth convergence producing different results. Nerlove (2000) also found that the conditional convergence rate is sensitive to the choice of estimation techniques. Lee et al. (1997) in their examination of the beta and sigma convergence observed substantial biases in the rate of convergence due to the ignorance of growth heterogeneity.

Quah (1996a) sees the empirical finding of convergence in the growth literature contrary to the evidence of global divergence in the inequality literature. In Solimano's (2001) view the strong assumptions of equality of determinant of convergence, whose differences are the core of differential growth performance across countries, limits the usefulness of conditional convergence. The heterogeneous development has given rise to uneven and complex regional convergence and divergence in GDP per capita and growth rates increases the world inequality driven by between country inequalities. The contribution from the between country growth have more impacts on the world distribution of income inequality than the within country component. This is also confirmed by Bourguignon and Morrisson (2002) who find evidence of a convergence process among European countries but also divergence among regions and an increasing concentration of world poverty in some regions. The empirical findings indicate the presence of convergence at least among countries with more homogenous development or sharing the same regional location, but also significant divergence in income inequality. For instance, there is evidence of strong convergence among more homogenous and integrated European countries and a weak convergence among Indian states and divergence among Chinese regions.

4.2. Openness, Growth and Inequality Relationships and Redistribution Policies

A number of cross-country studies investigate the relationship between openness and growth (see e.g. Edwards 1998; Sachs and Werner 1995; Rodriguez and Rodrik 1999; and Dollar and Kraay 2001a and 2001b). In general they find a positive correlation between openness and growth but the effect declines over time and it is less beneficial to the poor countries. On the other hand the results do not indicate the presence of a systematic relationship between changes in trade and changes in inequality. Trade does not redistribute income among different income groups. Fast growth reduces poverty, but countries and regions who are not participating in the integration are falling farther behind, reducing their prospects of growing out of poverty. Researchers also face methodological difficulties in the measurement and in establishing the causal relationship from openness and integration to growth, inequality and poverty. A number of other studies analyse the relationship between inequality and growth (Person and Tabellini, 1994; Alesia and Rodirk, 1994; Ravallion, 1995;

and Peroti, 1996). A negative relationship between initial inequality in distribution of income and growth is found.

Sylwester (2000) investigates how the change in government policies can lower the negative impact of income inequality on economic growth. In particular, he explores how income inequality affects spending on public education and how education affects growth. Results show that current education expenditure has a negative impact upon contemporaneous growth, but previous expenditure has a positive impact on growth. The negative impact of inequality on growth is found to be only a short-run cost and it is offset by the long-run positive effects of education. One major shortcoming of the literature described above is that the causal relationship between these variables has often been neglected. Application of a co-integration test and the establishment of linkage and direction of causality among the key variables will determine whether these relations must be estimated using single equation, recursive or as a system of equations. The unavailability of time series data limits application of this approach. In recent studies, Addison and Heshmati (2004) and Gholami et al. (2006) tested for causality between FDI, GDP growth, openness and ICT. Empirical results based on countries with different development levels suggest that ICT infrastructure and ICT investment increases inflow of FDI to developing countries with implications for their economic growth.

The interaction between growth and inequality is examined by Deininger and Squire (1998) where they investigate how those two factors in turn affect efforts to reduce poverty in the course of economic development. The robustness of the inequality-growth relationship is tested by estimation of growth as a function of inequality conditioning on a number of variables like initial GDP, investment, black market premium, education and asset represented by land. The Kuznets hypothesis is tested, which postulates an inverted-U relationship between income and inequality according to which the degree of inequality would increase first and than decrease with the level of economic growth. Three main results emerge from the study by Deininger and Squire. First, there is a strong negative relationship between initial inequality in assets distribution and long-term growth. Second, inequality reduces income growth for the poor but not for the rich. Third, the available data provide little support for the Kuznets hypothesis. The heterogeneous relationship between income inequality and economic development is investigated by Savvides and Stegnos (2000). The empirical results based on threshold regression provide weak evidence of the existence of negative inequality-development relationship, but the relationship is described by a two-regime split of the sample based on per-capita income measure of development.

An establishment of the link between economic growth, inequality and poverty is not the ultimate goal, but the redistribution that it follows. In this respect Ravallion (2001) prefers the investigations based on micro data to identify effective growth-oriented policies. Outcomes of policy measure are heterogeneous in their impacts on different income groups. Depending on the initial position of the poor and diversity of impacts the poor might gain more from redistribution, but also suffer more from economic contraction compared to the rich. In regard to heterogeneity in impacts in an earlier study Ravallion (1998) showed that aggregation can bias conventional tests of the negative relationship between inequality and growth. Bigsten and Levin (2000) in their review of the literature did not find any systematic patterns of changes in income distribution during recent decades or any links from fast growth to increasing inequality. However, recent evidence tended to confirm the negative impact of inequality on growth. In two recent collections of essays (van der Hoeven and Shorrocks,

2003; Shorrocks and van der Hoeven, 2004) aggregate growth is seen as both necessary and sufficient for reducing poverty, but the concern is that the benefits of growth are not evenly distributed at the national level. Thus in the analysis the consequences of growth for poverty, the level and distributional impacts of growth needs to be taken into account. There is need for diverse strategies, where initial conditions, institutions, specific country structures, and time horizons should all play a role in the creation of national solutions to the problem of poverty reduction.

4.3. Other Factors Contributing to Inequality

Several studies focus on the impact of globalization, economic openness, import competition from low-wage countries, and technical change biased to skilled labor on wage inequality in industrialized countries. The results indicate a widening of wage differentials in favor of skilled labor and high-income earners in the USA and UK during the last two decades. This suggests a positive association between openness and wage inequality in industrialized economies. However, wage inequality patterns can differ among industrialized countries suggesting that policy matters. With regard to the above wage explanations to inequality Atkinson (1999) shows that the world is working in a more complex ways than this simple explanation of inequality. He refers to changes in social norms away from redistributive pay norms to one where market forces dominate the wage settings. Progressive income taxation and social transfers can offset rising income inequality arisen from the market place wage settings and unemployment (Atkinson 2000). The critics of globalization point to the fact that growth may have an anti-poor effect, emphasizing the role of policy and institutions to promote pro-poor distribution of growth. It has increased less in Europe than in USA and UK for the same period (Linder and Williamson, 2001). Aghion (2002) argues that the Schumpeterian Growth Theory, in which growth is driven by innovations, can provide explanations to the observed increases in wage inequality between educational groups.

Several other factors, than those discussed above, affect inequality both at the national and global levels. Acemoglu and Ventura (2002) offer an alternative framework to the new classical growth model for analyzing the world income distribution. They show that international trade based on specialization leads to a stable world income distribution. The dispersion of the world income distribution is determined by the forces that shape the degree of openness to international trade and the extent of production specialization. Calderon and Chong (2001) show that the intensity of capital controls, the exchange rate, the type of exports, and the volume of trade affect the long-run distribution of income. The result shows a link between trade and wage inequality. The export of primary goods from developing countries increases their inequality, while manufacturing exports from developed countries decreases their inequality. Al-Marhubi (1997) finds that developing countries with greater inequality have higher mean inflation. Inflation is found to be lower in countries that are more open to trade and stable. Microdata-based studies show evidence of presence of permanent and transitory wage inequality. They find a positive relationship between initial earnings and subsequent earnings growth indicating increasing divergence in earnings over the working career. Education, gender, marital status and race are the main factors contributing to earnings inequality.

4.4. Recent Empirical Evidence

In a recent study Heshmati (2006a) investigates trends in inequality and the presence of a relationship between growth and inequality and also tests the Kuznets inverted-U hypothesis. Modified versions of the two frequently used linear and reciprocal specifications of the inequality growth relationship are specified and estimated:

$$GINI_{it} = \alpha_0 + \alpha_1 INC_{it} + \alpha_2 (1/INC_{it}) + \sum_j \alpha_j X_{jit} + \sum_m \alpha_m Z_{mit} \qquad (2)$$
$$+ \lambda_t + \mu_r + \varepsilon_{it}$$

$$GINI_{it} = \beta_0 + \beta_1 \ln INC_{it} + \beta_2 (\ln INC_{it})^2 + \sum_j \beta_j \ln X_{jit} + \sum_m \beta_m Z_{mit} \qquad (3)$$
$$+ \lambda_t + \mu_r + \varepsilon_{it}$$

where $GINI$ is the average income inequality represented by Gini coefficient. The specification here is conditional, where INC is the real per capita GDP, X_{jit} is a vector of j other determinant variables like education, openness and population for country i in period t, Z is m vector of data characteristics, and λ_t and μ_r are unobservable time-specific and regional-specific effects. The conditional versus unconditional versions of the model can jointly or individually be tested, $H_0 : \alpha_j = 0$ and $H_0 : \beta_j = 0$, using F-test based on residual sum of squares.

The data used in the empirical part are obtained from several sources. One main source is the WIDER's World Income Inequality Database (WIID) which contains information on income inequality, income shares, and a number of variables indicating the source of data for 146 industrialized, developing, and transition countries observed mainly from 1950 until 1998. The Gini coefficient as in an inequality measure is measured in percentage points. Several alternative models based on the equations above are estimated assuming a fixed effects model. The estimated results shows that the relative explanatory power of the macro variables compared to the regional and time heterogeneity effects is small. Depending on the way the income variable is given (non-logarithmic, logarithmic or reciprocal) six models are estimated. The test results suggest that models incorporating macro variables, data characteristic variables, and controlling for time and regional effects are the preferred model specifications. The null hypothesis of a simple linear specification versus Kuznets (added square of income or alternatively reciprocal of income) is obtained by testing the hypothesis $H_0 : \alpha_2 = \beta_2 = 0$.

Conditional empirical results provide evidence of the existence of a negative and significant inequality-development relationship. The effect is stronger when development is defined as inverse of real GDP per capita or transformed to logarithms. The Kuznets hypothesis represents a global U-shape relationship. All six models produce uniform indications. The weakness is, however, the few brief times with frequent interruptions that each country has been observed. Several developing countries have been observed during only one single period. Wan (2002) estimates unconditional inequality growth relationship using transitional countries data. The Kuznets hypothesis is rejected by the data, but a first half U-pattern is found to be adequate for describing the growth-inequality relationship among the transition countries.

4.5. Concluding Summary to the Growth-Inequality Relationships

There exists a comprehensive body of literature investigating the relationship between openness, growth, inequality and poverty. In general there exists a positive relationship between openness and growth but the effect declines over time and is different in its impact on distribution of income. One major shortcoming of the literature is that the simultaneous and direction of a causal relationship between these key variables has empirically been neglected. The empirical findings indicate the presence of convergence in per capita income but divergence in income inequality. There is evidence of strong convergence among more homogenous and integrated advanced countries but also divergence among less developed countries or geographic regions. The between country contribution is much higher than within country contribution to world inequality. Different regions have differently managed to couple growth and inequality.

The existing empirical results on the relationship between growth, inequality and poverty, show that outcomes of policy measures are heterogeneous. Depending on the initial position of the poor and diversity of impacts, the poor might gain more from growth and redistribution, but may also suffer more from economic contraction. Results based on micro data indicate that asset inequality affects negatively consumption growth and the effect usually vanishes in the aggregate growth models. In general it is rather difficult to measure the effects of inequality and growth on the efforts to reduce poverty in the course of economic development. In sum, economic growth benefits the poor but in the absence of effective redistribution policies it might initially deteriorate the income distribution. Initial conditions, institutions, specific country and demographic structures, and time horizons each play a significant role in targeting policies to make economic growth pro-poor. Globalization, openness and technical change have been biased to skilled labor in industrialized countries widening their wage differentials. Regression results based on the WIID database suggest that income inequality is declining over time. There is significant regional heterogeneity in the levels and development over time. The Kuznets hypothesis represents a global U-shape relationship between inequality and growth. A possible solution to the Kuznets hypothesis at the country level would be to aggregate the data to the world level by using population shares as weights. However, entry and exit of countries with a large population or GDP affects stability of the inequality and development series and regression results.

5. Foreign Direct Investment

5.1. Introduction to FDI

Foreign direct investment (FDI) plays an increasingly important role to the developing countries in their efforts to achieve a higher level of economic development. In addition to foreign exchange and investment capital, FDI supplies the developing countries with advanced management, skills and technology. Combined with abundant low-cost labor, FDI contributes to competitiveness of multinational corporations (MNC) and their local subcontractors. In 2000 developing countries as a group received US$266.8 billion in FDI inflows, while the outflow amount to $143.8 billion. The corresponding numbers for 2005 were $334.3 billion and $117.5 billion. The share of developing countries in FDI inflows has also increased from 18.9% in 2000 to 36.5% in 2005, and the corresponding shares of outflow have increased from 11.6% to 15.1% (UNCTAD 2006). The scale and character of FDI flows to developing countries have been affected by new inventions and adoption of new technologies. The revolution in ICT is facilitating a global shift in the service industries and expanded in- and outsourcing activities, in which MNC are increasingly relocating service production activities to low-cost developing countries. This follows the earlier shift in manufacturing production and global political change that also affected FDI flow patterns. The democratization and the opening up of political systems has also been a catalyst for economic reforms that have favored foreign investors (Addison and Heshmati, 2004).

In the World Investment Reports (WIR, 1991-2005), the main forces of flow of FDI between 1991 and 2005 are associated with transnational corporations (TNC). TNCs are seen as engines of growth because of factors including their employment, competitiveness, market structure, competition policy, cross-border mergers and acquisitions (Mand A), export competitiveness, internationalization of Rand D, development challenge, and linkages and the shift towards services. The new global forces of ICT and democratization must be seen alongside the longstanding and traditional determinants of FDI flows to developing countries. The traditional determinants include natural-resource endowments, geographical characteristics, human capital, infrastructure and public and private institutions. Differences in these factors have also contributed to a highly skewed distribution of FDI across countries. FDI to the less developed countries (LDC) has been concentrated in natural resource sectors of mining, oil and gas with limited effects on output and employment in the rest of the economy. Economic reform and other policy measures that improve the investment climate and availability of ICT infrastructure and capability have become increasingly important in the location decisions of foreign investors. Thus, any empirical assessment of the determinants of FDI flows must take account of new developments alongside the more traditional determinants. Aside from a supportive policy framework, human capital and its ability and cost influences FDI flows and the associated technology transfer (Saggi, 2002).

From a receivers' perspective growth impact of FDI is important. However, there is no clear consensus on the presence of a positive relationship between FDI and economic growth, but there has been a growing view in recent years that FDI is positively correlated with economic growth. This view has been supported by recent developments in growth theory which highlight the importance of improvements in ability, technology, efficiency, and productivity in stimulating economic growth. In this regard, FDI's contribution to growth comes through its role as a channel for transferring advanced technology and management practices by foreign firms from industrialized to developing economies. This knowledge diffusion or spillover leads to improvements in productivity and efficiency in local and subcontracting firms. Thus, FDI provides better access to technologies for the local economy and it also leads to indirect productivity gains through spillover effects. Empirically, there is sufficient evidence that FDI efficiency spillovers exist. For developed countries, the evidence indicates that the productivity of domestic firms is positively related to the presence of foreign firms (Globerman et al., 2000). For developing countries, the results are also generally positive, although somewhat mixed (Kokko, 1994; Kokko et al., 1996; and Sjoholm, 1999). There is also evidence that economic growth in turn is a crucial determinant of attracting FDI (Cheng and Kwan, 1999; Coughlin and Segev 2000; Fung et al., 2002).

Several studies analyze the causal relationship between FDI and economic growth. Nair-Reichert and Weinhold (2001) find that the relationship between investment and economic growth in developing countries is highly heterogeneous and stronger in more open economies. Kumar and Pradhan (2002) find a positive effect of FDI on economic growth, but the direction of causation is unclear. Chowdhury and Mavrotas (2005), in examining the causal relationship between FDI and economic growth, find both uni-directional and bi-directional causality between the two variables. Gholami et al. (2006) examine the relationship between FDI and ICT where the causality test indicates that there is a significant short-run causal relationship between the two variables. However, the results differ according to the country's level of development. In developed countries, existing ICT infrastructure attracts FDI, but in developing countries the direction of causality instead goes from FDI to ICT, which means that ICT capacity must be built up first in order to attract more FDI inflows. The studies described above were at the aggregate country level. Shiu and Heshmati (2006) estimate at the disaggregate level the rate of technical change and total factor productivity (TFP) growth of 30 Chinese provinces. FDI and ICT and other infrastructure investments are found to be significant factors contributing to the TFP growth and its differences among the provinces.

5.2. Global and Regional Development of FDI Flows[3]

A. Global Development of FDI

In the World Investment Report (WIR) it is stated that FDI in 2005 grew for the second consecutive year and it was a worldwide phenomenon (see WIR 2006, Table 1). Inflows of FDI in 2004 and 2005 rose by 27% and 29%, respectively, to reach $916 billion in 2005, but far below the peak of $1,400 billion in 2000. UK and USA were the largest recipients of inward FDI among developed nations, while China and Hong Kong China, Singapore, Mexico and Brazil were the largest recipients among the developing countries. The EU remained the favorite FDI destination. Global FDI outflows reached $779 billion. It should be noted that, the gap between inflows and outflows is due to differences in the data reporting and collection methods of the member countries. Developed countries mainly the Netherlands, France, UK and US remained the leading sources of FDI outflows. There were also significant outflows from several developing countries led by Hong Kong, China.

The recent boom in cross-border Mand A and increasing deals undertaken by collective investment funds especially those involving companies in developed countries, have spurred the increase in FDI. The value of cross-border Mand A rose by 88% over 2004 and reached $716 billion. A new feature of the Mand A boom is increasing investment by collective investment funds, $135 billion in 2005. Direct investment abroad seems to be influenced by low interest rates and increasing financial integration. Services, particularly finance, telecommunication and real estate, gained from the surge of Mand A and FDI flows. Most

---

3 The source of statistics in this section is WIR (2006) unless stated.

private TNCs undertake FDI, as do many state-owned enterprises from developing countries by expanding abroad. According to UNCTAD, the universe of TNCs spans some 77,000 parent companies with 770,000 foreign affiliates. It is dominated by the triad of EU, Japan and the US, home to 85 of the world's top 100 TNCs. France, Germany, UK, US and Japan account for 73 of the 100 top firms, while only 5 were from developing countries, namely Hong Kong (China), Malaysia, Singapore, Korea and mainland China. The trend of liberalization in the form of regulatory changes to facilitate FDI continues, but some protectionist tendencies are also emerging. Such negative tendencies are a result of growing security concerns in the US and EU about foreign acquisitions in certain areas. On the other hand, the positive changes involve simplified administrative procedures, enhanced incentives, reduced taxes and greater openness to foreign investors.

Table 2. FDI inflows, by region and selected countries, 2000-2005, (Billions of dollars and %)

Region/country	2000	2001	2002	2003	2004	2005
Developed economies	1133.7	599.3	441.2	358.5	396.1	542.3
Europe	721.6	393.1	314.2	274.1	217.7	433.6
European Union	696.1	382.0	307.1	253.7	213.7	421.9
Japan	8.3	6.2	9.2	6.3	7.8	2.8
United States	314.0	159.5	74.5	53.1	122.4	99.4
Other developed countries	89.7	40.4	43.4	25.0	48.3	6.5
Developing economies	266.8	221.4	163.6	175.1	275.0	334.3
Africa	9.6	19.9	13.0	18.5	17.2	30.7
Latin America and the Caribbean	109.0	89.4	54.3	46.1	100.5	103.7
Asia and Oceania	148.3	112.2	96.2	110.5	157.3	200.0
Asia	148.0	112.0	96.1	110.1	156.6	199.6
West Asia	3.5	7.2	6.0	12.3	18.6	34.5
East Asia	116.3	78.8	67.4	72.2	105.1	118.2
China	40.7	46.9	52.7	53.5	60.6	72.4
South Asia	4.7	6.4	7.0	5.7	7.3	9.8
South-East Asia	23.5	19.6	15.8	19.9	25.7	37.1
Oceania	0.3	0.1	0.1	0.4	0.7	0.4
South-East Europe and the CIS	9.1	11.5	12.9	24.2	39.6	39.7
South-East Europe	3.6	4.2	3.9	8.5	13.3	12.4
CIS	5.4	7.3	9.0	15.7	26.3	27.2
World	1409.6	832.2	617.7	557.9	710.8	916.3
Memorandum: percentage share in world FDI inflows						
Developed economies	80.4	72.0	71.4	64.3	55.7	59.2
Developing economies	18.9	26.6	26.5	31.4	38.7	36.5
South-East Europe and the CIS	0.6	1.4	2.1	4.3	5.6	4.3

Source: UNCTAD, World Investment Report 2006, Overview, Table 1.

B. Regional Development of FDI

Africa faced difficulties in the past in attracting FDI outside natural resource areas. Asiedu (2002) in her study of the determinants of FDI in developing countries found Africa different. In 2005 Africa attracted much higher levels of FDI but these went mainly into natural resources, especially oil, as well as services, e.g., banking and cross-border Mand A. In addition to the EU and US as dominant investors, India, China and Malaysia invested $15 billion in six African oil producing countries. African manufacturing has not been successful in attracting FDI although some countries like South Africa attracted export-oriented production. The fragmented markets, poor infrastructure, lack of skilled labor, quotas, and weak linkages between export sectors and the rest of the economy by building and fostering domestic capabilities in areas of physical infrastructure, production capacity and supportive institutions cause divestments. In recent years, positive developments in regulatory regimes, bilateral agreements related to investment and taxation are observed. However, these improvements are not sufficient to enhance competitive production capacity, and thus, better market access is required to increase the inflow of FDI.

The South, East and South-East Asia are still the main magnet for FDI inflows into developing countries. The FDI inflow reached $165 billion in 2005 which is 18% of the world inflows. India received the highest level ($7 billion), particularly into services. Manufacturing, especially, automotive, electronics, steel and petrochemical industries, attracted most FDI to the region. Chinese FDI outflows increased and seem to rise further over time. West Asia received an unprecedented level of FDI inflows ($34 billion), which soared by 85%. High oil prices, the liberalization of the regulatory regime, and the privatization in power, water, transport, banking and telecommunication services caused the increased FDI inflows. West Asia by tradition has been a significant outward direct investor. Instead of bank deposits and portfolio purchases, most of the region's petrodollars, unlike in previous years, went into services in developed and developing countries as a result of stronger economic ties with China and India. Latin America and the Caribbean continued to receive substantial FDI ($104 billion). High economic growth and high commodity prices were contributory factors. However, the development was not similar among the countries. The outflows from Latin America and Caribbean increased by 19% (to $33 billion), mainly acquiring assets in telecommunication and heavy industries.

FDI flows to South-East Europe and the Commonwealth of Independent States (CIS) remained relatively high (at $40 billion). The inflow was mainly concentrated on the Russian Federation, Ukraine and Romania. The outflow from CIS increased, reaching $15 billion. There was an upturn in FDI (37%) to developed countries and it reached $542 billion or 59% of the world total. The UK ($165 billion), France ($116), the US ($99), the Netherlands ($44) and Canada ($34) emerged as the main recipients. FDI into all three sectors of primary, manufacturing and services increased. In sum, the development in the first half of 2006 suggests that FDI should continue to grow further in the short term. This prediction is based on continued economic growth, increased corporate profits, and increase in stock prices, the boosted value of Mand A and a continued liberalization policy.

C. South-South Perspective on Investment

TNCs from developed countries account for the bulk of global FDI and private and state owned firms from developing and transition economies have emerged as significant outward investors, generating considerable South-South investment flows. To some of the recipient countries the new source of capital represents new competition. Data on cross-border Mand A show an increasing share of greenfield and expansion projects invested in business, finance, trade and manufacturing activities as well as in the primary sectors. The geographical composition of FDI from developing countries has shifted from Latin American to Asian countries. The largest stock of outward FDI was in Hong Kong, the British Virgin Islands, the Russian Federation, Singapore and Taiwan. Based on the UNCTAD outward FDI performance index, Hong Kong's index was 10 times larger than expected. Other economies with high values were Bahrain, Malaysia, Panama and Singapore, while Brazil, China, India and Mexico showed the lowest values. It should be noted that the bulk of South-South FDI is interregional in nature. New global and regional players are emerging, especially firms from Asia.

The majority of TNCs from the South are small, but several large ones with global ambitions have also appeared. There is high concentration in some countries, e.g., South Africa, Mexico and Brazil, Russian Federation, but less concentration among Asian countries. The number of companies from developing and transition economies listed in the Fortune 500 increased from 19 in 1990 to 47 in 2005. The industrial distribution differs by region and is dominated by the primary sector, financial services and infrastructure services. The cluster of automotives, electronics, garment and IT services are most exposed to global competition. In the WIR 2006 types of pull and push factors and other factors that help to explain the drive for internationalization by developing countries TNCs are presented. Firstly, market related factors push the corporations out of their home countries and pull them into host countries. Secondly, rising costs of production in the home country are a particular concern. Thirdly, competitive pressures are pushing them to expand overseas. Fourthly, home and host government policies influence their outward FDI decisions. The first major development factor is the rapid growth of many large developing countries (India and China), while the second factor is behavioral change among the TNCs. UNCTAD in a survey show that the four main motives influence investment decisions by TNCs are their seeking for market, efficiency, resources and asset creation.

Increased competitiveness is one of the prime benefits that developing country TNCs can derive from their outward FDI activities. Undertaking outward FDI is a complex and risky process requiring the upgrading of technology, building bands, learning new management skills, facing cultural, social and institutional differences, organizational and environmental complexities, and linking up with advanced global value chains. The overall economic and non-economic effects of overseas investment depend on the long-term motivation for the investment. Developing host countries may also gain from the rise in South-South FDI in the form of a broad range of capital, technology and management skills. In addition to an increased FDI inflow, it is an additional channel for further South-South economic cooperation. There is a better fit of the technology and business model of developing countries from FDI inflow easing the technology absorption process. In comparison with FDI by developed countries' TNCs, the FDI from developing countries' TNCs has greater employment generation potential by being more oriented towards labor intensive industries. The expansion of outward FDI from developing countries is paralleled by important changes in policies in home countries governing FDI and related matters. Various policy responses in host countries are adopted to influence the behavior of foreign affiliates and in the design of strategies to attract desired kinds of inward FDI.

D. The Success of the Chinese FDI Policy

One important part of the Chinese economic reform has been to promote FDI inflows. The economic reform and its FDI policy have made China one of the most important destinations for foreign direct investment. The evolution of the Chinese FDI is divided into initial, development and high growth phases. The initial phase involves the period 1979-1985. The Sino-foreign joint ventures investment law of 1979 opened up the market to the world's corporations. The law provided the legal framework for foreign investors to form equity joint ventures with Chinese partners. A number of related laws and regulations with regard to labor management, taxation, registration and foreign exchange followed. In 1979, Guangdong and Fujian were granted autonomy in dealing with foreign trade and investment and in 1980 four special economic zones (SEZ) were established within the two provinces. The SEZs were established with the objectives of attracting foreign capital and advanced technology, promoting export-led growth, creating employment, generating foreign exchange, serving as policy laboratories and enhancing the link between Hong Kong, Macao and Taiwan with mainland China. In 1984, 14 coastal port cities open to foreign trade and development were announced, with the autonomy to plan the legal framework and regulations for foreign investment (Fu, 2000).

The development phase in China covers the period 1986 to 1991. In 1986, the state promulgated two important laws, namely the "Law on Enterprises Operated Exclusively with Foreign Capital" and the "Provision on Encouraging Foreign Investment." These laws were introduced to lift the existing restrictions on foreign ownership and new incentives were implemented to remove uncertainties for foreign investors. The policies dramatically increased FDI and tax revenues from exports. In December 2001, China became a member of the World Trade Organization (WTO) and committed itself to a wide range of reforms such as enhancing transparency, improving intellectual property protection and reducing tariffs. As a result of improved investors' confidence, from 2002 to 2005 the annual realized FDI inflows grew to US$50-60 billion. China is currently the largest FDI recipient among developing countries by attracting 25-30% of total FDI inflow to developing countries. The MNCs invest principally in the manufacturing sector, where foreign equity capital mainly consists of fixed assets. Foreign capital has played a positive role in China's economic development during the reform period. It has generated more benefits in the form of spillover growth effect by improvement of efficiency and productivity of domestic firms in addition to helping to solve China's capital shortage. Wang (2007) finds that FDI fluctuates more than economic growth. The growing FDI has been accompanied by China's progress in foreign trade and economic growth. The average annual rate of GDP growth in China during 1978-2003 was around 9%.

The number of studies investigating the effects of inward FDI on economic growth in China is increasing. Some are descriptive while others use more advanced methods. Liu and Song (1997) argue that FDI promotes China's economic growth via its influence on the demand and supply conditions, business strategies and competition. Dayal-Gulati and Husain (2000) attempted to identify possible structural variations over three sub-periods and find that FDI had a much more positive and significant impact on China's economic growth during the period of 1993-97. Zhang (2001) found that the impact of FDI on growth increased with growth in FDI. Liu (2002), by using manufacturing data in the Shenzhen SEZ, finds FDI to have significant spillover effects by raising the level and growth rate of productivity. Shan et al. (1997), in testing the causal link between the inflow FDI and real output growth, find a two-way causality suggesting that FDI and growth reinforce each other. While Liu et al. (2002) find bi-directional causality between economic growth, FDI and export, Wang (2007) uses provincial level data and captures regional heterogeneity in FDI inflows and its impacts on economic growth. Heterogeneity is a major source of regional inequality in development and welfare in China. It is desirable that the policy of attracting FDI should focus more attention on promoting technology spillover and inflow of FDI in particular than to less developed regions.

5.3. Empirical Research on FDI Flows

The data used in studies of FDI are at different levels of aggregation. The most frequent used dataset is the World Bank's World Development Indicators (WDI). WDI is a time series of cross sections consisting of a sample of 207 countries observed from 1960 onwards. It is often complemented by other data sets such as Penn World Tables and International Financial Statistics. These datasets are mostly unbalanced and each suffers from missing information on the key variables which reduces the effective sample size used in the empirical studies. The variables used are classified as dependent, independent, and country characteristic variables. The independent variables include those perceived to be determinants of FDI such as: tax incentives, wage subsidy, demand poll, export support, openness, GDP growth, government consumption, wages, inflation, education, returns on savings and investment, ICT investment and infrastructure variables. The country characteristic variables include the degree of industrialization, investment risk, natural resources, political instability, and a number of dummy variables associated with regional location, income groups, the degree of indebtedness and democratization.

In order to identify and to estimate the impacts of determinants of FDI on its flows, following the empirical literature, some measure of FDI is regressed on a number of variables identified as determinants of FDI. The model is written as:

$$FDI_{it} = \alpha_0 + \sum_j \alpha_j X_{jit} + \sum_k \gamma_k Z_{kit} + \sum_g \delta_g M_{gi} + u_{it} \qquad (4)$$

where FDI is for example the FDI share of GDP of country i ($i = 1,2,.....,N$) in period t ($t = 1,2,.....,T$), α, γ and δ are vectors of unknown parameters measuring the impacts of the determinants on FDI flows that are to be estimated, X is vector of exogenous determinants of FDI, Z is a vector of country-characteristic variables, M is a vector of variables that vary by country but are constant over time, and u is the error term. The error term follows a two-way error component structure and it can be broken down into the components: an unobservable country-specific effect (μ_i), a time-specific effect (λ_t) and a random error term (v_{it}). The model is estimated using panel data econometrics methods.

Empirical results based on estimation of the above model by using a large sample of countries in Addison and Heshmati (2004) is summarized as follows. In sum, the results support many of the findings of previous research in this area. In particular, there is a positive relationship between the flow of FDI and economic growth; openness to trade has a positive impact on FDI flows; and the level of risk affects FDI negatively. For a recipient country being highly in debt is a significant deterrent to FDI. In addition the results indicate the presence of regional and income group heterogeneity in FDI flows, which is to be expected since the motives for FDI vary considerably across regions. Regarding the main hypothesis about recent global developments, they find that both democracy and ICT have significant positive effects on FDI. The results indicate that the international community needs to step up its assistance to the creation of ICT infrastructure and necessary training in poor countries. Poor countries have insufficient public resources to fund ICT and many are unable to attract private funding for ICT. This is because they are viewed as largely unattractive investment possibilities and left in a low-level ICT equilibrium trap. If such assistance is provided, it will help them to attract FDI which, in turn, will lead to further cumulative ICT investment and economic growth.

5.4. A Concluding Summary to the FDI Flows and their Impacts

The global flow of foreign direct investment has increased dramatically in the last two decades. However, the distribution of FDI is highly unequal and countries are involved in a fierce competition to attract foreign investors. FDI is increasingly important to developing countries in their efforts to develop their economies. In addition to increased export revenues and investment capital, it supplies the receiving countries with advanced management and technology. Thus, FDI is considered as a viable development factor for capital-scarce but labor-abundant developing countries. The scale and character of FDI flows to developing countries have been affected by a number of successive waves in the invention and adoption of new technologies. ICT has facilitated a global shift in the service industries and MNC now increasingly relocate their production activities to developing countries. The longstanding determinants of FDI flows to developing countries are their natural-resource endowments, geographical characteristics and low-cost human capital. Existing investments are often concentrated in natural resource sectors, particularly in minerals, oil and gas and these in general have had limited multiplier effects on output, employment and spillover effects in the rest of the economy.

Currently, there is no clear consensus on the presence of a positive relationship between FDI and economic growth, but there is a growing view that FDI is positively correlated with economic growth. Recent developments in the literature highlight the importance of improvements in labor's ability, technology spillover, efficiency and productivity in stimulating economic growth. The FDI's contribution to economic growth comes through a transfer of advanced technology and management practices by MNCs. This knowledge diffusion leads to improvements in the productivity and efficiency of local firms which gradually in turn increases the rate of technical progress in host countries. FDI provides better access to technologies for the local economy and it leads to indirect productivity gains through spillover effects. Empirically, there is sufficient evidence on the FDI efficiency spillover effects. The feedback from economic growth is found to be a crucial determinant in attracting FDI.

The WIR predicts global FDI growth. The UK and the USA are the largest recipients of inward FDI among developed nations, while China and Hong Kong, Singapore, Mexico and Brazil are the largest recipients among developing nations. The EU remained the favorite FDI destination and developed countries as a result of shifts in technology remained the leading source of FDI outflows. There were also significant outflows from developing countries. A recent boom in cross-border Mand A and increasing investment by collective investment funds has spurred the increase in FDI. Finance, telecommunications and real estate gained most from the surge of Mand A and FDI flows. The share of manufacturing declined while the share of FDI into the primary and in particular energy sector increased. The number of TNCs from developing countries is increasing slowly enhancing South-South FDI flows. The trend of liberalization in the form of regulatory changes to facilitate FDI continues, but some protectionist tendencies in developed countries are also emerging as a result of growing security concerns around Mand A, Positive changes observed involve simplified procedures, incentives, reduced taxes and greater openness to foreign investors.

At the regional level, Africa faced difficulties in the past in attracting FDI outside natural resource extraction areas. In 2005 Africa attracted much higher levels of FDI but these went mainly into natural resources and services. Positive developments in regulatory regimes, bilateral agreements related to investment and taxation were observed, but a better market access and infrastructure is required. South Asia, East Asia and South-East Asia are still the main magnets for FDI inflows into developing countries. China remained as one of the main recipients of FDI. India received significant FDI, particularly into services. Manufacturing, especially, automotive, electronics, steel and petrochemical industries, attracts most FDI to the region. Chinese FDI outflows increased and seemed to rise further over time. West Asia received an unprecedented level of FDI inflows. High oil prices, the liberalization of the regulatory regime and the privatization of utilities and services caused the increased FDI inflows. Latin America and the Caribbean continued to receive substantial FDI. High economic growth and high commodity prices were the main contributing factors. However, the development was not similar among the countries. FDI flows to South-East Europe remained relatively high.

Private and state owned firms from developing and transition economies have emerged as significant outward investors generating considerable South-South investment flows. Data on cross-border Mand A show increasing investment in business, finance, trade and manufacturing activities as well as in the primary sector. Developing host countries gain much from the rise in South-South FDI in the form of capital, technology and management skills, as well as developed South-South economic cooperation. There is a better fit of the technology and business models of developing countries from FDI inflow easing the technology absorption process. FDI from developing countries has greater employment generation potential by being more oriented towards labor intensive industries. One important aspect of the Chinese economic reform has been to promote both within and between regional FDI flows. The economic reform and FDI policy have made China one of the most important destinations for direct investment. Through a new investment law China provided the legal framework for foreign investors to form equity joint ventures with Chinese partners. A number of related laws and regulations followed. The establishment of special economic zones helped the local government in these zones to draw up and implement established FDI friendly development plans.

6. INSOURCING AND OUTSOURCING

6.1. Introduction to Outsourcing

In recent decades production, research as well as technology outsourcing has expanded rapidly. The empirical evidence very often is based on aggregate country or industry level data and originating from industrial countries. The growing importance of the service sector has induced increasing concern about its performance. Different methods have intensively been used in the evaluation performance of private and public services foremost in provision of health care, banking and education (Balk, 1998; Griliches, 1992; Griliches and Mairesse, 1993; Heshmati, 2003). Despite the comprehensive literature on the issues of growth, productivity, efficiency, competition and outsourcing on each subject separately, very little can be found on their linkages and causal relationships. Heshmati and Pietola (2007) contribute to the literature by empirically investigating such multi-dimensional causal relationships among the above variables, and thus attempt to fill in the gap by investigating the relationship between corporate competitiveness strategy, efficiency, productivity growth, innovation and outsourcing.

Among factors leading to implement outsourcing are contracting out production of goods and services to a firm with competitive advantages in terms of reliability, quality and cost (Perry, 1997), managing reasons (Young and Macneil, 2000), improving strategic focus, achieving numerical functional flexibility, changing the organizational structure, enhancing inter-firm co-operations in outsourcing (Suarez-Villa, 1998), measuring allocated capacity (De Kok, 2000) and increasing flexibility for the freed-up human and capital resources (Benson, 1999). Outsourcing is used to describe all the subcontracting relationships between firms (Eggert and Falkingner, 2003; Fixler and Siegel, 1999; Gilley and Rasheed, 2000). Glass and Saggi (2001) investigate the issues of innovation and the wage effects of international outsourcing. They find reductions in the costs of adopting technologies for production in low-wage countries, increases in production taxes in high-wage countries, and increases in production subsidies or subsidies to adopt technologies in low-wage countries as main forces explaining an increasing extent of international outsourcing. The next section aims to overview the recent development of the literature on outsourcing and the causal relationship between outsourcing and its impacts on the performance of firms.

6.2. Review of the Outsourcing Literature and Measurement of Outsourcing

The recent developments in the industrial, communication and technology areas have resulted in major changes in the ways products and services are planned, produced and distributed. As a measure to improve efficiency, firms allocate their resources to activities for which they enjoy comparative advantage, while other activities are increasingly outsourced to domestic or foreign external suppliers. Outsourcing is expected to reduce production cost relative to internal production because outside suppliers benefit from economies of scale, smoother production schedules and centralization of expertise (Chalos, 1995; Roodhooft and Warlop, 1999; Williamson, 1989). However, the choice between internal or external production requires more considerations than pure production cost differences. For instance, according to the transaction cost economics, outsourcing is desirable only when the cost of asset-specific investments is lower than the production cost advantage of outsourcing. This is a result of the fact that outsourcing makes previous investments a sunk cost to the firms.

Arnold (2000) in studying the design and management of outsourcing finds the transaction cost and core competencies approach to complement each other. The decision to invest in internal knowledge or to consume external knowledge is affected by a multiple of factors. Gavious and Rabinowitz (2003) in determining optimal knowledge outsourcing policy find that the lower the ability to develop internal knowledge, the more favorable external knowledge becomes. Barthelemy (2003) in analyzing the contracts and the trust in the relationship with IT outsourcing management finds that both factors are keys to the success of outsourcing. Eggert and Falkinger (2003), in examining the distributional effects of international outsourcing, find that the interplay between the cost-saving and substitution effects determines the nature of the outsourcing equilibrium and its distributional consequences. Despite the internationalization of outsourcing and its frequent utilization by multinational companies, in an international survey of outsourcing contracts, Kakabadse and Kakabadse (2002) find significant differences in behavior between the European and USA companies. The American companies undertake more value-added sourcing strategies, while Europeans focus more on gaining economies of scale through outsourcing.

In discussing globalization the focus has been on increased trade in goods and services and mobility of labor and financial assets. Declining prices of international services, knowledge of potential supplier and awareness of legal systems increase the role played by separate and smaller firms connected only by the rules of the international market place (Jones and Kierzkowski, 2000). Grossman and Helpman (2002b) investigated the extent of outsourcing and FDI in an industry in which producers need specialized components that can be produced by external suppliers across national markets. In such situations a consideration of how various cost factors affect the organization of industry production is needed (Grossman and Helpman, 2002a). The trend in outsourcing activities during recent decades has been globally and continuously increasing. These activities enhance the competitiveness and efficiency of firms within countries and across borders. Despite the remarkable increase in outsourcing, empirical studies of the subject are still rare. Previous research is mainly theoretical in nature. Feenstra (1998) finds an increasing trend in the integration of the global economy through trade, but also disintegration in production processes. Holmström and Roberts (1998) analyzed the boundaries of firms and how agency issues can affect the boundaries of an organization.

Despite an increasing number of studies on outsourcing, there is limited literature on the measurement of outsourcing and there is disagreement about how it is defined. Gilley and Rasheed (2000) identified three definition of outsourcing in the management literature. One definition sees outsourcing as the contribution in the physical and human resources by external vendors to the IT infrastructure in the user organization (Loh and Venkatraman, 1992). Another is the products supplied to multinational firms by independent suppliers (Kotabe, 1992). The third is reliance on external sources for value-adding activities (Lei and Hitt, 1995). Gilley and Rasheed conclude that outsourcing is not simply a purchasing decision, but it represents the decision to reject the internalization of activities. They propose that outsourcing may arise in two ways: through the substitution of external purchases for internal activities, and through abstention when a firm purchases goods and services that have not been completed in-house in the past. Temporary help supplies employment, as a flexible arrangement in avoiding the costly adjustment of labor to changes in economic conditions and the need of expertise is seen as one way to measure insourcing as an alternative to outsourcing.

6.3. Outsourcing Impacts

As discussed above, outsourcing can be related to production of intermediate goods or hiring temporary labor. According to a two-sector model, during recent decades the service sector has grown much faster than the goods sector with negative impacts on economic growth (Baumol, 1967; Baumol et al., 1985). In this model, manufacturing is the progressive and technologically advanced sector, while the service sector is stagnant. The negative effect is due to the high labor intensity in the service sector and its low incentives to introduce technological change. However, technology that is specific for use in the service sector is advancing and eliminating previous gaps. There are a number of studies that focus on explaining the difference in productivity growth rates in the two sectors. Abraham and Taylor (1996) found that firms contracting out services with the objectives of smoothing production cycles, benefited from specialization and realized potential labor cost savings. Siegel and Griliches (1992), in reviewing selected services, find weak evidence that outsourcing leads to overstatement of manufacturing productivity growth. Estevão and Lach (1999) estimate the extent to which the manufacturing sector is outsourcing temporary labor from the service sector. The results show increasing intensity in the use of temporary labor, which explains the flatness of manufacturing employment. Ten Raa and Wolff (1996) found a positive association between outsourcing and productivity growth in the goods sector.

More recently Fixler and Siegel (1999) focus on the internal generation, the buying or outsourcing decisions for selected services, and the effects of outsourcing on manufacturing services productivity growth. The propensity of the firm to outsource is a function of the difference between the marginal cost of the external suppliers and the marginal cost of in-house production. A firm will outsource if the marginal cost of internal production is higher (Inman 1985). Jacobson et al. (1993) in their analysis of wages following a shift of workers from manufacturing to services found that wages declined and outsourcing resulted in an increased productivity differential between manufacturing and services. Fixler and Siegel (1999) present five testable hypotheses in their empirical results. They investigated the productivity growth of service and manufacturing industries in the US. The results are consistent with the hypothesis and indicate that a positive correlation between wage growth and growth in outsourcing in manufacturing industries, a positive correlation between growth in manufacturing productivity and the rate of outsourcing, and growth in real output in service industry is positively correlated with manufacturing outsourcing.

I have already mentioned several factors with strong implications for outsourcing. A number of studies (Dritna, 1994 and Lacity et al., 1996) suggest that decision makers in general overestimate the production cost advantages of outsourcing and underestimate the role of transaction costs. Furthermore, Feenstra and Hanson (1996) argue that outsourcing, defined as the share of import of intermediate inputs in the total purchased materials by domestic firms, has contributed to an increase in the relative demand for skilled labor in the US. Outsourcing was the firms' response to import competition by moving non-skilled intensive activities abroad. Falk and Koebel (2000) examined the effects of outsourcing of services and imported materials on demand for labor in German manufacturing. The results showed little effects on labor demand for unskilled labor, but the shift in demand towards skilled labor can be explained by capital-skill complementarities and skill-biased technological change. Sharpe (1997) argues that outsourcing arose to reduce the adjustment costs of responding to economic changes. It has been argued that outsourcing has resulted in falling wages of the less-skilled workers in relation to the more-skilled US workers, causing wage inequality (see also Feenstra and Hanson, 1995 and 1996).

The issue of competitive strategy is important in strategic management. Porter (1980) defined three generic competitive strategies: cost leadership, differentiation, and focus. Nayyar (1993) reviewed studies measuring Porter's competitive strategies when firms emphasize various competitive dimensions. The top five reasons for outsourcing based on a large survey of companies were identified by Deavers (1997) as: (1) to improve company focus, (2) to gain access to world-class capabilities, (3) to accelerate benefits from reengineering, (4) to share risks and (5) to free resources for other purposes. However, Chen et al. (2003) show that trade liberalization may create incentives for strategic international outsourcing. Unlike the outsourcing motivated by cost savings, strategic outsourcing can have a collusive effect and raise prices in both the intermediate-good and final-good markets. Quelin and Duhamel (2003) view outsourcing as a choice that lies in corporate policy, not just business strategy. They review different elements characterizing strategic outsourcing, examine motives and risks associated with outsourcing and provide key points in implementation of strategic outsourcing operations. The results from a number of large surveys suggest that outsourcing is seen more as a corporate competitiveness strategy that leads to major improvements in the performance of the company (Deavers, 1997). Sharpe (1997) finds that outsourcing as a management tool addresses organizational competitiveness in an efficient way by moving towards business strategies based on core competencies and outsourcing other non-core activities and services.

6.4. The Causal Relationships among the Key Variables

Heshmati and Pietola (2007), using the Swedish community innovation survey data and the framework introduced by Griliches (1990) that was further developed by Crepon et al. (1998) in which one accounts for selectivity and simultaneity biases, investigate the effects of outsourcing, efficiency and competitive strategy on innovation and productivity of firms. The model is a system of equations consisting of four equations. The first two equations which represent innovativeness and innovation inputs are estimated separately as a generalized tobit model where observations on both innovative and non-innovative firms are included. The last two equations are estimated as a system using three stages least squares (3SLS) method. The endogenous innovation output variable is limited to innovative sample with strictly positive innovation output. The four-equation model is written as:

$$IN_i^* = \beta_0^1 + \sum_n \beta_n^1 \ln X_{ni}^1 + \beta_{OUTS1} OUTS1_i + \varepsilon_i^1 \tag{5}$$

$$\ln II_i = \beta_0^2 + \sum_m \beta_m^2 \ln X_{mi}^2 + \varepsilon_i^2 \tag{6}$$

$$\ln IO_i = \beta_0^3 + \sum_l \beta_l^3 \ln X_{li}^3 + \beta_{RD} II_i + \beta_{MR} MR_i + \beta_{EFF} EFF_i + \beta_Q \ln Q_i$$
$$+ \beta_{COM} COMP_i + \beta_{OUTS2} OUTS2_i + \varepsilon_i^3 \tag{7}$$

$$\ln Q_i = \beta_0^4 + \sum_j \beta_j^4 \ln X_{ji}^4 + \beta_{IO} IO_i + \beta_{EFF} EFF_i + \beta_{OUTS1} OUTS1_i + \varepsilon_i^4 \qquad (8)$$

where IN^* is a latent innovation decision variable, the observable counterpart $IN = 1$ when $IN^* > 0$; i.e. if the firm is engaged in innovation, else zero, II represents innovation input, IO innovation output, Q productivity, and MR inverted Mill's ratio introduced to correct for possible sample selection bias, X is an explanatory variable including employment, physical capital, human capital and various indicators, EFF, $COMP$, $OUTS1$ and $OUTS2$ are variables representing productive efficiency, competitiveness and outsourcing, respectively, and the $\beta : s$ are unknown parameters to be estimated. $OUTS1$ is outsourcing based on hiring temporary labor while $OUTS2$ is outsourcing defined as purchase of external innovations related services.

The dependent variables include log innovation input per employee, II, log innovation sales per employee, IO, and log productivity, Q. Productivity is measured as the growth rate in turnover between 1996 and 1998. The determinants of innovation input labeled as the x^1 vector consist of growth in employment, profitability, capital stock intensity, capital and knowledge intensive technologies and firm size. The x^2 variables in the selection equation consist of hired temporary supply labor, profitability, capital investment intensity, indebtedness, export share of turnover, capital and knowledge intensive technologies and firm size classes based on the number of employees. The determinants of innovation output labeled as the x^3 vector consist of predicted value of innovation input, inverted Mill's ratio, predicted value of firm performance, logarithm of Rand D intensity, growth in employment, purchase of innovation-related outsourcing services, efficiency in production and firm size. In addition the set of variables includes a number of composite indices on hampered project and hampering factors, sources of product and process innovations, competitive strategy, the importance of innovation cooperation and importance of location of innovation cooperation partners. The x^4 vector entering the productivity equation contains information on predicted value of innovation output, the temporary hired share of labor, efficiency in production, Rand D intensity, capital investment intensity, capital stock intensity, profitability, indebtedness and size. All equations include industrial sector dummy variables.

Empirical results show that there is a negative relationship, and at an increasing rate, between inefficiency in production and size of the firm. Profitability and investment intensity per employee, outsourcing defined as share of temporary hired labor and Rand D investment intensity enhances efficiency in production. The mean technical efficiency is 0.834 indicating that on the average, there is potential that for a given level of capital and other factors the firms could produce 16.4 per cent more output by using the best practice production technology. Efficiency in production is positively correlated with innovations input, innovations output, productivity growth and temporarily hired labor. The hired labor measure is positively correlated with innovation output and growth in value added and efficiency, while the expenditure measure is positively correlated with both innovations input and output but not with growth in value added or efficiency in production. The industries differ by degree of outsourcing. Outsourcing of products, services and processes is more intensive than in-sourcing or hiring labor on temporarily basis. The expenditure share of outsourcing is an increasing function of the size of firm. Outsourcing is also found to be positively associated with the degree of innovativeness.

6.5 Summary of the Key Results

In this part I summarized the methods used and empirical results obtained from studies of the link between corporate competitive strategy, efficiency, outsourcing, innovation and productivity growth at the firm level. A new method with a view to dealing with the issues of sample selection and simultaneity biases in innovation studies was employed to Swedish firm level innovation data.

The empirical results from an estimation of a stochastic frontier production function suggest that firms are relatively efficient, although the output can further be increased by using the best practice technology. Efficiency in production is positively correlated with innovation input, innovation output and productivity growth. There is positive association between size of firm, profitability, investment, outsourcing and efficiency in production. It is rather difficult to represent corporate competitiveness strategy in a proper way. A simple composite competitive strategy index was estimated using principal component analysis. It indicates the level and state of competitiveness among the firms. I identified a number of determinants of decisions of investment in innovation activities, how much to invest, innovation output and productivity growth. The systems of four equations estimated in a multi-step procedure accounting for both sample selection and simultaneity biases is found to be superior to alternative simpler methods. Internal financial sources, knowledge intensive production technology and size of firms are major determinants of investment in innovations. Variation in innovation output is to a large extent explained by variations in innovation input. The interactive positive and significant coefficients of innovation output and productivity equations indicate the presence of a two-way causality relationship between innovation output and productivity growth among innovative firms.

7. TRANSFER OF TECHNOLOGY AND MANAGEMENT

7.1. Introduction to Capability, Incentives and Technology Transfer

This section focuses on the management practices and strategies toward technology transfer and evaluation of their outcomes. In addition I deal with issues such as the internal organization and external environment that affects these practices and strategies including public policy developments, incentives, regulatory and legal issues, and development of global trends. In reviewing the literature I briefly present their major findings.

It is widely believed that the potential for developing countries to grow by using technology already developed by the industrialized countries is considerable (Goh, 2005). Some of these knowledge spillovers that take place in various forms of exchanges are passive and can occur at relatively low costs through trade in intermediate goods embodying the technology, while the rest are active in the sense that agents from the developed countries need to incur resource costs to access and transfer the technology. In addition the agents need also to make efforts to adapt and gain mastery over the technology received (Pack and Westphal, 1986; Mansfield and Romeo, 1980). Thus, different countries can grow at very different rates depending on their capabilities and institutional barriers and the incentive measures that the countries provide for the transfer and mastery of technology through trade, licensing, FDI, joint ventures, subcontracting activities, and capability enhancing research and training activities.

In discussing how to build up the right incentive systems for encouraging greater transfer and mastery of foreign technology Goh (2005) suggests that policy makers need to have a good understanding of what determines foreign firms' willingness to transfer their technology and the domestic firms' investment in mastery of imported technology. Two factors are widely cited as important in affecting the incentives for technology transfer. These are the ease of knowledge diffusion/imitation and the level of absorptive capacity in the recipient country. Both of these factors can be influenced by active public technology policies. Several factors including tied intellectual property rights, labor market regulations, trade relations and location of industries ease the diffusion of knowledge. The absorptive capacity and capability in modification for local needs can also be enhanced by investment in education, public Rand D subsidy and training of labor and management.

7.2. The University-Industry Relationship and Technology Transfer

One main area of research on technology is the university-industry relationship. The research in this area emphasizes the university-industry collaboration and heterogeneity in university incomes generated from transfer and commercialization of technology. Several studies investigate how to couple technology finance and technology transfer activities in private-to-private transfer cases. Here the financial institutions of the innovation system like venture capital acts as searcher, investor and an assistant for innovative companies. The effectiveness of public innovation policies to stimulate private Rand D investment is another related area of interest. The presence of possible trade offs between public and private investments are examined. In a recent study Bercovitz and Feldman (2006) offer a framework to illuminate the role of universities in systems of innovation and in the creation of a knowledge-based innovation system. Organization structure has been found to have strong impacts on technology transfer outcomes. The influences of university organizational structure and the technology transfer offices on their technology transfer performance are examined by Bercovitz et al. (2001). Empirical results provide evidence of the existence of alternative organizational structures and impacts where organizational capabilities result in differences in technology transfer outcomes. Caloghirou et al. (2001) investigate the characteristics of university-industry collaboration in a large set of European research joint ventures. Firms involved report that the most important benefit from such collaboration has been the positive impact on their knowledge base.

In a university-industry related study Meyer (2006) places the academic start-up phenomenon in the broader context. Based on Finnish academic inventions data, a considerable share of university-related patents are utilized in start up companies, but still most academic patents are utilized in established and large enterprises. Differences in utilization patterns are also found in different fields of science and technology. Thursby et al. (2001) describes results of a survey of licensing at a large sample of research universities.

They consider a number of attributes in their study including ownership, incomes, stage of development, marketing, license policies, and the role of the inventor in licensing. They analyze the relationship between licensing outcomes and both the objectives of the technology transfer offices and the characteristics of the technologies transferred. Results show that: patent applications grow with disclosures, sponsored research grows with licenses executed, royalties are positively related to the quality of the faculty, additional disclosures generate smaller percentage increases in licenses and these generate smaller percentage increases in royalties. In their introduction to the special issues on regional development in the knowledge-based economy Cooke and Leydesdorff (2005) seek to clarify two key concepts: the idea that knowledge is an economic factor and a system of reference for knowledge-based economic development. Here the university-industry-state relations at various levels are considered linked to industry organization with respect to patents and licensing.

7.3. FDI, Knowledge Diffusion and Technology Transfer

Analysis of the impact of knowledge diffusion on technology transfer via FDI or licensing has been the focus of great attention in the technology literature. There has been great interest for instance in studying the impact of knowledge diffusion on technology transfer (Radosevic, 1999) and international fragmentation of production (Hummels et al. 2001). Flow of FDI into developing countries, upstream and downstream type of technology diffusion with different implications for technology transfer process are considered in Saggi (2002). Giroud (2003) reviews the theory of vertical integration and the literature on TNCs' investments in the Asian nations. Giroud studies how alternative government policies affect economic outcomes. Governments in these countries actively seek to encourage foreign and domestic investment to promote economic growth and development. FDI has a number of benefits beyond domestic investment for the reasons related to balance of payments, spill-over benefits, technology transfer and labor force training. In practice, a liberalization of the direct investment has changed the ownerships structure of corporations in the aftermath of the Asian crisis.

Davis and Sun (2006) view business development as a corporate entrepreneurial capability that has emerged in the IT industry to support the industry in the practice of creation of value process with its external environment. Empirically the authors examine business development functions in SMEs in the IT industry in Canada. Results show that the principal local business development functions are finding profitable opportunities in business in recognizing and responding to customer needs. However, the non-local regional and export markets require different business development capabilities. In a related study Ivarsson and Alvstam (2005), study use firm-level data from the heavy truck and bus plants of AB Volvo and its local component suppliers in Brazil, China, India, and Mexico. They investigate the extent to which domestic suppliers are able to compete with international suppliers, and improve their operations through technological assistance from their TNC customer. The finding shows that technology transfers from industrialized to developing economies are to a large extent based on local inter-firm linkages arising from regular production activities. Results show that long-term relationships are more important in inter-firm learning than short-term relationships for domestic suppliers.

7.4. Innovation Research and Technology Valuation and Transfer

In the literature there are different perspectives on technology transfer to developing countries. In the evolutionary perspective, foreign TNC are contributors to technology transfer and upgrading of technology among their local suppliers. Lall (2000) views one reason for different perspectives on technology transfer is that most developing countries have none or only a limited capacity to generate new indigenous technology. Thus, external technology transfer is a major source of imports of technology (UNCTAD, 1999). In several studies (Dunning, 2000; Narula and Dunning, 2000; World Bank, 1998) the countries and their local firms capacity to identify, to absorb, to generate, and to disperse technological competence are found crucial to the transfer of technology. Two broad types of theories are identified in this respect (Nelson and Pack, 1999). These are the neoclassical accumulation and the evolutionary perspective of technology assimilation theories. The first stresses the role of physical and capital investments, while the latter focuses on learning in identifying, adapting and operating imported technologies. The locally developed elements are important to the success of investments (Nelson, 1990; Lall, 1992; Bell and Pavitt, 1993). Learning and development of routines are incremental and require a collective learning of technology.

In a different way technology transfer can also be distinguished by internalized or externalized characteristics of the process. Internalized transfers from TNC to their foreign affiliate are often part of the FDI package providing access to the ranges of technological, management, organizational and knowledge assets. Externalized technology transfers, are made to firms outside direct ownership and or control, in form of licenses and subcontracting. Externalized technology transfers have a stronger long-term effect (UNCTAD, 1999), but measurement of impact of technology is a rather difficult task. In particular there is a positive relationship between the soft natures of technology embodied in people and the difficulties in measuring the impact of technology transfer in such cases. Through the backward linkages between foreign affiliates and local suppliers, TNCs can improve technological development in host countries by complementing domestic investments and by undertaking transfers of knowledge, skills, and technology (see also Lall and Montimore, 2000; UNCTAD, 2001). Foreign TNCs provide their suppliers with extensive product and process related and technological assistance to meet the requirements of the home market. Due to growing demand for technological capabilities, reduced production costs, and increased delivery precision, domestic suppliers face competition from follow-source suppliers.

In general, technology transfer and innovation takes place most effectively when they are carried out within dynamic networks and conditional on effective public-private partnerships. The role and management of intellectual property and innovation can be handled through licensing techniques. Understanding technology assets and their acquisition based on consideration of capabilities, competencies and strategies for global competition are key issues. Managers play a key role in a company's success in the technology market. In addition to Rand D and acquisition of new equipment, the manager must account for the dominant role of human, technology, information and organization factors during different phases of development. The influential factors that determine the economic value of a technology must be identified and the underlying properties of technology valuation to be examined. In doing so one must account for technology risk premium in the estimation of risk-adjusted discount rate for the technology valuation. The objective is to estimate the cost of debt and equity for different sized classes of firms.

7.5. The New Era of Globalization and Technology Transfer

China and its technology capability development is a good example of the new era of globalization of technology. In the last two decades China's foreign trade and its industrially manufactured exports have diversified and expanded rapidly. Lemoine and Unal-Kesenci (2004) reported that China achieved an exceptional performance thanks to its strong involvement in international segmentation of production processes. A key factor contributing to the success was that China's specialization in assembly trade has given rise to a highly competitive and internationalized manufacturing sector, which has been the main channel of technology transfers. Their analysis of trade by stages of production and by technology contents shows that intermediate goods have played a crucial part in the technological upgrading of China's foreign trade. A negative development in their view is that the outward-oriented sector has had relatively limited linkage or spillover effects with the rest of industry. They find a systematic patterns in the development process where the development of East Asian economies has proceeded in waves, starting from Japan and followed by the first tier of new industrialized economies (South Korea, Taiwan, Singapore, Hong Kong), then by the second tier (Thailand, Malaysia, Philippines), and, finally, by the third tier (China and Indochina). Each of the countries has gradually shifted its specialization from labor-intensive industries such as textiles and footwear toward higher-technology sectors like electrical machinery and telecommunication equipment. See also ESCAP (1991), UNCTAD (1996) and Kojima (2000) for more details.

The recent wave of globalization process has enhanced the reorganization of production. Production processes have become highly internationally fragmented and participating firms take part in the production at different stages of the value-added chain, which is split-up across countries and firms. Countries and participating firms comparative advantages determine the in and outsourcing activities and countries involvement in stages of production. China and India provide two important case studies which highlight how latecomers can enter globalization and especially how China can carve out its place in the international division of labor. China has experienced innovation in the development of its technology market and employed strategic technology transfer policy combined with supporting innovation elements to build up its technology market. The technology market development needs to accelerate and improve to correspond to the need for and the rapid expansion of China's foreign trade and on-going reorganization of production in the region. Factors contributing to the fact that China has become a production base for Asian industrial firms include a rapid rise in exports, the development of an electrical and electronic industry based on foreign technology, and an accelerated economic growth of Southern coastal provinces (Wu, 1999; Lardy, 2002). Lemoine and Unal-Kesenci (2004) provide evidence that at the end of the 1990s, China's foreign trade was still highly dualistic where processing trade and ordinary trade display quite different patterns. Processing trade has been the engine of the rapid upgrading of China's foreign trade but domestic firms' foreign trade is still lagging behind. This suggests that the internationalized and competitive sector has not helped the modernization of the rest of the economy. China's entry into the WTO might serve as an important step towards the unification of the foreign trade regime and even a better access to foreign technology.

7.6. Summary of Key Conclusions and Policy Implications

The collected volume by Heshmati et al. (2007) is a recent contribution to the existing literature on commercialization and transfer of technology. A significant part of the collection focuses on the university-industry collaborations to promote commercialization and transfer of technology with the aim of creating knowledge-based development. The case studied shows that university cooperation has a positive influence on the innovative activity of large firms. Cooperation also affects the firms' ability to exploit market innovations originating in the university laboratories and it improves firms' internal innovative capacity and innovation efficiency by reducing the costs and risks associated with internal research. However, results show that universities in their research and innovation cooperation gain differently. The differences in financial gains for research universities in relation with technology transfer are attributed to differences in internal and external and research infrastructure factors. For a harmonization of technology finance, the financial organization, especially venture capital, is found to be the critical partner for private-to-private technology transfer system by concluding the agreement between the two parts as well as by investment in risky technology transfer activities. An investigation of the effectiveness of public innovation policy to stimulate private investment shows that public funds contribute positively to an increase in the firms' total Rand D efforts and it rejects the crowding out effects hypothesis.

In relation to business licensing of a patent portfolio, significant preparation is required to successfully transform the information and technology supported strongly by intellectual property. Real Option Analysis in licensing negotiations is found to be a useful tool in the preparation for negotiated deals. The important steps in the preparation do involve financial analysis using technology valuation management system to determine the value of the technology and to use quantitative measuring tools to identify competitive commercial products in the market. The objective is to create win-win scenarios for the negotiating parties of technology transfer. The approach is in particular important for business licensing technology valuation in cases where public financial support to universities is reduced or abolished. In general, creative measures that strengthen collaboration between university, government and enterprises to promote research activities and to accelerate the transfer of technology outcomes from the university to the industrialization of technology are encouraged. Estimation of the discount rate for the technology valuation indicates that reliability of the technology valuation in parts depends on the reliability of the discount rate estimates. Accounting for technology risk premium is suggested to improve the estimation of the risk-adjusted discount rate and crucial to venture capital firms.

Firm level analyses of the extent of international intra-firm transfer of management by Japanese MNCs suggest that top management has not been transferred to MNCs affiliates, but labor management has. Management technology has been transferred at European affiliates but not much at their Asian affiliates. The length of operation, provision of an FDI-friendly environment and improving labor quality has positively impacted the transfer of management technology. In addition, the strategies of the parent firm, their affiliates, the host countries, resources and development capability are all important determinants of the extent of technology transfer. In particular, policy and mechanics for technology transfer to SMEs is important for their survival, growth and performance, as well as subsidiaries and infrastructure for large corporations and the process of industrial development. Intellectual property as a barrier plays an important role in Rand D innovation and technology transfer to the developing countries. Thus, management of intellectual technology is critically important for the survival and growth of all enterprises in the new competitive and increasingly interdependent world economy. Analyzes of the development of technology market and technology transfer to China shows a good picture of the temporal patterns of recent waves of globalization of technology. The role of technology, capital, personnel, culture, policy, and intellectual property protection environments are key determinants of a successful technology transfer to create favorable circumstances for enterprises to participate in international competition.

8. RECENT DEVELOPMENTS IN THE FEDERAL REGION OF KURDISTAN

This chapter aims to review recent trends in economic development and development economics research. The areas of development considered includes information and telecommunications technology, globalization, economic growth, inequality, poverty and their linkages, direct foreign investment, in and outsourcing, spillover and transfer of technology and management. Here I investigate the development conditions and outcomes with reference to the areas listed above in the Federal Region of Kurdistan (FRK) from the beginning of the 1990s and onwards. There is a lack of statistics and research in each area. Thus, the analysis reflects my personal observations of the current state of the region.

8.1. Introduction

Kurdistan names the land that prior to the withdrawal of the British and French colonial forces from Middle East was divided between Iran, Iraq, Syria and Turkey. Kurds are the people who populate the land.[4] The total population of Kurds is estimated to be around 40 million of which more than 2 million live in Europe and North America. There are no statistics on the Kurdish population and its structure as such statistics in each country are not collected or reported. For centuries and in particular in 19th and 20th centuries the Kurds, like others in the Middle East, have been struggling to gain independence. The Kurds in Northern Iraq suffered heavily from oppression imposed by the regime of Saddam Hussein. The Iraqi army and security police among others destroyed 4000 of 4500 villages, displaced more than 1.5 million out of a total of 5 millions Kurds in the region, used chemical and biological weapons on the Kurds, mined the farmland and killed, as part of a campaign called Anfal in 1988 and 1989, more than 180,000 mainly Kurdish males.

As a result of international pressure to stop the Iraqi government's inhuman treatment of the Kurds, the USA and UK in 1990 established a no-fly zone in the North of Iraq. Enforcement of the zone was maintained by the USA and UK as part of the efforts by the international community, led by the USA, with the objective of disarming Iraq and preventing the country from developing weapons of mass destruction. Establishment of the no-fly zone facilitated a full withdrawal of the Iraqi army and security forces from the Kurdistan Region and the region gained some form of independence from the central government. There is a

---

4 Minorities populating the Southern part of the region include Arabs, Asyrians, Armenians, Yazidies and Turkemans.

desire and legal support through the 2005 election outcome that Iraq is to be cast as a federal system. However, in practice some self-interested forces are opposing such a type of governance. Despite being landlocked and undergoing active and persistent hostility from the neighboring countries, the Kurdistan Region has managed to build up necessary institutions and infrastructure and it has remained self-ruled. The region has a President, Prime Minister, regional parliament, regional government, regional ministries and many traditional and modern public service institutions.

8.2. Development in the Area of ICT Connectivity

The Kurdistan Region's communications with the outside world were cut off in 1988. The postal and telephone services ceased to operate. Lack of communication resulted in the intensive use of satellite services in the media, broadcasting and telecommunication. The presence of many non-governmental organizations (NGOs), the implementation of the oil for food program and comprehensive regional development programs, together with the large number of Kurds living abroad and advancements in communications technology, led to unique and profitable business opportunities to facilitate intensive use of information and telecommunication technologies in the region. Unlike fixed phones, connectivity in the form of computers and cell phones is relatively high. All connections are satellite-based and the use of broadband for lack of cooperation with neighboring countries is underdeveloped. Currently there are three providers of cell phone services[5] providing services to isolated areas of Hawler (Erbil), Sulymania, Kirkuk and other Kurdish cities. However, these are operating as pure regional monopolies and not providing services across their regions of operation. The condition has been very ineffective resulting in loss of welfare and is quite harmful to the regional development cooperation. The computer connectivity rate is high and, despite efforts made by the Korean development forces, NGOs and public sector efforts, the use of computers in public services is quite low. Universities are also not using their computer capacity fully. In general the development of the ICT sector is attributed to the satisfaction of the needs of NGOs to operate in the region. Similar to other countries, the Kurdistan Region sees this new sector as a major contributor and significant infrastructure and enabler to economic development.

8.3. Inflow of Foreign Direct Investment

The KRG has made serious efforts to provide official guidelines for investment activities in the region by introducing an Investment Law (KRG, 2006) which is aimed at the creation of good conditions for promoting investment in the Kurdistan Region. The law refers indiscriminately to both national and foreign capital sources and it removes key legal obstacles to investment activities. Various incentive measures in the form of land plots and other facilities and tax and duties exemptions and also regulations are introduced to promote investment activities. The law covers general provisions, exemptions and obligations, the investment hierarchy, and licensing and arbitration.

---

5 Korek, Asia and Sanatel are the three cell phone regional monopoly operators in the Kurdistan Region.

From the investor's point of view, there are a number of factors positively attributed to the law (see also Heshmati and Davis, 2007). The first important issue is the selection of areas of investment which cover the main economic and priority sectors including agriculture, manufacturing, services and various utilities and infrastructures. A second factor of strength is the non-discriminative treatment of capital by its source. Allocation of plots of land is the third and most important factor. The fourth key incentive factor is tax and customs duty exemptions for duration of ten years. The fifth strength factor is the provision of legal guarantees which account for insurance, employment, repatriation of profits, money transfers, and issues of security. Clarification of the investor's obligations and legal procedures in the case of contravention are to be considered as a sixth positive factor. The organizational structure and tasks of various agencies involved are to be seen as a seventh positive factor. The outlined procedures for licensing and risk of arbitration and finally provision of the transfer of duplicated investment laws to a unified one are among the eighth and ninth positive factors, respectively.

From the receiver's point of view, there are also several weaknesses in the law that gradually should be resolved. The first weakness is the lack of a strong emphasis on the transfer of technology, skills and management as basic conditions for the provision of investment incentives. The possibility of misuse of land plot allocation is a second weakness of the law. The lack of a patent register and non-existence of law enforcement and protection of intellectual property rights is a third key factor negatively affecting the flow of production-oriented FDI to the region. In order to attract technology-embodied investment, protection of intellectual properties is a factor that must be emphasized and the region's law enforcement capacity strengthened. Flow of oil revenues to the region inflated by recent years of high oil prices has raised the public and private income levels and consumption power and have, as a fourth factor, affected the trade balance negatively. In particular, development has been not only unfavorable but also destructive to local production. The KRG should promote local production through the imposition of duties on products and services that are or can be made available locally, while promoting only the import of technology-embodied capital. Thus, differentiated incentives and policy measures should be applied to capital by accounting for the nature of products and local production possibilities.

8.4. Development of Infrastructures

Education plays an important role in the development in the Kurdistan Region. Alongside the previous public institutions several new institutions have been established in the region. The governmental ministries of lower and higher educations plan and implement the region's educational policy. The Region has five universities located in the main cities of Hawler, Sulaymania, Dohuk, Koya and Kirkuk.[6] The policy of the universities organized under the umbrella of the regional Ministry of Higher Education and Scientific Research are old and inconsistent with a modern system of education and management. The quality of education has remained low, the system is highly bureaucratic, ineffective and not able to produce

---

6 The majority of residents of the oil rich city of Kirkuk are Kurds but the city was located outside the fly-free zone and subsequently not under the control of the Kurdistan Regional Government. A referendum is planned in late 2007 to bring clarity to the issue of integration of Kirkuk into the Federal Region of Kurdistan and its status as the new capital city of the Federal Region of Kurdistan.

graduates with the ability to be creative. They are unable to provide education of a high quality that corresponds to the needs of a modern society, particularly with regard to development. The difficulties in reforming the highly politicized higher education system have led to the establishment of new universities that are managed differently and with more autonomy in their operation. The public University of Kurdistan-Hawler and the recently established private American University at Sulaymania are two such examples. The needed labor market-oriented vocational education has not yet developed well.

A number of infrastructures are a prerequisite to the inflow of FDI and effective use of capital investments. The Financial Market and its functions are crucial to the success of the FDI policy. The financial policy of the KRG and its instruments are to be carefully determined. Another important infrastructure for inward FDI is the size and potential of small and medium enterprises (SME) and start-ups policies. SMEs serve as infrastructure for large enterprises. The focus should be on the optimal size of SME businesses, design of policies, to build up support institutions and guidelines to support the establishment of SMEs. The labor market policy options and a number of measures to promote the development programs of the region are the third category of infrastructure measures. The factors of interest include: mismatch of education and skills required; low quality education and creation of new job opportunities; high wage rate, low labor productivity and competitiveness; relatively high capital investment risk; high profitability of import compared to local production; and finally the absence of well-functioning labor market institutions and policy measures to promote production and employment creation. The fourth infrastructure factor is the formulation of a model for industrial development in the FRK (see Heshmati, 2007). The focus should initially be on the current policy and institutions, the conditions, potential and pitfalls and quantification of the resources available and needed, industrial policy instruments to improve security and self-sufficiency as well as infrastructure organizations. The establishment of Science Parks as a fifth factor is a necessary condition for the region's economic development. Science Parks are found to have a positive effect on productivity growth, technology, management and skill transfer.

8.5. Reconstruction Capacity Building

Iraq has been subjected to years of sanctions, war and destruction. The Kurdistan region has, however, enjoyed relative peace in recent years. The shared oil revenues after 2003 have allowed the region to start its reconstruction and development programs much earlier than other regions. KRG should take advantage of the existing peaceful conditions to build up capacity, not only to rebuild the Kurdistan region, but also to undertake reconstruction of the cities of Kirkuk and Mosul. An assessment of the past and current conditions in Iraq is vital to post-conflict rehabilitation and reconstruction of the country. Kurdistan, emerging from decades of conflict, needs to build up the capacity to recover itself and also actively participate in the recovery of the neighboring regions, in particular the Kirkuk region. FRK participation in the reconstruction of Kirkuk will help the FRK's manufacturing and service sectors to develop and become a player in Iraq's reconstruction program. It is important to evaluate the failure and success of the Investment Law. One motivation for developing countries to attract FDI is by obtaining advanced technology to enhance its domestic capability. Kurdistan is different and policies successful in other countries may not be as successful in Kurdistan. The result above suggests that the KRG should identify local specific factors that are determinants of inward FDI to the region and promote investment by national investors.

The increasing rate of inflation and devaluation of the domestic currency are identified as two key factors negatively affecting the inflow of FDI to developing countries. The FRK is using dual currencies: the US dollar and the Iraqi dinar. Since all transactions can be made entirely in US dollars, the risk of losing invested capital due to devaluation and transactions cost are minimized. So far, the currency factor has not been fully emphasized in the KRG arguments to attract inward FDI to the region. The security situation in Iraq is such that TNCs with an interest in participation in the Iraqi reconstruction program steer clear of the region. The regions capital city of Hawler[7] with its location and existing peaceful conditions can serve as the headquarters for many TNCs expecting participation in Iraq's reconstruction process. The KRG should attract these firms to boost the region's economy. It will help in building up the manufacturing and service sectors and their capacity, as well as technology, skill and management transfer. For instance the KRG should take advantage of the presence of Korean peace-keeping troops to facilitate the transfer of Korean technology to the region. Korea is a good partner for cooperation, in particular with their advanced oil, agriculture, communications, manufacturing, governance and institutional technologies. The Korean model of industrialization has shown in practice to be superior and a realistic way of development.

The inflow of private capital by repatriated Kurds and other private investors from the neighboring countries into the service sectors have been impressive. The regional government also has made comprehensive investment programs in building up development infrastructures in the form of international airports, universities, hospitals, public institutions, recreation, roads, job training, security, information and communication, banking and pubic utilities like energy and water. In recent years the economy has been booming and a large number of businesses have accumulated significant capital. In parallel with the accumulation process the businessmen have gained experience from doing business and have also been informed about investment opportunities elsewhere. Several Gulf countries also have established financial markets which attract interregional investors. Thus, the businessmen's expectations are high and the KRG must change its policy in response to changes in the environment and the financial markets. It is argued that a country's economic performance is to a great extent determined by its political, institutional and legal environment. Institutions and policies are referred to as governance infrastructure defining its investment environment. The KRG should adopt its institutions and governance to a higher and international standard by intensive training of its civil servants.

As a final checklist and in order for the FRK to encourage inward FDI and simultaneously to discourage outward FDI, the KRG should undertake a number of proactive policy measures to strengthen the necessary infrastructures and to affect investment behavior in the region. The region is rich in natural resources - a vital development factor, but the issue of the authority to use them is not settled yet. A clarification of this issue is an important agenda for the KRG. There is an Investment Law, but its strengths and weakness have not been investigated or tested. The newly developed banking system, in addition to being an FDI attraction factor, might have led to an increasing trend in outward FDI. Governance is weakly

---

7 For more information see the Kurdistan Regional Government official website at: http://www.krg.org/.

operated and most institutions are in place but are running ineffectively. Many new development infrastructure components are under construction. Currently there are no vocational training programs manifested in lacking skilled labor in the region. More important than the factors of governance, institutions and their operations are the low work morale, work discipline and respect for authority, a weak sense for national interest in work and decision patterns, and finally there is no economic development plan that integrates different activities. Construction of such a plan is underway under the supervision of the Ministry of Planning. Among other negative economic factors important to the inflow of FDI and the competitiveness of business and service sectors are high wages and low labor productivity. Efforts should be made to standardize wages to reflect the level of education and skills of the labor force. This will provide necessary tools for the government to support certain sectors in the form of wage subsidies to enhance self-sufficiency. Among other economic factors to emphasize strongly are the provisions of guarantees and securities and the dual currency conditions that are quite favorable to investors.

8.6. Globalization, Outsourcing and Local Production

The Kurdistan Region is an active participant of the new wave of globalization. The participation is in respect to international politics, migration, movement of skilled labor, information and communications technology and openness to trade relations. The society is open to the outside world through its many free media channels. The capital city of Hawler is a gateway to northern Iraq and it provides a safe environment for businesses, NGOs, tourism and refugees. I have already mentioned above the significant progress and investments made in the areas of education, infrastructures and information and communication. The regional government has made significant efforts to invest in building up a modern governance institutional structure. It has facilitated recognition of Kurds as a power in the region and changing views about Kurds and their existence and legitimate rights and demands. The interest and literacy rate in the English language has opened up new opportunities and participation in the globalization process. However, the unstable and post conflict conditions in Iraq have made the personal interactions with the outside world remain rather difficult. The living conditions for the majority of the population, and for females in general has improved and they occupy a significant share of the regional parliament, education and labor market. Despite the progress made there is still space for much improvement in their demands for equality and equal opportunities in all aspects of life.

Among the negative aspects of globalization worth mentioning are the foreign cultural dominance and the unbalanced development in the urban and rural areas. The booming construction sector has absorbed unskilled workers from the rural areas causing the low productive agriculture difficulties to compute and to produce goods with a high capacity to meet the increasing consumption demand. Lack of collection, transportation and storage facilities for agricultural products and investment in modern production technologies to produce and to supply round-the-year agricultural goods has made imported goods and services a significant part of the trade harming agriculture. Absence of a supportive agriculture and trade policy to promote domestic production and to limit the import of locally producible products and services has limited the development of the agricultural sector. In particular the openness and trade relations have undermined the local production to such an extent that it endangers the self-sufficiency and security of the region.

The rapid development has not resulted in a sufficient level of technology, skill and management transfer rather than a high dependency on imported skilled and unskilled workers to build up and to maintain the existing infrastructure. In-sourcing of labor has been significant in the form of imported labor in the construction and service areas, while most production previously produced domestically is outsourced to neighboring countries and countries in the East Asia. The rapid development not combined with taxation and redistribution has generated inequality among sub-groups of the population and it has raised poverty and its concentration among certain groups with low ability to adapt to the new conditions and to take advantages of the economic development. The direction of policy should change such that it encourages globalization to gain from it but at the same time to use in and outsourcing only to make the operation of businesses effective and less costly and to increase the rate of spillover and transfer of technology and management and to benefit from the relocation of production, contracting out activities, direct investments and joint ventures. The FRK in its policy should account for the potential and pitfalls in taking full advantages of the above factors in a small open economy with the minimum of restrictions and in the presence of many incentives to attract direct foreign investment and local production activities.

9. SUMMARY AND CONCLUSION

In this study I have provided a comprehensive review of the recent trends in development economics and related developments economics research. The focus has been on the development in the recent decades as a result of increased globalization of knowledge, technologies and economies. In particular I looked at the development in a number important areas including in-sourcing and outsourcing of production and services, the increased flow of direct foreign investment and its heterogeneous regional and sector distributions, the increased public investment in ICT as infrastructure for development, the importance of commercialization and transfer of technology, and increased income inequality and concentration of severe poverty in certain regions and among population sub-groups. In addition I investigated the development in the Federal Region of Kurdistan since its gained self-governance in 1991 as a small open economy case study with reference to the above developments.

In conclusion to the ICT as investment in infrastructure for development, this review suggests that ICT will continue to have an impact on performance for two reasons. First, productivity growth in the ICT-led areas and productivity improvements has continued to be strong; the ICT technology development will further encourage ICT investment and support further productivity growth. Second, the diffusion and impacts of ICT differ across economies. The largest economic benefits of ICT will be observed in countries with high levels of ICT diffusion. In order to derive the full economic benefits of ICT, other factors such as the regulatory environment, skills, ability to change organizational set-ups as well as innovations in ICT applications affect the ability of firms to seize the benefits of ICT technology. The contribution of ICT to economic growth is positively related to the level of development and adoption of complementary policies. These polices include basic infrastructure, competitive market, market opening, effective laws, regulations, law enforcement and the educational system. In general, for the developing countries, it is rather difficult to find any systematic evidence about such relationships. A longer period is required to establish a link between IT investment and economic growth and in particular, for ICT to be effective, it should be spread such that it reaches the critical mass point.

There are few studies that quantify the level and development of globalization. The indices computed are related to four main components: economic integration, personal contact, internet technology, and political engagements, each developing differently over time. Some of the indices are nonparametric while others are parametric in estimating the components weights. The results show that internal and external conflicts reduce the globalization prospects of the developing countries. The low rank of countries is often associated with political and technology factors, while the high-ranked countries share similar patterns in various index components distribution. The economic and technology factors play an important role in the ranking of the geographic and economic regions. The current versions of the index are only partial measures. A number of extensions to overcome the shortcomings are proposed. These concern the methodology and identification and incorporation of more relevant dimensions. A decomposition of the total variation in globalization into between and within country components is important. The within-country factors can provide useful information about the distributional shifts within different population groups, sectors and regions. Globalization is considered a possible source of inequality differences across countries and over time.

One major shortcoming of the literature on the relationship between growth, inequality, poverty and openness is that the simultaneous and direction of the causal relationship between these key variables has empirically been neglected. In general there exists a positive relationship between openness and growth, but its impact on distribution of income differs. There is evidence of strong convergence in per capita income and among more homogenous and integrated advanced economies but also divergence in income inequality and among less-developed countries or geographic regions. The between country contribution is much higher than within country contribution to world inequality. Different regions have differently managed to couple growth and inequality. The empirical results on the above relationships show that outcomes of policy measures are heterogeneous. Depending on the initial position, the poor might gain more from growth and redistribution, but they may also suffer more from economic contraction. In general it is rather difficult to measure the effects of inequality and growth on poverty reduction in the course of economic development. In sum, economic growth benefits the poor but at the absence of effective redistribution policies it might initially deteriorate the income distribution. Initial conditions, institutions, specific country and demographic structures, and time horizons each play a significant role in making economic growth pro-poor.

The global flow of foreign direct investment has increased dramatically but its distribution is highly unequal and countries fiercely compete to attract foreign investors. The positive changes involve simplified procedures, incentives, reduced taxes and greater openness to foreign investors. FDI is important to developing countries as it increases export revenues and investment capital, it supplies with advanced management and technology and it is a viable development factor for capital scarce but labor-abundant countries. The scale and character of FDI flows to developing countries have been affected by the invention and adoption of new technologies. ICT has facilitated a global shift in the service industries and relocation of many production activities. The determinants of FDI to developing countries are their natural-resource endowments and low-cost labor. However, the existing investments are often concentrated in natural resource sectors with limited multiplier effects on output and employment in the rest of the economies. There is a growing view that FDI is positively correlated with economic growth. It improves efficiency and productivity through transfer of advanced technology and management practices. A recent boom in cross-border mergers and acquisitions, increasing investment by investment funds, increasing number of TNC from developing countries, regulatory changes has spurred the increase in FDI enhancing South-South investment flows. Developing host countries gain much from the rise in South-South FDI and economic cooperation. There is a better fit of the technology and business models of developing countries from FDI inflow easing the technology absorption process. FDI from developing countries has being more oriented towards labor intensive industries. The economic reform, FDI policy and establishment of special economic zones have made China one of the most important destinations for FDI.

In this paper I provided a review of the methods used and empirical results obtained from studies of the link between corporate competitive strategy, efficiency, outsourcing, innovation and productivity growth. Results from a new method with a view to dealing with the issues of sample selection and simultaneity biases in innovation studies based on firm level innovation data was also presented. Results suggested that firms are relatively efficient, although the output can further be increased if firms use best practice technology. Efficiency in production is positively correlated with innovation and productivity growth. Furthermore, there was a positive association between size of firm, profitability, investment, outsourcing and efficiency in production. A simple composite competitive strategy index was estimated which indicates the level and state of competitiveness among the firms. I also identified a number of determinants of decisions of investment in innovation activities, innovation output and productivity growth. The systems of equations estimated accounting for both sample selection and simultaneity biases is found to be superior to alternative simpler estimation methods. Internal financial sources, knowledge intensive production technology and size of firms are major determinants of investment in innovations. There was a positive and two-way causality relationship between innovation output and productivity growth.

The university-industry collaboration is important to promote commercialization and transfer of technology. It has a positive influence on the innovative activity of large firms and it affects the firms' ability to exploit market innovations originating in the university laboratories and as well as firms' internal innovative capacity. Universities in their research and innovation cooperation gain differently. The differences in financial gains are attributed to differences in their research infrastructure factors. Venture capital is found to be the critical partner for technology transfer system by investment in risky technology transfer activities. Public innovation policy is found to stimulate private investment in Rand D with no crowding out effects. In relation to business licensing of a patent portfolio, Real Option Analysis is found to be a useful tool in the preparation for negotiated deals to create win-win scenarios for the negotiating parties. Estimation of discount rate for the technology valuation indicates that reliability of the technology valuation in parts depends on the reliability of the discount rate estimates. Accounting for technology risk premium improves the estimation of the risk-adjusted discount rate. Firm level analyses show that labor management is easier to be transferred than top management to MNCs affiliates and the degree of transfer differ by the countries origin. The length of operation, provision of FDI-friendly environment and improving labor quality has positively impacted on the transfer of management technology. In addition, the strategies of the parent firm, their affiliates, the host countries resources and development capability are all important determinants of the extent of technology transfer. Analyses of the development of technology market and technology transfer to China shows that the role of technology, capital, personnel, culture, policy, and intellectual property protection are key determinants of technology transfer.

This chapter also aimed at investigating the development conditions and outcomes with reference to the areas listed above in the Federal Region of Kurdistan. The Kurdistan Region was in 1988 cut off from communication with the outside world and it gained its independent governance in 1991. Intensive use of satellite services, broadcasting and telecommunication, the presence of many NGOs, comprehensive regional development programs together with technology advancement led to unique and profitable business opportunities to transfer new communication technologies to the region. The connectivity in the form of computers and cell phones is relatively high, but lack of cooperation among service providers and ineffective public institutions has led to underutilization of the resources. In similarity with other countries the Kurdistan Region sees this new sector as a major contributor and significant infrastructure and enabler to economic development.

The KRG has made serious efforts to provide official guidelines on investment activities in the region by introducing a new Investment Law. Various incentive measures in the form of land plots, tax and duties exemptions and also regulations are introduced to promote investment activities. From the investor's point of view, the factors positively attributed to the law are: the broad selection of areas of investment, the non-discriminative treatment of capital by its source, allocation of plots of land, tax and customs duty exemptions, provision of legal guidance, clarification of the investor's obligations and legal procedures, the organization and tasks of various agencies involved. From the receiver's point of view, the weaknesses of the law are: the lack of a strong emphasis on the transfer of technology, skills and management and local employment as basic conditions for provision of investment incentives, the possibility of misuse of land plot allocation, the lack law enforcement and protection of intellectual property rights and the raised public and private income levels and consumption that has affected negatively the trade balance and local production. The KRG should promote local production through the imposition of duties on products and services that can be produced locally, while promoting only the import of technology-embodied capital.

Education plays an important rule to development in the Kurdistan Region. The ministries of education are and should plan and implement a new educational policy consistent with a modern system of education and management. The universities are unable to provide education of high quality that corresponds to the needs of a modern society. In parallel with the reform of existing universities new public and private universities are established that are managed differently. The labor market oriented vocational education has not yet been developed. A number of infrastructures are a prerequisite to the inflow of FDI and the effective use of capital investments. These include the financial market and its functions, the size and potential of SMEs, the start-ups and labor market policies, measures to promote development in the region, formulation of a model for industrial development and establishment of Science Parks and economic free zones.

The Kurdistan region has enjoyed relative peace in recent years and high oil prices. The shared oil revenues after 2003 have allowed the region to start its reconstruction and development programs much earlier than expected. The KRG should take advantage of the existing peaceful conditions to build up capacity to rebuild both Kurdistan region and also undertake reconstruction of the neighboring cities. The KRG should identify local specific factors that are determinants of inward FDI to the region and promote investment by national investors. The increasing rate of inflation and devaluation of the domestic currency are identified as two common key factors negatively affecting the inflow of FDI. The FRK is using dual currencies: the US dollar and the Iraqi dinar but the advantages of currency factor in reducing investment risk have not been fully emphasized. The region's capital city of Hawler with its location and existing peaceful conditions can serve as the headquarters for many TNCs expecting participation in Iraq's reconstruction process. The KRG should take advantage of the presence of Korean peace-keeping troops to facilitate the transfer of Korean technology to the region. Korea is a good partner for cooperation, in particular with their advanced petrochemical, agriculture, communications, manufacturing, governance and institutional technologies. The Korean model of industrialization has been shown in practice to be a realistic way of development.

The regional government also has made comprehensive investment programs in building up development infrastructures. It is argued that a country's economic performance is to a great extent determined by its political, institutional and legal environment. Thus, the KRG should adopt its institutions and governance to a higher and international standard by intensive training of its civil servants. In order for the region to encourage inward FDI and simultaneously to discourage outward FDI, it should undertake a number of proactive policy measures to strengthen the infrastructures and to affect investment behavior. These include: a clarification of authority to use natural resources, evaluation of the strengths and weaknesses of the Investment Law, improvement in the function of the financial market, vocational training, governance and institutions, the low work morale, work discipline, the weak sense of national interest, economic development plan, the high wages and low labor productivity, provisions of guarantees and securities and improvement in equality.

Among the negative aspects of globalization worth mentioning are the foreign cultural dominance, the unbalanced development in the urban and rural areas, high dependency on imported labor, difficulties facing agriculture to compete in the absence of supportive agriculture and trade policy and openness and trade relations have undermined the local production to such an extent that it endangers the self-sufficiency and security of the region. The rapid development has not resulted in a sufficient level of technology, skill and management transfer rather than a high dependency of imported labor to build up and to maintain the existing infrastructure. In-sourcing of labor has been significant in the construction and service areas, while most production previously produced domestically is now outsourced. Rapid development not combined with taxation and redistribution has also generated inequality among sub-groups of the population and it has raised poverty especially with its concentration among certain sub-groups with little ability to adapt to the new conditions.

ACKNOWLEDGEMENT

I would like to thank Ms. Rhona Davis and Dr. Robert Doebler for his careful reading of the paper and suggesting improvements to the text; Ms Chiman S.J. Bajalan, Professor Jeong-Dong Lee; and participants at joint seminar held at Techno-Economics and Management Program at Seoul National University, Seoul; and Information and Communication University, Daejeon, South Korea for their comments and suggestions. Data on global diffusion of ICT from Mr. Minkyu Lee is highly appreciated.

ABOUT THE AUTHOR

Almas Heshmati is a Professor of Economics at the University of Kurdistan Hawler and founder and Director for the Hawler Institute for Economic and Policy Research, Federal Region of Kurdistan, Iraq. He held similar position at the RATIO Institute (Stockholm), Seoul National University (Seoul) and MTT Economic Research (Helsinki). He was Research Fellow at the World Institute for Development Economics Research (WIDER), The United Nations University (Helsinki) and Associate Professor at the Stockholm School of Economics. He has a Ph.D. degree in economics from the University of Gothenburg. E-mail: almas.heshmati@ukh.ac and heshmati@snu.ac.kr

REFERENCES

Abraham K. and T. Taylor (1996), Firms' use of outside contractors: theory and evidence, *Journal of Labor Economics* 14, 394-424.

Acemoglu D. and J. Ventura (2002), The world income distribution, *Quarterly Journal of Economics* CXVII(2), 659-694.

Addison T. and A. Heshmati (2004), The new global determinants of FDI flows to developing countries: the importance of ICT and democratization, *Research in Banking and Finance* 4, 151-186.

Agénor P.R. (2003), Does Globalization Hurt the Poor?, World Bank, Unpublished manuscript.

Aghion P. (2002), Schumpeterian growth theory and the dynamics of income inequality, *Econometrica* 70(3), 855-882.

Aghion P. and J.G. Williamson (1998), *Growth, Inequality and Globalization: Theory, History and Policy*. Cambridge: Cambridge University Press.

Alesina A. and D. Rodrik (1994), Distributive politics and economic growth, *Quarterly Journal of Economics* 109, 465-490.

Al-Marhubi F. (1997), A note on the link between income inequality and inflation, *Economics Letters* 55, 317-319.

Andersen T.M. and T.T. Herbertsson (2003), Measuring Globalization. IZA Discussion Paper. 2003:817. Bonn: IZA.

Antonelli C. (1990), Information technology and the derived demand for telecommunications services in the manufacturing industry, *Information Economics and Policy* 4: 45-55.

Arnold U. (2000), New dimensions of outsourcing: a combination of transaction cost economics and the core competencies concept, *European Journal of Purchasing and Supply Management*.6, 23-29.

Asiedu E. (2002), On the Determinants of Foreign Direct Investment to Developing Countries: Is Africa Different?, *World Development*, 30(1), 107-119.

Atkinson A.B. (1999), Is rising inequality inevitable? A critique of the transatlantic consensus, The United Nations University, WIDER Annual Lectures 3, Helsinki: UNU/WIDER.

Atkinson A.B. (2000), Increased income inequality in OECD countries and the redistributive impact of the Government budget, WIDER Working Papers 2000/202, Helsinki: UNU/WIDER.

Babones S.J. (2002), Population and Sample Selection Effects in Measuring International Income Inequality. *Journal of World-System Research*. 8(1), 7-28.

Balk B. (1998), *Industrial price, quality, and productivity indices. The micro-economic theory and applications,* Kluwer Academic, Boston.

Barthelemy J. (2003), The hard and soft sides of IT outsourcing management, *European Management Journal* 21(5), 539-548.

Barro R.J. (1997), Determinants of economic growth: a cross-country empirical study, MIT press, Cambridge, MA.

Barro R.J. and X. Sala-i-Martin (1995), Economic Growth, McGraw-Hill Inc.

Bata M. and A.J. Bergesen (2002a). Global Inequality: An Introduction to Special Issue on Global Economy: Part I. *Journal of World-System Research*. 8(1), 2-6.

Bata M. and A.J. Bergesen (2002b). Global Inequality: An Introduction to Special Issue on Global Economy: Part II. *Journal of World-System Research*. 8(2), 146-48.

Baumol W.J. (1967), Macroeconomics of unbalanced growth: the anatomy of urban crisis, *American Economic Review* 57, 415-426.

Baumol W.J., Blackman, A.B. and E.N. Wolff (1985), Unbalanced growth revisited: asymptotic stagnancy and new evidence, *American Economic Review* 75, 806-817.

Beer L. and T. Boswell (2002), The Resilience of Dependency Effects in Explaining Income Inequality in the Global Economy: A Cross National Analysis, 1975-1995. *Journal of World-System Research*. 8(1),29-59.

Bell M, and K. Pavitt (1993), Technological accumulation and industrial growth: Contrasts between developed and developing countries, *Industrial and Corporate Change* 2(2), 157–210.

Benson J. (1999), Outsourcing, organisational performance and employee commitment, *Economic and Labour Relations Review* 10(1), 1-21.

Bercovitz J. and M. Feldman (2006), Entrepreneurial Universities and Technology Transfer: A Conceptual Framework for Understanding Knowledge-Based Economic Development, *Journal of Technology Transfer* 31(1), 175-188.

Bercovitz J., Feldman M., Feller I. and R. Burton (2001), Organizational Structure as a Determinant of Academic Patent and Licensing Behavior: an Exploratory Study of Duke, Johns Hopkins, and Pennsylvania State Universities, *Journal of Technology Transfer* 26 (1/2), 21-35.

Bergesen A.J. and M. Bata (2002), Global and National Inequality: Are They Connected?. *Journal of World-System Research*, 8(1), 129-44.

Bevan D.L. and A.K. Fosu (2003), Globalization: An Overview. *Journal of African Economies*. 12(1),1-13.

Bhagwati J. (2000), Globalization and Appropriate Governance. *WIDER Annual Lecture* 4. Helsinki: UNU/WIDER.

Bigsten A. and J. Levin (2000), Growth, income distribution and poverty: a review, Department of Economics, Göteborg University, Working Paper in Economics No. 2000:32.

Bornschier V. (2002), Changing Income Inequality in the Second Half of the 20th Century: Preliminary Findings and Propositions for Explanations. *Journal of World-System Research* 8(1), 99-127.

Bourguignon F. and C. Morrisson (2002), Inequality among world citizens: 1820-1992, American Economic Reviews 92(4), 727-747.

Calderon C. and A. Chong (2001), External sector and income inequality in interdependent economics using a dynamic panel data approach, *Economics Letters* 71, 225-231.

Caloghirou Y., Tsakanikas A. and N. S. Vonortas (2001), University-industry Cooperation in the Context of the European Framework, *Journal of Technology Transfer* 26 (1/2), 153-161.

Chalos P. (1995), Costing, control, and strategic analysis in outsourcing decisions, *Journal of Cost Management*, Winter, 31-37.

Chen Y., Ishikawa J. and Z. Yu (2003), Trade liberalization and strategic outsourcing, *Journal of International Economics* 63(2), 419-436.

Cheng L. K. and Y. K. Kwan (1999), Foreign capital stock and its determinants, *Foreign Direct Investment and Economic Growth in China*, ed. by Wu, Y. MPG Books, Great Britain.

Chowdhury A. and G. Mavrotas (2005), FDI and growth: a causal relationship. *Research Paper of World Institute for Development Economics Research*, United Nations University, No. 2005/25.

Collier P. and D. Dollar (2001), Can the World Cut Poverty in Half? How Policy Reform and Effective Aid Can Meet International Development Goals. *World Development*. 29(11), 1787-802.

Collier P. and D. Dollar (2002), Aid Allocation and Poverty Reduction. *European Economic Review*. 46, 1475-500.

Cooke P. and L. Leydesdorff (2005), Regional Development in the Knowledge-Based Economy: The Construction of Advantage, *Journal of Technology Transfer* 31(1), 5-15.

Cornia G.A. and J. Court (2001), Inequality, Growth and Poverty in the Era of Liberalization and Globalization. *WIDER Policy Brief* 4. Helsinki: UNU/WIDER.

Coughlin C. C. and E. Segev (2000), Foreign direct investment in China: A Spatial econometric study, *World Economy* 21(1), 1-23.

Crepon B., Duguet E. and J. Mairesse (1998), Research, innovation, and productivity: an econometric analysis at the firm level, NBER Working Paper, no. 6696.

Davis C. and E. Sun (2006), Business Development Capabilities in Information Technology SMEs in a Regional Economy: An Exploratory Study, *Journal of Technology Transfer* 31(1), 145-161.

Dayal-Gulati A. and A. M. Husain (2000), Centripetal forces in China's economic take-off. *IMF Working Paper* WP/00/86.

De Kok T.G. (2000), Capacity allocation and outsourcing in a process industry, *International Journal of Production Economics* 68, 229-239.

Deavers K.L. (1997), Outsourcing: a corporate competitiveness strategy, not a search for low wages, *Journal of Labor Research* 18(4), 503-519.

Deininger K. and L. Squire (1998), New ways of looking at old issues: inequality and growth, *Journal of Development Economics* 57, 259-287.

Dewan S. and K.L. Kraemer (2000), Information technology and productivity: evidence from country-level data, *Management Science* 46, 548-562.

Dollar D. and A. Kraay (2001a), Trade growth and poverty, Development Research Group, The World Bank.

Dollar D. and A. Kraay (2001b), Growth is good for the poor, Policy Research Working paper 2001:2199, Development Research Group, The World Bank.

Dollar D. and P. Collier (2001), Globalization, Growth and Poverty: Building an Inclusive World Economy. Oxford: Oxford University Press.

Dowrick S. and J.B. DeLong (2003), Globalization and convergence, In: Bordo M.D., A.M. Taylor and J.G. Williamson (eds.), Globalization in historical perspective, Chicago, University of Chicago Press.

Dreher A. (2005), Does Globalization Affect Growth? Empirical Evidence from a New Index. Department of Economics, University of Konstanz, Unpublished Manuscript.

Dritna R.E. (1994), The outsourcing decision, *Management Accounting*, March, 56-62.

Dunning J.H. (Ed.) (2000), Regions, globalization, and the knowledge-based economy, Oxford: Oxford University Press.

Edquist H. and M. Henrekson (2007), Technological Breakthroughs and Productivity Growth, *Research in Economic History* 24.

Edwards T.H. (1998), Openness, productivity and growth: what do we really know, *Economic Journal* 108, 383-398.

Egger H. and J. Falkinger (2003), The distributional effects of international outsourcing in a 2x2 production model, *North American Journal of Economics and Finance* 14, 189-206.

ESCAP UN (1991), Industrial restructuring in Asia and the Pacific, Bangkok: United Nations.

Estevão M. and L. Lach (1999), Measuring temporary labor outsourcing in U.S. manufacturing, NBER Working Paper, no. 7421.

Falk M. and B. Koebel (2000), *Outsourcing of services, imported materials, and the demand for heterogeneous labour: an application of a Generalized Box-Cox function*, Centre for European Economic Research (ZEW) Discussion Paper no. 2000:51, Mannheim.

Feenstra R.C. (1998), Integration of trade and disintegration of production in the global economy, *Journal of Economic Perspectives* 12(4), 31-50.

Feenstra R.C. and G.H. Hanson (1995), Foreign investment, outsourcing and relative wages, NBER Working Paper, no. 5121.

Feenstra R.C. and G.H. Hanson (1996), Globalization, outsourcing, and wage inequality, *American Economic Review* 86(2), 240-245.

Fixler D.J. and D. Siegel (1999), Outsourcing and productivity growth in services, *Structural Change and Economic Dynamics* 10, 177-194.

Fu J. (2000), Institutions and investments: foreign direct investment in China during an era of reforms, University of Michigan Press U.S.

Fung K.C., Iizaka H., Lin C. and A. Siu (2002), An econometric estimation of locational choices of foreign direct investment: The case of Hong Kong and U.S. firms in China, Asian Development Bank Institute.

Gavious A. and G. Rabinowitz (2003), Optimal knowledge outsourcing model, *Omega The International Journal of Management Science* 31, 451-457.

Gholami R., Tom-Lee S.Y. and A. Heshmati (2006), The Causal Relationship Between Information and Communication Technology and Foreign Direct Investment, *The World Economy* 29(1), 43-62.

Gilley K.M. and A. Rasheed (2000), Making more by doing less: an analysis of outsourcing and its effects on firm performance, *Journal of Management* 26(4), 763-790.

Giroud A. (2003), Transnational Corporations, Technology and Economic Development: Backward Linkages and Knowledge Transfer in South East Asia, Edward Elgar, Cheltenham, UK.

Glass A.J. and K. Saggi (2001), Innovation and wage effects of international outsourcing, *European Economic Review* 45(1), 67-86.

Globerman S., A. Kokko and F. Sjoholm (2000), International technology diffusion: evidence from Swedish patent data, *Kyklos* 53, 17-38.

Goh A. (2005), *Knowledge diffusion, input supplier's technological effort and technology transfer via vertical relationships*, Journal of International Economics 66(2), 527-540.

Goudie A. and P. Ladd (1999), Economic growth, poverty and inequality, *Journal of International Development* 11, 177-195.

Griliches Z. (1990), Patent statistics as economic indicators: a survey, *Journal of Economic Literature* 28(4), 1661-1707.

Griliches Z. (1992), Introduction, in *Output measurement in the service sector* ed. Z Griliches, pp. 1-22, NBER and University of Chicago Press.

Griliches Z. and J. Mairesse (1993), Introduction, *The Journal of Productivity Analysis* 4, 5-8.

Grossman G. and E. Helpman (2002a), Outsourcing in a global economy, NBER Working Paper 2002:8728.

Grossman G. and E. Helpman (2002b), Outsourcing versus FDI in industry equilibrium, NBER Working Paper 2002:9300.

Heshmati A (2003), Productivity growth, efficiency and outsourcing in manufacturing and service industries, *Journal of Economic Surveys* 17(1), 79-112.

Heshmati A. (2006a), Conditional and Unconditional Inequality and Growth Relationships, *Applied Economics Letters* 13, 925-931.

Heshmati A. (2006b), Measurement of a Multidimensional Index of Globalization, *Global Economy Journal* 6(2), Paper 1.

Heshmati A. (2006c), The Relationship between Income Inequality Poverty, and Globalization, in M. Nissanke and E. Thorbecke, *The Impact of Globalization on the World's Poor*, Palgrave Macmillan.

Heshmati A. (2007), A Model for Industrial Development of the Federal Region of Kurdistan: Science and Technology Policy, Instruments and Institutions, Hawler Policy Report 2007:04 and IZA Discussion Paper 2007:3213.

Heshmati A. and R. Davis (2007), The Determinants of Foreign Direct Investment Flows to the Federal Region of Kurdistan, Hawler Policy Report 2007:05 and IZA Discussion Paper 2007:3218.

Heshmati A. and K. Pietola (2006), The Relationship between Corporate Competitiveness Strategy, Innovation, Increased Efficiency, Productivity Growth and Outsourcing, in P. Bararrar and R. Gervais, *Global Outsourcing Strategies: An International Reference on Effective Outsourcing Relationships*, Gower Publishing, pp. 77-116.

Heshmati A., Y-B. Sohn and Y-R. Kim (2007), Eds. *"Commercialization and Transfer of Technology: Major Country Case Studies"*, New York: Nova Science Publishers.

Heshmati A. and A. Tausch (2007), Eds. Roadmap to Bangalore: Globalization, the EU's Lisbon Process and the Structures of Global Inequality. Huntington NY: Nova Science Publishers, Inc.

Holmström B. and J. Roberts (1998), The boundaries of the firm revisited, *Journal of Economic Perspectives* 12(4), 73-94.

Hummels D., Ishii J. and K-M. Yi (2001), The Nature and Growth of Vertical Specialization in World Trade, *Journal of International Economics* 54, 75-96.

Inman R.P. (1985) Introduction and overview, in *Managing the Service Economy: Prospects and Problems*, ed RP Inman, Cambridge University press, Cambridge, MA, pp. 1-24.

Islam N. (1995), Growth empirics: a panel data approach, *Quarterly Journal of Economics* 110, 1127-1170.

Ivarsson I. and C.G. Alvstam (2005), Technology Transfer from TNCs to Local Suppliers in Developing Countries: A Study of AB Volvo's Truck and Bus Plants in Brazil, China, India, and Mexico, *World Development* 33(8), 1325–1344.

Jacobson L., Lalonde, R and D. Sullivan (1993), Earnings losses of displaced workers, *American Economic Review* 83(3), 685-709.

James J. (2002), *Technology, Globalization and Poverty*. Cheltenham: Edward Elgar.

Jones C.I. (2002), Introduction to economic growth, Second Edition, W.W. Norton and Company.

Jones R.W. and H. Kierzkowski (2000), *A framework for fragmentation*, Tinbergen Institute Discussion Paper TI 2000-056/2.

Jorgenson D.W. (2001), Information Technology and the US Economy, *American Economic Review* 91(1), 1-32.

Kakabadse A. and N. Kakabadse (2002), Trends in outsourcing: contrasting USA and Europe, *European Management Journal* 20(2), 189-198.

Kearney, A.T., Inc., The Carnegie Endowment for International Peace. (2002). Globalization's Last Hurrah?. *Foreign Policy*. January/February: 38-51.

Kearney, A.T., Inc., The Carnegie Endowment for International Peace. (2003), Measuring Globalization: Who's Up, Who's Down?. *Foreign Policy*. January/February: 60-72.

Khan A.R. and C. Riskin (2001), *Inequality and Poverty in China in the Age of Globalization*. Oxford: Oxford University Press.

Kojima K. (2000), The flying gees model of Asian economic development: origin, theoretical extensions, and regional policy implications, *Journal of Asian Economics* 11, 375–401.

Kokko A. (1994), Technology, market characteristics, and spillovers, *Journal of Development Economics* 43, 279-293.

Kokko A., R. Tansini and M. Zejan (1996), Local technological capability and spillovers from FDI in the Uruguayan manufacturing sector, *Journal of Development Studies* 34, 601-611.

Kotabe M. (1992), *Global sourcing strategy: Rand D, manufacturing, and marketing interfaces*, Quorum, New York.

Kumar N. and J. P. Pradhan (2002), Foreign direct investment, externalities, and economic growth in developing countries: some empirical explorations and implications for WTO negotiations on investment. *RIS discussion papers, Research and Information System for Non-aligned and Other Developing Countries.*

Kurdistan Regional Government (2006), Law of Investment in Kurdistan Region – Iraq, Law No. 4 of 2006, KRG.

Lacity M.C., Willcocks, L.P. and D.F. Feeny (1996), The value of selective IT outsourcing, *Sloan Management Review*, Spring, 13-25.

Lall S. (1992), Technological capabilities and industrialization, *World Development* 20(2), 165–186.

Lall S. (2000), Technological change and industrialization in the Asian newly industrializing economies: Achievements and challenges, In L. Kim and R. R. Nelson (Eds.), Technology, learning and innovation, Experiences of newly industrializing economies. Cambridge: Cambridge University Press.

Lall S. and M. Mortimore (2000), Competitiveness, restructuring and FDI: An analytical framework. In UNCTAD: The competitive challenge: Transnational corporations and industrial restructuring in developing countries, Geneva: United Nations Conference on Trade and Development.

Lardy N. (2002), Integration China into the global economy, Washington, DC: Brookings Institution Press.

Lee K., M.H. Pesaran and R. Smith (1997), Growth and convergence in a multi-country empirical stochastic Solow model, *Journal of Applied Econometrics* 12, 357-392.

Lee M-Y. and A. Heshmati (2007), World Economy, Information and Communications Technology, Princeton Encyclopedia.

Lei D. and M. Hitt (1995), Strategic restructuring and outsourcing: the effect of mergers and acquisitions and LBOs on building firm skills and capabilities, *Journal of Management* 21(5), 835-859.

Lemoine F. and D. Unal-Kesenci (2004), Assembly Trade and Technology Transfer: The Case of China, *World Development* 32(5), 829-850.

Lindert P.H. and J.G. Williamson (2001), Does Globalization Make the World More Unequal?, University of California, Davis and Harvard University.

Liu Z. (2002), Foreign direct investment and technology spillover: evidence from China, *Journal of Comparative Economics* 30, 579-602.

Liu X., P. Burridge and P.J.N. Sinclair (2002), Relationships between economic growth, foreign direct investment and trade: evidence from China, *Applied Economics* 34, 1433-1440.

Liu X. and H. Song (1997), China and the multinationals: a winning combination, *Long Range Planning* 30(1), 74-83.

Lockwood B. (2004), How Robust is the Foreign Policy-Kearney Globalization Index?, *The World Economy* 27, 507-523.

Lockwook B. and M. Redoano (2005), The CSGR Globalization Index: An Introductory Guide. CSGR Working Paper 155/04.

Loh L. and N. Venkatraman (1992), Determinants of information technology outsourcing: a cross-sectional analysis, *Journal of Management Information Systems* 9(1), 7-24.

Madden G. and S.J. Savage (1998), CEE telecommunications investment and economic growth, *Information Economics and Policy* 10, 173-195.

Maddison A. (2001), The World Economy: A millennial perspective, Development Centre Studies. Paris: OECD.

Mahler V.A. (2001), Economic Globalization, Domestic Politics and Income Inequality in the Developed Countries: A Cross-National Analysis. *Luxembourg Income Study Working Paper*. 2001:273. Luxembourg.

Mankiew N.G., D. Romer and D.H. Weil (1992), A contribution to the empirics of economics growth, *Quarterly Journal of Economics* 107, 407-438.

Manning S. (1999), Introduction to Special Issue on Globalization, *Journal of World-Systems Research*. 5(2), 137-41.

Mansfield E. and A. Romeo (1980), Technology Transfer to Overseas Subsidiaries by U.S. Based firms, *Quarterly Journal of Economics* 95, 737-749.

Meyer M. (2006), Academic Inventiveness and Entrepreneurship: On the Importance of Start-up Companies in Commercializing Academic Patents, *Journal of Technology Transfer* 31(4), 501-510.

Milanovic B. (2002), Can We Discern the Effect of Globalization on Income Distribution? Evidence from Household Budget Surveys, *World Bank Policy Research Paper* 2876, Washington DC: World Bank.

Mussa M. (2003), Meeting the Challenges of Globalization, *Journal of African Economies*. 12(1), 14-34.

Nair-Reichert U. and D. Weinhold (2001), Causality tests for cross-country panels: a new look at FDI and economic growth in developing countries, *Oxford Bulletin of Economics and Statistics* 63(2), 153-171.

Narula R. and J.H. Dunning (2000), Industrial development, globalization and multinational enterprises: New realities for developing countries, *Oxford Development Studies* 28(2), 141–167.

Nayyar P.R. (1993), On the measurement of competitive strategy: evidence from a large multiproduct U.S. firm, *Academy of Management Journal* 36, 1652-1669.

Nelson R.R. (1990), On technological capabilities and their acquisition. In R. E. Evenson and G. Ranis (Eds.), Science and technology: Lessons for development policy (pp. 71–80). Boulder, CO: Westview Press.

Nelson R.R. and H. Pack (1999), The Asian miracle and modern growth theory, *The Economic Journal* 109, 416–436.

Nerlove M. (2000), Growth rate convergence, fact or artifact? An essay on panel data econometrics, in J. Krishnakumar and E. Ronchetti, eds., Panel Data Econometrics: Future Directions, pp. 3-34, Amsterdam: North Holland.

Nissanke M. and E. Thorbecke (2006), *The Impact of Globalization on the World's Poor*, Palgrave Macmillan.

O'Rourke K.H. (2001), Globalization and Inequality: Historical Trends, NBER 8339, Cambridge MA: NBER.

O'Rourke K.H. and J.G. Williamson (2000), Globalization and History: The Evolution of a Nineteenth-Century Atlantic Economy. Cambridge MA: MIT Press.

Organization for Economic Co-operation and Development (2004), *The economic impact of ICT: measurement, evidence, and implication*, OECD.

Oliner S.D. and D.E. Sichel (2000), The Resurgence of Growth in the Late 1990s: Is Information Technology the Story, *Journal of Economic Perspectives* 14(4), 3-22.

Pack H. and L.E. Westphal (1986), Industrial Strategy and Technological Change: Theory versus Reality, *Journal of Development Economics* 22, 87-128.

Perotti R. (1996), Growth, income distribution, and democracy: what the data say, *Journal of Economic Growth* 1(3), 149-187.

Perry C.R. (1997), Outsourcing and union power, *Journal of Labor Research* 18(4), 521-534.

Persson T. and G. Tabellini (1994), Is inequality harmful for growth? *American Economic Review* 84, 600-621.

Porter M.E. (1980), *Competitive strategy*, Free Press, New York.

Pohjola M. (2001), Information Technology and Economic Growth: A Cross-Country Analysis, In Matti Pohjola, ed., *Information Technology, Productivity, and Economic Growth: International Evidence and Implications for Economic Development*, Oxford: Oxford University Press.

Quah D. (1996a), Twin Peaks: growth and convergence in models of distribution dynamics, *The Economic Journal* 106(437), 1045-1055.

Quah D. (1996c), Empirics for economic growth and convergence, European Economic Review 40, 1353-1375.

Quah D. (2001), Some simple arithmetic on how income inequality and economic growth matter, Paper presented at WIDER conference on Growth and Poverty, 25-26 May 2001, Helsinki.

Quelin B. and F. Duhamel (2003), Bringing together strategic outsourcing and corporate strategy: outsourcing motives and risks, *European Management Journal* 21(5), 647-661.

Radosevic S. (1999), International Technology Transfer and Catch-up in Economic Development, Edward Elgar, Cheltenham, UK.

Ravallion M. (1995), Growth and poverty: evidence for developing countries in the 1980s, *Economics Letters* 48, 411-417.

Ravallion M. (1998), Does aggregation hide the harmful effects of inequality on growth?, Economics Letters 61, 73-77. Ravallion M. (2001), Growth, inequality and poverty: looking beyond averages, *World Development* 29(11), 1803-1815.

Ravallion M. (2001), Growth, inequality and poverty: looking beyond averages, *World Development* 29(11), 1803-1815.

Ravallion M. and S. Chen (2003), Measuring pro-poor growth, Economics Letters 78, 93-99.

Ravallion M. and G. Datt (2000), When growth is pro-poor? Evidence from the diverse experience of Indian states, World Bank Policy Research, WP 2263

Rodriguez F. and D. Rodrik (1999), Trade policy and economic growth: a skeptic's guide to the cross-national evidence, NBER 1999:7081.

Roodhooft F. and L. Warlop (1999), On the role of sunk costs and asset specificity in outsourcing decisions: a research note, *Accounting, Organization and Society* 24, 363-369.

Sacks J. and A. Warner (1995), Economic reform and the process of global integration, Brookings Papers on Economic Activity 1:95.

Saggi K. (2002), Trade, Foreign Direct Investment, and International Technology Transfer: A Survey, *World Bank Research Observer* 17(2), 191-235.

Savvides A. and T. Stegnos (2000), Income inequality and economic development: evidence from the threshold regression model, *Economics Letters* 69, 207-212.

Seshanna S. and S. Decornez (2003). Income Polarisation and Inequality Across Countries: An Empirical Study. *Journal of Policy Modeling* 25(4), 335-358.

Shan J., G.G. Tian and F. Sun (1997), The FDI-led growth hypothesis: further econometric evidence from China. Working Paper, Economics Division, Research School of Pacific and Asian Studies, The Australian National University.

Sharpe M. (1997), Outsourcing, organizational competitiveness, and work, *Journal of Labor Research* 18(4), 535-549.

Shiu A. and A. Heshmati (2006), Technical Change and Total Factor Productivity for Chinese Provinces: A Panel Data Analysis, *IZA Discussion Paper* 2006:2133.

Shorrocks A. and R. van der Hoeven (2004), Eds., Growth, inequality, and poverty: Prospects for pro-poor economic development, Oxford: Oxford University Press.

Siegel D. and Z. Griliches (1992), Purchased services, outsourcing, computers, and productivity in manufacturing, in *Output measurement in service sector*, ed Z Griliches, University of Chicago Press, Chicago, IL, pp. 429-458.

Sjoholmn F. (1999), Technology gap, competition, and spillover from direct foreign investment: evidence from establishment data, *Journal of Development Studies* 36(1), 53-73.

Solimano A. (2001), The evolution of world income inequality: assessing the impact of globalization, Unpublished manuscript, ECLAC, CEPAL – Serie Macroeconomica del desarrollo No. 11, Santiago, Chile.

Suarez-Villa L. (1998), The structure of cooperation: downscaling, outsourcing and the networked alliance, *Small Business Economics* 10(1), 5-16.

Sylwester K. (2000), Income inequality, education expenditures, and growth, *Journal of Development Economics* 63, 379-398.

Talbot B. (2002), Information, Finance, and the New International Inequality: The Case of Coffee. *Journal of World-Systems Research*, 8(2),213-50.

Tausch A. and P. Herrmann (2002). *Globalization and European Integration*, Huntington NY: Nova Science Publishers, Inc.

Ten Raa T. and E.N. Wolff (1996), *Outsourcing of services and the productivity recovery in US manufacturing in the 1980s*, Center for Economic Research Discussion Paper, Tilburg University, September.

Thursby J. G., Jensen R. and M. C. Thursby (2001), Objectives, Characteristics and Outcomes of University Licensing: a Survey of Major U.S. Universities, *Journal of Technology Transfer* 26 (1/2), 59-72.

United Nations Conference on Trade and Development (1996), Trade and development report 1996, New York and Geneva: United Nations.

United Nations Conference on Trade and Development (1999), World investment report: Foreign direct investment and the challenge of development, New York and Geneva: United Nations.

United Nations Conference on Trade and Development (2001), World investment report: Promoting linkages, New York: UNCTAD.

United Nations Conference on Trade and Development (2006), World Investment Report 2006, UNCTAD.

U.S. Department of Commerce (2003), *Digital Economy 2003*, U.S. Department of Commerce.

Van der Hoeven R. and A. Shorrocks (2003), Eds., Perspectives on growth and poverty, United Nations University Press, Tokyo, Japan.

Wan G.H. (2002), Income inequality and growth in transition economies: are nonlinear models needed?, WIDER Discussion Paper 2002/104, Helsinki: UNU/WIDER.

Wang B. (2007), The Causal Relationship Between FDI and Economic Growth: Results Based on Chinese Provincial Data, in A. Heshmati (ed.), *Recent developments in the Chinese economy*, New York: Nova Science Publishers.

Williamson J.G. (2002), Winners and Losers Over Two Centuries of Globalization. *WIDER Annual Lecture* 6. Helsinki: UNU/WIDER.

Williamson O.E. (1989), Transaction cost economics, in *Handbook of Industrial Organization*, vol. 1, eds R Schmalensee and RD Willig, Elsevier, Amsterdam, pp. 136-181.

Woods N. (1998), Editorial Introduction. Globalization: Definitions, Debates and Implications. *Oxford Development Studies* 26(1), 5-13.

World Bank Development Research Group (1998), World development report: Knowledge for development, Washington, DC: World Bank.

World Bank Development Research Group (2002), Globalization, Growth and Poverty: Building an Inclusive World Economy, Washington DC: World Bank and Oxford University Press.

World Bank (2006), *World Development Indicators 2006*, World Bank, Washington DC.

Wu Y. (1999), (Ed.) Foreign direct investment and economic growth in China, Cheltenham, UK: Edward Elgar.

Young S. and J. Macneil. (2000), When performance fails to meet expectations: managers' objectives for outsourcing, *Economic and Labour Relations Review* 11(1), 136-168.

Yusuf S. (2003), Globalization and the Challenge for Developing Countries. *Journal of African Economies*. 12(1), 35-72.

Zhang K. H. (2001), How does foreign direct investment affect economic growth in China?, *Economics of Transition* 9(3), 679-693.

Zhu J. (1996), Comparing the effects of mass media and telecommunications on economic development: a pooled time series analysis, *Gazette* 57: 17-28.

In: Development Economics Research Trends
Editor: Gustavo T. Rocha, pp. 65-95

ISBN 978-1-60456-172-2
© 2008 Nova Science Publishers, Inc

Chapter 2

ALLEVIATING POVERTY FOR SUSTAINABILITY IN NEPAL: A SOCIAL ACCOUNTING APPROACH

Surendra R. Devkota[*]

Department of Economics, Rensselaer Polytechnic Institute, New York

ABSTRACT

This paper attempts to examine the socioeconomic structure of Nepal based on social accounting matrices (SAM) that utilizes some available macroeconomic information. Nepal is struggling to meet basic human needs such as an adequate supply of food, water, health care, shelter, and minimum education to majority of population. At least one fourth of households deprived of basic endowments like land, or skills (education). As the SAM coefficients reveal, investment in household sectors have high multipliers, and it is imperative to intervene at the household level to enrich human capital in order to alleviate poverty particularly at the socio-economically deprived households. Poverty alleviation through a trickle down approach has been a major planning theme since few decades, but it is yet to reach to the needy households. Planners and policy makers should realize that least developed country like Nepal does not need to follow an exact economic growth model adopted by the developed countries; they would rather focus on indigenous needs, skills, and resources and build a sustainable system.

Keywords: *Poverty, Socioeconomic structure, Sustainability, Nepal*

INTRODUCTION

The modern socioeconomic development in Nepal started only after 1950s from a very low level socioeconomic capital endowment. Socioeconomic development of past decades has not turned out as expected, particularly if compared to neighboring countries. Nepal has the highest poverty level in South Asia, which suggests an insignificant improvement in the

---

[*] Email: devkota@alum.rpi.edu.

average living standards. The Nepal Living Standard Survey (NLSS) 2003/04 conducted by the Central Bureau of Statistics (CBS) reveals that about 31 percent of the population (26.4 million in 2007) is poor compared to 42 percent in 1995/96. Though the incidence of poverty declined mainly due to remittance money, Gini coefficient between these two periods increased from 0.34 to 0.41. Poverty in rural areas is about 35 percent, while that in urban area is limited to 10 percent of the population.

UNDP (2000) summarizes the causes and effects of poverty in Nepal, and says the major reasons for the perpetuation of poverty in Nepal are low economic growth, inadequate social and economic infrastructure, relatively high population growth, low access to land, low access to non-agricultural income, deep-rooted cultural and historical practices, institutional weaknesses at both the government (central and local) and non-government level, and a lack of good governance. Further, growth has been concentrated primarily in the urban areas and particularly in the Kathmandu valley, largely excluding the 85 percent of the population who live in rural areas, where per capita agricultural production has grown minimally and the overall level of economic activity has been sluggish. Why there exists a persistent poverty in Nepal in spite of decades of national and international efforts? Why income inequality increased despite economic growth? Where and how to intervene to reduce both poverty and income inequality?

This paper aims to examine the structure of the Nepalese economy in order to find the answers of above mentioned questions and also analyses whether the ongoing 10th Five Year Plan of Nepal will achieve its goal of poverty reduction. First, a general overview the economy is discussed and followed by social accounting matrix model that is used to examine the economic structure and to forecast income level after the Plan is accomplished by 2007.

OVERVIEW OF THE NEPALI ECONOMY

Majority of population (78 percent according the NLSS) are dependent upon subsistence agriculture, though its contribution to gross domestic product (GDP) is declining. For instance, share of agriculture to GDP was nearly 65 percent in 1964, and that is reduced to 39 percent in 2004. Since 70 percent employment is dependent upon agriculture, an agrarian economy is still prevalent, but country entered into market economy only in early nineties. Prior to that a mixed economy of centrally planned Marxist type, also known as Panchayati system enforced by King Mahendra in 1961 after overthrowing an elected government. Khadka (1994) discussed about the Panchayati economics, and Mahat (2005) presents an elaborative picture of economic growth after the introduction of multiparty polity in 1990. Different politico-economic philosophies introduced by different regimes in Nepal are also discussed by Pandey (1999) and Devkota (2005).

Bhattarai (2003) by studying sectoral (agriculture, industry, and trade) and spatial differentiation of the Nepali economy claimed that the spatial unevenness in development in Nepal can be seen as the function of both the conservative monopolistic structure and uneven penetration of the capitals. Blaikie, Cameron, and Seddon (1979, 2001) after studying Nepal's economic growth over the decades concluded "far reaching structural change is required if the mass of people in Nepal are to be assured of their basic needs."

In earlier days, the "basic needs strategy" endorsed by the United Nations was a very routine political rhetoric in Nepal, though majority of people still lack of it. Subsequently, different governments in Nepal attempted to incorporate the Program for the Fulfillment of Basic Needs during the Seventh Plan period (1985–1990), but political upheavals interrupted its implementation. After restoration of democracy in 1990, poverty became a principal objective of the National Planning Commission. The Ninth Plan (1997–2002) mentioned poverty as the sole development objective. Likewise, the Tenth Plan (2002-2007) reiterates the emphasis on poverty alleviation. Despite more than two decades of development planning about poverty, the results are not encouraging. The 2003/04 Household Survey reported that the bottom fifty percent of the population has consumes less than 20 percent of total output, while the top 30 percent consumes more than 60 percent of the total. The situation in South Asia is like in India where the top 10 percent consumes about 33 percent of the total. Likewise, in Bangladesh the highest 10 percent consumes about 29 percent, Pakistan 27.6 percent, and Sri Lanka 28 percent (World Bank, 2002).

Following the philosophy of modernization, the government of Nepal is determined to increase the rate of economic growth so that the poor will benefit as directly as possible from economic development. To promote the growth agenda, a variety of strategies, polices, plans were put forward, although no one is really clear about how to achieve the kind of economic growth outlined in the five-year plans. What is the difference between the new Plan and old versions? The old Plans also had the same goals of socioeconomic development, but they failed. For example, in the last five decades, despite the investment of billions, if not trillions of Rupees on population stabilization efforts, the population growth rate has not declined since the 1950s. For example, in 1951/52 the population growth rate was 2.3 percent and the latest Census of 2001 shows it is 2.24 percent, which means that the annual population stabilization efforts had insignificant impact. The actual population growth rates are in stark contrast to the aims of the Five Year Plans. The Sixth Five-year Plan of Nepal (1980-85) aimed to reduce population growth rate to 1.6 percent in 1990, and 1.2 percent in the year of 2000. The Seventh Five-year Plan (1985-90) reiterated the same objective of population stabilization. Further, at the end of the Ninth Five-year Plan (1997-2002), population growth rate was still above two percent. By this account, it can be inferred that the Plans were unsuccessful. Henceforth, it is necessary to examine the economic structure that lies behind economic production, consumption, and investment, which will help to devise appropriate policy measures in order to follow a sustainable development path. There is a general consensus that the social accounting matrix is an appropriate tool to explore the socioeconomic structure and transactions of a circular flow economy.

THE SOCIAL ACCOUNTING MATRIX

The social accounting matrix (SAM) analyzes the structure of an economy. Richard Stone, a Noble Laureate in Economics in 1984, pioneered work on social accounting in the sixties and paved the way for the SAM. Stone (1986) perceived that social accounting is a systematic quantitative description of a socioeconomic system. Later, Pyatt and Thorbecke (1976) formalized the concept of the social accounting into social accounting matrix. Now,

SAM is practiced in many disciplines of humanities and social science such as demography, education, economics, regional sciences and health (Hewings and Madden, 1995).

SAM is an expanded version of the input-output (IO) model. IO analysis focuses on the structure of production, the activity taking place in the upper left corner of Figure 1, but does not provide much detail about final users. Final demand describes only in terms of the major components household consumption of final products, government consumption, trade (consumption by out-of area users), and investment. While the IO table describes production in terms of hundreds of industries, households are presented by a single sector in final demand, even though they account for most of final demand and are the driving force in the economy. This restricted treatment of households limited the ability of the IO model to address such issues as income distribution or environmental impacts of changing economic patterns.

The need for a more detailed treatment of households led researchers, beginning with the work of Richard Stone in the 1960s, to expand the IO system (Pyatt and Round 1985) to a Social Accounting Matrix (SAM). Figure 2 provides a simplified version of a SAM. The purpose of a SAM is to provide within the IO framework a more detailed description of the dual role that households play as consumers and as suppliers of labor and capital. Households are disaggregated into many columns according to criteria relevant to the policy question at hand. Often, households are disaggregated according to income category. As suppliers of labor and capital, the value-added block may also be disaggregated for different categories of labor according to wage group or by occupation. The connections between the source of income (household supply of labor and capital) and consumption (household purchases of final demand) are represented by another matrix showing the flows between final demand and value added.

With a growing need for analysis linking economic and environmental effects, the basic IO/SAM framework has been expanded to incorporate environmental and natural resource accounts (United Nations, 1993; Lange, 1999). Thorbecke (1998) describes SAM as a comprehensive, consistent, complete and disaggregated data system that is useful for policy analyses. SAM depicts a static image of the country's economic structure. Its double entry bookkeeping system reveals incoming and outgoing accounts (King, 1985).

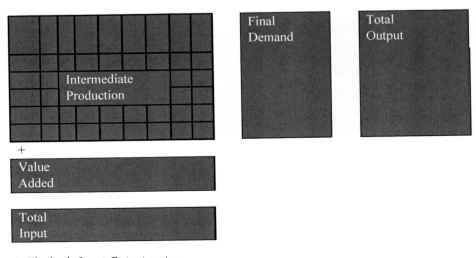

Figure 1. The basic Input-Output system.

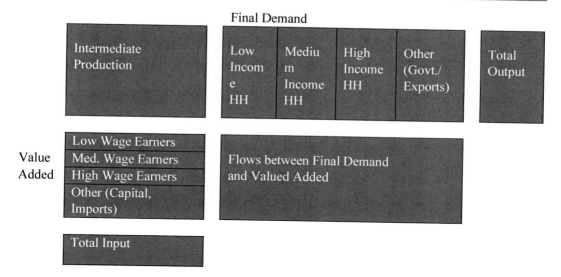

Figure 2. A general structure of a Social Accounting Matrix.

SAM is an efficient way of presenting a fundamental law of economics: every income has corresponding expenditure (Pyatt, 1988). It is a square matrix in which rows represent income and columns reveal expenditure. Structurally, a SAM is comprised of institutes, assets, and transactions to describe the factors of production, factor income, and consumption (Pyatt, 1991; Thorbecke 1998). Pyatt further says that SAM is a framework both for models of how the economy works as well as for data, which can be used to monitor its workings. Pyatt (1990, and 1999) discusses how statistics over time can be integrated into a social accounting matrix representation of economic activity. A further advancement of SAM is the exploration of the relationship between commodity balances and input-output tables. Robinson, Cattaneo, and El-Said (2001) used a "cross entropy" approach to estimate a consistent SAM starting from inconsistent data estimated with error, a common experience in many countries. Golan and Vogel (2000) developed a framework for estimating the entries of a SAM, or any large matrix of expenditures, and trade or income flows. SAM is used to develop a price-model that captures the interdependence among activities, households and factors to provide a complete set of accounting prices (Roland-Holst and Sancho,1995). Keuning (1991) discussed how flow accounts, which could be a part of the next system of national accounts, can be embedded easily in a SAM framework. Defourny and Thorbecke, (1994) reviewed the SAM framework as a basis for multiplier analysis, multiplier decomposition, element of structural analysis and, more particularly, the transmission of economic influence within a structure. SAM is helpful for uniform valuation of inputs for meaningful manipulation of the input-output table contained in a SAM, as well as to assess the real effects of changes in demand (Greenfield and Fell, 1979. A general guideline for building a SAM is suggested by Keuning and de Ruijter (1988) who suggest the steps of overall design of the system, identification of sources, choice of base year, defining classification, preparation of tabulation plans, derivation of initial estimates, correction of errors, and reconciliation.

Country SAMs

Pyatt and Roe (1977) executed the first SAM for the Sri Lankan economy. Chander et al., (1980) developed of a SAM for Malaysia for 1970 in which the distribution of income between different factors and socioeconomic groups is identified. Rand (2002) constructed a SAM for Vietnam to find the links between trade and income in the country. Eckaus and Mohie-Eldin (1981) discussed the implications of the accounting system, sources of progressiveness in the fiscal system, comparison of distribution of taxes and subsidies of rural and urban households in terms of income of 1976 for Egypt. The role of migration and the impacts of alternative economic integration policies on income, employment, and expenditures in a small migrant-sending region of rural El Salvador analyzed by Taylor, Zabin and Eckhoff (1999). Lizardo, Navarro and Suazo (1999) built the Honduran SAM for 1991 and several simulations were run to assess the impact of selected policy changes. Khorshid (1991) used a stylized SAM based long-term economy wide model for long term policy issues facing a Gulf Cooperation Council (GCC) country, Kuwait. Dubcovsky (1999) created a SAM for Nicaragua based on 1991 data, and the most relevant aspects of structural adjustment are presented: exchange policies, tariff policies, and fiscal policies. Mujeri and Alauddin (1993) examined savings, consumption and investment behavior of social classes in Bangladesh in urban and rural areas with the help of input-output analysis and information from a social accounting matrix. Banouei (1993) gave a history of input-output tables in Iran, compilation of input-output flow, import and export tables, and the use of social accounting matrix for Iran. Adelman, and Robinson (1986) built a SAM for the United States agricultural sector. Roland-Holst and Sancho, (1992) used a SAM to explore the income generation process and its distributional effects. Hanson and Robinson (1991) discussed the use of SAM and its relationship between the existing national economic accounts for the United States. Alarcon, Van Heemst, and De Jong (2000) used SAM as a basis for extensions with non-monetary data addressing social and environmental concerns for Bolivia. Den Bakker, de Gujt and Keuning (1994) described a historical SAM for the Netherlands, including related non-monetary tables on demographic characteristics, and employment.

SAM is employed by many international agencies for different purposes. For instance, the World Bank did a symposium for SAM in 1985 (Pyatt and Round, 1985). In the early nineties, the Cornell Food and Nutrition Policy Program accomplished several SAM analyses of African countries such as Cameroon, Madagascar, Nigeria, Gambia, and Tanzania (http://www.he.cornell.edu/cfnpp/). Since 1989, Canada based International Development Research Center (http://www.idrc.ca/ nayudamma/ mimap_e.html) created the 'Micro Impacts of Macroeconomic and Adjustment Policies' (MIMAP) program to assist countries in the South to develop alternatives to traditional macroeconomic policies by compatible policy analysis with poverty monitoring. The goal is "to help developing countries minimize the negative impact of structural adjustment programs on the poor- currency devaluation, public expenditure reductions, trade liberalization, and other policies designed to improve the long-term economic outlook." MIMAP projects at the country level in Bangladesh, Benin, Burkina Faso, India, Lao PDR, Morocco, Nepal, Pakistan, the Philippines, Sri Lanka and Vietnam. In some countries SAM is utilized to monitor and analyze the poverty level. For example, SAM is executed for India (Pradhan et al., 1999) and CGE for Bangladesh, India, Pakistan, Sri Lanka and Nepal (http://www.mimap.org/).

The International Food Policy Research Institute (IFPRI) (http://www.ifpri.org/), Washington D.C based institute conducts researches on economic growth and poverty alleviation in low-income countries. It identifies and analyzes policies for sustainably meeting the food needs of the developing world, improvement of the well being of poor people, and sound management of the natural resource base that supports agriculture. With the help of SAM, this institute conducted a detailed analysis of the links between macro policies and distributional outcomes, including poverty. So far, IFPRI executed a SAM for Bangladesh (1993/94), Egypt (1997), Malawi (1998), Morocco (1994) Mozambique (1994/95), Tanzania (1992), Thailand (1998), Vietnam (1996/97), Zambia (1995), and Zimbabwe (1991).

A social accounting matrix for Europe was developed by Round (1991). Reinert and Roland-Holst (2001) examined a three-country SAM of the North American economy to conduct a linear multiplier analysis of industrial pollution linkages in North America. Thorbecke, and Jung (1996) presented a multiplier decomposition method focusing on poverty alleviation. Kim and Ahn (2002) studied the effects of regional income disparity in Korea on the allocation of investments using a dynamic multi-regional SAM model. Rural-urban spillover effects using a bi-regional SAM model developed by Roberts (2000) allows for flows of commodities and factor incomes between the two areas. Esparza (1989) used a SAM for the Californian economy to evaluate industrial-occupational linkages and the relative impact of defense expenditures in a regional economy. A macroeconomic impact model of restructuring public spending using a multi-sectoral dynamic computable general equilibrium model calibrated to a South African SAM by Gibson and Van Seventer (1997).

Sam Fiscal Accounting

A financial SAM was constructed for Cameroon with a clear distinction of financial assets and liability accounts (Emini, 2002). Kilkenny (1999) examined a SAM approach to documenting multi-regional and multi-jurisdiction in fiscal accounts. Kilkenny studied a fiscal SAM of rural, urban, and metro areas of Iowa, USA to describe and compare the benchmark net fiscal situations of interdependent regions. Crossman (1988) examined SAM, assigning reliability weights to the items in the accounts, and using an elegant balancing method advanced by Stone.

Village SAM

The SAM approach has been widely used to explore the structure of the village economy. Taylor and Adelman (1996) used a village based SAM based village economy to analyze the effects of policies, market changes, and ecological shocks on a rural economy. Subramanian, and Sadoulet (1990) showed how three factors: technical change, output fluctuation and government policy, affect income distribution and poverty in the Indian villages. Parikh, and Thorbecke (1996) explained the impact of rural industrialization on village life and economy in India. A village SAM is constructed using 1982 household data from a major migrant-sending village in Central Mexico by Adelman, Taylor and Vogel, (1988). This SAM was used to analyze the economic structure of a migrant-sending rural economy and the village matrix multiplier. Decompositions are derived from the SAM and are used in policy scenarios of the production, value added, income, and investment flows of the village.

SAM and Sustainability

Although the System for Integrated Environmental and Economic Accounting (SEEA), adopted by the UN since the 1992 Rio Summit, and Input Output tables are basic components, SEEA is yet to be an integral part of the national accounting system. There are several opinions about SEEA (Holub et al., 1999). Likewise, the other tools to measure sustainability are also lagging to integrate the social, economical and environmental entities *in toto*. For example, income disparity, and environmental quality vis-à-vis pollution index are yet to be adjusted with the national accounting identity in order to pursue the path of sustainability. There are hopeful signs that the SAM framework could some day be an effective tool to integrate all major entities of sustainability.

Pan (2000) extended the SAM into a social and ecological accounting matrix (Table 1) to derive an environmentally adjusted net domestic product. Based on the empirical analysis, Pan concluded that, considering the net losses of natural resources and environmental assets, China must reduce its GDP growth rate to 3.4 percent to have an ecologically sustainable domestic product. The following equations show the basis for deriving the sustainable output level considering the population, economy, society, resources, production, consumption, and environmental protection.

Table 1. Structure of social and environmental accounting matrix

	Supply	Household	Government	Trade	Capital	Resource	Environment
Supply	AX	C	G	E	I	V	Z
Household	Y					VH	ZH
Government		T					
Trade	M						
Capital		SH	SG		F		
Resource	N						
Environment	K						

Where,
C: household consumption; G: government expenditure; E: Export; I: investment; V: recovered resources by industrial activity; Z: recovered environment assets by industrial activity; VH: final demand of resources; ZH: final demand of environmental assets; M: import; N: input of resources, K: inputs of environmental assets; SH: household saving; SG: government saving; F: foreign investment; T: net tax.

Ecological domestic product $(Y) = C + I + G + (E - M) - (N - V) - (K - Z)$
$Y = C + SH + T - VH - ZH$
$I = SH + SG + F$, and $T = G + SG$
$M = E + F$
$N = V + VH$ $(VH = N - V)$
$K = Z + ZH$ $(ZH = K - Z)$

SAM's strength to integrate national income and resource and environmental accounting offers a good insight of policy analysis. One of the problems with integrating social, ecological, and economic indicators is the lack of compatibility between the monetary and physical values. This may hinder analysis of the complex interaction between these indicators. However, SAM can make this task easier because it can include both monetary and non-monetary values. Alarcon, Heemst and de Jong (2000) concluded that it is feasible to extend the SAM using both physical and monetary indicators. They also observed that addressing the problem of sustainability requires detailed information about stocks and flows along with social indicators.

A SOCIAL ACCOUNTING MATRIX FOR NEPAL

The SAM for Nepal is constructed based on 1999 the Input-Output database (Shrestha and Sapkota, 1999) for the 10th Plan. In addition to the IO table, other required supplementary information is taken from the publications of the Ministry of Finance (www.mof.gov.np), and the Central Bureau of Statistics (CBS) (www.cbs.gov.np). A thematic SAM structure is presented in Table 2. Since there is no universal standard format for SAM, it is customary to build a SAM with respect to the availability of information and the objective of analysis. To this regard, a SAM model developed for developing countries (Cohen, 2002) is followed. In general, the SAM system includes following major accounts.

- Wants include basic needs such as food, non-food, and housing.
- Factors of production include land, labor, and capital.
- Accounts of economic agents such as households, firms, government, and rest of the world are grouped as institutions.
- Products accounts are structured according to taxonomy of sectors.
- National capital accounts record the flow of savings and investment of the economy.

Since the main objective of the present SAM is to investigate the extent and magnitude of poverty, primary emphasis is on wants and the household sectors. Both wants and households are further disaggregated (Table 3). The general objective of disaggregating the SAM is to explore the relation between production and consumption in the economy, and particularly the wants of different deciles of households and factors of production. Although government of Nepal pursued different development policies in order to enhance economic growth and to alleviate poverty, income disparity is widening. Hence it is necessary to examine the economic structure lying behind the economic transactions between production, consumption, and investment. This will help to guide appropriate policy measures so that a sustainable development path could be followed.

To construct the SAM, it is assumed that the latest survey on per capita average consumption in deciles also reflects the households' average income. So wants are expanded into food, non-food, housing and other sectors, and households are categorized by income deciles. A disaggregated SAM (26 x 26) is computed based on the information available in the IO table, economic surveys, and CBS sources

Table 2. Thematic SAM structure

	Wants	Factors	Households	Firms	Government	Capital	Production	Rest of world
Wants			HH spending					
Factors							Value added	Factor pay
Households		Wages			Transfer to HH			Transfer
Firms		Profit						
Government		Profit PE	HH direct tax	Direct tax			Indirect tax	Transfer
National capital			HH saving	Saving	Public saving		Depreciation	Deficit
Gross production	Consumption				Public Consumption	Investment	Intermediate	Export
Rest of world					Public Transfer		Imports	

Table 3. An Aggregate SAM for Nepal

(Million Rupees)

		Wants	Factors	Households	Firms	Government	National capital	Gross Production sector	Rest of world	Total
	Wants	0	0	342037	0	0	0	0	0	342037
	Factors	0	0	0	0	0	0	390363	-75653,1	314709,9
Institutions	Households	0	132508,2	0	0	525	0	0	273214,6	406247,8
	Firms	0	182774,4	0	0	0	0	0	0	182774,4
	Government	0	-572,7	8228,8	34665,4	0	0	24898	12738	79957,5
	National capital	0	0	55982	148109,4	36700	0	-15517,4	5627,4	230901,4
Activities	Gross production	342037	0	0	0	42732	92682	84740,4	51623	613814,4
	Rest of world	0	0	0	0	0	138219,4	129330,4	0	267549,8
Total		342037	314709,9	406247,8	182774,8	79957	230901,4	613814,4	267549,9	2437992,2

Since there is a discrepancy in import and export data, a residual method is employed to balance them. Likewise, there is a lack of complete recording of incoming as well as outlays of donor agencies, residual techniques are used to balance them. That's why the exact matching of income rows and expenditure columns is lacking in Table 3.

Likewise, another of major problem with the economic data in Nepal is the incomplete accounting of remittances from abroad. Dahal (2000), and Nepal (2002) discussed the opportunity cost of the flow of remittance in Nepal sent by Nepalis working abroad. They estimated about Rs. 75 billion (1 USD = Rs. 71) in currency could have entered Nepal in 1999/2000, and this SAM also complements that estimation (Table 3). As of now, The Nepal Rastra Bank (2006) estimates that the Nepali economy in 2004/05 earned over US Dollars 922 million in remittances from overseas workers – accounting for 12.4 percent of national gross domestic product.

THE SAM MODEL AND MULTIPLIER ANALYSIS

Since a SAM documents the circular flow of the income and expenditures of an economy, a change in the income of one sector will affect households and other sectors both directly and indirectly because of inter and intra transactions of different kinds of sectors and demands such as factor demand, intermediate demand, household demand, and government demands. Hence, it reveals a link between production activities and household consumption. To this regard, a SAM needs to be divided into endogenous and exogenous accounts. In general, government, capital, and rest of the world are exogenous accounts, and the other parameters such as households and their consumption (wants), and production and its factors become endogenous accounts. Exogenous accounts are assumed as fixed for the analysis. So, the model behaves like a demand driven Keynesian model as supplies are assumed to adjust to the demand. It also satisfies Walras' Law that total income is equal to the total expenditure in the system (Pradhan, and Sahoo, 1996).

The disaggregated SAM Table 3 is further simplified as Table 4. The exogenous sectors are denoted by X and are comprised of flows of export, investment demands, income transfers from abroad, and government. The endogenous accounts of the 23 x 23 sub-matrix show the flows from endogenous to endogenous sectors (Table 4).

Table 4. A schematic SAM

		Wants	Factors	Institutes	Activities	Exogenous Govt., Capital, ROW	Total
Endogenous	Wants			T_{13}		X_1	Y_1
	Factors				T_{24}	X_2	Y_2
	Institutes		T_{32}	T_{33}		X_3	Y_3
	Activities	T_{41}			T_{44}	X_4	Y_4
Exogenous							
	Total	Y_1	Y_2	Y_3	Y_4		

In Table 4, T13 is the matrix of household spending, T24 reveals a matrix of value added generated by the various production sectors, T32 reflects institutional income, T41 shows household consumption, and T44 is the input-output transaction matrix. Each flow of the endogenous account of 23 x 23 matrices is divided by its respective column in order to obtain the SAM multipliers.

Table 4 can be interpreted in a simple matrix format as follows. A matrix of coefficients is derived by dividing each element in the T_{ij} by the corresponding sum of the column vector Y_j.

$$\begin{vmatrix} Y_1 \\ Y_2 \\ Y_3 \\ Y_4 \end{vmatrix} = \begin{vmatrix} 0 & 0 & A_{13} & 0 \\ A_{21} & 0 & 0 & 0 \\ 0 & A_{32} & A_{33} & 0 \\ A_{41} & 0 & 0 & A_{44} \end{vmatrix} \begin{vmatrix} Y_1 \\ Y_2 \\ Y_3 \\ Y_4 \end{vmatrix} + \begin{vmatrix} X_1 \\ X_2 \\ X_3 \\ X_4 \end{vmatrix}$$

$A_{ij} = T_{ij} Y^{-1}, j = 1, 2, 3, 4$

X is the vector of row sum of respective sub-matrix.
It can be written as;

$Y = AY + X$

$Y = (I-A)^{-1} X$, which is analogous to input-output model. Now, Y1, Y2, Y3, and Y4 can be derived through the inverse of $(I-A)^{-1}$.

The equation $Y = (I-A)^{-1} X$, $(I-A)^{-1}$ gives an aggregate or total multiplier of SAM (23 x 23 matrix), which can be expressed as;

$(I-A)^{-1} = Ma X$

This total or aggregate multiplier is further decomposed into sub-matrices (Table 4) as

$Ma X = M_3 M_2 M_1 X$.

M_1 is called the "transfer multiplier", M_2 is known as the "own effect multiplier", and M_3 is the "cross-effect multiplier." The transfer multiplier, M1, depicts the effects of direct transfers within the production activities. M2, also known as open loop effect, indicates interactions from production to institutions, wants, and factors. M3, the closed loop effect, insures the circular flow of income from production to factors to institutions to wants and back to activities in the form of consumption demand (Cohen, 2002 a, b).

Based on above discussion of the SAM model, complete SAM multipliers are presented in Table 5, which is further decomposed and discussed below.

Table 5. SAM Multipliers

		1	2	3	4	5	6	7	8	9	10
1	Food	1,463312	0,463918	0,466217	0,449401	1,150662	1,123464	1,114938	1,10089	1,098109	1,107505
2	Non-food	0,221047	1,221337	0,222433	0,21441	0,421865	0,436603	0,45892	0,477622	0,474481	0,467526
3	Housing /others	0,08083	0,080936	1,081337	0,078403	0,193403	0,205937	0,192103	0,187445	0,193392	0,190933
4	Factors	1,82065	1,823033	1,832065	1,765985	1,822412	1,82259	1,822486	1,822477	1,822537	1,822493
5	1st Decile Household	0,030375	0,030414	0,030565	0,029463	1,030404	0,030407	0,030405	0,030405	0,030406	0,030405
6	2nd decile	0,039689	0,039741	0,039938	0,038498	0,039728	1,039732	0,039729	0,039729	0,03973	0,039729
7	3rd decile	0,046596	0,046657	0,046888	0,045197	0,046641	0,046645	1,046643	0,046643	0,046644	0,046643
8	4th decile	0,053572	0,053642	0,053907	0,051963	0,053623	0,053629	0,053626	1,053625	0,053627	0,053626
9	5th decile	0,060894	0,060974	0,061276	0,059066	0,060953	0,060959	0,060955	0,060955	1,060957	0,060955
10	6th decile	0,069215	0,069306	0,069649	0,067137	0,069282	0,069289	0,069285	0,069285	0,069287	1,069285
11	7th decile	0,079938	0,079442	0,079836	0,076956	0,079415	0,079423	0,079418	0,079418	0,07942	0,079418
12	8th decile	0,092828	0,092949	0,09341	0,090041	0,092918	0,092927	0,092921	0,092921	0,092924	0,092922
13	9th decile	0,113178	0,113326	0,113887	0,10978	0,113287	0,113298	0,113292	0,113291	0,113295	0,113292
14	10th decile	0,179505	0,17974	0,180631	0,174116	0,179679	0,179697	0,179686	0,179686	0,179692	0,179687
15	Firms	1,055461	1,056842	1,062078	1,023771	1,056482	1,056586	1,056525	1,05652	1,056555	1,056529
16	Agriculture	0,883775	0,85978	0,773494	0,363627	0,866556	0,864821	0,865811	0,865875	0,865295	0,865733
17	Manufacturing industries	0,621971	0,636677	0,69284	0,266336	0,632893	0,633997	0,633346	0,633291	0,633666	0,633389
18	Construction	0	0	0	0	0	0	0	0	0	0
19	Gas, electricity, water	0,023264	0,02385	0,026075	0,009974	0,023698	0,023742	0,023716	0,023714	0,023729	0,023718
20	Trade, Hotel, Restaurant	0,312839	0,319873	0,346704	0,133839	0,31806	0,318587	0,318276	0,31825	0,318429	0,318297
21	Transport &Communication	0,314088	0,320771	0,346298	0,134247	0,319052	0,319554	0,319258	0,319233	0,319403	0,319278
22	Banking & real estate	0,296457	0,300302	0,310134	0,12567	0,298767	0,298995	0,298891	0,2989	0,298969	0,298908
23	Community, Social service	0,055461	0,056842	0,062078	0,023771	0,056482	0,056586	0,056525	0,05652	0,056555	0,056529

Table 5 (Continued)

	11	12	13	14	15	16	17	18	19	20	21	22	23
1	1,092578	1,075094	1,061592	0,989269	0	0,450352	0,452965	0,4856	0,451655	0,453645	0,452486	0,45496	0,4658
2	0,49494	0,494631	0,519554	0,601738	0	0,214864	0,216111	0,231681	0,215486	0,216435	0,215882	0,217063	0,222234
3	0,178413	0,196291	0,18484	0,175015	0	0,078569	0,079025	0,084719	0,078796	0,079144	0,078941	0,079373	0,081264
4	1,822415	1,822618	1,822547	1,822631	0	1,769722	1,779989	1,908235	1,774842	1,782665	1,778107	1,787831	1,830428
5	0,030404	0,030408	0,030406	0,030408	0	0,029525	0,029696	0,031836	0,029611	0,029741	0,029665	0,029827	0,030538
6	0,039728	0,039732	0,039731	0,039732	0	0,038579	0,038803	0,041599	0,038691	0,038861	0,038762	0,038974	0,039902
7	0,046641	0,046646	0,046644	0,046646	0	0,045292	0,045555	0,048837	0,045423	0,045624	0,045507	0,045756	0,046846
8	0,053624	0,053629	0,053627	0,05363	0	0,052073	0,052375	0,056149	0,052224	0,052454	0,05232	0,052606	0,053859
9	0,060953	0,06096	0,060957	0,06096	0	0,05919	0,059534	0,063823	0,059362	0,059623	0,059471	0,059796	0,061221
10	0,069282	0,06929	0,069287	0,06929	0	0,067279	0,067669	0,072545	0,067474	0,067771	0,067598	0,067967	0,069587
11	1,079415	0,079424	0,079421	0,079424	0	0,077119	0,077566	0,083155	0,077342	0,077683	0,077484	0,077908	0,079764
12	0,092918	1,092928	0,092924	0,092929	0	0,090231	0,090755	0,097293	0,090492	0,090891	0,090659	0,091154	0,093326
13	0,113287	0,1133	1,113296	0,113301	0	0,110012	0,11065	0,118622	0,11033	0,110816	0,110533	0,111138	0,113785
14	0,179679	0,1797	0,179692	1,179701	0	0,174484	0,175497	0,188141	0,174989	0,17576	0,175311	0,17627	0,180469
15	1,056484	1,056602	1,056561	1,056609	1	1,025937	1,031889	1,106235	1,028905	1,03344	1,030798	1,036435	1,061129
16	0,866455	0,864493	0,865157	0,864269	0	1,422954	0,576382	0,445428	0,367985	0,372762	0,368152	0,372234	0,392247
17	0,632906	0,634167	0,633722	0,634234	0	0,31178	1,408468	0,528998	0,280611	0,277929	0,275207	0,288675	0,355856
18	0	0	0	0	0	0	0	1	0	0	0	0	0
19	0,023699	0,023749	0,023731	0,023752	0	0,010816	0,021557	0,014118	1,026797	0,016647	0,012966	0,012595	0,014448
20	0,318066	0,318669	0,318456	0,318702	0	0,164156	0,226335	0,22224	0,154765	1,239841	0,314553	0,161939	0,205026
21	0,319058	0,319631	0,319429	0,319661	0	0,173215	0,258438	0,237471	0,156874	0,231528	1,259121	0,159864	0,220929
22	0,298843	0,299086	0,299025	0,299207	0	0,185343	0,226198	0,206335	0,292573	0,201172	0,292337	1,169362	0,176553
23	0,056484	0,056602	0,056561	0,056609	0	0,025937	0,031889	0,106235	0,028905	0,03344	0,030798	0,036435	1,061129

HOUSEHOLDS INCOME AND PRODUCTION ACTIVITIES

Household income inequality and distribution is analyzed through the SAM multipliers: namely aggregate, transfer, open, and closed multipliers. The overall equation can be written as;

$$M_{a,34} = [M_{3,33}] \quad [M_{2,34}] [M_{1,44}]$$
Total multipliers = (Closed)   (Open)   (Transfer) multipliers

The algebraic derivation of the above mentioned decomposed multiplier is also found in Thorbecke and Jung (1996), and Cohen (2002 a, b). The aggregate (total) SAM multipliers presented in Table 5 indicate demand thrust in the production activities. This implies that a unit of demand injection in certain production activities will have total multiplier effects.

The wants sub-matrix in Table 5, i.e., rows 1 to 3 indicates the effects of an injection from activities on wants. Impacts of injections in agriculture, and households are high on food items compared to injection in production sectors (see rows 1 to 3). SAM propensities for food for low-income households are higher than those for high-income households. The latter has high coefficients on non-food items. 8th deciles households have high saving and housing coefficients, among others.

The impact of injections on the factor accounts (row 4) show that both construction (1.908) and community and social services (1.830) have high multiplier effects. Agriculture has minimal impacts (1.769) on the factor accounts. It should be noted that agriculture is the main activity for subsistence for about 90 percent of the population.

Rows 5 through 14 show the impact of injections in activities on households (this is separately discussed below). However, rows 5 to 10 reveal interesting multiplier effects. Low-income households retain high multiplier values in construction and social services. Injection into other production sectors has a smaller multiplier impact than found in the food and households sectors. Altogether, rows 1 through 15 reveal aggregate income multipliers, whereas rows 16 to 23 indicate aggregate output multipliers.

Agriculture has the lowest (1.769), and the construction sector has the highest income multiplier effects (1.908). Interestingly, banking and real estate have the lowest output impact (2.201) compared to all other production sectors. Both construction and manufacturing industries are the leading sectors having high output multipliers (Table 6). Injection in production sectors, on the average, will add to income by an additional 40 percent and output by 60 percent. Agriculture sectors' aggregate income multiplier (1.769) and output multiplier (2.294) are smaller than those found in Korea, Pakistan, India, Sri Lanka, and Indonesia. These income and output multipliers for the Nepali economy (Table 6) are comparable with those of an African country. Similarly, the average income multiplier (1.801) and output multiplier (2.458) is more or less equal with Kenya, Surinam, and Egypt, but less than India (income = 3.684; output = 5.946), Pakistan (income = 4.028; output = 8.770), Sri Lanka (income = 2.055; output =3.090), and Indonesia (income = 2.119; output = 3.390) (Cohen, 2002 a). It might be noticed that the output multipliers for Nepal are relatively homogeneous. Cohen also found a homogeneous pattern of output multipliers in the less developed countries he studied.

TRANSFER MULTIPLIERS

As discussed earlier, transfer multipliers capture impacts resulting from direct transfers within the endogenous accounts, that is, between production sectors. Table 7 shows the transfer multipliers. Manufacturing industries (2.749) and construction sectors (2.761) have high transfer effects, whereas banking and real estate (2.201), and agriculture (2.294) are at the bottom of transfer multiplier impact in the Nepalese economy.

An addition of 1 unit in agriculture will lead to a multiplier effect of 2.294, out of which 62 percent adds to agriculture, 13.5 percent manufacturing, 8 percent banking, 7.5 percent transport, and 7 percent in the trade, hotel, and restaurant sector.

Likewise, out of total transfer effects of manufacturing industries (2.749), an injection of 1 unit will lead to impact industries (61 percent), agriculture (25 percent), transport (11 percent), banking (10 percent), and trade, hotel and restaurant (10 percent).

The construction sector has the highest transfer multiplier (2.761); an introduction of 1 unit will add 43.5 percent to construction, 23 percent to industries, 19 percent to agriculture, 10 percent to transport, 9 percent on banking, and 10 percent on trade, hotel, and restaurant.

An injection of 1 unit into banking results in a transfer impact by 2.201, out of which 51 percent adds to the banking sector, 16 percent to agricultural sector, 12.5 industries, and 7 percent on the trade, hotel, restaurant and transportation sectors.

OPEN-LOOP MULTIPLIERS

The open loop multiplier, or cross multiplier effect, describes the transactions from production to households, factor and wants. Table 8 depicts the open loop multipliers. As the table indicates, agriculture has the lowest effect (1.769), whereas construction, and community and social services have high cross multiplier effects, 1.908 and 1.830 respectively. Only these two sectors have high multiplier effects on the lower deciles households compared to other sectors.

Injection of one unit into any of the production sectors will have differentiated impacts. Based on table 9, a comparison is drawn between the low-income and high-income households. A one unit introduction in any of the production sectors will have only nominal multiplier effects on the low-income households. For example, investment of one million Rupees in the agriculture sector will increase the average income of the upper 20 percent of households by 28.45 percent whereas 50 percent lower income households' average income will add only 22.46 percent (Table 9).

Table 7. Transfer multipliers

	Agriculture	Manufacturing industries	Construction	Gas, Water Electricity	Trade, Hotel, Resturant	Transport Communication	Banking Real estate	Community, Social service
Agriculture	1,42295374	0,576381595	0,445428144	0,367984692	0,372761509	0,36815245	0,372234113	0,39224747
Manufacturing industries	0,311779613	1,408467577	0,528998287	0,280610686	0,277928532	0,275207013	0,288674904	0,35585571
Construction	0	0	1	0	0	0	0	0
Gas, electricity, water	0,010815996	0,021556808	0,014118462	1,026796707	0,016646915	0,012966103	0,012595016	0,01444794
Trade, Hotel, Resturant	0,164155548	0,226334622	0,222240089	0,15476546	1,239840762	0,314552756	0,161938663	0,20502592
Transport &Communication	0,173214536	0,258437827	0,237470796	0,156874215	0,23152787	1,259120847	0,159864175	0,22092906
Banking & real estate	0,185343476	0,226198352	0,206335072	0,292573133	0,201171866	0,292337215	1,169361716	0,17655264
Community, Social service	0,025936936	0,031889042	0,10623513	0,028905382	0,033440085	0,030798029	0,036435055	1,06112916
Total	2,294199844	2,749265824	2,760825979	2,308510275	2,373317539	2,553134414	2,201103641	2,4261879

Table 8. Open-loop multipliers

	Agriculture	Manufacturing industries	Construction	Gas, Water Electricity	Trade, Hotel, Resturant	Transport Communication	Banking Real estate	Community, Social service
1st Decile	0,029525077	0,029696371	0,031835951	0,029610505	0,029741008	0,029664973	0,029827199	0,03053786
2nd decile	0,03857906	0,038802882	0,041598572	0,038690685	0,038861207	0,038761855	0,038973829	0,03990242
3rd decile	0,045292367	0,045555136	0,048837317	0,045423416	0,045623611	0,045506971	0,04575583	0,04684601
4th decile	0,052073031	0,052375139	0,056148691	0,052223699	0,052453865	0,052319763	0,052605879	0,05385927
5th decile	0,059190483	0,059533884	0,063823213	0,059361745	0,05962337	0,059470939	0,059796162	0,06122087
6th decile	0,067279007	0,067669335	0,072544811	0,067473672	0,067771049	0,067597788	0,067967454	0,06958685
7th decile	0,077118828	0,077566243	0,083154777	0,077341964	0,077682834	0,077484233	0,077907963	0,0797642

Table 8 (Continued)

	Agriculture	Manufacturing industries	Construction	Gas, Water Electricity	Trade, Hotel, Resturant	Transport Communication	Banking Real estate	Community, Social service
8th decile	0,090231106	0,090754593	0,097293328	0,090492181	0,090891008	0,090658639	0,091154415	0,09332626
9th decile	0,110011785	0,110650033	0,118622205	0,110330093	0,110816352	0,110533043	0,111137504	0,11378547
10th decile	0,174484226	0,175496519	0,188140785	0,174989078	0,175760309	0,175310967	0,176269673	0,18046947
Firms	1,025936936	1,031889042	1,10623513	1,028905382	1,033440085	1,030798029	1,036435055	1,06112916
Total	1,769721905	1,779989177	1,908234779	1,774842418	1,782664696	1,778107199	1,78783096	1,83042782

Table 9. Impact of injection on household

	Households	
	Lower 50%	Upper 20%
Agriculture	22.46	28.45
Manufacturing industries	22.59	28.61
Construction	24.22	30.67
Gas, electricity, water	22.53	28.53
Trade, Hotel, Restaurant	22.63	28.65
Transport andCommunication	22.57	28.58
Banking and real estate	22.69	28.74
Community, Social service	23.23	29.42

CLOSED-LOOP MULTIPLIERS

Closed- loop multipliers capture the inequality of household income. These multipliers catch the effects resulting from production activities to households to wants to factor and back to production activities through consumption demand. Then, it completes the circular flow of income. Table 10 depicts the closed-loop multipliers, which are closely related to the consumption patterns of households. Cohen (2002 a) describes the closed-loop effect phenomena: "the increase in income resulting from open loop effects are used mainly to purchase consumer goods, which increase output, and increase factor income, that is paid out as institutional income, which is again spent mainly on consumption, and so on." In general, closed loop multipliers are fairly constant which may be due to a similar pattern of household consumption and savings. Cohen (2002 a, b) also observed a similar relationship in developed and developing countries such as the Netherlands, Colombia, Surinam, and Pakistan. But these are higher than open loop multipliers, which indicate that consumption is larger than other categories of final demand (Table 10). It shows that an increase of income of one unit by any type of household will add to total income from 2.8224 to 2.8226 through the closed-loop effects which are higher than the open–loop multiplication.

Closed loop effects are also known as indirect effects. They capture the value added generated with each type of household by a one unit increase in disposal income exogenously generated. Each column total is equivalent to a Keynesian multiplier that implies an increase in the overall income of each group of households if their disposal incomes are increased by one unit. Row totals (Table 10) indicate the multiplier effect on the income of each class of household due to a one-unit increase in income of all groups of households. For example, if all ten types of household income increased by one unit initially, then, finally, their income would increase by the row total multipliers. Based on this notion, firms have a high-income redistribution potential (10.565). If income redistribution potential is compared among the households, there is only an 8 percent difference of multipliers (1.493) between the lowest and the highest income households. Hence it can be inferred that if the government wishes to redistribute the land from households, say 10th deciles to 1st deciles, it may not deliver a significant change in the income of poor households. Further, the other factor to note is the multiplier effects of the agriculture sector, which has the lowest multipliers (Tables 5, 6, 7 and 8).

POVERTY REDUCTION STRATEGY

The long-term vision of the National Planning Commission (NPC) is to reduce the incidence of poverty down to ten percent within the next two decades, i.e. by 2020. The NPC assumes that both economic growth and macroeconomic stability are necessary conditions for poverty reduction. Broad based economic growth and pro-poor policy measures are expected to enhance all sectors of the economy including trade and investment, fiscal and monetary policies, financial and capital markets and other economic and social sectors. The 10th Plan (2002-2007), also the Poverty Reduction Strategy Paper of the government of Nepal, aims to achieve the following major goals:

(i)   Broad-based high economic growth in the agriculture and manufacturing sectors with involvement of private sectors,
(ii) Social sector development for creating employment opportunities, reducing poverty and for accelerating broad-based growth These groups can be the hard-core poor, asset-less people, disadvantaged groups, indigenous people, people living in remote or isolate areas, female-headed households and women.
(iii) Targeted programs for the backward and vulnerable groups and safety nets. The major components of targeted programs include technological adaptation and advisory services in agriculture and livestock, rural infrastructure, rural access program, sustainable natural resource utilization, access to markets, land reform (already announced), micro-finance, micro-enterprises, and skill/vocational training.
(iv) Good governance through decentralization by: (i) promoting transparency, accountability, and responsiveness in the local institutions, (ii) improving the capacity of local bodies to identify their needs, mobilize resources, plan, prepare and implement projects and programs, and report accounting and expenditures, (iii) clarifying the responsibilities of both local bodies and line ministries and transforming the authority from central to local and (iv) fiscal decentralization (NPC, 2002).

The Plan anticipates a 6.1 annual growth rate of the gross domestic product. In order to meet that growth rate, total investment requirement is estimated about Rs. 596.5 billion, which increases steadily from Rs. 85 billion in 2002 to Rs. 145 billion in 2007. The sectoral investment requirement is presented in Table 11, where investment share is compared to the multipliers. Leontief multipliers are considered equal to SAM's transfer multipliers (Cohen, 2002).

As table 11 reveals, manufacturing is one of the leading sectors for multiplier effects on the economy, although it receives the second lowest investment projection share. Though construction has a high multiplier value, its inter-industry transaction is relatively low (Table

5). However, community and social services receives the highest investment share, and it has a high multiplier value.

Table 11. Multipliers and share of investment prioritization

Sectors	Multipliers		Investment projection in
	SAM (Total)	Leontief	10th Plan (%)
Agriculture	6.577	2.294	14.57
Manufacturing industries	7.057	2.749	6.06
Construction	7.379	2.761	12.52
Gas, Electricity, Water	6.604	2.308	1.86
Trade, Hotel, Restaurant	6.687	2.373	7.85
Transport andCommunication	6.856	2.553	18.33
Banking and real estate	6.528	2.201	15.55
Community, and Social service	6.856	2.426	23.26

If the investment projection requirements for the 10th plan are fulfilled as planned, that will boost the production sectors vis-à-vis income of households and firms. In fact, open-loop effects portray the interaction between production sectors and institutions. Now, if all estimated investment requirements are injected until 2007, Table 12 depicts changed nominal income scenarios of households and firms. The column sums indicate the output of each sector (Figure 3), and sum of the rows gives each group of household total income due to investment as planned in all sectors (Figure 4).

As Figure 3 illustrates, community and social sectors have a large share of output compared to other sectors, which also receive a high investment priority (Table 11). Agriculture, though it receives 14.57 percent of total planned investment, ranks third as a contributor to total output (Figure 4). Out of the total estimated income due to the open multiplier effect, firms will share 58 percent of it (Table 12), and the rest will be allocated among the classes of households. The overall impact is a rise in the income level of households (Figure 4) with nearly five times difference between the lowest and the highest income households.

Investment obviously will have multiplier effects, but there are a few noteworthy considerations. For example, nearly two-thirds of Nepal's annual budget is supported by the kindness of donors or by different types of loans, which may or may not be available as expected to meet the targeted level of investment. Further, there are certain barriers to socioeconomic development like political conflict, corruption, lack of institutional support and donor driven psyche (Devkota, 2007). Although the country is on last lap of the 10th Plan, it seems that it has already lost its base due to political instability (Pyakuryal, 2006) that started in mid-nineties, which, in fact, has affected the implementation of both 9th and 10th plans. In 2005, NPC in its second assessment of the Plan realized that several factors such as absence of elected bodies at the local level and ongoing conflict and political instability hindered the accomplishment of its goals (see details on http://www.npc.gov.np/tenthplan/assessment.htm as of March 30 2007).

Table 12. Changed income of institutes due to investment injection in the 10th Plan

	Agriculture	Manuf. industries	Construction	Gas, Water Electricity	Trade, Hotel, Restaurant	Transport Communication	Banking Real estate	Community, Social service	Total income
1st Deciles	2566,6	1074,62	2377,85	328,25	1392,36	3243,71	2766,35	4237,003	17986,74
2nd deciles	3353,6	1404,16	3107,05	428,912	1819,33	4238,41	3614,67	5536,29	23502,42
3rd deciles	3937,2	1648,5	3647,72	503,55	2135,92	4975,96	4243,67	6499,69	27592,21
4th deciles	4526,7	1895,3	4193,81	578,93	2455,69	5720,91	4878,99	7472,75	31723,08
5th deciles	5145,4	2154,35	4767,03	658,06	2791,34	6502,85	5545,86	8494,14	36059,03
6th deciles	5848,5	2448,75	5418,46	747,99	3172,78	7391,48	6303,71	9654,89	40986,56
7th deciles	6703,9	2806,89	6210,93	857,38	3636,81	8472,52	7225,66	11066,96	46981,05
8th deciles	7843,7	3284,14	7266,96	1003,16	4255,17	9913,07	8454,21	12948,64	54969,05
9th deciles	9563,3	4004,1	8860,046	1223,08	5188	12086,25	10307,57	15787,27	67019,62
10th deciles	15167,9	6350,71	14052,47	1939,87	8228,43	19169,4	16348,32	25039,4	106296,5
Firms	89184,6	37341,07	82626,14	11406,13	48381,74	112712,7	96125,31	147227,3	625005
Total Output	153841,4	64412,59	142528,466	19675,312	83457,57	194427,26	165814,32	253964,333	1078121

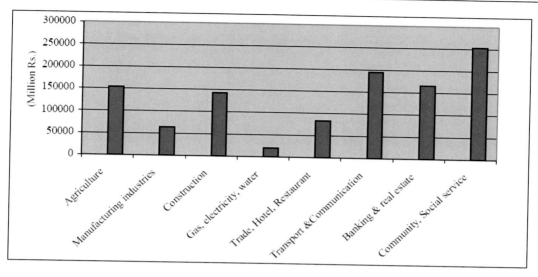

Figure 3. Sectoral output due to the total investment during the 10th Plan period.

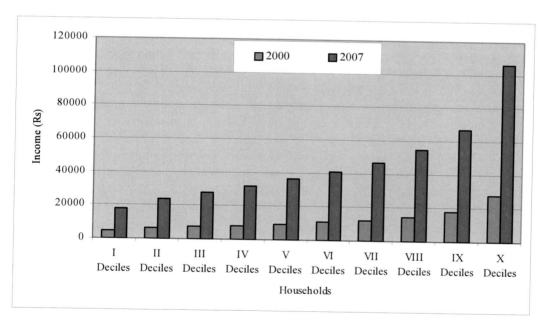

Figure 4. Projected income rise of household due to total investment in the 10th Plan period.

Emergency, insurgency, instability, and lack of a credible government advanced the politico-economic crisis. The Asian Development Bank (2005) estimated an account of cost of conflict in Nepal. For example, economic growth slowed to an average of 1.9 percent over the period of 2002-2004, and if it will be the trend for future years (2005-2009) then the country will lose about 57 percent of the economic growth due to decline in development expenditure. Local production of goods and services were far below the potential level. The World Bank in its Global Economic Prospects 2007 report cites Nepal economic growth rate for 2006 was 1.9 percent. This is less then population growth rate and indicates a return to the situation of the 1970s. Further direct and indirect consequences of the insurgency such as cost of displaced people, damages of infrastructure, forgone opportunities, and lost of thousands of lives are yet to be accounted for. In fact, a valid figure of people who lost (15,000 is an average estimation) their lives in ten years insurgency including Maoists is still to be accounted for.

Additionally, the fundamental problem is whether the increased nominal income level will alleviate poverty in real terms. There are a few factors like price level changes that always pose problems to low-income households. It is expected that from 2000 to 2007 the GDP deflator will rise by 76 percent, which will obviously impact investment. Further, between 1995/1996 to 1999/2000 the national average inflation rate was 35 percent. These facts will obviously set back real income growth, particularly for low-income families.

There are a few additional factors that may hamper the investment – income multiplier scenarios. For instance, investment in agriculture demands a high priority due to the fact that 90 percent of the people depend on agriculture, and it contributes 40 percent of GDP. The Labor Force Survey of 1998/1999 estimated that out of 9.5 million employed people, the agriculture sector employs 6.4 million people. The problem is further complicated by households' land holding capacity. The average land hold size in 1991/1992 was 0.68 hectare in mountain, areas 0.77 in hills, and 1.26 hectare in the Terai. About 69.5 percent of the landholdings are less than one hectare and agricultural productivity has been stagnant for decades. The total cultivated land in the country is 2.6 million hectares, and 30 per cent of the cultivated area is comprised of farms less than one ha. The latest Population Census of 2001 reveals about 24.4 percent of population does not have any land. The prevailing land holding pattern means no or low possibility for income generating chances for poor households. The cumulative impacts of such factors will reduce the investment-income multipliers, and will increase income disparity. Government initiated land reform measures in the past did not deliver any significant results.

Since land is one of the resource constraints, an alternative option is to intervene at the household level. To this regard, human capital enrichment strategies could the most useful option as the closed–loop multipliers indicate. Thorbecke and Jung (1996) used a multiplier decomposition method to analyze poverty in Indonesia and concluded that, "human capital of the poor must be enhanced through education and vocational training." Khan (1999) also reiterated that both economic growth and increasing the capital stock of the poor by appropriate skill enhancement may help to alleviate poverty.

Human capital - the skill, knowledge, and education acquired by an individual - development goal in Nepal requires revision of existing education policy at both secondary and tertiary education levels. Primary focus should be paid towards vocational education and training opportunities for low income households because according to the latest NLSS survey of 2003/04 only 51 percent of population (63 percent male and 39 percent female) can read and write. Further, it also reveals that literacy rate amongst the poor households is limited to 25 percent. Likewise, 31 percent of male and 56 percent of female population never attended school. Rural areas have much high rate of un-attending school (48 percent) than urban areas (25 percent). According to the Survey, reasons such as 'too expensive' for 27 percent and 'parents did not allow' for 38 percent are noteworthy. Nearly 60 percent of girls and 40 percent of boys both under-19 are not attending the school. In such prevailing context, it is highly imperative to invest primarily on vocational education and training targeting to the households that fail to complete secondary school. As Ramacharan (2004) argues that wrong type of education have little impact on development, so investment on both secondary and tertiary schooling is important. Nepal has already faced a crisis of waste of human resources as indicated by Bista (1994), so an equal opportunity should be provided to socio-economically deprived households in order to break the poverty cycle and reduce the income inequality gaps. Because human capital is the fundamental key of economic growth, and a vast majority of literature reveals a strong correlation between human capital and rise of employment, productivity and income (Wheeler, 2006; Jolliffe, 2002). Barro and Lee (2000) conclude that human capital is the main engine of economic growth, which is further justified by the findings of Jones and Schneider (2006) "A 1 point increase in a nation's average IQ is associated with a persistent 0.11 percent annual increase in GDP per capita." Based on the U.S. study, Krueger (2003) observed that education and training of disadvantaged could reduce inequality. He further suggests to invest in low income areas that may result high pay off, and such a task could be executed by the local government. Skar and Cederroth (1997) observed that the greatest challenge for the government of Nepal is the provision of occupational training for national self-sufficiency that in turn can help to alleviate unemployment - a strategy of enriching human capital.

CONCLUSION

The economic structure of Nepal examined through the SAM multipliers, namely aggregate, transfer, open-loop, and closed-loop multipliers indicates a huge gap of household income disparity as also justified by the NLSS survey. Among the production activities, the agriculture sector has the lowest income coefficients where as community and social services, and construction activities have high total income multipliers. Regarding the output coefficients, the banking sector has the lowest, and industries and construction activities have high aggregate output multipliers.

The Tenth Plan envisions a huge investment so that the standard of living of the poor may be raised. Investment in the community and social sectors will deliver a high output due to these sectors' high multiplier values. The investment – income multiplier scenarios indicate that the income level of households may increase during the Plan period, keeping many factors mute such as bad governance, high corruption, increasing inflation, and ill-defined sources of investment funding. Further, poor households' earnings will still be at least five times lower than upper ones at the end of the Tenth Plan.

Economic growth is, of course, a basis to augment the income level of people. But that may not necessarily be the sole, or even the most important, factor in reducing poverty. In addition, there exist many households deprived of basic endowments like land, or skills (education), and even economic sustainability would be impossible for them. As the SAM coefficients reveal, investment in household sectors have high multipliers, and it is imperative to intervene at the household level to enhance human capital. To this end, investment in community and social services at least the 1st, 2nd, 3rd and 4th deciles households seems an urgent need. That may include households socio-economically discriminated against – *Dalits,* which are the so-called untouchables as well as some indigenous ethnic minorities. In other words, poverty alleviation programs should exclusively target these households, say all types of *Dalits,* to enrich their human skill as well as quality of life, and break the vicious circle of poverty.

The Tenth Plan, based on the gross output of $ 9.03 billion in 1999 anticipates that by the end of 2007 gross output should be about $ 14.21 billion, which is an increment of fifty seven percent. Within the Plan period, from 2002 to 2007, it is expected that the overall contribution of the agriculture sector will be increased by twenty two percent, industrial sector (35 percent) and other sectors (47 percent). The annual growth rate of aggregate gross output for the plan period is estimated to be 6.3 percent based on a medium pace of growth. In fact, over these years annual growth rate did not even exceed three percent due to political instability and conflict. Hence it can be inferred that most of the objectives set by the 10th Plan could be half-baked only. It also raises a question of efficacy of a centralized planning system that controls both demand and supply of resources without ordinary people's accessibility. Is it worthwhile to continue such a planning system?

Nepal is struggling to meet basic human needs such as an adequate supply of food, water, health care, shelter, and minimum education, which needs to be sustained economically, environmentally, and socially. Repetition of past successive five-year development plans would be futile, since these plans are based on unsuccessful development models. Such plans cannot deliver the outcome demanded by local residents. Planners and policy makers should realize that economically poor countries do not need to follow a similar route of development adopted by the developed countries. They need to revise policy models in the context of their own socioeconomic structure, value systems and cultures. Henceforth, development plans, policies, and programs should emphasize other pillars of development — human and social capitals as well as ecological capital — because sustainability cannot be achieved in parts, it should address the whole system (Gowdy and O'Hara, 1997). Economic growth could be complemented by human, social and ecological capitals development. Augmentation of social capital is possible by focusing on enriching human capital, particularly focusing on the deprived classes of society who will ultimately determine the future of sustainability. In the words of the late visionary leader of the Nepali Congress Shree B. P. Koirala "Our capital is the people. We don't have machinery, and we don't have financial capital, we have labor. So we have got to motivate our people for development purposes. And that motivation can be provided only by institutions that are democratic and responsible to the people and reflective of the aspirations of the people[1] ." In the 21st Century, Nepal would be better off had she been able to enrich human capital vis-à-vis social sustainability to complement sustainable economic development.

REFERENCES

Adelman, I., Robinson, S., (1986), US Agriculture in a General Equilibrium Framework: Analysis with a Social Accounting Matrix, *American Journal of Agricultural Economics*, 68 (5), 1196-1208.

Adelman, I., Taylor, J. E., Vogel, S., (1988), Life in a Mexican Village: A SAM perspective, *Journal of Development Studies*, 25(1), 5-25.

1 B P Koirala, Worldview Jan/Feb, 1978 (also see on http://www.nepalicongress.org.np/contents/general/about_bp /nav.php?show=interview#) (As of March 10 2007).

Alarcon, J. Van Heemst, J. De Jong, N., (2000), Extending the SAM with Social and Environmental Indicators: An Application to Bolivia, Economic Systems Research, 12(4), 473-497.

Asian Devlopment Bank (2005), Measuring the Economic Cost of Conflict: The effect of Declining Development Expenditure, Working Paper No. 2, Kathmandu: Asian Development Bank.

Banouei, A. A., (1993), Input Output tables in Iran: Compilation, Use, Prospects, Economic Systems Research, 5(3), 335 - 342.

Barro, R. J. and J.-W. Lee, (2000), International Data on Educational Attainment: Updates and Implications, CID Working Papers 42, Center for International Development at Harvard University. http://www.economics.harvard.edu/faculty/barro/papers/p_jwha.pdf

Bhattarai, B.R. (2003), The Nature of Underdevelopment and Regional Structure of Nepal: A Marxist analysis, Delhi: Adroit Publishers.

Bista, D. B. (1994), Fatalism and Development, Calcutta: Orient Longman.

Blaikie P.M., Cameron, J., Seddon, J., (1979), Crisis in Nepal: Growth and Stagnation at the Periphery, Oxford: Oxford University Press.

Blaikie P.M., Cameron, J., Seddon, J., (2001), Nepal in Crisis: Growth and Stagnation at the Periphery, Delhi: Adroit Publishers.

Central Bureau of Statistics (1999), Nepal Labor Force Survey, Kathmandu.

Central Bureau of Statistics (2006), Statistical Year Book of Nepal, Kathmandu.

Central Bureau of Statistics (2004), Nepal Living Standard Survey, Kathmandu. (www.cbs.gov.np)

Chander, R., Gnasegarah, S., Pyatt, G., Round, J.I., (1980), Social Accounts and Distribution of Income: The Malaysian Economy in 1970, Review of Income and Wealth, 26(1), 67 - 86.

Cohen, S. I., (2002 a), Social Accounting and Economic Modeling for Developing Countries: Analysis, Policy and Planning Application, Burlington: Ashgate.

Cohen, S. I., (2002b), Social Accounting for Industrial and Transition Economics: Economy-wide Models for Analysis and Policy, Burlington: Ashgate.

Crossman, P., (1988), Balancing the Australian National Accounts, Economic Record (Australia), 64 (184), 39 - 47.

Dahal, R., (2000), Nepal's Remittance Bonanza, Himal South Asia, 13, 3.

Defourny, J., Thorbecke, E., (1984), Structural Path Analysis and Multiplier Decomposition within an Accounting Matrix Framework, *Economic Journal*, 94 (373), 111 - 137.

Den Bakker, G. P, De Gujt, J., Keuning, S. J.., (1994), An Historical Social Accounting Matrix for the Netherlands (1938), *Review of Income and Wealth*, 40(2), 175 -181.

Devkota, S.R. (2005), 'Politics of Poverty in Nepal: Structural Analysis of Socioeconomic Development in Nepal', Heidelberg Papers in South Asian and Comparative Politics, Working Paper no 25, South Asian Institute, University of Heidelberg, Germany. (URL: http://www.ub.uni-heidelberg.de/archiv/5294).

Devkota, S. R. (2007), Socioeconomic Development in Nepal: Past Mistakes and Future Possibilities, *South Asia Economic Journal* (forthcoming in September Issue).

Dubcovsky, G., (1999), Nicaragua: Structural Adjustment Policy Analysis in the Nineties, *North American Journal of Economics and Finance*, 10(1), 169-406.

Eckaus, R. S., Mccarthy, F.D., Mohie-Eldin, A., (1981), A Social Accounting Matrix for Egypt 1976, *Journal of Development Economics*, 9(2), 183 - 204.

Esparza, A., (1989), Defense Impact Analysis within a Social Accounting Framework, Growth and Change, 20 (3), 63-80.

Emini, C.A., (2002), Designing the Financial Social Accounting Matrix Underlying the Integrated Macroeconomic Model for Poverty Analysis: The Cameroon Country Case, CREFA, Quebec.

Golan, A., Vogel, S. J., (2000), Estimation of Non-stationary Social Accounting matrix Coefficients with Supply side Information, *Economic Systems Research*, 12(4), 447 -472.

Gowdy, J., O'Hara, S. (1997), 'Weak Sustainability and Viable Technologies', Ecological Economics, 22(3): 239-247.

Greenfield, C.C., Fell, H.A., (1979), The Estimation of Price Effects in A Social Accounting Matrix, Review of Income and Wealth, 25(1), 64 - 82.

Hanson, K.A., Robinson, S., 1991, Data Linkages and Models: US National Income and Product, *Economic Systems Research*, 3(3), 215-233.

Hewings, G.J.D., Madden, M., (1995), Social and Demographic Accounting, New York: Cambridge University Press.

Holub, H. W., Tappeiner, G., Tappeiner, U., (1999), Some Remarks on the System of Integrated Environmental and Economic Accounting of the United Nations, Ecological Economics, 29, 329-336.

Jolliffe, D., (2002), Whose Education Matters in the Determination of Household Income? Evidence from a Developing Country, Economic Development and Cultural Change, 51: 287-312.

Jones, G., Schneider, W.J., (2006), Intelligence, Human Capital, and Economic Growth: A Bayesian Averaging of Classical Estimates Approach, *Journal of Economic Growth*, 11, 71-93.

Keuning, S. J, (1991), Proposal for a Social Accounting Matrix, *Economic System Research*, 3 (3), 233-249.

Keuning, S. J., De Ruijter, W. A., (1988), Guidelines to the Construction of a Social Accounting Matrix, Review of Income and Wealth, 34(1), 71-101.

Khadka, N. (1994), 'Politics and The Economy during Nepal's Partyless Panchayat System (1961-1990): A Study in Retrospect', Asian Affairs, 94: 25 (1): 47-59.

Khadka, N. (1994), Politics and Development in Nepal: Some Issues, New Delhi: Nirala Publications.

Khan, H.A. (1999), 'Sectoral Growth and Poverty Alleviation: A Multiplier Decomposition Technique Applied to South Africa', World Development, 27(3): 521 – 530.

Khorshid, M., (1991), A Social Accounting Matrix based Long-term Model for a Gulf Cooperation Country, *Economic Systems Research*, 3(3), 299-315.

Kilkenny, M., (1999), Inter-regional Fiscal Accounting, Growth and Change, 30 (4), 567-590.

Kim, E., Ahn, J., (2002), Spatially Optimal Allocation of Investment: An Application of the Dynamic Multi-regional Social Accounting Matrix, Review of Urban and Regional Development Studies, 14 (1), 41-59.

King, B. B., (1985), What is SAM? In Pyatt and Round (editors) Social Accounting Matrices: A Basis for Planning, A World Bank Symposium, Washington, D.C.

Krueger, A. B. (2003), Inequality, Too Much of a Good Thing, In Heckman, J.J. and Krueger, A.B., (Editors) Inequality in America: What Role for Human Capital, p. 1-75, Cambridge: The MIT Press.

Lange, G. M., (1998), Applying an Integrated Natural Resource Accounts and Input –Output Model to Development Planning in Indonesia, *Economic System Research*, 10 (2), 113-134.

Lizardo, M., Navarro, J., Suazo, E., (1999), Honduras: Application of a CGE Model, North *American Journal of Economics and Finance*, 10(1), 149-169.

Mahat, R. S. (2005), In Defense of Democracy: Dynamics and Fault Lines of Nepal's Political Economy, New Delhi: Adroit Publishers.

Ministry of Finance (2006), Economic Survey 2005/06, Kathmandu.

Mujeri, M. K., Alauddin, M., (1993), Consumption, Saving and Investment by Social Class in Bangladesh, *Journal of Development Studies*, 30 (1), 226-246.

National Planning Commission (1998), The Ninth Plan (1997-2002), Kathmandu.

National Planning Commission (2002), Concept Paper on Tenth Plan/ Poverty Reduction Strategy Paper, NPC, Kathmandu (http://www.ndf2002.gov.np/

Nepal Rastra Bank (2006), A Glimpse of Nepal's Macroeconomic Situation, Paper presented at the 35th Meeting of the board of the governors, Asian Clearing Union, (May 22-23 2006) Kathmandu. (www.nrb.org.np).

Nepal, K, (2002), Remittance Economy, The Nepali Times, 104, 4.

Pan, X., (2000), Social and Ecological Accounting Matrix: an Empirical Study for China, paper presented for the Third International Conference on Input – Output Techniques, and for Leontief memorial Prize, Macerata, Italy, August 21-25, 2000.

Pandey, D. R. (1999), Nepal's Failed Development: Reflections on the Mission and the Maladies, Kathmandu: Nepal South Asia Center.

Parikh, A. Thorbecke, E., (1996), Impacts of Rural Industrialization on Village Life and Economy: A Social Accounting Matrix Approach, Economic Development and Cultural Change, 44(2), 351-378.

Pradhan, B.K., Sahoo, A., (1996), Social Accounting Matrix and Its Multipliers for India, MARGIN, 28 (2), 153 – 169.

Pyakuryal, B. (2006), Dimensions of economic restructuring, The Kathmandu Post, November03 2006. (http://www.kantipuronline.com/kolnews.php?andnid=90315)

Pyatt, G. (1985), Commodity Balances and National Accounts: A SAM Perspectives, Review of Income and Wealth, 31(2), 155-170.

Pyatt, G., (1988), A SAM Approach to Modeling, *Journal of Policy Modeling,* 10(3), 327-352.

Pyatt, G., (1990), Accounting for Time Use, Review of Income and Wealth, 36(1), 33-53.

Pyatt, G. (1991), Fundamentals of Social Accounting, *Economic Systems Research*, 3(3), 315 –342.

Pyatt, G., (1999), Some Relationship between T Accounts, Input –Output Tables, and Social Accounting Matrices, *Economic Systems Research,* 11(4), 365-388.

Pyatt, G., Roe, A., (1977), Social Accounting for Development Planning with Special Reference to Sri Lanka, Cambridge: Cambridge University Press.

Pyatt, G., Round, J. I., (1979), Accounting and Fixed Price Multiplier in a Social Accounting Matrix Framework, *Economic Journal*, 89(356), 850-874.

Pyatt, G., Round, J.I., (1985), Social Accounting Matrices: A Basis for Planning, A World Bank Symposium, Washington, D.C.

Pyatt, G., Thorbecke, E., (1976), Planning Techniques for Better Future, Geneva: International Labor Office.

Ramacharan, R., (2004), Higher or Basic Education? The Composition of Human Capital and Economic Development, IMF Staff Paper, 51(2), 309-326.

Rand, J. (2002), Trade and Income Growth in Vietnam: Estimates from a New Social Accounting matrix, *Economic Systems Research*, 14 (2), 157-184.

Reinert, K. A., Roland-Holst, D. W, (2001), Industrial Pollution Linkage in North America: A Linear Analysis, *Economic Systems Research*, 13(2), 197-209.

Roberts, D., (2000), The Spatial Diffusion of Secondary Impacts, Land Economics, 76 (3), 395-403.

Robinson, S., Cattaneo, A., El-said, M., (2001), Updating and Estimating Social Accounting Matrix Using Cross Entropy Methods, *Economic Systems Research*, 13(1), 47-64.

Roland-Holst, D. W, Sancho, F., (1995), Modeling Prices in a SAM Structure, Review of Economics and Statistics, 77(2), 361-372.

Roland-Holst, D. W., Sancho, F., (1992), Relative Income Determination in the United States: A Social Accounting Perspectives, *Review of Income and Wealth*, 38(3), 311-238.

Round, J.I., (1991), A SAM for Europe: Problems and Perspectives, *Economic Systems Research*, 3(3), 249-269.

Shrestha, D. L., Sapkota, P. (2002), Integrated Macroeconometric and Input Output Model of Nepal, Report Developed for the Formulation of the Tenth Plan, National Planning Commission/ Nepal.

Skar, H.O., Cederroth, S. (1997), Development Aid to Nepal, Nordic Institute of Asian Studies, Report no 35. Curzon.

Stone, R., (1986), Social Accounting: The State of Play, Scandinavian Journal of Economics, 88(3), 453-472.

Subramanian, S., Sadoulet, E., (1990), The Transmission of Production Fluctuations and Technical Change in a Village Economy, Economic Development and Cultural Change, 39(1), 131-174.

Tarp, F., Ronald-Holst, D., and Rand, J., (2003), Economic Structure and Development in an Emergent Asian Economy: Evidence from a Social Accounting Matrix for Vietnam, *Journal of Asian Economics*, 13, 847 – 871.

Taylor, J. E., and Adelman, I., (1996), Village Economies: The Design, Estimation and Use of Village Economic Models, New York: Cambridge University Press.

Taylor, J. E., Zabin, C., Eckhoff, K. (1999), Migration and Rural Development in El Salvador: A Micro-economy wide Perspectives, *North American Journal of Economics and Finance*, 10 (1), 91-115.

The World Bank, (2002), World Development Indicators 2002, Washington, D.C.

Thorbecke, E., (1998), Social Accounting Matrices and Social Accounting Analysis, in Isard W. et al., (eds.) Methods of Interregional and Regional Analysis, Vermont: Ashgate Publishing Company.

Thorbecke, E., Hong-Sang J. (1996), 'A Multiplier Decomposition Method to Analyze Poverty Alleviation', *Journal of Development Economics,* 48: 279 – 300.

UNDP Poverty Report (2000), Overcoming Human Poverty, New York (http://www.undp.org.np/keydoc/poverty2000/pr2000.htm)

UN, (1993), System of National Accounts: Prepared Under the Auspices of the Inter Secretariat Working Group on National Accounts, Commission of the European Communities/ International Monetary Fund/ Organization for Economic Cooperation and Development/ United Nations/ World Bank, Washington D.C.

Wheeler, C.H. (2006) Human Capital Growth in a Cross Section of U.S. Metropolitan Areas, Federal Reserve Bank of St Louis Review, 88 (2), 1130132.

In: Development Economics Research Trends
Editor: Gustavo T. Rocha, pp. 97-121

ISBN 978-1-60456-172-2
© 2008 Nova Science Publishers, Inc.

Chapter 3

FRAGILE STATES OF THE WORLD: AN ECONOMIC SECURITY QUESTION FOR TOMORROW, TODAY

Rosario A. Turvey
Department of Geography and Geology,
Nipissing University, Ontario, Canada

When a group of people is in dire need anywhere, we cannot ignore our obligation to help them: we must act.

- Michael Morgan, 2006

ABSTRACT

In recent years, the dilemma of weak, failing and fragile states has been at the center of global development research and policy development on issues concerning the small, less developed and poor countries. Regarded as one of the greatest economic and social challenges to humankind, questions on the conception of state fragility within the framework of global development and security are complex and analytically difficult, but are too important to ignore, hence the need to place the fragile states in the spotlight as problematic development spaces on Earth. This Chapter reviews the notion of state fragility as another concept used to describe the world's poorest countries and raises the economic security question in the study of development economics and geography. Fragile states are invariably referred to as weak and potentially failing states, places that are highly vulnerable to internal and external shocks, and pressures, and areas at risk and at the brink of further decline- or even failure. Here, the less examined but vital aspect of economic security as a pragmatic, down-to-earth approach for protecting the fragile states and fragile peoples of the world is discussed to understand their functioning in many respects. It reviews the changing landscape of global development vis-à-vis state fragility in terms of emerging frameworks on country classification. Its central task is to provide an understanding of the directions and nature of growth and development of the poor developing states from the standpoint of state fragility and economic security. Broadly, the purpose is to explore and stimulate thought and discussion on the economics of development with respect to fragility and the relevance of economic security as the critical missing link in tackling poverty in developing economies.

I. INTRODUCTION

The state of the world's security environment in the post-Cold War era has changed tremendously with the rise of new concerns and complex challenges that differ from the past but likely to shape the course of the 21st century. Across the globe, pressing challenges to security have influenced the interplay of power relations and various factors in the international system and the world economy. Some of the challenges are the changing nature of war, new terrorism with a worldwide reach, global maladies due to complex forms and types of new deadly diseases and impacts of globalization to peoples and places. In recent times, the dilemma of weak, failing and fragile states has been at the center of global development research and international development.

Questions about the conception of fragility of states within the framework of global security are complex and analytically difficult, but are too important to ignore- hence the need to place them in the spotlight as problematic development spaces on Earth. Increasingly, the security question has been raised in the literature with the fragile states invariably referred to as weak and potentially failing states, places that are highly vulnerable to internal and external shocks and pressures, areas at risk and at the brink of further decline- or even failure. Although there is neither a universal definition nor a standard list of fragile states to date, the World Bank estimates at least half a billion people living in these states with most of them living in extreme poverty. Another important concern is the rise of the number of fragile states that would be at risk to crime and instability not only within national spaces but also regionally and internationally [WB, 2005].

Of greater concern to the security arena is the perception that fragile states are likely to threaten regional and global stability- if and when they fall and fail, and turn into breeding grounds for criminal activity and terrorist networks. Therefore, it is not surprising to find multiple conceptions on what these states are about- even if we have yet to agree on the listing of fragile states [Moreno-Torres and Anderson, 2004]. Although existing discourses and scholarly writings on fragility provide no textbook definition of fragile states, given a multiplicity of meanings and operational frameworks, the focus is not so much about conceptualization or debate on terminology but on approaches toward implementing workable and effective solutions to the current 'fragile-state' conundrum in tackling economic and social vulnerability today.

This Chapter considers the notion of state fragility within the broad frameworks of place and security with the less examined but vital aspect of economic security as a pragmatic, down-to-earth approach for protecting the fragile states and fragile peoples of the world. While it is not intended to add to the long list of definitions, 'fragile states' are referred here as places or countries with high risk or extreme vulnerability to internal and external shocks and pressures in spatial and temporal terms. In the literature, there is a great interest to save these states from falling, given the nature, scale and complexity of problems and risks from state failure. Statements that call for urgent, decisive, and alternative actions and measures to resolve their serious security threats are broad and complicated that neglecting them would raise serious implications beyond their national borders or neighbouring areas and regions [WB, 2005; DFID, 2006].

The difficult situation in many fragile states of the developing world is compelling that there is a pressing need to adopt a 'building on-the-ground capacity' approach- one that takes perspectives from below or from within the community. Another fundamental point is an emphasis upon providing a stable environment (to avert failure or collapse) which, as the World Bank [2005] articulates, should go from a 'move from reaction to prevention' of risks and crisis situations. The world's response could involve adopting a 'pragmatic, down-to-earth' approach to economic security (ES) to save the fragile states, many of which are among the world's poorest and most vulnerable countries. This is not to suggest that donors and the international development community have no place and role in resolving the stability questions and related development issues of the fragile states. In fact, they do- but how? The short answer is to assert the importance of both the internal and external forces/actors in this global project of saving, not losing fragile states from possible state failure. In advancing ES, the rationale is to contribute toward the pressing task of building a secure future whether in terms of capacity and institution building, development partnerships, humanitarian intervention, peace and stabilization and securitization efforts in both the national and local community level. The focus is on strengthening the local capacity to achieve ES and thereby avert a likely state collapse. But first is a review of existing terminology and conceptual frameworks on fragile states before a discussion of place and economic security.

II. STATE OF KNOWLEDGE: FRAGILITY, FRAGILE STATES AND FAILED STATES

In this section, the concepts of fragility, fragile states and failed states are reviewed based on recent state of knowledge in the context of place and economic security (ES). From what has been written on the subject, a distinction has been made between fragile states and failed states or collapsed states [Gross, 1996; Helman and Ratner, 1993; Zartman, 1995; Ignatieff, 2002; Khan, 2002; World Bank, 2003; Francois and Sud, 2006]. Whether examined by theme, focus and problem area, impacts and implications, there has been a significant interest on the rise of fragile states and the phenomenon of failed states. At the outset, this paper focuses on ES as a goal for 'saving fragile states' from economic collapse where prevention is a key strategy. Here, fragile states are not used interchangeably to mean failed states as an 'either or' case or situation. As Francois and Sud [2006] clarified, in practice there is "...a continuum with fragile states at one end and failed/collapsed states at the other" [p. 143]. This continuum is adopted to point out how fragile states are perceived differently vis-à-vis the failed states for developing an economic security framework.

Over the last few years, the term 'fragility' is found in a burgeoning security and development literature as yet another descriptor on the world's poor countries with many also classified as least developed countries (LDCs) and economically vulnerable with low growth if not poorly performing or volatile economies [Briguglio, 1995; UN, 2003]. Discourses on the notion of fragility and the state-of-affairs of fragile states often focus on issues of instability or conflict, low economic performance and poverty, institutional and structural weakness, poor governance and security threats. From Afghanistan to Zimbabwe, the problems of fragile states have received much interest in academic research, policy and development cooperation (see Annex 1). Except for a few, the situation of these countries indicates where they are- if we are to position them in global development terms, particularly based on current measures of poverty, security and economic classification. Without a doubt, they are also the focus of international initiatives for 'making poverty history' and the focus of the Millennium Development Goals (MDG) by 2015. Any world country or state listed in an empirical survey and /or assessment of 'fragile states' puts them on the spotlight as they take on new gravity of dealing with the complex pressures of preventing state failure, if not total collapse. If they are in the list of recent surveys (e.g., WB and DFID) of fragile and failed states, it is imperative to sustain global efforts to address their multi-faceted security and development needs.

Past writings have analyzed fragility and related conceptual frameworks on fragile states not only to recognise their dismal state-of-affairs but also to accord them with high priority in research, foreign aid and international development. For example, McGillivray's [2006] research on aid allocation and effectiveness found that fragile states are "not only under-aided but aid flows have also been twice as volatile as those to other low income countries" [p. 1]. He referred to fragile states as "difficult development environments and/or difficult partnership countries but also recognised the potential to increasing absorptive capacity… prior to government-wide reform"[p. 5]. In the World Bank's Country Policy and Institutional Assessment [CPIA, 2002; 2005] their situational analysis raised the urgency, severity and complexity of issues besetting fragile states. But first are definitions of the term.

Fragile States: Failing or Falling?

For decades, fragile states have become a serious preoccupation of the international community [Rotberg, 2006]. With a diversity of definitions for poor and precarious countries, there is a continuing debate over terminology and analytical frameworks [Moreno-Torres and Anderson, 2004; DFID, 2005; Norris, 2006; Francois and Sud, 2006]. As Norris [2006] pointed out, there is no consensus on the "best way to conceptualize, define and measure these polities" (p.7) However, there are commonly shared views on the dilemma of these states, particularly those that convey a notion of risk society, extreme vulnerability of places, political deficiency (governance and stability) countries in the borderline of the world economy. Further, many are considered difficult environments and/or partnerships in the context of the donor community and in terms of development cooperation frameworks [Moreno and Anderson, 2004; McGillivray, 2006]. Others described them with precarious economies that are ranked as low-income countries of risk, under stress, and poor performance [WB, 2003; DFID, 2005; USAID, 2005].

In this Chapter, the meanings of fragile states that are development-based are adopted. Terms like difficult partnerships or difficult environments by some authors suggested the need to assess and improve development cooperation frameworks and strategies. In taking a development-oriented view, Moreno and Anderson [2004] defined these states with difficult environments given the challenges surrounding aid and partnerships in the so-called 'transformational development'. A common finding is that these states are under-aided in development cooperation and foreign policy terms [McGillivray, 2006]. As a group, they are not only low-income countries but in need of external aid based on recent assessments for development cooperation by the international/donor community [OECD, 2006; McGillivray,

2006]. Current literature classified them not only among the poorest, but one with weak, ineffective institutions and likely to have dismal growth prospects for poverty reduction [WB, 2003; Moreno and Anderson, 2004; Vallings and Moreno-Torres, 2005]. From the donors' perspective, these states are difficult partners based on their perceived inability and ineffectiveness to use domestic and international resources for poverty reduction. In the OECD [2006] document, they are reportedly less strategic, with less aid and little attention. In the World Bank report [2005], they are not only faced with 'grave poverty' but with development challenges as well. Broadly, it is imperative to respond to the call for good international engagement in these states because as OECD [2007] puts it: Have they been left behind?

Variously described as weak, unstable and vulnerable to criminal and terrorist networks, such descriptors virtually produced a picture of poor countries at the margins that deserve urgent attention by internal and external agents of national and global development. Indeed, terms such as poorly performing and volatile states are in wide use as frames of description as it was in the past with a persistent economic security question on the growing low-income, poor countries of the world. Since their problems are diverse and complex, greater attention has been paid through programs for economic cooperation, humanitarian and security programs. The people in these states are struggling to survive with insecure, unstable governments, harsh environments and ineffective functioning of states [Moreno and Anderson, 2004; DFID, 2006]. Further, Moreno and Anderson have stressed how vital these states are to the overall operation of the world economy since many are among the poorest and most vulnerable. Although each state's situation varies from place to place, their geographies of representation in the world economy and the political arena are constructed as spaces of development at best and precarious states at risk from failure at worst. Below are selected definitions from the literature.

AUSAID, 2006

Fragile states are countries that face particularly grave poverty and development challenges and are at high risk of further decline- or even failure. Government and state structures lack the capacity (or, in some cases the political will) to provide public safety and security, good governance and economic growth for their citizens.

DFID, 2006

Fragile states are those where the government cannot and will not deliver core functions to the majority of its people including the poor. Fragile states are often characterized by high levels of insecurity.

Norris, 2006

...fragile states: understood here as a range of poorer developing nations facing serious risks of political instability, conflict, and in extreme cases even state collapse.

OECD, 2006

Fragile states face problems in a wide range of domains, indicating the need for a mix of actors, instruments, incentives and interventions. Political, security, economic and social spheres are interdependent: failure in one risks failure in all.

The World Bank, 2005

Defined as low-income countries under stress (LICUS), all 'fragile States' are different and many reasons can cause their fragility but features they share are weak governance, failing public institutions, inability or conflict- all of which contribute to dismal growth prospects.

Francois and Sud, 2006

Fragile states...are states that are prone to failure in the future. The term failing could be used to denote a deteriorating situation in which a fragile state moves towards collapse.

McGillivray, 2006

Fragile states as a group have not only been under-aided but aid flows have been twice as volatile as those to other low income countries, even when changes such as the onset or cessation of conflict and large performance changes are taken into account.

Moreno Torres and Anderson, 2004

Fragile states ...with a range of problems such as poverty and conflict; with 'difficult environments grounded in the role of the state in development effectiveness'. Difficult environments are *those areas where the state is unable or unwilling to harness domestic and international resources effectively for poverty reduction'*.

Defining Failed States

A survey of literature indicates that state failure is interchangeably viewed to mean weak, fragile, failing and failed and collapsed states [Francois and Sud, 2006]. Already, academics, policy makers and development specialists have made scholarly contributions in examining this phenomenon based on the nature, causes and dire consequences. Failed states are perceived as politically chaotic states of anarchy and instability in an otherwise orderly and regulated sea of international relations [Hough, 2004; Andersen, 2006, p. 3]. Several authors have expressed concerns over the rising criminal and political violence; hostilities in ethnic, religious, linguistic and cultural lines; incidents of terrorism and widespread corruption; collapsed social services, extreme poverty and starvation in failed states [WB, 2005; Francois and Sud, 2006; Rhodes, 2006; Rourke, 2006]. As it is well known, international security is derived in part from the capacity of states to provide or deliver political and public goods and services, primarily those on national and individual security and public order. As Rhodes [2006] noted, 'if states cannot provide it or government refuses to do so, failure looms'.

Concerns on the effects of failed states include for example the global spread of disease as it encourages migration if not influx of refugees in terms of human security. If we look at the post-Cold war, attention has been paid on why, when and which states have failed with serious impacts within their own territory and their neighbouring states. In the aftermath of the Cold War, relations have improved between Russia and the US with the softening of superpower competition for influence. However, in reflecting on the case of Afghanistan, Hough [2004, p. 10], the world has yet to tackle the rise on the phenomenon of failed states since the 1990s, 'where domestic sovereign control breaks down indefinitely'. Afghanistan is held as one that is yet to save itself from its status as a failed state which Rourke [2006, p. 110] described as "a country so fragmented ...it cannot be said to exist as a unified political or national entity". This phenomenon of failed states is not really new but considered to be more worrisome than before [Rotberg, 2006, p. 132]. Other case-studies in the real world dilemma of state failure include the Ethiopia-Eritrea war and the internal conflicts in Somalia and the Sudan now the 'hallmarks of 'New World Order' global indifferences [Hough, 2004, p. 49].

In outlining the problem of weak and failed states, Coyne [2006, p. 343] referred to them as states that produce 'potential chaos ... as they pose a threat to global political and economic security and stability.' Unfortunately, the policy and practice in the real world is more of a 'reaction' to crises, emergencies and others, and less of 'prevention' wherein states and the international community become engaged in post-conflict reconstruction efforts. This means exactly the opposite, ie., the pre-conflict schemes within typical programs for capacity and institution-building in governance, economic management. On the other hand, Maull [2006: 73] argued that state building" can be seen in the context of failed and deficient statehood. Coyne's perception of reconstruction meant 'occupation' to create and restore physical infrastructure, facilities, and minimal social services...fundamental social change through reform in the political, economic, social and security sectors. This is true in Afghanistan, Bosnia, Cambodia, Haiti, Kosovo and Somalia where the policy agenda and development practice focus on reconstruction, not stabilization. Further, Coyne believed that foreign intervention and the focus on reconstruction efforts can fail or do more harm than good.

Along a different school of thought, Khan's [2002] version of failed states is based on Ann Krueger's [1990] two-pronged definition of state (government) failure in terms of economic performance. One side consisted of 'errors of omission', when the state fails to do things that could have improved economic performance, and the other due to 'errors of commission' when the state does things which worsens economic performance. Accordingly, Khan framed his two conceptual models for examining state failure with the first being a 'service-delivery' model. The range of services or functions as listed in a standard textbook that nation-states should deliver include law and order, public goods, social security and market regulation. Khan's other model is called the 'social transformation model' which is driven by the 'lack of institutional capacities with pre-existing distributions of power' [2002, p. 2.]. Again the emphasis is on the inherent role and responsibilities of the state at the central level. However, in case of failure by the state, the question is this: What should be an alternative structure in case the state malfunctions or unable to keep service delivery and transformation processes running in these so-called 'fragile states'?

III. FRAGILE STATES IN DEVELOPMENT AND SECURITY FIELDS: THE 'OTHER PLACES'?

Fragility and security need not be construed as 'strange bedfellows' in the nexus of poverty, fragility, development and security. The first two terms in the fragility nexus suggest their state-of-affairs *vis-a-vis* the nature and causes of fragility while 'development' is a dynamic transformative process involving a mix of actors, agencies and institutions at various levels (state or central government, regional and local) to achieve the objectives of poverty reduction, mitigation of risks and threats and so on. Security, in its broad sense, is associated with long-term safety, stability, peace and well-being. World attention to the state-of-affairs of fragile states as a critique to current thinking is derived *writ large* from discursive analysis that tend to suggest a conception of 'other places' in dire need of either rescue or freedom from the risk of falling and failing for one reason or another. Recent studies on this group of states reflect which places are at risk and which ones have problematic geographies. These states are under pressure to deal with questions of instability and pervasive corruption, poor economic performance, difficult environments and partnerships, stress and internal conflicts as discussed in current literature [Moreno and Anderson, 2004; Vallings and Moreno-Torres, 2005; World Bank, 2005; Francois and Sud, 2006; McGillivray, 2006; Norris, 2006].

The various definitions and labels suggest an idea of 'otherness' as opposed to developed economies with stable, safe, dynamic states of prosperity, given an emphasis on their fragility as a spatial representation of development of poor countries. Many fragile states are sites of vicious wars, human rights abuses, abject poverty and disease and lost opportunities. Whether we like it or not, fragile states are not imaginary geographies, rather real places at risk within the periphery of global development. Their multiple challenges to development demand flexible, effective and immediate action- from framing strategies and solutions to help and save them from falling. If the inevitable happens, the shift from fragile to failed states could take place and turn into what Zartman [1995] calls the 'collapsed states' with zero state functionality and lost legitimacy. But of course the traditional approach is to strengthen state capacity which is often aimed at the central, not sub-national or local government. Thus, the world cannot turn its back from them because they need a wide-ranging support to strengthen their economies and institutions for security, governance and economic growth for tomorrow, today. Next is a summary of the basis for prevailing themes on fragile states before the discussion of vulnerability and economic security.

IV. SHARED THEMES- THE CONCERNS OF FRAGILE STATES

Three relevant themes prevail from current research, approaches and policy recommendations in addressing the concerns of fragile states. The first recognizes the important role of international organisations, both intergovernmental and non-government actors. Recent scholarly writings and published works by international development institutions ranging from the World Bank to UNU-WIDER[1] support the important role of the international development/donor community for tackling the pressing issues of fragile states. The global effects of doing nothing about the fragile states are well known [Hough, 2004; World Bank, 2005; Andersen, 2006; Francois and Sud, 2006; Rotberg, 2006]. Since the fragile states have become a preoccupation of the international community, OECD[2] [2007] has pointed out the 'need for a mix of actors, instruments and interventions' to deal with their wide array of problems today and in the future.

Second is to appreciate the involvement of local actors for capacity and institution-building whether to improve the economy, strengthen governance or policy institutions'. For example, Francois and Sud [2006, p. 142] argued that "...the international community must involve local actors much more substantively in the process and provide resources in a way that promotes the construction of sustainable national institutions." Similarly, the World Bank [2005, p. 6] initiatives to build capacity and reduce the risk of fragility if not state failure, recommended among others, the approaches to decentralization to strengthen local or community capacity with 'well-designed community-based development approaches to state capacity and institution building initiatives'. More importantly, the Bank's community-driven development programs are seen as critical instruments not only in peace-building but in economic and development interventions in volatile countries of Angola, Comoros and Nepal. In addition to the role of local actors in capacity building, the Bank's document on the Principles for Good International Engagement in Fragile States has raised the need for synchronizing local priorities and systems in pursuing the country's development [WB, 2005, p. 32].

Third is to focus attention on the poorly performing if not failing economy, by aiming for economic growth in the immediate term. The World Bank's [2005] report on good practice in country assistance strategies for fragile states, stressed that common fragility in terms of weak state policies and institutions as well as risks of conflict and political instability are challenges that are closely link or interrelated. They identified among others, the erosion of state capacity which could lead to failure in generating economic growth. Apart from the Bank's focus on building core economic and development competencies, a unified approach that considers the whole spectrum of the economy, peace and security and development linkages has been adopted in engaging their client governments [WB, 2005, p. 7]. These are strategies that are

---

[1] UNU-WIDER- United Nations University World Institute for Development Economics Research .

consistent with what is being articulated for framing the notion of economic security toward preventing state failure in fragile states. Next is a discussion of security and its links with state fragility in development economics and geography.

V. LINKING THE FRAGILE STATES AND THE 'GEO' FACTOR IN SECURITY ISSUES

1. Security: Meaning and Conceptual Issues

1.1. The Security Concept

The field of security studies in international relations and politics shows no shortage of 'conceptual literature' to explain what 'security' means according to its nature and characteristics [e.g., Wolfers, 1952; Ullman, 1983; Digeser, 1994; Tickner, 1995; Baldwin, 1997; Buzan et al., 1998]. In a standard dictionary, 'secure' means to make something, somebody or somewhere safe, or untroubled by fear or danger, reliable, and certain not to fail. Closely related terms to suggest insecure and unstable conditions such as fragility and vulnerability to risks and threats are probably sufficient reasons to capture the underlying forces for certain actors and spatial units to adopt security measures which in this paper focuses on fragile states. Pertinent security studies indicate that current definitions of 'security' vary by context, focus and philosophical basis. In global politics, state security in conventional terms is about national security within the international system of power relations. In this sense, security is posited as a principal goal of the states- in the national security context with the state as prime unit of analysis [Waltz, 1979, Tickner, 1992; Rengger, 2000; Smith, 2000].

In this new dynamic field of security studies, the concept of security is not limited to the question of 'what is to be secured' (e.g.., the state), but also 'for which values' and 'for whom.' Early writings by Wolfers [1952] viewed security to be value-laden and that it holds objective and subjective dimensions of acquired values in national security. Security from an objective lens according to Wolfer is measured by the *absence of threats* to acquired values while the subjective view is the *absence of fear* when acquired values are attacked. In matters of national security, examples of values and vital interests for protection are territorial integrity and economic welfare. A more nuanced conceptualization of security by Buzan [1991] relates to the international system in which it depends on the ability of states and societies to maintain their independent identity and functional integrity. Others like Wheeler and Booth [1992] argued for a stable security achieved not at the expense of others but as a process of emancipation. From the standpoint of emancipation, Booth [1991, p. 319] privileges the individual rather than the state as the referent of security and asserts '...emancipation, power or order as 'true security'. Theoretically, Booth [1991] claims that emancipation is security itself which means freedom from want (poverty) and freedom from political oppression (fear). Others advanced a survivalist notion of security. In particular, Waltz [1993] interprets 'security' with regard to conditions of anarchy and the need for an assurance of survival. He asserts that the goals of tranquillity, profit and power could be

---

[2] OECD- Organization for Economic Cooperation and Development.

achieved only if states are assured of survival in conditions of anarchy. Presumably, this condition of anarchy points to the existence of threats and disturbances to security, hence the concern for survival.

In the developing world, Thomas [1987] disagrees with a rather simplistic yet persistent military orientation of security from a Western (developed world) standpoint. Her contribution to the literature asserts a more inclusive view of the concept in relation to the state's existence. In differentiating the internal from the external types of security, Thomas argues that the internal security of the state through nation building is just as relevant and that the search for secure systems of food, health, money and trade are equally important to matters of external security. As work on meaning construction and measurement continues, a revisit of the conceptual issues on contemporary security is imperative.

1.2 Explicating the Spatial Dimension in the Field of Security

In asserting a spatial dimension of security with respect to fragile states, the concept of place is proposed here as a way to link the twin goals of economic growth and security. A close look at the meaning of 'place' in development terms is compelling when dealing with economic and social issues of immense interest to fragile states. The term 'place' is easily understandable to everyone and everywhere and it is often assumed that we already know what the term 'place' means in the growth and development of the local and/or national economy. Past writings about 'place' invariably asserted the diversity of places, the spatial dimension of social phenomena, and the importance of place in understanding our world from different contexts and theoretical positions [Hartshorne, 1979; Gregory, 1989; Massey, 1994]. In geographic texts, places are invariably held with spatial-temporal dimensions and described with the basic notions of location, scale, direction and distance, physical and cultural aspects, distribution, changing attributes and nature of interactions with other places [Fellmann et al., 2004].

The geographer's interest in 'place' is evident in various philosophical and methodological accounts on spatial organisation, sense of place, specificity of place, environment and society relations, and forms of geographic representation- mapping and naming places [Bunge, 1966; Smith, 1989; Entrikin, 1991; Cloke et al., 1991]. In phenomenology for example, it is expressed in writings on the everyday geographies and in framing a sense of place in discussions of space, place and environment [Relph, 1976; Agnew, 1987; Entrikin, 1991; Williamson et al., 2002]. In a critique of the everyday-people-place relations in human geography, Cloke et al., [1991, p. 81] viewed a 'sense of place' as '...a rudimentary understanding of how this place 'works' and a nagging feeling towards this place of liking, disliking, loving, hating, accepting, rejecting or whatever.'

To Entrikin [1991], a sense of place may be derived from both its historical (passive) and developmental (active) presence in human affairs. He asserts the active role that human consciousness plays in the representation of place and views the conception of place as contexts for our actions and as an important component of our sense of identity, both as individuals and as member of groups. Further, he contends that: "As 'moral agents, we are part of place, community and culture, no matter if our goal is preservation or transformation" [Entrikin, 1991, p. 14]. Accordingly, the concept of place as context with an active role and presence in our local worlds, whether to initiate, take action and transform the organisation of, and interactions in space is vital to economic development and for asserting our goals for growth and well-being, prosperity and security.

Place is central to geography and fundamental to economic analysis as a process because it defines *'where'*, *'how'* and *'why'* development occurs. It may mean specific places in the process of becoming and coping with changes, adjustments and/or reconstruction. 'Development' according to Agnew and Knox [1989, p. 24], is a normative concept that "involves values, goals and standards that make it possible to compare a particular situation against a preferred one". Viewed not only in terms of income and consumption but also to people's health, education, security, civil rights and so on, Agnew and Knox [1989] describes development as a process of political, social, economic and cultural transformation to enhance social well-being and quality of life. Since development does not occur in a vacuum, place is a building block, an essential component of any local initiative to establish spatial and social relations and networks in business and industry, to make connections and to engage in economic activities- from production to distribution and consumption. Within the project of economic growth and development, it is an end by itself as measured by the transformation of the economy, quality of life and other non-economic factors considered in deciding the place preferences of potential residents and for making choices in the location and investment decisions of firms.

Place in economics and geography, may be framed in three-tiered ways of thinking (space-place-region) and often geographically defined (villages, towns, counties, cities) at the local level. Terms like 'locality' and 'community' are key organising and planning concepts to interpret the site, setting and function as well as relations, connections and interactions between and among places in local development. To Cooke [1989, p. 296], 'localities' play an active role in transforming and shaping their destiny and this means "… not simply places or even communities: they are the sum of social energy and agency resulting from the clustering of diverse individuals, groups and social interests in space." Mason [2000, p. 21] proposes what he called an 'ordinary' conception of community to be "constituted by a group of people who have a range of values, a way of life, identify with a group and its practices and recognise each other as members of that group". To Shaffer [1989, p. 3], a 'community' is a 'group of people in a physical setting with geographic, political and social boundaries and with discernible community linkages.' Increasingly, the term 'community' in local economic development stresses the role of active local agencies, the nurturing of civil society, and mutual recognition within a community's economic life.

Adopting a 'place perspective' to security assessment and development involves a consideration of place that could provide insights to the contemporary struggles, contributions and participation of human communities to the economy. In sum, 'place' is a fundamental aspect of the development process in the real world context- not merely as settings in historical sense, but as key component of community life that actively shapes, reshapes and influences our experiences of the world- including matters of security- whether local, regional or global.

2. Economic Security in Development

Throughout the field's intellectual history, various labels and types of security by actors, sectors or areas of concern are found in the literature. Recent writings indicate a trend toward policy shifts in foreign policy and security agenda. Conceptual literature on national security includes discussions on human security, collective security versus common security in the policy agenda and non-traditional/ critical security studies. In the so-called family of security terms, various kinds of security include economic security, environmental security, social security, identity security and physical security [Buzan and Waever, 1997; Baldwin, 1997; Williams, 2003]. One security variant that has gained significant attention in the form of policy analysis, community development project and empirical research is 'economic security' [www.sfu.ca/economicsecurity project; www.policyalternatives.ca; Manley, 2005]. This paper focuses on the notion of economic security and discusses its spatial links with development. Interest on economic security within the broad umbrella of security studies is not entirely new. The web has a collection of useful meanings that present a direct but practical version, e.g., 'Wikepedia' which describes economic security in terms of probability of continued solvency, predictability of the future cash flow and employment security. In this section, the state of knowledge on economic security is reviewed within the purview of international and local affairs.

2.1. Economic Security in International Affairs

Security in an age of terrorism denotes a complex and broad policy agenda at both international and national levels. Broadly, the notion of 'security' in international affairs is categorised into economic security, food security, health security, environmental security as well as personal, community and political dimensions [UNDP, 1994; DFAIT, 2000]. Evidence in recent years showed increasing economic instability if not greater incidence of economic crises in one country after another in an era of 'globalization' [ILO, 2004]. In a capitalist economic system, this paradox is said to exist since states are expected to feel insecure and therefore have to compete to achieve economic well-being [Buzan, 1996, p. 95]. There are also concerns for insecurity from one state to the other within the dynamics of global, regional and continental change. In broadening the unit of analysis beyond the level of the state, Collins [2003] viewed economic security to mean access to resources, finance and markets and maintenance, and increase in the levels of welfare and prosperity.

According to UNDP [1994], 'human security' from a broad notion of security, is concerned with the well-being of political constituencies, the disadvantaged and the vulnerable groups at the local level. As central tenet within the United Nations (UN) system, the concept of economic security is integral to human security in terms of policy development and publications of the UN and its specialized agencies. From a basic needs approach, the UN [1994] version describes economic security in the international development context as it related to the world's poor living on the edge- as having the means to live a stable and fulfilled lifestyle plus the money to meet basic needs including basic health care and education. To a working person in the developing world, a secure work means having income, access to credit and loans and privileges that people in the developed world sometimes take for granted.

At the policy level, the United Nations Development Programme (UNDP) was first among the international agencies to articulate 'economic security' as a key concern under the umbrella of human security which privileges the human community rather than the state. UNDP's view of human security has focused on two key areas namely, a) safety from the chronic threats of hunger, disease and repression and, b) protection from sudden and harmful disruptions in the conduct of daily life [Collins, 2003]. This definition also identified seven types of human security namely economic security, political security (freedom from political oppression) and community security (survival of cultural identity). UNDP's version of human security in the 1994 Human Development Report is consistent with the critical security studies (CSS) positing emancipation (e.g., Booth, 1991) and freedom from poverty or economic security. The first major statement on human security came in the 1994 Human Development Report from the United Nations Development Programme (UNDP). The People's Security Survey (PSS) under the auspices of the International Labour Organization (ILO) was conducted in 2002 in which 'economic security' is labour-force oriented with its emphasis on basic security, work-related security and employment security [ILO, 2002].

Drawn from the PSS survey of 48, 000 people in 15 countries, ILO reports that many conventional policies for anti-poverty programmes have failed to reach the poor [ILO, 2002]. In the survey, *basic security* pertains to income security and voice representation security while *work-related security* refers to income security, representation security and labour market security, employment security, job security, work security and skill reproduction security. ILO [2002] views basic security as a development goal and socio-economic right. Basic security means reducing the impact of uncertainties and risks that people face everyday, providing a social environment so people can belong to a range of communities, have fair access to opportunities and develop capacities for decent work [www.ilo.org/PSS]. From the perspective of the developing world, economic security is largely development-based in approach and orientation.

In international politics, the concept is applied to explain the behaviour of states in capitalist economies where the concern is based on capacity building and in creating favourable conditions to secure the economy [Dent, 2001; Collins, 2003]. Arguments in support of the workings of the concept are framed from the functions of state to maintain survival, economic capacity, persistent improvement and protection. From a survivalist stance, economic security refers to a "state's ability to provide sufficient capacity to survive in what is a hostile, competitive, capitalist environment" [Collins, 2003, p. 112]. The goal for survival is a function of the state's economic capacity to maintain military capabilities. In an insecure environment, the state's survival based on economic capacity depends on their access to markets, finance and supplies. The second element to ensure the state's survival pertains to economic capacity. To Dent [2001], the state's goal for economic security is to maintain its economic capacity and ability to increase economic growth and prosperity.

Defining economic security in the classic state-centric view as a concept is synonymous with the objective for capacity improvement which depends on the country's ability to create favourable conditions for continued economic growth and development [Dent, 2001, pp. 6-7]. The idea of prosperity becomes an element in security and this means safeguarding the structural integrity and prosperity-generating capabilities and interests of the 'politico-economic entity in the context of various externalized risks and threats that confront it' [Dent, 2001, p. 6]. The external capacity of the state is established to show that a state has extraterritorial economic interests and its concerns are not tied to its own territory because its capacity must access to markets, finance and supplies [Collins, 2003, p. 112]. In a similar line of thought, Mandell [1994, p. 61] refers to economic security as the "extent to which a nation's goods and services maintain and improve a society's way of life through performance at home in the international marketplace." As Collins [2003, p. 111] argued, economic security is characterized by the general condition of insecurity. As such, the goal is to change insecurity to achieve security.

In the twenty-first century, pressing concerns on global issues such as population growth, resource capacity and markets have encouraged more attention to economic security issues in international relations and development. Issue-oriented frameworks for advancing ES tend to look at the role of the state in functional terms. As Bayliss and Smith [2005] point out, problems associated with deprivation and poverty are sources of internal conflicts that tend to produce tensions between states and in effect, economic insecurity. These perspectives, whether functional, extraterritorial or sectoral in setting policy agenda are important for understanding economic security from an international lens.

2.2. Dynamic and Productive Economy: Local Agency

Community responses to achieve ES generally reflect the collective desire of a democratic society to safeguard their quality of life and to sustain their local economies. In the case of fragile states, the question of economic security is more crucial to the people and communities in localities experiencing stagnant and poorly performing economies, shifts and changes in their economic geographies- e.g., adverse realities of unemployment, precarious governance, and insecurity of livelihoods and income sources and dismal growth prospects on trade. Concerns on the economy are deeply embedded in our aspirations, expectations and hopes for the future as individuals, political constituents and communities. The goal to achieve ES in a locality is an inherent, everyday functioning of society and the economy.

In practice, there are three forces at work to make ES a feasible goal and project at a particular place which in the context of this paper concerns the fragile state. These forces are set toward achieving economic diversity, the active participation of local agencies/actors and enhanced quality of the place to live, play, work and invest. Local agencies refer to individuals, institutions and new economic relationships in particular places. By strengthening capacities for local growth and economic development, the focus should be on meeting the development needs of local economies regardless of their economic structure and potential. The local economy, as it relates to the nature and scope of economic structures and role of local agencies, are shaped and reshaped by the actions, policies and institutions of people. But it is possible to determine if a place is moving toward ES as measured by the economic performance and quality of life indicators, by the dynamics of the economy, and by the prospects for the future as envisaged by the locality.

2.3. Economic Security at the Community Level

The framework of economic security at the community level asserts a spatial perspective of economic development. Broadly, the geographical dimension of security analysis varies widely by country, whether the country is economically developed or developing. Here, economic security at the community level means identifying the sources and causes of threats and risks and mitigating them to protect, nurture and sustain the stability and viability of the economy. The notion of local economic security has a conceptual and practical appeal that may work at the community level. Security in a community focuses on the concerns of the locality, at the municipal or local governance level- in the village, township, town, city and others to be economically secure today, tomorrow and in the future. In geographical contexts, questions of which place is secure may be viewed as follows:

- *Spatial-* global, national, regional, local, community or household
- *Temporal-* short-term, long-term, annual and/or relevant time frame
- *Sectoral-* security of income, work, job, resource capacity
- *Political-* policy basis, organizational and institutional structures

- *Vulnerability*- susceptibility to economic collapse, threats, risks in planning and managing communities for a secure future

The spatial characteristics of ES can be implemented or experienced locally or over a wide area (regional, provincial and national). In today's interdependent world, the location, the site and situation are explicit spatial characteristics of security. In the rubric of national security, ES follows a place-based approach by focusing on the security of a locality as described by its temporal, local conditions and spatial characteristics. The local conditions to which it may take place fall into three broad temporal categories of medium-term (five years), long-term (multi-year, decadal variability) and isolated extreme events or severe economic conditions associated with natural causes, disasters and other factors. A place-based approach to local economic security is an integrative complex of physical, institutional and societal strategy for development in a given geographic space with boundaries. A place-based analysis of local economic security requires a definition or delineation of the scope, boundaries, and limitations in terms of spatial scale whether it concerns a small town, a large city or urbanized area. In general, economic security in terms of its spatial characteristics can be described or experienced locally or over a wide area (regional, provincial and national). In operational terms, a place-based approach to economic security may mean shaping a locality with some if not all of the following attributes of a secure future:

1. Maintenance, conservation and management of resources
2. (natural, physical and human-made resources)
3. Stable population and labour force
4. Skilled, knowledgeable and trained labour
5. Gender approach to development
6. Satisfaction of human needs, material and non-material
7. Capacity for fair competition
8. Equalization of opportunities in a just, fair society
9. Cultural justice and human rights
10. Safety (freedom from fear) and emancipation (freedom from want)

Delineating which community is economically secure involves assessing the overall state of the local economy in relation to sub-national and national economies. In development-based studies, this means evaluating the capacity of place and the community to cope with risks, threats and extreme events (level of resistance) and the ability to recover from damages and losses in the economy (level of resilience). Clearly, any systematic process to attain economic security needs to specify what, where and why it should be addressed. The common experience is in the naming and labelling of places, i.e., from 'boom towns' to 'ghost towns' and so at the state level, the fragile and failed states as descriptors to define the state or the community's economic situation. Boom towns may mean dynamic local economies (in some sort of economic paradise) whose economic growth and development can be measured by the high employment patterns, levels of productivity, increased income and job opportunities and growing tax base. Ghost towns are to describe towns facing economic collapse and difficulties in employment and income patterns, population and tax base, youth exodus and limited economic opportunities. In an ideal world, the vision of a locality is to foster an 'economic paradise' (not an economic collapse or disaster due to the shutdown of a community's major employer or the restructuring of industry). In the real world, a locality is economically secure if it is protected from current conditions of fierce competition, pressures arising from insecurity and future challenges, and vulnerability to economic risks, threats and shocks from a hostile, capitalist environment.

2.4. Economic Security Is Value-Laden

Economic security is value-laden and this is strongly reflected in the development policy and goal for every community whether small, medium or large in land area and population, urban and rural, heartland or hinterland. A locality may have core and non-core values with the former deemed more important than others in terms of asset management, resource allocation, priority setting and protection. Broadly defined, security is valued by the community, by individuals, families, local government and non-government actors and interest groups. Values maybe determined by the community as reflected in their respective economic development plan, vision and mission statement. The primacy of security can be justified in linguistic terms, in policy regimes or in decisions for shaping economies. Values are also articulated as economic well-being and stability, safety and retention of the quality of life.

Security in the context of the community as they apply to 'fragile states' involves much more than dealing with risks, threats and uncertainty or sense of insecurity. Security at the local community level means more than survival, more than meeting basic needs, more than just economic growth, safety, stability, prosperity for all sectors and groups. Here, community security is a function of the contributions and participation of all actors in a bottom-up process of development for economic well-being through various local initiatives. By focusing on the internal strengths and the external linkages and addressing the potential risks and threats, the locality will remain a strong, viable, dynamic place to live, work and invest for a secure future.

There are two aspects to be considered in adopting ES in development practice from a local, place-based perspective. First is the nature of localities and then the transformative practices for community reinvention and/or renewal and reshaping relationships to place and the environment in this global era. The nature of localities means the state of the local economy, whether resource dependent in respect of livelihoods, single-industry community, small town, or economically depressed community. The locality must regularly monitor the sources of pressures, causes and nature of risks and threats to define the state of the local economy for the community's future. Sources of risks and threats in recent times vary from vulnerability to external economic shocks, structural weakness and intrinsic factors, susceptibility to extreme events and threats arising from natural disasters, terrorism, organised crime and so on.

The transformative practices of communities could take the form of local stabilization, adaptation and mobilization to achieve economic resilience. Local stabilization means preventing disruptions to community services based on tenable working and living conditions, as well as reducing risks and constraints to community economic stability. Stabilizing the locality in economic development means the ability of the locality (place) to maintain a functioning and healthy behaviour of the economy within acceptable levels and scale. Stability includes resource capacity derived from adequate protection, conservation and management of natural resources and the environment, fiscal assets, human resources, energy and water resources, food resources to meet the daily conduct of business, sustenance, service provision and effective operation of infrastructure.

Community adaptation to attain local resistance entails adjustments to conditions from the external environment (e.g., fierce competition; linking university research to private enterprises) and coping with changes and challenges (e.g., branch plant closures and job losses from traditional economic base). Local resistance means adjustability and/or the locality's ability to cope with and respond to pressures, risks, change. The forms of adaptation may be structural, institutional, regulatory, financial and technological and they vary according to the nature of the problem or issue. Though localities compete for material wealth, not for insecurity, they must maintain their response capabilities and flexibility to adjust to change and competition. Mobilization to achieve local resilience demands community leadership and cooperation in setting development goals and priorities and in implementing programs and projects for creating opportunities and building social and economic relations. Local resilience refers to the security of the locality as a result of planning and managerial efforts for economic development. The locality is engaged with security practices which occur when a group of people or actors cooperate, interact and enter into partnership toward shaping the local economy for a secure future. If we adopt this economic security strategy, we can be more optimistic about saving fragile states, otherwise, we face the risk of losing them. Why? As Rotberg [2006] recently wrote, "...these states pose dangers not only to themselves and their neighbours but also to peoples around the globe" [p. 132]. He warned that preventing state failure and reviving those that fail are strategic and moral imperatives. Based on the work of Francois and Sud [2006], ideas about helping fragile states have been acknowledged based on several international initiatives by development and donor agencies [World Bank, 2003, 2005; OECD, 2003; USAID 2005; DFID, 2003]. Their strategies are often aimed to promote peace with infusion of modest levels of foreign aid and strengthening civil society in the context of good governance. However, there are arguments to suggest that internal will and commitment are fundamental to finding alternative delivery mechanisms that work where aid is channelled through other means below the state level. In an attempt to list down which LDCs are economically vulnerable and which ones are fragile states, Appendix 1 provides a checklist using results from selected assessment studies.

VI. CONCLUSION

This concept paper initially reviewed the state of knowledge on terminology and conceptual frameworks regarding fragility and fragile states. While there are differentiated and shared meanings of 'fragility' and fragile states, the literature implies that this group of states are situated as 'the others' in global economic development. In defining this group of poor economies, the continuum of setting apart the fragile states from failed states is adopted so as to assert the importance of moving towards prevention rather than reaction to the dilemma of fragile states if and when there are reasons for a low-down (state failure). What is asserted here is the importance of internal and external forces to produce the best results in the interest of saving fragile states. Notably, the problem lies not in the vast array of issues ranging from political instability to weak economies. Neither is it a question of advancing a new way of classifying the world's poor countries nor is it about a matter of ranking them as though they have gone downward spiral within the international political and economic systems. At issue is a crucial need for the world to sustain attention, frame constructive arguments and carry out immediate actions to save the millions of lives and livelihoods of these precarious, difficult, insecure and threatened spaces of development. The question is not about what, why and when we should pay them with much deserved attention and response. The question is where and how we can work together to resolve their difficult situations, challenges and constraints.

The notion of state fragility has been considered within the broad framework of place with the less examined but vital aspect of economic security as a pragmatic, down-to-earth approach for protecting the fragile states and fragile peoples of the world. The state-of-affairs in many fragile states indicate an urgent need to find alternative approaches and mechanisms to deal with their development and economic security questions. By suggesting an 'on-the-ground capacity' approach, the idea is to encourage discussions on non-traditional partnerships and frameworks of cooperation where external donors and actors are actively but indirectly engaged in developing their economies by building local capacities to 'make poverty history' and attain economic security. Drawing from what has already been advanced in the literature, there are suggestions to engage local actors, other than the state-focused orientation to capacity and institution building. In constructing ES, resistance (coping from crisis situations) and resilience are elements of state-building and prevention of state failure. By adopting a community-based, locally driven approach to ES, it is fair to say that fragile states can save themselves- if only we build capacities at the base (as foundations) for economic growth, local governance and participation. Through a bottom-up approach to forestall state failure, this essential yet viable process could make places less vulnerable, safer and economically secure in the long-term.

Annex 1. Country Listing: LDCs and Fragile States

Country	Fragile States (DFID, 2006)	WB LICUS (2005)	Economic Vulnerability (Briguglio, 1995)
LDC N=50	N= 46	N=26	Rank
1. Afghanistan	X	X	X
2. Angola	X	X	
3. Bangladesh			X
4. Benin			X
5. Bhuttan			
6. Burkina Faso			
7. Burundi	X	X	
8. Cambodia	X	X	
9. Cape Verde			X
10. Central African Republic	X	X	
11. Chad	X	X	X
12. Comoros	X	X	X
13. Dem. Rep of Congo	X	X	
14. Djibouti	X	X	
15. Equatorial Guinea			
16. Eritrea	X		
17. Ethiopia	X		
18. Gambia	X		X
19. Guinea	X	X	

Annex 1.(Continued)

Country	Fragile States (DFID, 2006)	WB LICUS (2005)	Economic Vulnerability (Briguglio, 1995)
20. Guinea-Bissau	X	X	X
21. Haiti	X	X	X
22. Kiribati	X	N	X
23. Lao People's Democratic Republic	X	X	
24. Lesotho			
25. Liberia	X	X	X
26. Madagascar			X
27. Malawi			X
28. Maldives			X
29. Mali	X		X
30. Mauritania			X
31. Mozambique			X
32. Myanmar	X	X	
33. Nepal	X		X
34. Niger	X		X
35. Rwanda			
36. Samoa			
37. Sao Tome and Principe	X	X	
38. Senegal			X
39. Sierra Leone	X		X
40. Solomon Islands	X	X	
41. Somalia	X	X	
42. Sudan	X	X	X
43. Timor-Leste	X	X	
44. Togo	X	X	
45. Tuvalu			
46. Uganda			
47. United Rep of Tanzania			
48. Vanuatu	X		X
49. Yemen	X		X
50. Zimbabwe	X	X	X
NON-LDC			
Azerbaijian	X	X	
Cameron	X	X	
Cote Ivoire	X		X
Dominica	X	X	X
Georgia	X		
Guyana	X		X
Indonesia	X		
Kenya	X		X
Nigeria	X	X	X
Papua New Guinea	X	X	X
Republic of Congo	X	X	X
Tajikistan	X	X	
Tonga	X		X
Uzbekistan	X	X	

Sources: Briguglio, 1995; World Bank, 2003, 2005; DFID, 2006.

Note: 'X' means the state is covered in the study.

REFERENCES

Andersen, L (2005). International Engagement in Failed States: Choices and Trade-Offs. *DIIS Working Paper No. 20*, Danish Institute for International Studies, http://www.diis.dk /graphics/Publications/WP2005/20_lan_ international_engagement.pdf (Retrieved January, 13, 2006).

Andersen, L. (2006). Security Sector Reform in Fragile States. *DIIS WorkingPaper No 2006/15*, Danish Institute for International Studies, http://www.diis.dk /graphics /publications/WP2006/15.

AustAID (Australian Agency for International Development). (2005). *Fragile States and Australia's Aid Program.* AUSAID website.

Agnew, J. (1987). *Place and Politics: The Geographical Mediation of State and Society.* Boston: Allen Unwin.

Agnew, J. and P.L. Knox. (1989). *The Geography of the World Economy.* London: Allen Unwin.

Baldwin, D. (1997). The Concept of Security Studies. *Review of International Studies 23 (1)*, 5-26.

Bayliss, J. and S. Smith (Eds). (2005). *The Globalization of World Politics.* Oxford and New York: Oxford University Press.

Booth, K. (1991). Security and Emancipation. *Review of International Studies* 17 (4), 313-327.

Bunge, W. (1966). Gerrymandering, Geography, and Grouping. *Geographical Review 56*, 256-263.

Buzan, B. (1993). Societal Security, State Security and Internationalization. In Ole Waever, B. Buzan, Kelstrup, M. and Lemaitre, P. *Identity, Migration and the New Security Agenda in Europe,* pp. 41-58. London: Pinter.

Buzan, B. (1991). *People, States and Fear: An Agenda for International Security Studies in the Post-Cold War Era.* Boulder: Lynne Rienner; London: Harverster Wheat Sheaf.

Buzan, B. (1984). Peace, Power and Security: Contending Concepts in the Study of International Relations. *Journal of Peace Research, 21,* 109-25.

Buzan, B., Waever, O. and J. de Wilde. (1998). *Security: A New Framework for Analysis.* Boulder: Lynne Rienner.

Buzan, B. and O. Waever. (1997). Slippery, Contradictory? Sociologically Untenable? The Copenhagen School Replies. *Review of International Studies 23 (2),* 241-250.

Buzan, B. (1991). *People, States and Fear: An Agenda for International Security Studies in the Post-Cold War Era.* Boulder: Lynne Rienner.

Buzan, B., Waever, O. and de Wilde, J. (1998). *Security: A New Framework for Analysis.* Boulder: Lynne Rienner.

Branyi, S. (2005). Fragile States and Sustainable Peacebuilding: an NSI Policy Brief. *The North-South Institute.* 2005, Ottawa NSI (http://www.nsi-ins.ca/english /research /progress/)

Canadian Centre for Policy Alternatives (CCPA) and Simon Fraser University. (2005). *Economic Security Project* (ESP). CCPA and SFU, British Columbia. (http//www.sfu.ca economicsecurityproject (Retrieved July 20, 2005).

Canadian Centre for Policy Alternatives (CCPA) and Simon Fraser University. (2005). *Economic Security Project* (ESP). CCPA and SFU, British Columbia. www.sfu.ca /economicsecurityproject (Retrieved July 20, 2005).

Carr, E.H. (1945). *Nationalism and After*. New York: MacMillan.

Clark, G. (1983). *Interregional Migration, National Policy, and Social Justice*. Totowa: Rowman and Allenheld.

Cloke, P., Philo, C. and Sadler, D. (1991). *Approaching Human Geography: An Introduction to Contemporary Theoretical Debates*. London: Paul Chapman Publishing.

Collins, A. (2003). *Security in Southeast Asia: Domestic, Regional and Global Issues*. Boulder: Lynne Rienner.

Coyne, C. (2006). Reconstructing Weak and Failed States: Foreign Intervention and Nirvana Fallacy. *Foreign Policy Analysis, 2 (4)*.

Cooke, P. (1989). *Localities: The Changing Urban and Regional System*. London: Unwin Hyman.

Dent, C. (2001). Singapore's Foreign Economic Policy: The Pursuit of Economic Security. *Contemporary Southeast Asia, 23 (1)*, 1-23.

DFID (Department of International Development). (2005). Why we need to work effectively in fragile states. London: DFID.

DFAIT (Department of Foreign Affairs and International Trade). (2000). *Freedom from fear: Canada's Foreign Policy for Human Security*. www.dfait- maeci.gc.ca/foreignp /HumanSecurity/HumanSecuritysBooklet-e.asp. (Retrieved January 12, 2005)

deGroot-Maggeti, G. (2000). Economic Security is Based on Justice. *The Catalyst* 1 2(1), Citizens for Public Justice (www.cpj.ca/child_pov/00)

Digeser, P. (1994). The Concept of Security. *Unpublished paper* delivered at the Annual Meeting of the American Political Science Association, 14 September, 1994.

Entrikin, E.N. (1991). *The Characterization of A Place,* Lecture delivered for the Wallace W. Atwood Lecture Series No. 5 Worcester: Clark University.

Foreign Affairs and International Trade, Government of Canada. (2005). *Failed and Fragile States*. Discussion Paper London: DFAIT January, 2005.

Foreign Policy (2005). The Failed States Index, pp. 56-65. *Foreign Policy* (July/August, 2005). Fund for Peace and the Carnegie Endowment for International Peace.

Francois, M. and Sud, I. (2006). Promoting Stability and Development in Fragile and Failed States. *Development Policy Review 24 (2)*, 141-160.

Fellman, J., Getis, A. and Getis, J. (2004). *Human Geography: Landscapes of Human Activities*. Toronto: McGrawhill.

Gallie, W.B. (1956). Essentially Contested Concepts, *Proceedings of the Aristotelian Society 56*, 167-98

Gray, J.N. (1977). On the Contestability of Social and Political Concepts. *Political Theory 5*, 330-48.

Gregory, D. (1989). Areal Differentiation and Post-Modern Human Geography, In Gregory, D. and Walford, R. (Eds). *Horizons in Human Geography*. Macmillan: London.

ILO (International Labour Organization). (2002). In-Focus Programme on Socio-Economic Security' www.ilo.org/public/english (Retrieved August 12, 2005).

Hartshorne, R. (1979). Notes Towards a Bibliography of the Nature of Geography. *Annals of the Association of American Geographers 69*, 63-76.

Held, D., McGrew, A, and Perrata, J. (1999). *Global Transformation, Politics, Economics and Culture*. Standford: Standford University Press.

Herd, G. (2001). Societal Security: the Baltic States and EU Integration. *Cooperation and Conflict 36(3)*, 273-296.

Huysmans, J. (1997). Revising Copenhagen, or About the Creative Development of a Securities Agenda in Europe. *European Journal of International Relations 4(4)*, 488-505.

Hough, P. (2004). *Understanding Global Security*. London and New York: Routledge. Jackson, R. H. (1987). Quasi-States, Dual Regimes, and Neoclassical Theory:

International Jurisprudence and the Third World. *International Organization* 41 id=355and1=1.

Kaplan, R. (1994). The Coming Anarchy. *Atlantic Monthly 273 (2)*, 44-65.

Khan, Mushtaq. (2002). State Failure in Developing Countries and Strategies of Institutional Reform. *Unpublished Paper* prepared for June Paper for World Bank ABCDE Conference, June 22- 24, 2002. Department of Economics, SOAS, University of London.

Knorr, K. (1973). National Security Studies: Scope and Structure of the Field', in Trager, F. and P. Kronenberg (Eds.). *National Security and American Society: Theory, Process and Policy*. Lawrence: K.S.

Knudsen, O. F. (2001). 'Post-Copenhagen Security Studies: Desecuritizing Securitization' *Security Dialogue 33 (2)*, 355-368.

Krause, K. and C. Williams. (1996). Broadening the Agenda of Security Studies: Politics and Methods. *Mershon International Studies Review 40*, 229- 254.

Mandell, R. (1994). *The Changing Face of National Security Studies: A Conceptual Analysis'*. Westport: Greenwood.

Manley, J. (2005). The Future of North America: Seeking a Roadmap. *International Journal LX (2)*, 497-508, Spring 2005.

Maull, H. (2006). The Precarious State of International Order: Assessment and Policy Implications. *Asia-Pacific Review 13 (1)*, 68-77

McGillivray, M. (2006). Aid Allocation and Fragile States. Discussion Paper No. 2006/01. Helsinki: UNU-WIDER, 1-23.

Mason, A. (2000). *Community, Solidarity and Belonging: Levels of Community and their Significance*. Cambridge: Cambridge University Press.

Massey, D. (1994). Space, Place and Gender. Cambridge: Polity Press.

McSweeny, B. (1996). Identity and Security. Buzan and the Copenhagen School. *Review of International Studies 22(1)*, 81-93.

McSweeny, B. (1999). *Security, Identity and Interests*. Cambridge University Press: Cambridge.

Menkhaus, K. (2004). Somalia: State Collapse and the Threat of Terrorism. Adelphi Paper 364. *International Institute for Strategic Studies*, London: ISSI.

Norris, P. (2006). Political Protest in Fragile States, paper for plenary panel PSO1 Political Action and Beyond. *Unpublished Paper* presented at the International Political Science Association World Congress in Fukouka, Japan, July 2006.

Ottaway, M. and Mair, S. (2004). States at Risk and Failed States. Putting Security First. *Policy Outlook*. Carnegie Endowment for International Peace and German Institute for International and Security Affairs, Washington.

Patrick, S and Kaysie Brown. (2006). Fragile States and US Foreign Assistance. *Working Paper 96* August 2006. Show me the Money Center for Global Development, (www. cgdev.org).

Rotberg, R. (2006). Failed States in a World of Terror, Chapter 5, pp. 129-137.In Rhodes, M. *Global Politics in a Changing World: A Reader* 3rd edition, Houghton Mifflin: Boston.

Rourke, J.,(2006). *International Politics on the World Stage*, 11th ed 2006. New York: McGraw-Hill.

Patterson, J., Kretzmann, E., and Smith, T. (2005). Global Security and Insecurity: Responses to Terrorism and Threats, pp. 71-88. In Snarr, M. T. and D. Neil Snarr, *Introducing Global Issues.* Boulder: Lynne Rienner Publishers.

Relph, E. (1976). *Place and Placelessness.* London: Pion.

Rengger, N.J. (2000). *International Relations, Political Theory and the Problem of Order: Beyond International Relations Theory?* London: Routledge.

Shaffer, R. (1989). *Community Economics: Economic Structure and Change in Smaller Communities.* Iowa: Iowa State University Press.

Smith, N. (1989). 'Geography as Museum: Private History and Conservative Idealism'. In Entrikin, J.N. and S. Brunn. *Reflections on Richard Hartshorne's The Nature of Geography*, pp. 89-120. Washington: Occassional Publications of the Association of American Geographers.

Smith, S. (2000). Wendt's World. *Review of International Studies 26 (1)*, 151-163.

Smith, F and Naim, M. (2000). *Altered States: Globalisation, Sovereignty and Governance.* Ottawa: International Development Research Center.

Stohr, W., and F. Taylor. (1981). *Development from Above or Below?* Chichester: John Wiley and Sons.

Swanton, C. (1985). On the Essential Contestedness. *Ethics 95*, 811-27.

Tickner, J.A. (1995). *Revisioning Security.* In Booth, K. and S. Smith (Eds). *International Relations Theory Today* pp. 175-197. Oxford: Oxford University Press.

Scheye, E. and Peake, G. (2005). To Arrest Insecurity: time for a Revised Security Sector Reform Agenda, pp. 295-327. In *Conflict, Security and Development, 5 (3)*. International Policy Institute: London.

Tickner, J.A. (1992). *Gender in International Relations: Feminist Perspectives on Achieving Global Security.* Columbia University Press: New York.

Thomas, C. (1987). *In Search of Security: The Third World in International Relations.*.Lynne Rienner: Boulder.

Torres-Moreno, M. and M. Anderson (2004). Fragile States: Defining Difficult Environments for Poverty Reduction. *PRDE Working Papers 1, Poverty Reduction in Difficult Environments Team,* Policy Division. DFID:London.

Turvey, R. (2005). Economic Security in E-Society: A Distinct Geo-Security Approach to Peace and Development of Asia's Political Economy, paper delivered for the Plenary Session, *13th Annual Conference of Canadian Consortium in Asia-Pacific Studies* (CANCAPS), Dec. 4, 2005. Ottawa (www. cancaps.ca).

Ullman, R. (1983). Redefining Security, *International Security 8*, 129-53.

United Nations. (1999). Report of Committee for Development Policy, Report on the First Session, 26-30 April. York: UN Economic and Social Council.

United Nations Development Programme (UNDP) (1994). *Human Development Report 1994.* New York: UN.

United Nations Development Programme (UNDP). (1994) *Human Development Report 1994.* UN: New York.

US Agency for International Development (2005). Fragile States Strategy. http://www.usaid.gov/policy/2005_fragile_states_strategy.pdf.

Vallings, C. and Moreno-Torres, M. (2005). Drivers of Fragility: What Makes States Fragile? *Working Paper No. 7.* PRDE Working Paper Series.

Waever, O. (1996). The Rise and Fall of the Inter-Paradigm Debate. In S. Smith, K. Booth and M. Salewski (Eds). *International Theory: Positivism and Beyond* pp. 149-185. Cambridge: Cambridge University Press.

Waever, O. (1998). Insecurity, Security and Asecurity in the West European Non-War Community. In E. Adler and M. Barnett (Eds), *Security Communities* pp. 69-118. Cambridge: Cambridge University Press.

Waltz, K. (1979). *Theory of International Politics.* Reading: Addison-Wesley.

Waltz, K. (1993). The Emerging Structure of International Politics', *International Security* 18, 44-79.

Weir, K. (2007). The Waning State of Sovereignty', pp. 40-48. In Rourke, J. *Taking Sides-Clashing Views in World Politics* 12th ed., Dubuque: McGraw-Hill.

Wheeler, N.J. and K. Booth. (1992). The Security Dilemma'. In J. Bayliss and N.J. Rengger (Eds). *Dilemmas of World Politics: International Issues in a Changing World.* Oxford: Oxford University Press.

Williams, M. (2003). Words, Images, Enemies: Securitization and International Politics. *International Studies Quarterly 47*, 511-531.

Williamson, T. Imbroscio, D. and Alperovitz, G. (2002). *Making a Place for Community: Local Democracy in a Global Era.* New York and London: Routledge.

Wolfers, A. (1952). National Security as an Ambigous Symbol', *Political Science Quarterly* 67, 481-502

World Bank (2002). *World Bank Group in Low-Income Countries under Stress: A Task Force Report.* World Bank: Washington DC.

World Bank (2005). Fragile States: The Low Income Countries under Stress (LICUS) Initiative. World Bank: Washington DC. http://web.worldbank.org/WBSITE /EXTERNAL/NEWS/0contentMDK: 20127382-menuPK34480-pagePK:34370-the sitePK:4607.00html.

In: Development Economics Research Trends
Editor: Gustavo T. Rocha, pp. 123-147

ISBN 978-1-60456-172-2
© 2008 Nova Science Publishers, Inc.

Chapter 4

DEVELOPING COUNTRY GROWTH, PRIMARY COMMODITY PRICES AND THE BALANCE OF PAYMENTS CONSTRAINT

Stephan Pfaffenzeller
University of Liverpool, England

ABSTRACT

This chapter reviews the theoretical foundations of the Prebisch Singer Hypothesis and the evolution of the associated empirical discussion. The review of the theory is set against the background of balance of payments constrained growth theory. The secular decline in the net barter terms of trade predicted by the Prebisch Singer Hypothesis implies a tightening of the balance of payments constraint. It has therefore historically been expected to counteract the convergence of *per capita* income levels between developed and developing economies and to limit the prospects of trade based development strategies.

The empirical validity of the Prebisch Singer Hypothesis has been assessed through the measurement of negative trends in the real price of primary commodities. At the onset, this discussion centred on the quality characteristics of the data series employed. At a later stage, the focus of the applied literature shifted towards the consideration of stationarity characteristics and the stability of the data series over time.

In so far as a consensus has been established in the empirical literature it tends to point towards a high degree of volatility as the main characteristic of commodity prices. Any trends that can be detected tend to be small by comparison. This conclusion has implications for the balance of payments constraint of commodity dependent developing countries. In addition to diversification out of the *agri*-sector, it now appears that in some cases diversification within the primary sector may be a useful intermediate step in the evolution of trade based development strategies.

From the post World War II era onwards, the growth performance of developing countries has attracted the attention of numerous economists, so much so that development economics emerged as a distinct field of enquiry during the 1950s. One of the hypotheses which emerged during this time and has been widely discussed until the present is the Prebisch Singer Hypothesis. This chapter will address the available evidence on this hypothesis and its predicted implications for developing economy growth. In doing so reference will be made to the original discussion as well as the more recent balance of payments constrained approach to modelling emerging market growth.

1. Introduction: The Basic Predictions of the Prebisch Singer Hypothesis

The core prediction of the Prebisch Singer Hypothesis is that of a sharp and secular decline in developing countries' net barter terms of trade (NBTT). The Prebisch Singer Hypothesis is based on the acceptance as stylized fact of the notion that developing countries have a comparative advantage in the export of primary commodities such as raw materials and agricultural products. Developed countries by contrast specialise in the production and trade of manufactured goods and advanced capital equipment. The comparative advantage based trade between developing and developed countries could therefore be seen as trade between geographically separated primary and secondary sector producers. The NBTT of developing countries –in their trade with developed countries– can accordingly be modelled in terms of the commodity terms of trade as in:

$$NBTT_{LDC} = \frac{P_C}{P_M} \tag{1.1}$$

where P_C and P_M are the prices of primary commodities and manufactures respectively expressed in a common numéraire currency[1]. The prediction from the seminal sources for the Prebisch Singer Hypothesis (Singer (1950) and Prebisch (1950)) is that the secular deterioration in the terms of trade will translate into a sustained real income transfer from slower growing economies to faster growing ones. In more recent discussions of this hypothesis, Bloch and Sapsford (1997) have highlighted the difference between Prebisch and Singer effects[2]. In this distinction, the Singer effect focuses on the contribution made by technical progress on the decay of relative commodity prices: technological innovations in developed countries tend to be raw material or labour saving, while innovations in LDCs tend to be factor neutral. The combined effect of these two structural factors is to shift world market demand towards the manufacturing sector in relative terms.

The structural shift implied by the Singer effect should of course not have been unexpected. It has long been a known fact, that the participation of the primary sector diminishes relative to the secondary sector as an economy develops[3]. On a national level at least, this shift in relative economic importance had frequently been observed. This process would naturally be expected to coincide with a decline in the relative price of primary sector output: it is this price signal after all which should divert productive resources into the expanding secondary sector. The emergence of an analytically similar reallocation process in the context of international trade can however give rise to additional problems.

---

[1] This specification avoids the explicit inclusion of a nominal exchange rate for the time being. The numéraire in question can of course be –and usually is– one of the trading partners' currencies.

[2] Bloch and Sapsford (1997) further point out that the Prebisch and Singer effects may be counteracted by a 'Ricardo effect' i.e. positive output growth.

[3] Cf. Ingersent and Rayner (1999), Ch1 for a review of this process.

The industrialisation of a given integrated economy tends to automatically imply the transfer of labour resources to its expanding secondary sector. No such transfer was observed or would be generally expected in the case of international trading relationships. If the contracting low productivity primary sector therefore becomes confined to a given geographic area, it is to be expected that the economy thus defined would persist in a situation of underdevelopment. A successful development process would then require diversification into a domestic high productivity sector which could pay a premium over the subsistence wage. Historically, this role has been attributed to the manufacturing sector.

The Prebisch effect by contrast highlights the role of market power and price setting behaviour (see Toye and Toye (2003) for an in-depth account of Prebisch' approach). Primary commodity markets are seen as generally competitive, forcing primary sector producers in general and exporters in particular to operate at minimum cost. Markets for the manufactured products of developed countries, as well as their export markets, are characterised by less intense competition to the point where manufacturers can engage in mark up pricing. Centre economy labour markets, meanwhile are highly unionised while those in the periphery are not.

This asymmetric market structure tends to produce higher prices in the goods exported by developed countries relative to those exported by (primary sector dependent) developing economies over the course of the business cycle: unionised workers in the centre are capable of defending wage gains made during a boom while manufacturers can pass on cost increases through mark-up pricing. No such process takes place in the more competitive periphery markets. The Prebisch effect therefore works in the same direction as the Singer effect and tends to reinforce it.

These differences in competitive market structure and in the impact of technological innovation are further compounded by the observed elasticity characteristics of developed and developing country exports. It is a widely accepted stylized fact, that demand for primary commodities tends to have a low (i.e. below unity) income elasticity. This regularity is known as Engel's law[4] in the classical literature. It implies that at higher levels of income, the proportion of income spent on primary products, such as food, will tend to fall relative to the proportion spent on other products such as manufactured goods.

Price elasticities also tend to be low for primary commodity exports (see Kaplinsky 2007). A similarly low elasticity for developing country imports of manufactured goods would tend towards reinforcing the presence of overall low trade elasticities and would produce a similar effect on the balance of payments (cf. the discussion below and Gandolfo (2002), p.86 on the notion of elasticity pessimism).

These low price and income elasticities thus have important implications for the income terms of trade and hence for developing countries' ability to fund manufactured goods imports for consumption or, in the case of capital goods imports, for investment. In the given case, the income terms of trade are defined as:

$$ICTT_{LDC} = \frac{Q_C P_C}{P_M} \tag{1.2}$$

---

[4] This is, to be precise, a somewhat simplified formulation of Engel's Law. For an in-depth discussion of Engel's original statements cf. Zimmerman (1930).

which is simply the value of commodity exports deflated by the price of manufacturing commodity imports. In a competitive commodity market, an increase in Q_C will produce a countervailing decline in P_C. With sufficiently low demand elasticities such an increase in the supply of primary commodity exports can translate into a depression of the real value of developing country exports if the decline in P_C/P_M outweighs the impact of a higher Q_C.

One key conclusion from the Prebisch Singer Hypothesis is therefore that the structural decline in the commodity terms of trade could trap developing economies in a position where they can't increase the real value of their export earnings on the basis of comparative advantage based trade. This position immediately limits the ability of the economy as a whole to mobilise resources for domestic industrialisation.

2. DEVELOPING COUNTRY GROWTH AND COMMODITY DEPENDENCE

The limitation observed with regards to one option for resource mobilisation is not in itself sufficient to explain persistent underdevelopment. A terms of trade deterioration would, within the given theoretical framework, serve to explain a direct welfare loss from the relative price decline, but would not suffice to predict the long term impact on economic growth. To fully appreciate the Prebisch Singer Hypothesis' implications for the observed developing country growth performance, its predictions have to be considered in the context of growth models typically applied to developing countries. This chapter will therefore turn to its interpretation against the background of the Lewis growth model and a balance of payments constrained growth model proposed by McCombie and Thirlwall (1994).

2.1. The Early Debate on Developing Country Growth Perspectives

A benchmark model for the analysis of developing country growth is the model introduced by Lewis (1954). The Lewis model characterises developing economies in a two sector setting with a subsistence sector and a structurally separate industrial sector. Labour in the subsistence sector is assumed to have a zero marginal product while the marginal product of labour in the industrial sector is assumed to be positive. This dualist economic structure implies that the subsistence sector can act as a labour reservoir for the industrial sector, and that wages –and thus the material standard of living of the modal worker—are determined by the subsistence wage. It also suggests that an increase in the wage, and thus in the working population's standard of living, is likely when industrial production expands to a point where the absorption of labour from the subsistence sector produces labour scarcity, thus driving up the wage level throughout the economy.

The Prebisch Singer Hypothesis scarcely predates Lewis' contribution and both theories were simultaneously at the centre of discussion in the development economics literature. Indeed, in some respects the two models can be seen as complementary. Singer (1950) already emphasised the dualist structure found in some developing economies when he pointed out that foreign investment projects often failed to integrate with the host economy. How far Singer's characterisation was and has remained appropriate is a different question though. Bhagwati (2004, p.163) pointed out more recently that Singer's critique is mainly descriptive of the impact of extractive industrial projects rather than foreign direct investment in general.

Whatever the judgement on the merits of the Prebisch Singer Hypothesis may be in the long term, the dualist view appeared to be a valid description of most developing economies at the time. The perception that trade receipts would be insufficient to generate investment income while foreign investment would fail to spill-over into the host economy led many to favour infant industry protection in the context of import substitution strategies. The main objective, after all, seemed to be the expansion of the industrial sector to the point of surplus labour exhaustion, and import substituting industrialisation appeared to offer a fast track solution for meeting this objective (*cf.* also Lewis (1954) on this point).

An issue that was not sufficiently addressed in the context of import substitution strategies was the qualitative dimension of investment strategies. The pre-eminent problems appeared to relate to the quantity of investment and the relative size of the secondary sector. Lewis (1954) even went so far as to point to soviet central planning as an example of successful investment promotion.

These protectionist strategies were progressively abandoned as the success of export oriented development strategies pursued by a number of East Asian economies became accepted (for an overview of this paradigm shift *cf.* Krueger (1997)). There had been warnings against state directed investment early on (*cf.* Hayek (2002) which was first published in 1968). A more modern rationalisation of this problem is provided by Krugman (1987) among others.

The question then arises as to why falling commodity trends should remain an issue of concern if successful development is to be reflected in a relative contraction of the primary sector. In some sense, the terms of trade should be expected to shift in favour of expanding economic sectors, if this is where resources need to be directed.

2.2. Thirlwall's Model of Balance of Payments Constrained Growth

Examples of successful export oriented development strategies became relevant at least from the 1980s onwards. The potential role that foreign direct investment could play in supporting the capital accumulation underlying the emergence of a native industrial sector should by then also have become apparent –indeed it forms the subject of well known contributions such as Young (1995) or Krugman (1994) who highlight the role of production factor accumulation in emerging market growth experiences. An inability to implement an industrialisation strategy from the income of comparative advantage based primary commodity exports would at first sight appear less serious against this background.

Commodity prices in the case of commodity dependent developing countries, would however retain their relevance to the extent that export led growth could be shown to be itself a function of export earnings. A stylized fact that points to the continued relevance of the value of export earnings is the observation of a close correlation between a country's growth rate and the ratio of the growth of its exports to the income elasticity of imports. The imputation of a causal link underlying this correlation does not immediately follow. Krugman (1989) dismisses the existence of such a causal link without further explanation in relation to intra-industry trade between developed economies.

The hypothesis of a causal link appears more plausible in the case of developing economies. The very concept of surplus labour does after all imply the availability of unused or underused production factors. If these have to be complemented by capital inputs and if foreign currency receipts from export earnings are crucial for an economy's ability to acquire foreign capital goods then growth prospects could be directly dependent on export earnings, at least for a given level of investment receipts.

Thirlwall's balance of payments constrained growth model (*cf.* McCombie and Thirlwall (1994)) follows a demand led approach and is based on a dynamic version of Harrod's trade multiplier. In its basic form, the (trade-) balance constraint is defined as:

$$p_d + x = p_f + m + e \tag{2.1}$$

where:

p_d is the growth rate of the domestic price of exports,
p_f is the growth rate of the price of imports denominated in foreign currency
x is the growth rate of exports
m the growth rate of imports, and
e is the rate of depreciation of the domestic currency, where the exchange rate is defined in price quotation.

Exports are defined as:

$$x = \eta\,(p_d - p_f - e) + \varepsilon z \tag{2.2}$$

where η is the price elasticity of export demand, ε its income elasticity and z the growth rate of world income. Imports, likewise are given by:

$$m = \psi\,(p_f + e - p_d) + \pi y \tag{2.3}$$

where ψ is the price elasticity of imports, π its income elasticity and y the growth rate of domestic real income. Substituting [2.2] and [2.3] into [2.1] then yields:

$$p_d + \underbrace{\eta(p_d - p_f - e) + \varepsilon z}_{x} = p_f + \underbrace{\psi(p_f + e - p_d) + \pi y}_{m} + e \tag{2.1'}$$

which can be solved for y to yield:

$$y_B = \frac{(1 + \eta + \psi)(p_d - p_f - e) + \varepsilon z}{\pi} \tag{2.4}$$

where y_B is now the balance of payments constrained growth rate of real income. In the particular case where relative purchasing power parity holds consistently, [2.4] reduces to:

$$y_B = \frac{\varepsilon z}{\pi} \tag{2.5}$$

since $p_d - p_f - e = 0$. Equation [2.5] then spells out the benchmark version of the model reflecting the core relationship between the long run sustainable growth rate, the growth of total export earnings, which is functionally dependent on foreign GDP growth, and the income elasticity of import demand.

A sustained *ceteris paribus* terms of trade deterioration-as implied by the Prebisch Singer Hypothesis-should then be reflected in a long term depreciation of the real exchange rate. In terms of [2.4], a secular decline in the relative price of exports implies that $p_f > p_d$ for a given rate of change of the nominal exchange rate. Given that $\eta, \psi < 0$ and, for normal goods, $\pi, \varepsilon > 0$ the directional implications of a sustained terms of trade deterioration for the balance of payments constrained growth rate depend on the magnitude of the price elasticities.

For sufficiently price elastic demand functions in traded goods markets, Thirlwalls's model would predict an easing of the balance of payments constraint to result from deteriorating terms of trade: so long as the Marshall Lerner condition holds (*i.e.* if $|\eta + \psi| > 1$)[5] the product $(1 + \eta + \psi)(p_d - p_f - e)$ in the numerator of [2.4] should be positive under deteriorating terms of trade, net-export demand is predicted to be higher and the rate of real income growth consistent with a balanced trade position should accordingly increase as well.

Prebisch and Singer's observations on low price elasticities in inter-industry trade between developed and developing economies therefore change the model prediction decisively. For $|\eta + \psi| < 1$, equation [2.4] predicts a lower rate of balance of payments constrained growth. In the case of commodity dependent developing economies engaging in inter-industry trade with developed economies the price of exports is assumed to be approximately represented by the price of primary commodities. Manufactured goods prices are accordingly viewed as approximately representative of the price of developing country imports. Formally we have: $P_C \approx P_d$ and $P_M \approx P_f$, where P_d and P_f are the price levels of exports and imports respectively. The predicted impact of a terms of trade deterioration then leads directly to the conclusion that falling commodity terms of trade should be expected to depress the externally sustainable growth rate of real income in commodity dependent LDCs.

Incorporating Foreign Investment

The model, as discussed so far, has been presented on the basis of a purely trade based external equilibrium. McCombie and Thirlwall (1994) and Hussain and Thirlwall (1982) extend their model to account for the possible role of foreign investment flows.

The balance of payments constraint then is represented by:

$$\theta(p_d + x) + (1 - \theta)f = p_f + m + e \tag{2.6}$$

---

[5] Strictly speaking, this condition needs to be fulfilled for the trade balance to move into surplus from an initial balanced position and under the assumption of elastic supply precluding price reactions. For an in-depth discussion of critical elasticities cf. Gandolfo (2002) *p.*82 ff.

where f indicates the rate of change of net foreign investment inflows and θ is the proportion of import costs covered by export earnings, such that the remainder of $(1-\theta)$ is covered by investment inflows.

According to McCombie and Thirlwall (1994), solving equation [2.6] for the balance of payments constrained level of real income growth yields:

$$y_B = \frac{(1+\theta\eta+\psi)(p_d - p_f - e) + \varepsilon z + (1-\theta)(f - p_d)}{\pi} \qquad (2.7)$$

where $(f - p_d)$ captures the rate of change of net investment inflows in real terms and all other variables are as above. An alternative form of writing equation [2.7] is given by:

$$y_B = \frac{(\theta\eta+\psi)(p_d - p_f - e) + (p_d - p_f - e) + \varepsilon z + (1-\theta)(f - p_d)}{\pi} \qquad (2.8)$$

where $(\theta\eta + \psi)(p_d - p_f - e)$ captures the quantity impact of relative price changes while $(p_d - p_f - e)$ represents what McCombie and Thirlwall call the terms of trade effect. It should be immediately obvious that, for a given level of investment flows, a terms of trade deterioration tends towards the same impact as in the purely trade based variety of the model. For the case of $\theta = 1$ equation [2.7] reduces to [2.4]. With intermediate values of θ however a reduction in the sustainable rate of real income growth can be avoided if shortfalls in export revenue are compensated by foreign investment flows.

Under the Prebisch Singer characterisation of commodity terms of trade trends, the effects of the sustained terms of trade deterioration could be contained or even reversed by a countervailing positive trend in investment flows. This property of investment flows follows immediately from equations [2.7] and [2.8]: with $(1+\theta\eta+\psi)(p_d - p_f - e) < 0$ a given balance of payments constrained growth rate can now be preserved if real net foreign investment flows grow at rate:

$$(f - p_d) = \frac{-(1+\theta\eta+\psi)(p_d - p_f - e)}{1-\theta}, \quad 0 \le \theta < 1 \qquad (2.9)$$

in which case [2.7] reduces to [2.5]. A number of points are worth noting at this point. The case of interest is the one where the Marshall Lerner condition does not hold. It can then be seen from [2.9] that economies with a larger initial share of export revenues in financing the cost of imports (i.e. with a high value for θ) require a larger foreign investment flow acceleration in response to a given deterioration in the terms of trade[6]. Formally, this follows from:

---

[6] The case of $\theta = 1$ is not considered here since this would simply yield $(f - p_d) \to \infty$ to reflect the fact that any increase over an initial base of zero approaches infinity.

$$\frac{\partial f}{\partial \theta} = \frac{-(1+\eta+\psi)(p_d - p_f - e)}{(1-\theta)^2} \tag{2.10}$$

The intuition behind this is straightforward: with a higher export share, θ, a given fall in the value of net exports creates a stronger need for investment based financing of the cost of imports. This prediction would imply that a particularly strong boost to financial inflows could be required in the case of trade and commodity dependent developing economies experiencing adverse terms of trade movements. In such cases, net foreign investment flows would often play a minor role initially –indeed, this is almost a corollary of commodity dependence. Moreover, these are most likely the very countries finding it hardest to attract a large amount of funds.

Nothing has so far been said about the nature of terms of trade movements or the qualitative composition of investment flows. The common interpretation of the Prebisch Singer Hypothesis results in the prediction of a strong, reasonably stable downwards trend in the commodity terms of trade. If this trend is to coincide with a stable balance of payments constrained real income growth rate, a corresponding steady acceleration of net foreign investment flows is required. Such an increasing inflow of foreign investment could reasonably be expected in rapidly industrialising emerging economies. To the extent that the industrial sector in those economies expands successfully, commodity dependence – and hence the need for steadily increasing foreign investment – should eventually be weakened.

The situation is different if the commodity terms of trade are mainly characterised by less uniform or shorter lived price movements. Such a situation could create a role for shorter term financial flows, a possibility which will be discussed in more detail below.

Having identified a number of potential problems of commodity price dependence and having placed them in the context of a recent balance of payments focussed growth model, one should ask what consensus – if any – there is with regards to the observed time series characteristics of the commodity terms of trade. The evidence to date will be discussed in the following section.

3. THE EMPIRICAL EVIDENCE ON THE COMMODITY TERMS OF TRADE

The discussion so far has covered theoretical models of developing economies. The Prebisch Singer hypothesis, while being partly motivated by induction, predicts a secular deterioration in developing country barter terms of trade on theoretical grounds. Lewis' concept of a dualist economy provides a background against which Thirlwall's demand led growth model appears relevant for some developing countries. For these LDCs, predictions from a balance of payments constrained growth perspective should be possible. The precise nature of theoretically anticipated growth and policy constraints should, however, depend on empirical observations on real commodity prices and the terms of trade. This topic will be discussed in the following section.

3.1. The Early Debate on Negative Commodity Price Trends

Prebisch and Singer supported their argument by reference to a series of British terms of trade data from about 1876-1947 (*cf.* Spraos (1980) for details on the data sources and Toye and Toye (2003) for a detailed account of the early use and promulgation of this data set). With the United Kingdom being a leading industrial power during much of this time, and during the earlier period in particular, it would have appeared plausible to regard the inverse of this series as an appropriate proxy for developing countries' terms of trade. Yet this very assumption was one point for which the findings of Prebisch and Singer were criticised. The seminal paper for a survey of this early debate is Spraos (1980) in which a number of criticisms are addressed.

Aside from the choice of UK trade data and the question of their inter-temporal reach, Prebisch and Singer's conclusions were seen as precarious since import prices would be consistently recorded on a *c.i.f.* basis, *i.e.* including transport costs, while export prices are usually recorded *f.o.b.* This discrepancy is a persistent problem in recording commodity prices, although it is not always clear what the net effect of the implied bias is for the composite index in question: not all commodity price indices use *c.i.f.* and *f.o.b.* data consistently for LDC exports or imports respectively, the Grilli and Yang data set for example uses *c.i.f.* commodity prices in some cases, *f.o.b.* prices in others (*cf.* Pfaffenzeller *et.al.* (2007)). A further problem, common to price indices in general, is the disregard for quality improvements and changes in product variety in the recorded price measures.

A further issue of concern is the 'time window' under consideration for the estimation of commodity price trends. Early discussions of the Prebisch Singer Hypothesis referred mainly to a UN data series extending back to 1900 and the inverse of Schlote's terms of trade index for the United Kingdom covering the period 1814-1938 (*cf.* Spraos (1980)). A later data set which received substantial attention in the discussion of commodity price movements was the index compiled by Grilli and Yang (1988). This data set covers a trade weighted average of 24 primary commodities over the period 1900-1986. The Grilli and Yang index is most frequently deflated by the MUV-G5 index, an index of export unit values based on exports by leading industrialised countries to developing economies.

To get an overview of the development of primary commodity prices against a background of spreading industrialisation, an updated version of the Grilli and Yang Commodity Price Index (GYCPI) as in Pfaffenzeller *et.al.* (2007) can be combined with the inverse of Schlote's (1938) terms of trade series for the United Kingdom. For the concatenation, the GYCPI has been deflated by the MUV index, as is by now customary, and has been appended to the inverse of the Schlote series from 1922 onwards. Following Sapsford *et. al.* (1992) the inverse of the Schlote index has been employed up to 1921 to avoid overstating a possible structural break in 1921 resulting from a war time interpolation of the MUV series[7].

There are of course issues surrounding data quality and appropriate representation of developing country terms of trade via composite commodity indices. Some of these issues are taken up below. For a detailed discussion of the data underlying the GYCPI *cf.* Grilli and Yang (1988) and Pfaffenzeller *et.al.* (2007).

---

[7] *Cf.* Sapsford *et.al.* (1992) for details. In contrast to Sapsford *et.al.*, both series have been indexed to their 1913 value rather than indexing the inverse of Schlote's series to equal the GYCPI in 1913.

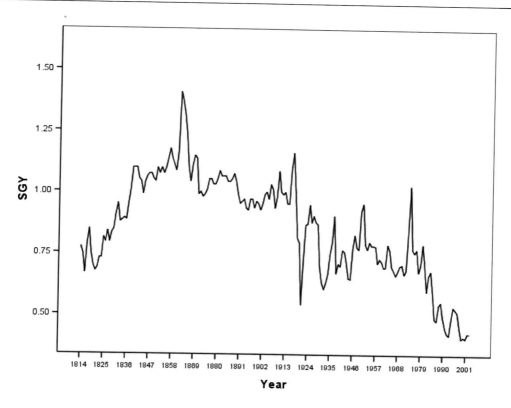

Figure 1.

The adequacy of inverting British terms of trade data to obtain a proxy for developing country terms of trade has itself been subject to debate and is discussed in some depth Spraos (1980).

The combined Schlote-Grilli-Yang series (or SGY index for short) is shown in Figure 1 and covers the period 1814-2003. In the early 19th century, the commodity terms of trade can be seen to increase before reaching a peak in 1861. From this point onwards, a general tendency to decline can be observed although commodity prices underwent temporary recoveries. Spraos (1980) argued, for example, that the decline observed by Prebisch and Singer is no longer apparent, once data for the 1970s are taken into account. As is obvious from Figure 1, the 1970s did see a recovery in the commodity terms of trade, but this was followed by another sharp decline from the 1980s onward.

The early development of commodity prices is not surprising of course. The initial price boom in the mid 19th century is exactly what one should expect if spreading industrialisation increases demand for raw materials. The subsequent decline is consistent with Singer's observation on raw material saving technological progress: the upswing in commodity prices, and hence the incentive for raw material saving innovations, began in the early 19th century, while the actual raw material saving innovations appear to have occurred with some delay. More recent accelerations in the decay of commodity prices have been attributed to the 1982 debt crisis and the market entry of transition economies (*cf.* Borzenstein and Reinhart (1994)).

Table 1 shows some illustrative trend estimates for the entire sample period and for a number of sub-periods. For the data series in natural logarithms, linear trends have been estimated in levels allowing for a first order autoregressive component in the series and are reported alongside alternative estimates which include a structural break dummy for 1921. These estimates are unlikely to give the most appropriate econometric specification[8], but rather provide the kind of simple model representative of early empirical studies on long run series such as Grilli and Yang (1988).

This approach is intended to illustrate how variations in the sample period considered can impact on trend measurements when simple estimation techniques are used. The sub-periods selected are the period from 1861-2003, *i.e.* the time interval following the peak of the mid 19th century commodity price boom, the period 1900-2003, starting from the same time as the original GYCPI and the 1876-1947 sub-period on which Prebisch' estimates were based according to Spraos (1980).

The trend estimate concerned is lower in absolute value for the full sample period than when the starting point of the sample is placed in either 1861 or 1900. Yet, the series with a later starting date, some time after the 1870s, is possibly more representative of modern price developments, since industrial demand for commodities is bound to have been far less pronounced prior to the mid 19th century. The starting point selected by Prebisch and Singer is therefore likely to be appropriate, although the later starting date used for the GYCPI does not mark a major departure from this benchmark since real commodity price movements during the late 19th century tended to be relatively modest.

Except for the full 1814-2003 sample period, similar trend estimates with a magnitude of $\beta = -0.006$ to -0.007 are obtained for all sub-periods considered, when no allowance is made for a structural break in 1921. Including a level shift dummy for the imputed 1921 structural break reduces the absolute value of the trend estimate to -0.004 for the 1861-2003 and 1900-2003 sub-periods while yielding statistically insignificant estimates of $\beta = -0.000$ and $\beta = -0.001$ for the 1876-1947 sub-period and the full sample period respectively.

Table 1. Estimated Trends in the Commodity Terms of Trade

Period	Constant	Trend	Dummy	ϕ
1814-2003	0.084	-0.003	..	0.913
t-ratio	*0.656*	*-2.840*	..	*30.402*
1814-2003	-0.004	-0.001	-0.375	0.911
t-ratio	*-0.033*	*-0.446*	*-4.592*	*29.016*
1861-2003	0.523	-0.006	..	0.776
t-ratio	*5.387*	*-8.186*	..	*14.432*
1861-2003	0.378	-0.004	-0.289	0.846
t-ratio	*2.691*	*-2.780*	*-3.448*	*19.710*
1900-2003	0.641	-0.007	..	0.755
t-ratio	*3.602*	*-5.603*	..	*11.593*
1900-2003	0.500	-0.004	-0.279	0.823
t-ratio	*2.138*	*-2.435*	*-2.978*	*15.659*
1876-1947	0.475	-0.006	..	0.633
t-ratio	*3.651*	*-4.604*	..	*6.756*
1876-1947	0.041	0.000	-0.294	0.648
t-ratio	*0.253*	*-0.215*	*-4.138*	*7.740*

---

[8] The main conclusions from the more extensive econometric literature on this topic, allowing for different stationarity characteristics and for a more general ARMA parameterisation of the residual term, are discussed below.

It is not surprising, that evidence for a secular decline in the commodity terms of trade is somewhat weaker for the full sample period than for the sub-periods considered subsequently, since the former commences from a price-level preceding the mid 19th century commodity price boom. The period following this high price period is –after all—the time interval to which Prebisch and Singer were referring in their analysis. Among the sub-samples considered in Table 1, the estimate for the 1876-1947 period considered by Prebisch appears to give the weakest support for a statistically significant secular decline in the commodity terms of trade. This is so since in spite of the preceding price decline, and in spite of the subsequent recovery during the 1970s the 1876-1947 time window does not account for further commodity price deteriorations observed during the 1980s and 1990s.

This sensitivity of the conclusions reached with respect to the time interval considered is a noteworthy aspect of the discussion. The core of Spraos' (1980) argument is precisely that the impression of a secular decline in the commodity terms of trade had arisen from a premature truncation of the time series under consideration. One should expect increasing sample length to eventually clarify the direction of a secular trend and developments over the remainder of the 20th century have indeed reinforced the impression of a sustained real commodity price decline. However, there are a number of issues, related to the statistical and economic dimensions of the problem, which have tended to add complexity to the Prebisch Singer debate instead of leading to a well defined consensus.

One long standing concern about empirical investigations into the commodity terms of trade has been the implicit assumption of close commodity price co-movement and co-movements between the commodity terms of trade and developing country terms of trade. Another aspect of the empirical debate has developed against the background of increasingly sophisticated statistical methods. The present discussion will address the question of uniform price movements first, before turning to developments in econometric implementation thereafter.

Commodity Price Developments

An attempt to investigate the evolution of developing country terms of trade through the commodity terms of trade necessarily entails an implied assumption of homogenous development among the commodity and manufactured goods prices used to obtain a measure of the commodity terms of trade. Over a short time horizon, this can be taken to refer to price co-movement or excess co-movement over time. A number of studies have addressed the question of commodity price co-movement, with different approaches leading to different conclusions (*cf. e.g.* Cashin *et.al.* (1999) and Leybourne *et.al.* (1994)). A brief survey of the evidence will be provided below.

The question of short term price co-movement is of course of direct policy relevance with respect to issues such as price stabilisation and possible diversification. In the context of the Prebisch Singer Hypothesis, however, the central question is one of long term trends. If the commodity terms of trade are to reflect the developments anticipated in the Prebisch Singer Hypothesis, a tendency toward long term real price decline should be common to primary commodities in general.

The question of whether such a common trend can in fact be observed has been discussed for almost as long as the Prebisch Singer Hypothesis itself. Kindelberger (1958) for example argued early on, that no such homogenous tendency could be observed among commodity prices. Kindelberger seemed to rely on a non-continuous set of region and product data. More recent studies have of course had the benefit of longer term continuous product price series, enabling a more formal analysis of long term price trends.

Long term studies of the time series characteristics of individual real commodity price series also tend to indicate that long term trend characteristics differ between primary commodities. Cuddington (1992) was one of the first authors investigating the real price trends for the individual commodity price series included in the construction of the GYCPI. He finds that trend estimates differ in terms of statistical significance, magnitude and even sign. The latter aspect is crucial in this context: If some commodity price series are estimated to have long run positive real price trends then the development of the relevant series could be seen as evidence against the Prebisch Singer thesis and their inclusion in a composite index would tend to counteract the downward trend observed for other constituent series.

Similar mixed results are found by *e.g.* Kellard and Woher (2006), Kim *et.al.* (2003), León and Soto (1997) and Newbold *et.al.* (2005). Grilli and Yang (1988) obtain different trend estimates for their various commodity sub-indices, with a positive price estimate for their tropical beverages price index. The various studies differ in their econometric approaches and in the number of negative real price trends identified. Yet, the general problem of non-homogeneity in long term price trends is generally confirmed: some price series follow negative trends, others have positive trend estimates or no significant trend at all. As a consequence, the adequacy of the very notion of the commodity barter terms of trade, based on a broadly defined commodity price aggregate, could be called into question.

3.2. Stationarity and Structural Stability of Commodity Prices

The trend coefficient estimates presented in Table 1 are obtained from a simple trend stationary model with:

$$p_t = \alpha + \beta t + u_t, \ (1 - \phi L)u_t = \varepsilon_t \tag{3.1}$$

applied to the real price series in natural logarithms, where p_t is the value of the SGY index in natural logarithms in period t, α is a constant, β the trend coefficient, u_t the correlated error term, ϕ the autoregressive coefficient, L the difference operator and $\varepsilon_t \sim N(0,\sigma)$ is a white noise error term assumed to have a constant variance σ.

The variant of [3.1], allowing for a structural break would accordingly be:

$$p_t = \alpha + \beta t + \psi + u_t, \ (1 - \phi L)u_t = \varepsilon_t \tag{3.2}$$

where $\psi = 0$ before the specified break date (1921) and $\psi = 1$ thereafter. The model specification in [3.1] and [3.2] makes fairly restrictive assumptions in that it only makes allowance for serial correlation in the form of a stationary first order autoregressive process. It has recently become more common to allow for a wider range of ARMA parameterisations for the residual process and to test the data for stationarity instead of merely assuming it.

It has been shown by Newbold and Granger (1974) that conventional significance tests are unreliable when a stationary model is estimated for a sample from a non-stationary time series. The conventional way of testing for stationarity would normally be based on a Dickey-Fuller type testing equation like:

$$(1-L)p_t = \alpha + \beta t + \rho^* p_{t-1} + \sum_{i=1}^{k=9} \gamma_i (1-L)p_{t-i} + \varepsilon_t \tag{3.3}$$

in which the t ratio on the coefficient estimate of ρ^* yields the Dickey fuller test statistic and γ_i is the coefficient on the ith lagged autoregressive term. One would then conclude that the series in question is stationary if the unit root null hypothesis $H_0: \rho^* = 0$ can be rejected at the appropriate critical value (these are discussed in Mackinnon (1991)).

   If a reliable conclusion on the stationarity of the series can be reached, the significance of a trend estimate should, in principle, be easy to assess. In the case of a stationary series a trend stationary model can be estimated as in:

$$p_t = \alpha + \beta t + u_t, \quad \left(1 - \sum_{i=1}^{p} \phi_i L_i\right) u_t = \left(1 - \sum_{j=1}^{q} \theta_j L_j\right) \varepsilon_t \tag{3.4}$$

where u_t is a general ARMA pq residual process and ϕ_i and θ_j are the autoregressive and moving average coefficients on the ith and jth lags respectively[9]. The first order autoregressive model in [3.1] is a special case of [3.4] where $p = 1$ and $q = 0$ so that: $\varepsilon_t = (1 - \phi L)u_t$. Alternatively, if the unit root null hypothesis can not be rejected, the data series can be differenced in order to render it stationary. The model to be estimated for this case would then take the general form:

$$(1-L)p_t = \beta + v_t, \quad \left(1 - \sum_{i=1}^{p} \phi_i L_i\right) v_t = \left(1 - \sum_{j=1}^{q} \theta_j L_j\right) \varepsilon_t \tag{3.5}$$

where β now captures the stochastic trend and v_t is the ARIMA residual process. For the special case where $\phi = 1$, $p = 1$ and $q = 0$ in [3.1] this would yield a random walk plus drift model:

$$(1-L)p_t = \beta + \varepsilon_t \tag{3.6}$$

   It is a fortunate property of a log-linear trend function that the average value of the differenced series captures the average rate of change and thus a variable conceptually equivalent to the deterministic trend coefficient. Still, there are added complications in assessing the significance of the stochastic trend term. Kim et.al. (2003) have shown that conventional t-tests on the drift coefficient can lack power if the ARIMA residual term is

---

[9] For a concise introduction to ARMA and ARIMA models, cf. Johnston and Dinardo (1997) Ch7.

under-parameterised. This can be corrected for by considering –and where appropriate fitting– more extensively parameterised model alternatives[10].

A more widely discussed problem is the reliability of unit root tests themselves. Conclusions on the statistical significance of the trend coefficient estimate are often conditional on the result of the unit root pre-test, so the reliability of the pre-test method used is crucial. The testing equation in [3.3] allows for trend and constant under the alternative hypothesis, but assumes parameter stability. It also aims to approximate any higher order ARMA pattern through the addition of autoregressive terms. Either can be shown to be problematic.

Agiakloglou and Newbold (1992) have shown that the presence of a large moving average component in the residual process can substantially inflate the size of the rejection region of the unit root test over its nominal size. This can be counter-acted through the inclusion of a sufficiently large number of autoregressive terms in [3.3], although such a measure – while reducing the type I error probability – will lead to a loss in power. There is no simple way of escaping this size power trade-off which, according to Agiakloglou and Newbold (1996), is exacerbated when a trend term is included in the testing equation. Newbold et.al. (2005) consider evidence across order of integration scenarios and obtain consistent results in some cases, while in others no consistent inference independently of pre-test results is possible.

The implied assumption of structural stability in [3.3] is likely to become a problem in the presence of structural breaks in the series. The role of structural breaks has been a factor in the debate on long term commodity price trends for some time. Sapsford (1985) argues that Spraos' (1980) failure to detect a significant long term trend in commodity prices can be explained by failure to account for structural instability. In the literature based on the Grilli and Yang index, the possibility of a structural break in 1921 has been discussed extensively and different break dates have been considered for individual price series.

Aside from their direct impact on possible trend measurements, structural breaks have received attention in the debate on the Prebisch Singer Hypothesis since they affect the reliability of the unit root pre-test. Perron (1989) shows that conventional unit root tests lack power in the presence of a one-time structural break in an otherwise stationary data generating progress. Perron's (1989) unit root test, allowing for a single structural break, has been used in the analysis of commodity price trends by Cuddington and Urzúa (1989). Sapsford et. al. (1992) obtain conflicting results based on a different version of the GYCPI: while Cuddington and Urzúa confirm the existence of a structural break in 1921 and attribute much of the measured commodity price decline to its presence, Sapsford et.al.(1992) argue that the price decline in 1921 is overstated in the GYCPI and that the relevant part of the index should be interpolated from Schlote's (1938) index.

Cuddington (1992) allowed for structural breaks in individual commodity price series, while León and Soto (1997) and Kellard and Wohar (2006) allow for endogenously inferred multiple structural breaks in individual price series when testing for stationarity. Kellard and Wohar, moreover consider segmented trends with possible changes in slope in this context. These various studies obtain mixed results on the stationarity characteristics of commodity price series and the prevalence of negative trends. Ocampo and Parra (2003) also consider stationarity and structural stability characteristics but finally conclude that the observed

---

[10] See Kim et.al. (2003) and Newbold et.al.(2005) for a more detailed discussion of this approach.

deterioration of commodity prices can frequently be attributed to discrete periods of price decline.

This overview of the empirical evidence is far from complete. The literature on the stationarity and structural stability of long run commodity price series is extensive, involving a number of data sets and covering co-integration based as well as univariate models. However, little would be gained by giving a more detailed overview of this particular sub-set of the literature.

The examples quoted provide a concise characterisation of the direction the statistical debate on the commodity terms of trade is taking. There is a general tendency towards the use of increasingly complex stationarity tests, allowing for varied and increasingly frequent structural changes. The approach taken by Kellard and Wohar in particular raises the question of just how secular a trend function should be judged to be if repeated changes in slope and even direction are considered in its estimation.

Univariate studies of commodity price trends then tend towards increasing methodological complexity, while there is no clear indication of a consensus or prevalent position on the statistical significance of a long term trend. There is more clarity on the question of *economic* significance though and this should be helpful in putting the unresolved issue of statistical significance into perspective.

3.3. Volatility, Co-Movement and Individual Country Terms of Trade

A number of studies have contrasted the magnitude of the trend coefficient estimates obtained with the volatility surrounding these trends and the emerging view is one of short term volatility as the dominant feature of long run commodity price series. The problem of commodity price fluctuation was acknowledged early on by Hans Singer, commenting on Kindelberger (1958). More recently, Cashin and McDermott (2002) have argued that the observed volatility is *the* salient feature of long term commodity price developments.

Using the Economist commodity price index, Cashin and McDermott show that observed commodity price fluctuations increased in amplitude following the end of the gold standard in 1899 while a higher frequency of price cycles was observed after the end of the Bretton Woods fixed exchange rate system in 1971. The magnitude of estimated trends is comparatively minor, suggesting that they are of less concern in a policy context, regardless of statistical significance.

This result is consistent with the observation of Newbold *et.al.* (2005) that estimated trends are of little use in forecasting many commodity price series. The 'small trends big variability' conclusion also appears to be unintentionally vindicated by the development observed in the academic discussion on the statistical significance of trend measurements: The very fact that the variations to the unit root tests employed are characterised by efforts to account for an increasing number of structural breaks and trend breaks is indicative of a volatile series rather than a well defined structurally stable data generating process.

The picture that emerges with respect to the trajectory of commodity prices in general is that of a weakly trending, highly volatile and highly correlated data series. The difficulty in deciding on the order of integration of the series or the statistical significance of the trend estimates should come as no surprise in this context and neither should the possible trend components' lack of economic importance over the short term.

A related discussion focuses on the suitability in practice of the commodity terms of trade as a proxy for developing country barter terms of trade. Bleaney and Greenaway (1993) and Lutz (1999) find some evidence of a long term relationship at the level of regional aggregates and in the case of Lutz (1999) for some individual countries. Cashin and Patillo (2006) look at country level evidence –referring to the Grilli and Yang data set for commodity prices– and find evidence of a stable long term relationship only for 11 of a sample of 42 sub-Saharan African countries.

Cashin and Patillo's recent results should be of particular interest since they suggest that widely defined commodity terms of trade measures are of limited use as a proxy for country terms of trade in a geographic region where narrowly focussed commodity dependence is a persistent and widespread phenomenon. This limited usefulness of the commodity terms of trade is consistent with the preceding comments on limited price co-movement and heterogeneous trend estimates for individual commodity price series. Since commodity dependent sub-Saharan African countries often have a very narrowly focused export profile (*cf.* Cashin and Patillo *op.cit.*) it should be unexpected for their terms of trade to be well represented by a broadly defined commodity aggregate.

The importance of the findings on country specific terms of trade is not confined to statistical technicalities however. Kaplinsky (2007) observes that relative commodity and manufacturing price developments are becoming increasingly differentiated. Manufactured products based on mature technologies have in some cases shown price behaviour similar to that originally imputed to primary commodity prices under the Prebisch Singer Hypothesis (*cf.* also Kaplinsky (1999) for an example of this phenomenon). At the same time, there is a countervailing development in some primary sectors: market segmentation through processes like the certification of purity standards has been observed to attract premium prices in niche markets. In these cases, some commodity prices can remain at a high level because product branding sustains entry barriers to the niche market (again, *cf.* Kaplinsky (2007)).

More generally, the sustained fast economic growth in China has put upwards pressure on prices over a range of commodities (*cf.* Kaplinsky (2007) and O'Connor *et.al.* (2007)). At the same time, China's competition is beginning to drive down the prices of some manufactured products (Kaplinsky (2007), Clyde-Hufbauer (2006)). This combination of influences can be expected to produce a sustained rise in the real price of at least a range of primary commodities although, as O'Connor *et.al.*(2007) point out, it is yet too early to reach that conclusion. The experience of the 1997 East Asian Crisis would also suggest that some caution is in order when extrapolating high continuous growth rates for emerging markets.

The observed developments in commodity and manufactured product markets, as well as the documented success of some emerging markets, point towards the need for re-assessing the Prebisch Singer Hypothesis in principle. It simply does not appear to be the case that broad primary commodity price aggregates can be taken to be representative of individual developing countries' terms of trade.

Hans Singer had already argued as early as 1971 (*cf.* Singer (1975)[11]) that the focus of the analysis of economically stagnant developing countries ought to shift from commodity prices to comparative innovation intensity. This shift in focus is consistent with the argument of Kaplinsky (1999) and Kaplinsky (2007) that the export profile of economies which persist in a state of underdevelopment tends to be biased towards either primary commodities which are

---

[11] This reference is to a re-print of a 1971 paper.

traded in competitive markets or manufactured products in the later stages of the product life cycle. The latter should be expected to exhibit price behaviour reminiscent of that traditionally attributed to primary commodities in general.

Conversely, developed countries should tend to have their exports concentrated in research and development intensive sectors, while successful emerging economies would be expected to eventually move into more innovation intensive sectors of the global economy.

A changed focus towards comparative innovation intensity of exports can help identify a potential situation of limited scope for resource mobilisation through trade in modern underdeveloped countries. This limitation in itself need not prevent economic growth and development, unless the additional assumption is made that foreign investment is either not forthcoming or fails to integrate with the domestic economy. Such a trade profile could, however, lead one to expect a constraint on export led growth in the given context of balance of payments constrained growth theory.

To bring the preceding analysis to its conclusion, one should therefore ask under what circumstances policy makers in developing countries should be concerned about a particular export profile. The underlying growth model should then offer some predictions about the likely nature of the anticipated impediments to growth.

4. CONCLUSION

The Prebisch Singer Hypothesis has conventionally been investigated empirically by testing for the significance of real commodity price trends. Studies of the structural or macroeconomic drivers of price movements have been the exceptions (*cf.* Borzenstein and Reinhart (1994) and Bloch and Sapsford (1997) for examples). This focus on primary commodity prices has probably been closely linked to data availability, particularly in the early stages of the debate, and may owe at least part of its sustained persistence to the self-sustaining momentum of an increasingly detached academic debate.

As mentioned above, a refocusing of the study of underdevelopment and export specialisation towards a comparison of relative innovation intensity has been suggested early on by Singer (1975). Data availability remains an issue for this direction of study, but the evidence provided by Kaplinsky (2007) and Kaplinsky (1999) as well as the evidence from the debate on commodity price trends and individual countries' terms of trade suggests that the simple use of broad commodity price aggregates as a proxy for developing country terms of trade in general is increasingly inappropriate.

To obtain a theoretical justification as to why terms of trade movements should impact on growth, the discussion of the Prebisch Singer Hypothesis has here been placed in the context of a balance of payments constrained growth model. On this basis one can then consider the relevant model predictions, bearing in mind that the model used does allow for investment flows and allowing for the possibility that the terms of trade may be characterised by volatility rather than secular trends.

Prior to a discussion of model predictions, it is worth outlining the general characteristics one would expect of a country case where the consideration of relevant commodity price developments as a determinant for growth would still be appropriate. Following the arguments in the main text, three conditions should be met in such a case:

(A) The developing country in question should have a dualist economic structure with a surplus labour supply.
(B) The growth of the economy should be constrained through limited access to foreign exchange.
(C) The country's export profile should show a specialisation in primary commodities or manufactured products *which display the kind of price behaviour traditionally ascribed to primary commodities.*

It can no longer be taken for granted that these conditions describe the situation of the typical developing economy. At the time of writing, a number of emerging market economies may for example no longer be realistically classified as foreign exchange constrained, although this condition could change in the near future (see Mohanty and Turner (2006) for a discussion of recent developments and likely prospects). One should also note the explicit reference to *relevant* commodity price developments above. This formulation takes account of the available evidence on general commodity aggregates and country terms of trade as discussed previously. Any product price indices taken into consideration in reference to condition (C) should therefore be specific to the relevant country's trade profile.

In countries were these conditions are met, a number of scenarios can be predicted from Thirlwall's balance of payments constrained growth model. For the traditional view of the Prebisch Singer case of a pronounced secular decline, the balance of payments constrained growth rate of income –as identified in equation [2.8] above- would simply fall below the counterfactual level for stable terms of trade at a given rate of change of the nominal exchange rate and of real investment flows.

It has been pointed out above that this impact could in principle be compensated by a countervailing inflow of foreign investment. In practice, this kind of investment inflow is most likely to be foreign direct investment. Singer's critique about the possible non-integration of investment projects with the local economy (*cf.* Singer (1950)) has to be borne in mind here. If foreign investment flows should indeed turn out to be mainly dedicated to economically isolated investment projects, it would by no means be certain how far such financial flows would eventually contribute to sustaining a higher rate of growth, even if the external constraint appears to be relaxed in balance of payments accounting terms.

The model under review does not formally address how investment flows feed into the local economy. Yet, common sense, as well as Singer's original critique, would suggest that some contribution to capital formation and to the diffusion of technological know how would be required to support sustained growth.

It should be remembered also that the predicted impact of a sustained terms of trade decline is predicted for a given rate of change of the nominal exchange rate. (In the possible case where this rate of change is zero, the prediction would of course apply to a given level of the nominal exchange rate.) In principle, a countervailing appreciation could compensate for the real depreciation produced by the terms of trade decline. It is because of the hypothesised low price elasticity values, that no such appreciation is expected.

The impact of a secular terms of trade deterioration and its possible containment are reasonably unambiguous in terms of model prediction and policy implication. The issue becomes more complex in the empirically likely case of export specialisation in a set of commodity like products which are characterised mainly by price volatility rather than stable and predictable trend movements.

In this case too there would be repercussions on either the balance of payments constrained growth rate of real income or the amount of real investment flows. Given the shorter duration of price movements and the likelihood of frequent changes of direction, their impact on both variables would be different in nature from a secular terms of trade deterioration.

Terms of trade fluctuations could in principle be reflected in either changing investment flows or changing income growth rates. It is a direct prediction of the Thirlwall model that in the absence of investment flows or for a given, stable level of real investment flows, terms of trade fluctuations in the presence of low price elasticities should translate into corresponding variations in the balance of payments constrained growth rate of real income. In other words: large terms of trade fluctuations are likely to be reflected in larger business cycles[12].

Such increased volatility in income growth rates can in theory be contained by accommodating changes in short term investment flows, which could stabilise the value of the balance of payments constraint at its original level. The mere fact that short term investment flows could have such a stabilising role does of course provide no reason why an investor should wish to undertake them. Short term investment flows, after all, tend to be some form of portfolio investment and their accrual in substantial amounts pre-supposes the existence of a sufficiently developed secondary capital market.

This is precisely the kind of financial infrastructure one would expect to be underdeveloped in commodity dependent LDCs. Moreover, portfolio capital flows which are large, relative to the overall size of the host economy's financial markets, and apt to reverse rapidly can have and have had a destabilising impact of their own (cf. Griffith-Jones and Pfaffenzeller (1998)). The large financial flows which would be required are both, a mixed blessing and unlikely to be forthcoming for those economies most in need of them.

An alternative strategy could target export earnings directly. Traditionally this has been attempted through stabilisation agreements, national marketing boards or multilateral funds (cf. Page and Hewitt (2001)). These attempts have had limited success and have largely been phased out (cf. Page and Hewitt (2001)). Furthermore, entry barriers in the relevant market segments tend to be too low and the markets tend to be too competitive for the formation of effective cartels that could stabilise or raise prices.

One possibility of mitigating the problem arises from the observation, discussed above, that the hypothesized degree of short term commodity price co-movement has been overstated. This raises the option of combining primary commodity production or trading pattern with a view to product mix diversification. Such a diversification could lead to risk spreading among commodities which do not register high covariance values for their inter-temporal price developments.

Where there is some choice over the product mix, as there may be in the case of certain agricultural commodities, diversification could take place at the producer level. A wider set of options could be attainable if earnings diversification is delegated to trading companies which act as an intermediary to local producers and use some of their earnings to contain price fluctuations.

---

[12] In terms of model prediction, this relationship between terms of trade movements and business cycles is likely rather than certain, since it is conceptually possible that the fluctuations in the balance of payments constraint just happen to counteract the domestic business cycle. It is however far from obvious that the required coincidence in magnitude and timing is a likely prospect.

The possibility of earnings diversification has as yet received little attention: it is briefly mentioned in Marinkov and Burger (2005) but otherwise appears to have been little researched. The lack of attention paid to this topic should not be surprising as such, given that serious doubts about pronounced commodity price co-movements are relatively recent. It is however a topic worthy of further research as earnings diversification could potentially contribute towards macro-economic stabilisation in those economies which are well characterised as commodity dependent and balance of payments constrained developing countries, in the sense outlined above.

ACKNOWLEDGEMENT

I am grateful to Prof. David Sapsford for advice received on an earlier draft of this paper, all errors and omissions are, of course, my responsibility.

BIBLIOGRAPHY

Agiakloglou and Newbold (1992) "Empirical Evidence on Dickey-Fuller Type Tests"*Journal of Time Series Analysis* Vol. 13, pp.471-483.

Agiakloglou, Christos, Newbold, Paul (1996) "The balance between size and power in Dickey-Fuller tests with data dependent rules for the choice of truncation lag" *Economics Letters* Vol. 52, pp. 229-234.

Bhagwati, Jagdish (2004) "In Defense of Globalisation" New York: *Oxford University Press*

Bleaney, Michael and David Greenaway (1993) "Long-Run Trends in the Relative Price of Primary Commodities and in the Terms of Trade of Developing Countries" *Oxford Economic Papers* Vol 45, pp 349-363.

Bloch, Harry and David Sapsford (1997) "Some Estimates of Prebisch and Singer Effects on the Terms of Trade between Primary Producers and Manufacturers" *World Development* Vol.25, pp.1873-1884.

Borzenstein, Eduardo, Carmen Reinhart (1994) "The Macroeconomic Determinants of Commodity Prices" *IMF Staff Papers* Vol. 41, pp.236-261.

Cashin, Paul and John McDermott (2002) "The Long-Run Behavior of Commodity Prices: Small Trends and Big Variability" *IMF Staff Papers* Vol.49, pp.175-199.

Cashin, Paul, McDermott, John, Scott, Alasdair (1999) "The Myth of Comoving Commodity Prices" *Working Paper of the International Monetary Fund* WP/99/169.

Cashin, Paul and Catherine Patillo (2006) "African terms of trade and the commodity terms of trade: close cousins or distant relatives?" *Applied Economics* Vo.38, pp.845-859.

Clyde Hufbauer, Gary, Yee Wong and Ketki Sheth (2006) "US-China Trade Disputes: Rising Tide, Rising Stakes" Washington D.C.: *Institute for International Economics*,

Cuddington, John (1992) "Long-run trends in 26 primary commodity prices" *Journal of Development Economics* Vol 39, pp 207-227

Cuddington, John and Carlos Urzúa (1989) "Trends and cycles in the net barter terms of trade: a new approach" *The Economic Journal* Vol. 99, pp. 426-442.

Gandolfo, Giancarlo (2002) "International Finance and Open Economy Macro-economics" Berlin:*Springer-Verlag* .

Griffith-Jones, Stephany and Stephan Pfaffenzeller (1998) "The East Asian Currency Crisis: A Survey of the Debate on its Causes and Possible Solutions" *Institute of Development Studies, Sussex*, mimeo http://www.ids.ac.uk/ids/global/Finance/easia.html

Grilli, Enzo, Maw Cheng Yang (1988) "Primary Commodity Prices, Manufactured Goods Prices, and the Terms of Trade of Developing Countries: What the Long Run Shows" *The World Bank Economic Review* Vol.2, pp. 1-47.

Hayek, Friedrich A. (2002) "Competition as a Discovery Procedure" *Quarterly Journal of Austrian Economics* Vol.5, pp. 9-23 .

Hussain, Nureldin and A.P. Thirlwall (1982) "The Balance of Payments Constraint, Capital Flows and Growth Rate Differences Between Developing Countries" *Oxford Economic Papers, New Series*, Vol. 34, pp. 498-510.

Ingersent, Ken A. and Anthony Rayner (1999) "Agricultural Policy in Western Europe and the United States" Cheltenham: *Edward Elgar.*

Johnston, Jack and John Dinardo (1997) "Econometric Methods" 2nd Edition, New York: *MacGraw Hill.*

Kaplinsky, Raphael (2007) "Revisiting the Revisited Terms of Trade" *World Development* Vol.34, pp.981-995.

Kaplinsky, Raphael (1999) "If you want to get somewhere else, you must run at least twice as fast as that!: The Roots of the East Asian Crisis" *Competition and Change* Vol.4, pp.1-30

Kellard, Neill and Mark Wohar (2006) "On the prevalence of trends in primary commodity prices" *Journal of Development Economics* Vol. 79, pp.146-167.

Kim, Thae-Hwan, Stephan Pfaffenzeller, Anthony Rayner and Paul Newbold (2003) "Testing for Linear Trend, with Application to Relative Primary Commodity Prices", *Journal of Time Series Analysis*, Vol. 24, pp 539.

Kindelberger, Charles P. (1958) "The Terms of Trade and Economic Development" *Review of Economics and Statistics* Vol. 40, pp. 84-89.

Krueger, Anne O (1997) "Trade Policy and Economic Development: How We Learn" *The American Economic Review*, Vol.87, pp 1-22

Krugman, Paul (1987) "Is Free Trade Passé?" *Journal of Economic Perspectives* Vol. 1, pp. 131-144

Krugman, Paul (1989) "Differences in Income Elasticities and Trends in Real Exchange Rates" *European Economic Review* Vol.33 pp.1031-1054.

Krugman (1994) "The Myth of Asia's Miracle" *Foreign Affairs* Vol.73, pp.62-77.

León Javier and Raimundo Soto (1997) "Structural Breaks and Long-Run Trends in commodity Prices" *Journal of International Development* Vol. 9, pp.347-366

Lewis, W.A. (1954) "Economic Development with Unlimited Supplies of Labour" *The Manchester School* Vol.22, pp.139-191

Leybourne, S.J., Tim Lloyd and Geoff Reed (1994) "The Excess Co-movement of commodity Prices Revisited" in: Sapsford, D., Morgan, W., (Eds.), *Economics of Primary Commodity Prices* pp. 30-49, Aldershot: Edward Elgar .

Lutz, Matthias (1999) "Commodity Terms of Trade and Individual Countries' Net Barter Terms of Trade: Is there an Empirical Relationship?" *Journal of International Development* Vol.11, No.6, pp.859-870.

MacKinnon, James (1991) "Critical Values for Cointegration Tests", in Engle, R. and Granger C., *Long-Run Economic Relationships*, pp. 267-276, Oxford: Oxford University Press.

Marinkov, Marina and Philippe Burger (2005) "The Various Dimensions of Commodity Dependence in Africa" *South African Journal of Economics* Vol.73, pp.269-291.

McCombie, J.S.L. and Thirlwall, A.P. (1994) "Economic Growth and the Balance-of-Payments Constraint" *Macmillan*, London.

Mohanty, MS. and Turner, Philip (2006) "Foreign exchange reserve accumulation in emerging markets: what are the domestic implications?" *BIS Quarterly Review*, September.

Newbold Paul and Clive Granger (1974) "Spurious Regressions in Econometrics" *Journal of Econometrics* Vol.2, pp.111-120.

Newbold Paul, Stephan Pfaffenzeller and Anthony Rayner (2005) "How Well are Long-Run Commodity Price Series Characterized by Trend Components?" *Journal of International Development* Vol. 17, pp.479-494.

Ocampo, José Antonio and María Ángela Parra (2003) "The terms of trade for commodities in the twentieth century" *CEPAL Review* Vol.79, pp.7-35.

O'Connor, John, David Orsmond and Max Layton (2007) "The Recent Rise in Commodity Prices: A Long Run Perspective" *Bulletin of the Reserve Bank of Australia*, April 2007, pp.1-9.

Page, Sheila and Adrian Hewitt (2001) "World Commodity Prices: still a problem for developing countries?" *odi special report* London: Overseas Development Institute

Perron, P., (1989) The great crash, the oil price shock and the unit root hypothesis, *Econometrica* Vol.57, pp.1361-1401.

Pfaffenzeller Stephan, Paul Newbold and Anthony Rayner (2007) "A short note on updating the Grilli and Yang Commodity Price Index" *The World Bank Economic Review* Vol.21, pp.151-163.

Prebisch, Raul (1950) "The Economic Development of Latin America and its principal problems" New York: *United Nations Department of Economic Affairs* .

Sapsford, David, P. Sarkar, Hans W. Singer (1992) "The Prebisch-Singer Terms of Trade Controversy Revisited" *Journal of International Development* Vol. 4, pp. 315-332.

Sapsford, David, (1985) "The Statistical Debate on the Net Barter Terms of Trade Between Primary Commodities and Manufactures: A Comment and Some Additional Evidence" *The Economic Journal*, Vol. 95, pp. 781-788.

Schlote, Werner (1938) "Entwicklung und Strukturwandlungen des englischen Außenhandels von 1700 bis zur Gegenwart" Kiel: *Institut für Weltwirtschaft* .

Singer, Hans W. (1975) "The Distribution of Gains Revisited" In: *The Strategy of International Development*, Singer (ed.) pp 58-66, London: Macmillan Press .

Singer, Hans W. (1950) "U.S. Foreign Investment in Underdeveloped Areas -the Distribution of Gains between Investing and Borrowing Countries", *American Economic Review - Papers and Proceedings*, Vol.40, pp. 473-485.

Spraos, John (1980) "The Statistical Debate on the Net barter Terms of Trade Between Primary Commodities and Manufactures" *The Economic Journal* Vol.90, pp. 107-128.

Toye, John and Richard Toye (2003) "The Origins and Interpretation of the Prebisch-Singer Thesis" *History of Political Economy* vol.35, pp.437-467.

Young, Alwyn (1995) "The Tyranny of Numbers: Confronting the Statistical Realities of the East Asian Growth Experience" *The Quarterly Journal of Economics* Vol.110, pp. 641-680.

Zimmerman, Carle C. (1930) "Ernst Engel's Law of Expenditures for Food" *Quarterly Journal of Economics* Vol.47, pp.78-101.

In: Development Economics Research Trends
Editor: Gustavo T. Rocha, pp. 149-164

ISBN 978-1-60456-172-2
© 2008 Nova Science Publishers, Inc.

Chapter 5

ASSESSING THE COMPETITIVENESS OF EUROPEAN COUNTRIES

Kyriaki Kosmidou[1], Michael Doumpos[2], Fotios Pasiouras[3] and Constantin Zopounidis[2]

[1]Department of International and European Economic Studies, Athens University of Economics and Business, Greece
[2] Department of Production Engineering and Management, Technical University of Crete, Greece
[3] School of Management, University of Bath, UK

ABSTRACT

The competitiveness of a country is an issue of particular importance to the managers of both firms and national economies. In this study, we investigate the factors that influence two of the main drivers of competitiveness, namely account balance and GDP growth. We also suggest an alternative methodology, namely PROMETHEE II, for assessing the competitiveness of EU countries in terms of their economic performance, government efficiency, business efficiency, and infrastructure. The results indicate differences in the determinants of GDP growth and account balance. As for the ranking of the countries, Luxembourg, Ireland and UK are included in top five in most of the cases, while the Southeuropean countries are ranked in the last positions.

1. INTRODUCTION

Competitiveness, and in particular the competitiveness of a country, has been characterized as an issue of key importance to the managers of both firms and national economies (Thomson, 2004). Obviously, the performance and success of firms is influenced by the environment in which they operate, and managers will need to be aware of the relative competitiveness of alternative potential locations for their firms. At the same time, policy-makers will be interested in making their country a relative competitive environment that will enhance the performance of local firms and attract foreign investments. Furthermore, there is a link between country competitiveness and the ability of an economy to create wealth for its citizens (Grilo and Koopman, 2006). Therefore, unsurprisingly, as Reinert (1995) highlights, competitiveness issues have been central in public policy for at least 500 years.

This interest is reflected in the efforts of various policy units and commissions (e.g. Commission of the European Communities, 1994; Department of Trade and Industry, 1998), as well as academics (e.g. Porter, 1990; Oral and Chabchoub, 1997; Zanakis and Becerra-Fernandez, 2005) to investigate country competitiveness. As Lall (2001) mentions this concern with competitiveness has also created a large industry that generates an output ranging from productivity and cost studies for specific activities and institutional analyzes to country strategy papers, cluster studies and so on.

However, there are two indices that truly dominate the field. The first is the Global Competitiveness Report (GCR) that is published annually by the World Economic Forum (WEF). However, GCR is based on the analytical framework of Porter (1990) that actually deals with productivity rather than competitiveness. As Zanakis and Berecca-Fernandez (2005) point out, although many view competitiveness as a synonym for productivity, these two related terms are in fact quite different since productivity refers to the internal capability of an organization (or country) whereas competitiveness refers to the relative position of an organization (or country) against its competitors (Cho and Moon, 1998). The second is the World Competitiveness Yearbook (WCY), computed and published annualy by the International Institute for Management Development (IMD). The methodology followed to calculated the WCY is based on simple weighted averages and Siggel (2006) characterizes the aggregation method used in WCY as "problematic". One common drawback in both reports is that it is not easy for the reader to analyse either index appropriately, first because the authors do not provide full details of the methodology and second because they slip over complex theoretical issues (Lall, 2001).

The objective of the present study is twofold. First, to investigate the factors that influence two of the main drivers of competitiveness, namely account balance and GDP growth. Second, to suggest an alternative methodology, namely PROMETHEE II, for assessing the competitiveness of EU countries in terms of their economic performance, government efficiency, business efficiency and infrastructure. We focus on the EU because the agreement reached in Copenhagen in December 2002, opened the way for 10 countries (i.e. Poland, Czech Republic, Hungary, Slovakia, Slovenia, Estonia, Lithuania, Latvia, Cyprus, Malta) to join the EU in May 2004. This EU enlargement has created not only a very large market, but has also increased the opportunities and threats of the member states and the firms within them, as firms can no longer expect competition only from firms from neighbouring countries. Furthermore, the EU has given particular emphasis in competitiveness, as this is reflected in the Lisbon Strategy that was adopted by the European Council in March 2000. This strategy aims to make Europe, by 2010, the most competitive and dynamic knowledge-based economy in the world, capable of sustainable economic growth, with more and better jobs and greater social cohesion.

Our study is of particular importance for at least two reasons. First, the PROMETHEE II, is a simple but efficient multicriteria methodology that is based on outranking relations and is well-suited for performance evaluation problems where multiple evaluation criteria are involved. Thus, it can contribute significantly towards making an integrated and rational evaluation and assessment of the competitiveness of EU countries. Second, while several studies examine individual countries such as Germany (Feldman, 1994), UK (Nachum et al., 2001), Bulgaria (Pashev, 2003) Ireland (Barry et al., 2005), Croatia (Malekovic and Frohlich, 2005), Former Yugoslav Republic of Macedonia (Gutierrez, 2006), very few studies have attempted a comprehensive comparison of multicountry competitiveness (Zanakis and Becerra-Fernandez, 2005). Furthermore, most of the multicountry studies either provide general discussions (e.g. Sharp, 1998; Lall, 2001; Grilo and Koopman, 2006) or attempt to replicate the rankings of the two leading indices (e.g. Oral and Chabchoub, 1997; Zanakis and Becerra-Fernandez, 2005) rather than provide alternative methodological frameworks.

The rest of the paper is as follows. In Section 2, we define country competitiveness while Section 3 reviews the literature. Session 4 discusses the sample and methodology, and Section 5 presents the empirical results. Finally, Section 6 concludes the study.

2. DEFINITION OF COUNTRY COMPETITIVENESS

Defining the competitiveness of nations is a controversial issue (Aiginger, 1998), and there is not universally accepted definition of competitiveness. Hence, given the various definitions that exist, it is appropriate to briefly discuss some of the main arguments at this point.

As Ketels (2006) mentions *"since the term competitiveness entered the public debate in force, it has been widely used by practitioners but viewed by scepticism by many academics"* *(p. 115)*. Indeed, there is a large number of economists, such as Krugman (1994, 1996) that reject the idea that nations compete with each other and argue that it is companies, rather than nations, that compete internationally. While much of the debate[1] started with the publication of Porter's (1990) *Competitive Advantage of Nations* (CAN), Porter also comes very close to the view that the term of competitiveness of a country makes no sense by arguing that *"the only meaningful definition of competitiveness at the national level is national productivity"* (p. 6). Nevertheless, Davies and Ellis (2000) argue that *"throughout CAN there is an elision between competitiveness as the productivity of a nation and competitiveness as the ability of some firms and industries to secure large shares of the global market"* (p. 1194).

Garelli (2006) contradicts the idea that nations do not compete and mentions that *"nations compete because world markets are open"* (p.3) and *"a significant part of the competitive advantage of nations stems from far-reaching incentive policies emphasizing tax breaks, subsidies, etc. which are designed to attract foreign investment"* (p.4). Reiljan et al. (2000) attribute the arguments against competitiveness to confusion in terminology and problems with the definition of competitiveness, and argue that these are not reasons to eliminate the term at all or ignore practical analyses and forecasts of competitiveness of different economic entities. Furthermore, they mention that *"competitiveness reflects a position of one economic entity (country, industry, enterprise, household) in relation to other economic entities by comparing the qualities or results of activities reflecting superiority or inferiority"* (p. 10) and provide both a narrow and a broader definition. Sharp (1998) also highlights that while Krugman might be right to criticize the "zero-sum-game" mentality of some of the debate over competitiveness, the broad concept of holding market share in the

---

[1] For a discussion of Porter's Competitive Advantage of Nations, that also outlines the main arguments of critics and supporters see Davies and Ellis (2000). Ketels (2006) also provides an interesting discussion.

face of competition has its uses. Ketels (2006) also identifies the "market share" based definition as the main rival to the productivity-based definition of competitiveness. In this case, competitiveness is related to the ability to sell on international markets and sustain an economy's overall external balance (Figueroa, 1998). Ketels also mentions that *"A criticism that disproportionally affects the productivity-based view of competitiveness with its fundamental interest in prosperity is that it is narrowly economic and takes no account of social and environmental prosperity"* (p. 117). Finally, according to Trabold (1995; cited in Reiljan et al., 2000) competitiveness is determined by four important aspects, namely ability to sell (export ability), ability to attract (location), ability to adjust, and ability to earn.

Policy makers tend to emphasize the relation between exports and standards of living that is similar to the definition of Scott and Lodge (1985) who argue that competitiveness is *"a nation state's ability to produce, distribute and service goods in the international economy...,and to do so in a way that earns a rising standard of living"* (p. 15). For example, OECD/TEP (1992) defines competitiveness as *"a country's ability to produce goods and services, which meet the test of foreign competition while simultaneously maintaining and expanding the real income of its people"* (p. 237). The Competitiveness Policy Council (1994) defines it as *"the ability to sell products on international markets, while incomes in the domestic markets increase in a sustainable way"*. The European Competitive Report published annually by the Commission of the European Communities defines competitiveness as a sustainable rise in the standards of living of a nation with the lowest possible level of involuntary unemployment. The 2000 report also highlights that *"More precisely, the level of economic activity should not cause an unsustainable external balance of the economy nor should it compromise the welfare of future generations"* (p. 26).

Thompson (2004) attributes the above differences to different underlying philosophies by distinguishing between economics, business scholars and managers. More precisely, Thomson mentions that for many economists, national competitiveness is a straightforward narrow issue of relative costs largely determined by exchange rages, whereas business scholars perceive national competitiveness as a complex of institutional and systematic factors relating to macro political-economy issues and the ways in which these affect the microeconomic activity of firms within their competitive environments. Finally, for managers the term represents a mixture of both these narrow and broad academic conceptions. Hence, the relative cost of doing business in a given location is a matter of key competitive importance, and so, too, is the institutional and systemic environment in terms of legal infrastructure, governmental processes, public policy and other factors affecting business activity.

3. LITERATURE REVIEW

As mentioned before, two of the most well known reports relative to competitiveness are the WCY and the GCR. This section provides a brief discussion of these two reports along with academic studies that attempt to replicate their rankings.

The most recent (2006) WCY provides rankings for 61 national and regional economies. More than 300 indicators are considered, covering the following four main categories: economic performance, government efficiency, business efficiency, and infrastructure. Each of these factors is divided into 5 sub-factors resulting in 20 sub-factors in total, each one accounting for 5% in the overall consolidation of the results, which leads to the overall ranking of the WCY. Two thirds of the criteria are hard (e.g. GDP) and one third are soft data collected from surveys.

The GCR currently covers 125 major and emerging economics. The rankings are produced from a combination of publicly available hard data and a comprehensive executive opinion annual survey conducted by the World Economics Forum. In total over 90 variables are used, of which two thirds are from the survey and one third from publicly available sources. The variables fall within the following nine categories: institutions, infrastructure, macroeconomy, health and primary education, higher education and training, market efficeincy, technological readiness, business sophistication, and innovation. The GCR is related to the work of Porter on national competitive advantage published in *The Competitive Advantage of Nations* in 1990. In his study, Porter (1990) proposed a methodology to analyze the competitiveness of countries and then developed an agenda for each of country to pursue in order to become internationally more competitive. The basic idea of his methodology is to analyze the economy of a country, sector by sector, in terms of the now familiar corners of the "national diamond": factor conditions, demand conditions, supporting and related industries, and firm strategy, structure and rivalry. The proposed methodology was applied on a sample of 10 countries (Denmark, Germany, Italy, Japan, Korea, Singapore, Sweden, Switzerland, the United Kingdom and the United States) and the obtained results were then transformed into a set of recommendations to form an agenda for each country to adopt.

Oral and Chabchoub (1996) use mathematical programming in an attempt to uncover the methodology used by the World Competitiveness Report (WCR) during 1992. They concentrate on OECD countries and develop various formulations of the model. They also explore alternative situations using hard and soft-data based indicators. Nevertheless, they conclude that the WCR rankings, neither at the factor nor overall competitiveness levels can be reproduced.

In a later study, Oral and Chabchoub (1997) use a more general formula, based again on mathematical programming, to replicate the WCR ratings. More precisely, they estimate a weight estimation model (WEM), which assumes that one might assign different weights to a given indicator for different countries, rather than imposing the same weight for all countries. Their results can be summarized as follows. First, the WCR rankings at all four levels can be reproduced by using the weighs obtained from WEM. Second, it is not necessary to use all of the indicators in order to replicate the WCR rankings. Third, one needs to use different sets of weights for different countries. Fourth, the presence of multiple optimal solutions indicates the existence of various sets of weights that reproduce the WCR rankings.

Ulengin et al. (2002) examine the 1999 World Competitiveness Index (WCI) ranking using a sample of 29 countries. The results indicate that it is possible to estimate the WCIs of any country based on power-related and objective attributes taken as independent variables. Furthermore, the prediction of WCI values is much more accurate when the countries are grouped according to high and low levels of WCI, respectively. For the countries with the highest WCI, they key explanatory variables were main ethnic group, urban and rural population, carbon dioxide emission, and inflation. For the lowest group of WCI countries, the most significant variables were life expectancy, internet use, level of GDP, unemployment rate, surrogate personnel, and marine force. The authors also suggest the use of hierarchical agglomerative clustering heuristics and self-organizing map neural networks to produce a grouping of countries based on their respective WCIs.

Zanakis and Becerra-Fernandez (2005) use a dataset of 43 countries from the 1999 WCY and 55 variables measuring economic, internationalization, governmental, financial, infrastructure, management, science and technology, as well as demographical and cultural characteristics. They employ several techniques such as stepwise regression (SWR), weighted non-linear programming (WNLP), artificial neural networks (NN) and classification and regression trees (CART) and attempt to identify important factors associated with competitiveness and develop knowledge discovery databases models to be used for prediction purposes. Their results indicate that the main drivers of competitiveness are higher computer usage and lower country risk rating, in entrepreneurial urbanized societies with less male dominance and basic infrastructure, with higher gross domestic investment, savings and private consumption, more imports of goods and services than exports, increased purchaser power parity GDP, larger and more productive but not less expensive labor force, and higher RandD expenditures. The out-of-training sample accuracy was assessed through a ten-fold cross-validation approach indicating SWR and NN as the best performers.

4. SAMPLE AND METHODOLOGY

4.1. Sample and Variables

The sample used in this study consists of 21 EU countries over the period 2000-2002. These are the 15 "old" members and 6 "new" members. The data have been collected from the database of IMD. Cyprus, Latvia, Lithuania, and Malta were excluded from the sample due to missing values for several variables.

In the first stage of the analysis, we employ OLS stepwise regression in an attempt to reveal the factors that influence two of the main drivers of competitiveness. The dependent variables are real GDP growth (GDPGR) and current account balance as a percentage of GDP (BALANCE). GDPGR has been selected because GDP growth is considered one of the basic factors influencing a country's competitiveness and a critical means of improving welfare and raising living standards. BALANCE has been selected because, if competitiveness means the ability of a nation to sell more in the world marketplace than it buys, then trade surplus should be considered a measure of its competitiveness (Ulengin et al., 2002). Our independent variables range between 39-45 (depending on year) and cover the following four categories: (i) economic performance (i.e. macro-economic evaluation of the domestic economy), (ii) government efficiency (i.e. extent to which government policies are conductive to competitiveness), (iii) business efficiency (i.e. extent to which enterprises are performing in an innovative, profitable and responsible manner, and (iv) infrastructure (i.e. extent to which basic, technological, scientific, and human resources meet the needs of business). Table 1 presents a list of all the variables.

In the second stage of the analysis, we use PROMOTHEE (see section 4.2) to provide a ranking of the countries with respect to their competitiveness. In this case, the input consists of nine variables selected on the basis of factor analysis (see section 5.1).

Table 1. List of Variables

Panel A: Dependent Variables - Stage 1	
Real GDP Growth	Current account balance
Panel B: Independent Variables - Stage 1	
ECONOMIC PERFORMANCE	
Domestic Economy (% GDP)	
Private final consumption expenditure	Government final consumption expenditure
Gross domestic investment	Gross domestic savings
Economic sectors / Agriculture	Economic sectors / Industry
Economic sectors / Services	
International Trade (% GDP)	
Current account balance	Balance of trade
Balance of commercial services	Exports of goods
Exports of commercial services	Imports of goods and commercial services
International Investment (% GDP)	
Direct investment flows abroad	Direct investment flows inward
Balance of direct investment flows	Net position in direct investment stocks
Employment	
Employment (% population)	
GOVERNMENT EFFICIENCY	
Public Finance (% GDP)	
Government budget surplus/deficit	Central government domestic debt
Central government foreign debt	General government expenditure
Fiscal Policy	
Collected total tax revenues (% GDP)	Collected capital and property taxes (% GDP)
Collected employer's social security contribution (% GDP)	Employee's social security contribution rate (%of income equal to GDP per capita)
Societal Framework	
Income distribution - lowest 20%	Income distribution - highest 20%
BUSINESS EFFICIENCY	
Productivity	
Overall productivity - real growth	
Labor Market	
Unit labor costs in the manufacturing sector (% change)	Labor force (% population)
Part-time employment (% population)	Female labor force (% of total employment force)
Finance	
Banking sector assets (% of GDP)	Stock market capitalization (% of GDP)
Stock market index (% change)	
INFRASTRUCTURE	
Basic Infrastructure	
Population under 15 years	Population over 65 years
Technological Infrastructure	
High-tech exports (% of total manufactured exports)	

Table 1. (Continued)

Health and Environment	
Total health expenditure (% GDP)	Urban population (% population)
Public expenditure on health (% of total health expenditures)	

Education	
Secondary school enrolment (% of relevant age group population receiving full time education)	Higher education achievement (% of population that has attained at least tertiary education - persons 25-34)

4.2. Promethee II

In the present study, we use the PROMETHEE II method (Brans and Vincke, 1985) that is considered one of the most efficient and simplest multicriteria methodologies and is well-suited for performance evaluation problems where multiple evaluation criteria are involved. PROMETHEE II is based on the outranking relations concept which was developed by Roy (1968, 1996). Roy defined the outranking relation as a binary relation **S** between alternatives (countries) a and b in a given set of alternatives A, such that aSb (a outranks b) if there are enough arguments to decide that a is at least as good as b, while there is no essential reason to refute that statement.

The construction of the outranking relation through the PROMETHEE II method involves the consideration of the performance of the alternatives (countries) on a set of n evaluation criteria (indicators). To each criterion j a weight $p_j \geq 0$ is given depending on its importance (the criteria weights sum up to 1, i.e., $\sum_{j=1}^{n} p_j = 1$). The higher the weight of a criterion, the more important it is for the evaluation of the overall performance of the alternatives. The criteria's weights constitute the basis for the assessment of the degree of preference for alternative a over alternative b. This degree is represented in the preference index $\pi(a, b)$ defined as follows:

$$\pi(a,b) = \sum_{j=1}^{n} p_j H_j(d_{ab})$$ (1)

The preference index for each pair of alternatives (a, b) ranges between 0 and 1. The higher it is (closer to 1) the higher is the strength of the preference for a over b. According to (1) the preference index is calculated as the weighted average of the partial preference of a over b on each criterion j. To measure the partial preference of a over b on a criterion j the function $H_j(d_{ab}) \in [0, 1]$ is used; this is an increasing function of the difference $d_{ab} = g_{aj} - g_{bj}$ between the performance of alternative a on criterion j (g_{aj}) and the performance of alternative b on the same criterion j (g_{bj}). $H_j(d_{ab})$ is a kind of preference intensity function (Vincke, 1992). In the case $d_{ab} = g_{aj} - g_{bj} \approx 0$ alternatives a and b have similar performance on criterion j and consequently the preference of a over b is expected to be low, i.e., $H_j(d_{ab}) \approx 0$.

Table 2. Forms of the preference function

Preference functions	Functional form	Graphical form	Parameters
Usual	$H(d) = \begin{cases} 0 & \text{if} \quad d = 0 \\ 1 & \text{if} \quad d > 0 \end{cases}$		-
Quasi	$H(d) = \begin{cases} 0 & \text{if} \quad d \leq q \\ 1 & \text{if} \quad d > q \end{cases}$		$q > 0$
Linear preference	$H(d) = \begin{cases} d/p & \text{if} \quad d \leq p \\ 1 & \text{if} \quad d > p \end{cases}$		$p > 0$
Level	$H(d) = \begin{cases} 0 & \text{if} \quad d \leq q \\ 0.5 & \text{if} \quad q < d \leq p \\ 1 & \text{if} \quad d > q \end{cases}$		$p > q > 0$
Linear preference and indifference area	$H(d) = \begin{cases} 0 & \text{if} \quad d \leq q \\ \frac{(d-q)}{(p-q)} & \text{if} \quad q < d \leq p \\ 1 & \text{if} \quad d > p \end{cases}$		$p > q > 0$
Gaussian	$H(d) = 1 - \exp\left(-d^2/2\sigma^2\right)$		$\sigma > 0$

Source: Brans et al. (1986).

On the other hand, the case $d_{ab} = g_{aj} - g_{bj} \gg 0$ designates that the performance of alternative a on criterion j is considerably higher than the performance of alternative b, and consequently it is expected that a is strongly preferred to b, i.e., $H_j(d_{ab}) \approx 1$. The function H_j can be of different forms, depending upon the judgment policy of the decision maker. Brans and Vincke (1985) proposed six general forms which cover a wide range of practical situations (Table 2). For the purposes of this study we use the Gaussian form of the H_j for all criteria, that requires the specification of only one parameter (σ). Furthermore, the Gaussian function is a generalization of all the other five forms, whereas the fact that it does not have discontinuities contributes to the stability and the robustness of the obtained results (Brans et al., 1986).

The results of the comparisons made for all pairs of alternatives (a, b) are organized in a directed graph (value outranking graph), such as the ones shown in Figure 1. The nodes of the graph represent the alternatives under consideration, whereas the arcs connecting pairs of nodes a and b represent the preference of alternative a over alternative b (if the direction of the arc is $a \rightarrow b$) or the opposite (if the direction of the arc is $b \rightarrow a$). Each arc is associated with a flow representing the preference index $\pi(a, b)$ as defined in (1). The sum of all flows leaving a node a is called the leaving flow of the node, denoted by $\phi^+(a)$. The leaving flow provides a measure of the outranking character of alternative a over all the other alternatives. In a similar way, the sum of all flows entering a node a is called the entering flow of the node, denoted by $\phi^-(a)$. The entering flow measures the outranked character of alternative a compared to all the other alternatives. The difference between the leaving and the entering flow $\phi(a) = \phi^+(a) - \phi^-(a)$ provides the net flow for the node (alternative) a which constitutes the overall evaluation measure of the performance of the alternative a. Assuming that m alternatives are considered, the net flow may range in $[-m, m]$. The case $\phi(a) \approx -m$ designates that alternative a is strongly outranked by the other alternatives, whereas the case $\phi(a) \approx m$ designates that alternative a strongly outranks the other alternatives. On the basis of their net flows the alternatives are ranked from the best (alternatives with high positive net flows) to the worst ones (alternatives with low net flows).

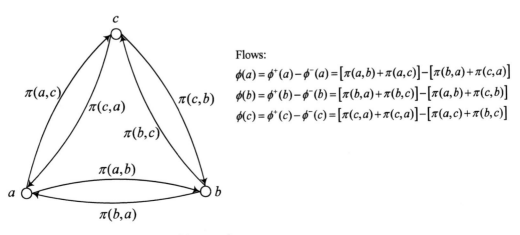

Flows:

$$\phi(a) = \phi^+(a) - \phi^-(a) = [\pi(a,b) + \pi(a,c)] - [\pi(b,a) + \pi(c,a)]$$
$$\phi(b) = \phi^+(b) - \phi^-(b) = [\pi(b,a) + \pi(b,c)] - [\pi(a,b) + \pi(c,b)]$$
$$\phi(c) = \phi^+(c) - \phi^-(c) = [\pi(c,a) + \pi(c,a)] - [\pi(a,c) + \pi(b,c)]$$

Figure 1. Example of a value outranking graph.

5. RESULTS

5.1. OLS Results

Table 3 presents the results of the OLS stepwise regressions when we use GDPGR as the dependent variable. The adjusted R^2 ranges between 0.567 (2000) and 0.814 (2001). We observe that different factors appear to influence GDPGR among the years. More detailed, while the real growth of overall productivity and general government expenditure are statistically significant in both 2001 and 2002 none of the two is significant in 2000. By contrast, imports of goods and commercial services and high-tech exports have both a positive and statistically significant impact on GDPGR only during 2000. Finally, population over 65 years is significant only in the case of 2001.

Table 3. Stepwise OLS regression results (Dependent Variable- Real GDP growth)

	2000	2001	2002
Imports of goods and commercial services	0.564***	---	---
High-tech exports	0.409***	---	---
Overall productivity-real growth	---	0.729***	0.641***
General government expenditure	---	-0.675***	0.433***
Population over 65 years	---	0.282***	---
R^2	0.611	0.842	0.745
Adjusted R^2	0.567	0.814	0.716
Stand. error of estimate	1.315	0.711	1.019
F	14.113	30.217	26.262

Table 4. Stepwise OLS regression results (Dependent Variable- Current account balance as % GDP)

	2000	2001	2002
Balance of trade	1.231***	---	---
Balance of commercial services	0.580***	---	---
Secondary school enrolment	0.282***	---	---
Government budget surplus/deficit	---	0.532***	---
Employee's social security contribution rate	---	0.296***	---
Exports of commercial services	---	-0.200***	---
Private final consumption expenditure	---	-0.532***	-0.456***
Gross domestic investment	---	-0.379***	-0.780***
Banking sector assets	---	-0.259***	---
Female labour force	---	-0.140***	---
R^2	0.944	0.979	0.819
Adjusted R^2	0.931	0.965	0.794
Stand. error of estimate	1.250	0.850	2.256
F	73.475	72.227	31.768

Table 4 shows the results when we use BALANCE as the dependent variable. The first observation relates to the values of the adjusted R² which are higher than the ones in Table 3 and now range between 0.794 (2002) and 0.965 (2001). Hence, our model is in better position to explain the current account balance (as a percentage of GDP) rather than the real GDP growth. Again, we observe particularly important differences among the years, which are even more severe in this case. The balance of trade, balance of commercial services and secondary school enrolment are significant only in case of 2000, while the government budget surplus/deficit, employee's social security contribution rate, exports of commercial services, banking sector assets and female labour force have a significant impact on Balance in 2001. Finally, the private final consumption expenditure and gross domestic investment are significant in 2001 and 2002.

5.2. Application of Promethee II

As previously mentioned, factor analysis was used prior to the application of PROMETHEE II to reduce the number of input variables. Nine factors were extracted explaining 83.6% of the variance. The variable with the highest loading was then selected from each factor. Thus, the following set of variables was used: Higher education achievement, overall productivity-real growth, balance of commercial services, public expenditure on health, exports of goods, income distribution –highest 20%, employer's social security contribution rate, government final consumption expenditure, unit labor costs in the manufacturing sector.

The discussion in section 4.2 illustrates that the application of PROMETHEE requires the determination of the appropriate evaluation criteria and also the shape of the H_j function for each selected evaluation criterion j. The shape of the H_j function that was selected for each criterion j, is the Gaussian form (Gaussian criterion) defined as $H_j(d) = 1 - \exp\left(-d^2/2\sigma_j^2\right)$. For the parameters σ_j 10 different scenarios were considered ranging between $0.25s_j$ and $2.5s_j$, where s_j is the standard deviation of all differences d_{ab} for all countries a and b on criterion j. When low values for σ are considered the preference for a country a over a country b can be high even when the performance of the two countries on the criteria are similar. On the other hand, when higher values for σ are employed, the preference for a country a over a country b will be high only if the performance of country a on the criteria set is considerably higher than the performance of country b.

A simulation approach was also employed for the criteria weights required to calculate the preference index in (1). More detailed, 50 random weighting scenarios were generated. In each scenario the criteria weights are considered as random numbers uniformly distributed in the interval [1, 100]. The combination of the 50 weighting scenarios with the 10 scenarios of the parameter σ resulted in the consideration of 500 scenarios, in total. In each scenario a different ranking of the countries is obtained according to the corresponding parameters of the PROMETHEE II method. Table 5 presents the ranking of the countries after averaging their scores over the 500 scenarios.

Luxembourg, Ireland, UK and Estonia are included in top five all the years, while Denmark is also ranked in the top five positions in 2000 and 2001.

Table 5. Results of PROMETHEE II (rankings on the basis of the average score obtained over 500 scenarios)

Country	2000	2001	2002
Estonia	1	2	4
Luxembourg	2	5	2
Ireland	3	1	1
Denmark	4	3	10
United Kingdom	5	4	5
Finland	6	16	6
Czech Republic	7	6	9
Belgium	8	10	7
Netherlands	9	9	12
Slovenia	10	12	11
Sweden	11	8	3
Poland	12	13	8
France	13	7	14
Germany	14	14	15
Austria	15	19	18
Slovak Republic	16	11	13
Spain	17	18	17
Portugal	18	15	16
Greece	19	17	19
Hungary	20	21	21
Italy	21	20	20

Finally, Sweden also makes it in the top five in 2002 when it is ranked 3rd. By contrast, Spain, Portugal, Greece, Hungary and Italy, are ranked in the last positions in most of the cases. Hence, the Southeuropean countries are, in general, in worse position even that the new members.

6. CONCLUSION

Competitiveness issues have been central in public policy for at least 500 years. As Ketels (2006) points out its growing importance is driven by changes in the nature of global competition that have increased the pressure on many locations to design sustainable strategies to support and improve prosperity.

In the present study we first investigate the factors that influence two of the main drivers of competitiveness, namely account balance and GDP growth. Then we propose a multicriteria methodology, namely PROMETHEE II, for assessing the competitiveness of EU countries in terms of their economic performance, government efficiency, business efficiency, and infrastructure. The results indicate differences in the determinants of GDP growth and account balance. As for the ranking of the countries we find that Estonia, Luxembourg,

Ireland and UK are included in top five in most of the cases, while the Southeuropean countries are ranked in the last positions.

The present study could be extended towards numerous directions in future research. First, it would be worthwhile to consider a larger time period, while distinguishing before and after the EU enlargement. Second, while the present analysis was limited to cross-section estimations, future research could re-estimate the models using panel data. The analysis could also be conducted separately for old and new members states. Finally, it would be interesting to rank countries on the basis of individual categories such as economic performance, government efficiency, infrastructure, and so on.

ACKNOWLEDGEMENTS

The study presented in this paper consists part of a research project "Operational Programme for Education and Initial Vocational Training Education" "PYTHAGORAS II: Funding of research groups in Technical University of Crete – M 2.2, co-financed by European Union through the Third Community Support Framework, co-financed by the European Social Fund.

We would also like to thank participants in the 3rd International Conference on Computational Management Science (Amsterdam) for their comments and suggestions. Dr. Pasiouras was Research Associate in the Financial Engineering Laboratory of Technical University of Crete when the research reported in this study was undertaken.

REFERENCES

Aiginger, K., (1998), A framework for evaluating the dynamic competitiveness of countries, *Structural Change and Economic Dynamics*, 9, 159-188.

Barry, F., Hannan, A., Hutson, E., Kearney, C., (2005), Competitiveness Implications for Ireland of EU Enlargement, Institute for International Integration Studies (IIIS) Discussion Paper No. 49, January, Trinity College Dublin, Ireland.

Brans, J.P., Vincke, Ph. (1985), A preference ranking organization method: The PROMETHEE method for multiple criteria decision-making, *Management Science*, 31, 6, 647-656.

Brans, J.P., Vincke, Ph., Mareschal, B. (1986), How to rank and how to select projects: The PROMETHEE method, *European Journal of Operational Research*, 24, 228-238.

Cho, D.S., Moon, H.C., (1998), A nation's international competitiveness in different stages of economic development, *Advances in Competitiveness Research*, 1 (6), 5-19.

Commission of the European Communities, (1994), An Industrial Competitiveness Policy for the European Union, Communication from the Commission the Council, COM (94) 318, fin Brussels, September.

Commission of the European Communities, (2000), European Competitiveness Report, Commission Staff Working Paper, 30 October, Brussels, available at: http://ec.europa.eu/enterprise/enterprise_policy/competitiveness/index_en.htm

Competitiveness Policy Council, (1994), Promoting long term productivity, Third report to the President and the Congress, Government Printing Office, Washington, D.C.

Davies, H., Ellis, P., (2000), Porter's Competitive Advantage of Nations: Time for the Final Judgement?, *Journal of Management Studies*, 37, 1189-1213.

Department of Trade and Industry, (1998), Our Competitive Future: Building the Knowledge Driven Economy UK Government Competitiveness, The Stationery Office (White Paper), London.

Feldman, R.A., (1994), Measures of External Competitiveness for Germany, IMF Working Paper 94/113 (September), Research Department, International Monetary Fund.

Figueroa, A., (1998), Equity, Foreign Investment and International Competitiveness in Latin America, *The Quarterly Review of Economics and Finance*, 38 (3), 391-409.

Garelli, S., (2006), Competitiveness of Nations: The Fundamentals, IMD World Competitiveness Yearbook.

Grilo, I., Koopman, G.J., (2006), Productivity and Microeconomic Reforms: Strengthening EU Competitiveness, *Journal of Industry, Competition, and Trade*, 6, 67-84.

Gutierrez, E., (2006), Export Performance and External Competitiveness in the former Yugoslav Republic of Macedonia, IMF Working Paper 06/261 (November), Policy Development and Review Department, International Monetary Fund.

Ketels, C.H.M., (2006), Michael Porter's Competitiveness Framework – Recent Learnings and New Research Priorities, *Journal of Industry, Competition and Trade*, 6, 115-136.

Krugman, P.R., (1994), Competitiveness: a dangerous obsession, *Foreign Affairs*, 73 (2), 28-44.

Krugman, P.R., (1996), Making Sense of the Competitiveness Debate, *Oxford Review of Economic Policy*, 12 (3), 17-25.

Lall S., (2001), Competitiveness Indices and Developing Countries: An Economic Evaluation of the Global Competitiveness Report, *World Development*, 29 (9), 1501-1525.

Malekovic, S., Frohlich, Z., (2005), Croatian Regional Policy Fostering Competitiveness, *Transition Studies Review*, 12 (1), 129-143.

Nachum, L., Jones, G.G., Dunning, J.H., (2001), The international competitiveness of the UK and its multinational enterprises, *Structural Change and Economic Dynamics*, 12, 277-294.

OECD/TEP, (1992), Technology and the economy. The key relationships. The technology/economy programme. Paris.

Oral, M., Chabchoub, H., (1996), On the methodology of the World Competitiveness Report, *European Journal of Operational Research*, 90, 514-535.

Oral, M., Chabchoub, H., (1997), An estimation model for replicating the rankings of the world competitiveness report, *International Journal of Forecasting*, 13, 527-537.

Pashev, K., (2003), Competitiveness of the Bulgarian Economy, Discussion Papers 34/2003, Bulgarian National Bank, August, ISBN 954-9791-68-8.

Porter, M.E., (1990), *The Competitive Advantage of Nations*, London: Macmillan.

Reijan, J., Hinrikus, M., Ivanov, A., (2000), Key issues in defining and analysing the competitiveness of a country, No. 561, University of Tartu, Tartu University Press.

Reinert, E.S., (1995), Competitiveness and its predecessors-a 500-year cross-national perspective, *Structural Change and Economic Dynamics*, 6, 23-42.

Roy, B., (1968), Classement et choix en présence de points de vue multiples: La méthode ELECTRE, *R.I.R.O*, 8, 57-75

Roy, B., (1996), *Multicriteria Methodology for Decision Aiding*, Kluwer Academic Publishers, Dodrecht

Scott, B.R., Lodge, G.C., (1985), U.S. competitiveness in the world economy, Harvard Business School Press, Boston.

Sharp, M., (1998), Competitiveness and cohesion-are the two compatible?, *Research Policy*, 27, 569-588.

Siggel, E., (2006), International Competitiveness and Comparative Advantage: A Survey and a Proposal for Measurement, *Journal of Industry, Competition and Trade*, 6, 137-159.

Thomson, E.R., (2004), National Competitiveness: A Question of Cost Conditions or International Circumstances?, *British Journal of Management*, 15, 197-218.

Trabold, H., (1995), Die internationale Wettbewerbsfahigkeit einer Voppswirschaft. Deutsches Institut fur Wirtschaftsforschung, Vierteljahrshefte zur Wirtschaftsforschung 2/1995 (Schwerpunktheft Internationale Wettbewerbsfahigkeit), Dunker and Humblot, Berlin, pp. 169-183.

Ulengin, F., Ulengin, B., Onsel, S., (2002), A power-based measurement approach to specify macroeconomic competitiveness of countries, *Socio-Economic Planning Sciences*, 36, 203-226.

Vincke, P., (1992), *Multicriteria Decision Aid*, John Wiley and Sons Ltd, New York.

Zanakis, S.H., Becerra-Fernandez, I., (2005), Competitiveness of nations: A knowledge discovery examination, *European Journal of Operational Research*, 166, 185-211.

In: Development Economics Research Trends
Editor: Gustavo T. Rocha, pp. 165-171

ISBN 978-1-60456-172-2
© 2008 Nova Science Publishers, Inc.

Chapter 6

GROWTH AND DEVELOPMENT IN THE PACIFIC ISLANDS: AN OVERVIEW OF ISSUES

Biman C. Prasad[1] and Kartick C. Roy[2]
[1]School of Economics, University of South Pacific, Suva, Fiji
[2]School of Economics, University of Queensland, Brisbane, Australia

1. INTRODUCTION

Pacific Island countries (PICs) are a very diverse group with varied culture, traditions and language. In addition, the diversity in the size of their economies presents special challenges for their development. Niue with a population of 1,700 is the smallest and Papua New Guinea with a population of about 5 million is the biggest and with the largest amount of natural resources. Almost all the PICs have in the last decade faced serious economic problems characterized by low levels of economic growth (see table 1.1). Unemployment, poverty and other social problems have been increasing in all these countries. The economic performance of the PICs has generally been weak despite high investment ratios recorded (ADB, 2000). The weak performance is attributed to both lower external demand due to global economic slowdown, and domestic structural problems relating to the small size of the economies, remoteness from the main markets, narrow resources base, political instability, civil unrest, market rigidities, depletion of already limited resources and dominance of the public sector (PIFS, 2002). Over the last six years up to 2004, the PICs have experienced variable but generally low growth rates. From a weighted average growth rate in GDP of 6 per cent in 1999, the GDP growth rate fell to -1 per cent in 2000 and -0.8 per cent in 2001. With a recorded GDP growth rate of 1 per cent in 2002, performance improved in 2003 and 2004 with average growth rates in GDP of 2.6 per cent and 2.7 per cent respectively. In the context of a predicted weaker international economic environment, it is expected that economic growth in the Pacific Region will decline to 2.3 per cent in 2005 (ADB, 2005).

Table 1.1. Growth Rate of GDP (% per year)

PICs	1996	1997	1998	1999	2000	2001	2002	2003	2004	2005*
Average	5.6	-3.4	-1.0	6.6	-1.0	-.08	0.9	2.6	2.7	2.3

Source: ADB Outlook, 2005 Update.
* provisional/estimates.

The challenges facing small island developing states (SIDS) in the Pacific and other regions have been articulated in a number of specific international forums (See for example UN, 2002). The first global conference on the sustainable development of SIDS was held in Barbados in 1994, followed by a call at the World Summit of Sustainable development in Johannesburg in September 2002 for a special conference for a programme of action. The Barbados +10 was held in Mauritius in January 2005. As pointed out by the UN in its Millennium Project (UN, 2005) implementation of the Barbados programme is vital for achieving the millennium development goals (MDG) goals. The Barbados programme was the first intergovernmental policy initiative to integrate the SIDS into the world economy. However, after a decade this has not been implemented due to the lack of external resources and commitments from the developed countries.

Two major global processes bring out the challenges more clearly and urgently for the PICs. The first includes the multilateral trade negotiations under the World Trade Organisation (WTO) and the second is the targets set by the United Nations under the MDG. These challenges therefore have to be considered within the framework of these two processes. It is important for policy makers and politicians to understand these processes more extensively if PICs are to develop policy prescriptions for sustainable development.

2. PROBLEMS AND PROSPECTS FOR GROWTH AND DEVELOPMENT IN THE PICS

Across the Asian Pacific region, the least developed and Pacific island countries remain marginalized, unable to participate fully in the region's dynamism. South Asia, where GDP growth rates have risen dramatically in the last two years, must sustain that growth and translate it into a better quality of life for the poor. Central Asian economies are making good progress, but integration into the wider global economy remains a daunting challenge. In East and South-East Asia, pockets of poverty continue to exist.

Pacific Island countries face many difficult problems as also do many other small economies around the world. For the Pacific Island these include physical disadvantages, remoteness, smallness and dispersion. These characteristics of PICs raise significantly the cost of doing business. As pointed out by Winters and Martin (2004) most small economies have cost of doing business disadvantages which put them in significant difficulties for achieving high levels of economic growth.

The ability of PICs to raise the performance of the services sector remains viable. Tourism development provides a particular opportunity for many them, as the potential for manufacturing in many smaller PICs is very small and limited. While the tropical island nature of the PICs provides better opportunities for tourism, significant investment in the development of infrastructure is needed in many of them to reap the full potential of the tourism industry.

Agriculture remains an important source of income and employment in the majority of the PICs, though investment in this sector needs to be raised significantly. For the bigger Melanesian countries such as Papua New Guinea, Vanuatu, Solomon Islands and Fiji, agriculture remains vital for their economic progress. Unfortunately, as pointed out by Reddy and Duncan (2006), the productivity in agriculture has been declining in the PICs. For the PICs to raise the level of agricultural production, the issue of productivity has to be addressed. Important constraints such as the management of land and the communal nature of property rights provides special challenges for the development of agriculture in the PICs.

Almost all PICs suffer from the lack of appropriate human resources and physical infrastructure. In addition many of the PICs suffer from monopolistic control of the delivery of public utilities. The lack of competition in this area has raised the price of these utilities and is one of the major costs of doing business. This affects the level of investment in these countries. The level and quality of human resources is affected by the quality of primary and secondary education. While many PICs have high enrolment rates in both primary and secondary levels, countries such as Papua New Guinea, Solomon Islands and Vanuatu lag behind. The lack of formal sector employment opportunities for youth in these countries also reduces the demand for primary and secondary education.

The tourism industry makes a significant contribution to many Pacific island economies. Tourism numbers have been increasing steadily in many of the countries, led by Fiji. The prospect for the tourism industry lies in the attractiveness of the PICs including their tropical climate and undisturbed beaches. It also includes a combination of factors, including the growing demand for safe destinations, increased marketing and increased air capacity and the entry of low-cost carriers. However, this is an industry that is also most vulnerable to political instability and natural disasters, and the threat of terrorism always remains a distant fear. Several of the PICs and most notably Solomon Islands, Fiji and Tonga, have been affected by political instabilities. Fiji has suffered 4 coups in the last twenty years and this has affected its potential to achieve its target of a billion tourists a year.

In addition to the tourism industry, remittances from Pacific Island migrants continue to be an attractive prospect for raising the level of living standards of PICs people. A recent World Bank (2006) report on the Pacific argues strongly for labour mobility and calls for policies to enhance this. It argues that PICs prospects for growth over the years have been elusive and it is increasingly difficult for the 40 per cent of the population who are youths to find employment in their own countries.

3. MDG TARGETS FOR THE PACIFIC ISLANDS

According to the Millennium Project report the following areas will need to be carefully considered if Small Island Developing States (SIDS) such the Pacific Islands are to achieve any of the goals by 2015. These are as follows: (1) Science and Technology. Developing appropriate information and communications technology can help PICs to overcome isolation, and barriers to scale, and to support the development of service based industries like tourism and financial services. PICs will have to use these reforms to move away from primary based industries to more manufacturing and service-based industries. Many of the PICs, however, have monopolistic structures in their communication industry and this keeps costs high and therefore affects the development of other industries. (2) Urban and Rural investment strategies for the Development of Infrastructure. Many of the PICs face serious problems with the infrastructure, such as poor roads, poor airport, sea port facilities and lack of clean water and sanitation. Improvements in these are crucial for attracting investment in key growth industries such as tourism and financial services. PICs would need support for the development of infrastructure- aid for infrastructure must precede aid for trade if trade is to be enhanced; (3) Climate Change and Environmental Management. Extreme climatic conditions and natural disasters impose a significant economic and social costs to PICs and often inhibits development. Appropriate infrastructure for disaster management and risk strategies would be required to mitigate against damages. In this area PICs would need support from developed countries. Many of the PICs have fragile environment and are affected by damage to ecosystems, depletion of fish stocks and coral reefs. They need to put in strategies for proper environmental management. (4) Regional and Public goods; these are important in delivering basic services to the poor. Regional cooperation and integration would and should provide opportunities for these countries to overcome some of the difficulties that may be created by smallness.

4. GLOBAL AND REGIONAL CHALLENGES

Apart from the problem areas noted above there are specific regional concerns, many of which overlap and are concerns in many of the PICs. The Millennium report, for example, identifies the issue of health services and education for the Caribbean region. In terms of health the report points out that HIV prevalence in the Caribbean is second only to Sub-Saharan Africa. The maternal mortality rate remains high, for example reaching 680 deaths per 100,000 births in Haiti. In terms of education, job training and skills development will be a major challenge in view of the erosion of preferences for bananas and textiles in the world markets.

Many of the Pacific Islands countries face similar challenges but national averages in some of these countries mask the disparities between urban and rural areas, and small and big islands within each the countries. The case of Solomon Islands is a good example of the government's inability to provide basic health and education facilities for its people. Investment in education and health is vital for many of the Pacific Island countries if they are to achieve some of the MDG goals.

The second global economic process, which poses difficult challenges but also opportunities for PICs, is the multilateral trade negotiations under the WTO. It is well recognized that international trade can be a powerful driver of economic growth and poverty reduction. It is, however, not a panacea for all economic ills of a country, in particular, if countries fail to adopt complementary policies such as investments in infrastructure, human capital, macroeconomic stability and institutional reforms. The current negotiations under the WTO involve trade in agricultural products, trade in services, non-agricultural market access, rules, trade facilitation, intellectual property (TRIPS Agreement), trade and environment, special and differential treatment and dispute settlement procedures. While all these are important for PICs, the main focus at the Hong Kong Ministerial meeting was on Agriculture, NAMA and Special and Differential treatment and trade in services.

The Monterrey Consensus outlined two areas on which MDG-based international trade policy should focus. The first is that market access and terms of trade should be improved for the poor countries and improving their supply side competitiveness for low-income countries exports through increased investment in the infrastructure such as roads, electricity, ports and trade facilitation.

The first issue that poses serious challenges in the negotiations is the preferential market access and erosion of preferences for PICs. It is well known that PICs are beneficiaries of many varieties of trade preferences, and generally deriving from their relationships with their former colonial powers. Many of the preferences available to PICs are through special programmes such as the Caribbean Basin Initiative, Cariban of Canada or SPARTECA of Australia and New Zealand, and the European Union grants special preferences to many PICs by virtue of Cotonou Partnership Agreement between African, Caribbean and Pacific (ACP) countries and members of the European Union. Some PICs are, however, beneficiaries of preferential agreements under the least developed countries (LDCs) categories. At the first WTO Ministerial Conference in 1996 members agreed on the importance of granting trade preferences to LDCs. This was followed through successive ministerial conferences and the 6[Th] Ministerial Conference in Hong Kong agreed to grant duty free access to LDC exports. Some of the PICs will be beneficiaries of this agreement.

Other preferential access is provided by the US and Japan and some PICs benefit from this as well. In 2000, for example, the US approved the Africa Growth Opportunity Act through which the Generalised System of Preferences (GSP) of the US was expanded to include the range of products including clothing and textiles. Japan also reviewed its GSP in 2000 to provide duty free access to the Japanese market for industrial products from LDCs. The Japanese GSP was further reviewed and extended for another decade until 31 March 2014 and LDCs Kiribati and Tuvalu were added to the list of beneficiaries. In 2003 Japan further improved its GSP and the number of agriculture and fisheries products under duty free and quota free treatment was increased from 300 to 500 items for LDCs.

In March 2001 the EU adopted the "Everything But Arms" (EBA) initiative to provide duty and quota free access to all products but arms and special trade regimes for bananas and sugar until preferences are phased out.[1] Small and Vulnerable economies as a group at the recent Hong Kong Ministerial meeting asked that banana, rice and sugar be brought under the 'sensitive' product category.

The new ACP-EU Cotonou agreement, which superseded the Lome IV Convention provides for an 8-year roll over of the preferences previously granted under the Lome IV, with minor improvements until 2008.

Canada also provides preferences under its GSP programme as well. In January 2003, Canada granted duty free and quota-free access to LDCs, except for dairy, eggs and poultry. Clothing and textile was added in 2003.[2] Australia and New Zealand provide important markets for Pacific SIDS and give duty and quota- free access to LDCs of the Pacific (Kiribati, Samoa, Solomon Islands, Tuvalu and Vanuatu). The South Pacific Regional Trade

---

[1] For Banana the phasing out period is 2002-2006 and for sugar and rice 2006-2009.
[2] For details of Canada's GSP and rules of origin see UNCTAD (2003) " Trade Preferences for LDCs: An early assessment and possible improvements".

and Economic Cooperation Agreement (SPARTECA) is a non-reciprocal agreement providing duty free and unrestricted concessionary access to their markets.

Despite all the preferential treatment granted by the developed countries, the effectiveness of the GSP remains questionable. Studies show that only a handful of countries really benefit from trade preferences.[3] Judging from the experiences of countries such as Fiji, and some of the Caribbean and Indian Ocean countries, it is clear that trade preferences have not been able to encourage investment and generate export diversification; rather, they have to some extent created preference-dependent export and preferential depended efficiencies. This is especially the case for ACP countries under the four Lome Convention and now under the Cotonou Agreement.

What is important now, however, for PICs is how to counter the continuing erosion of trade preferences and policies to integrate their economies into the international economy and reap the benefits of global trading regimes.

Since the creation of the WTO, which is a major force for trade liberalisation, high rates of trade preferences have diminished and further negotiations will eventually mean more erosion and in some case no preferences at all. For example, many countries are now taking disputes to the WTO and these disputes when settled are likely to erode preferences. Some of the disputes are (1) Banana Dispute (2) Sugar Dispute- Brazil and Australia/Thailand and the EU over subsidies in the EU sugar regime (3) The Thailand-Philippines/EU, over margins for preference for canned tuna from Fiji, Mauritius, Papua New Guinea, Fiji and Seychelles; and (4) the current negotiations over the fisheries subsidies under the WTO, could undermine the revenue potential of small island economies, many of them dependent on access fees for their revenue.

The Pacific Plan adopted in 2004 is a result of the review of the state of regionalism by the Pacific Island Leaders in view of new global and regional economic challenges. This plan has been adopted also in recognition of the fact that PIC economic performance has been on the slide for the last 5 years. In addition, poor governance, corruption, political and social instability has put further pressures to re-look at regional cooperation. The plan further puts emphasis on strengthening regional cooperation and promoting sustainable development in the region. The long-term the challenge for PICs is to create capacity to reap the benefits and opportunities that may be available through increasing global economic integration. Many PICs will continue to face significant economic problems in future as they make adjustment to the various pressures of global trading regimes and changing global economic environment. To meet these challenges PICs would have to put more emphasis on raising productivity and improving the governance structures, which remain poor in comparision to economies that have done well. These challenges have also been highlighted in the Pacific 2020 plan, developed by the Australian Government (AusAID, 2006).

In addition, Pacific Island countries have been characterized by increasing political instability, bad governance and corruption. In particular, recent political instability in Tonga, Solomon Islands and Fiji has exposed a fear that the whole region may be politically unstable. This already has serious impacts on tourism, foreign investment and economic growth. PIC policy makers and political leaders have serious choices to make in terms of polices that ought to be pursued to bring economic prosperity to their countries. This will not be an easy

---

[3] See for example Inama (2003).

choice in the current economic and political climate and it may take considerable time for many of them to recover from serious economic decline.

REFERENCES

Asian Development Bank (ADB). (2000) *Development Banking in the Pacific- Experience and Alternatives*, ADB, Manila

Asian Development Bank (ADB). (2005) *Outlook 2005, Publication Highlights*, Oxford University Press

AusAID (2006) *Pacific 2020: Challenges and Opportunities for Growth, Australian Department of Foreign Affairs and Trade:* AusAid: Canberra.

Inama, S. (2003) "Trade Preferences and the World Trade Organization Negotiations on Market Access." *Journal of World Trade,* 37(5): 959–76.

Pacific Islands Forum Secretariat (PIFS). (2002) *Economic Outlook*, Suva (*http://www .forumsec.org.fj)*

Reddy, M and R. Duncan (2006) "Productivity of Pacific Islands Agriculture: Issues and Challenges", *ICFAI Journal of Agricultural Economics*, 3(2):16-31.

UN (2002) "Review of Progress in the Implementation of the Programme of Action for the Sustainable Development of Small Island Developing States", *Report of the Secretary General.* E/CN.17/2004/1. Economic and Social Council, New York.

UNCTAD (2003) "Trade Preferences For Ldcs: An Early Assessment Of Benefits And Possible Improvements." Unctad/ITCD/TSB/2003/8. Geneva.

Winters, A. and Martin, J. (2004) *When Comparative Advantage Is Not Enough:* Business Costs in Small Remote Economies: Centre for Economic Policy Research, London and Centre for Economic Performance, London School of Economics, Department of Economics, University of Sussex, Brighton.

World Bank (2006) *Expanding Job Opportunities for Pacific Islanders Through Labour Mobility at Home and Away,* World Bank: Sydney.

In: Development Economics Research Trends
Editor: Gustavo T. Rocha, pp. 173-196

ISBN 978-1-60456-172-2
© 2008 Nova Science Publishers, Inc.

Chapter 7

THE DIFFERENTIAL IMPACT OF THE ECONOMIC CRISIS ON THAILAND, INDONESIA AND SOUTH KOREA

Chung Sang-Hwa

Institute of East and West Studies, Yonsei University, Korea

INTRODUCTION

Korea began the process of industrialisation in the late 1960s, followed by Thailand and Indonesia in the mid-1970s. Despite variations in resource endowments, all three countries had recorded such impressive records of industrialisation[1] that international society loudly applauded their economic successes. In the late 1990s, however, the Asian economic crisis had entered a totally new phase, spawned by the July 1997 foreign currency crisis in Thailand. 'Currency crisis', defined as a large drop in the value of currency in a short period of time, had spread to Southeast Asia, and eventually reached Korea. Among the victims, Thailand, Indonesia and South Korea (hereafter Korea) asked the International Monetary Fund (IMF) for rescue loans, but Malaysia, which also had been hard hit by the crisis, closed its foreign exchange market instead of requesting the IMF for help.

The three Greater East Asian countries had several characteristics in common when they encountered economic crisis: they relied on trade in the process of economic development; enjoyed high levels of liquidity; had recently introduced financial liberalisation; and had opaque corporate and banking systems.[2] After they accepted the IMF stabilisation programs, they also faced such problems together as the precipitate decline of currency value, the instability of financial sectors, market contractions, decreases in investment, and increases in unemployment. As of early 2001, the economic crisis appears to be contained in Korea, but it

---

[1] Korea had poor natural resources, but it could develop its economy thanks to skilled manpower and the effective governmental policies of the time. Indonesia and Thailand had rich natural endowments and could invite generous foreign investments to encourage speedy industrialisation.

[2] However, it is also true that each country had its own political and economic specificities as will be discussed later in detail.

still scratches Indonesia with its fingernails, and Thailand is located somewhere between the two.

Although there has been much research on the Asian economic crises, many issues still remain unclear and unanswered. Were the crises unavoidable? What was the decisive cause(s) of the foreign exchange crises? Were the IMF interventions adequate? What were the political and economic consequences of the crises? Should and can Asian countries reform their political and economic management styles? Which international political economy approach, for example, the interdependence school, neomercantilism, or structuralism, more adequately explains the crises?

This analysis examines the economic crises of Indonesia, Thailand and Korea in order to understand better their causes, processes and consequences. A comparative study has an advantage in that it clarifies the issue by contrasting similarities and differences. In the next section, the pre-crisis political and economic developments are compared. The following section explores the causes of the three countries' economic crises. Then, IMF programs and each country's reform efforts, and the consequences of the economic crises, are surveyed. The last section critically assesses the nature of the Asian economic crises based on the discussions of the previous parts, and presents theoretical and policy implications.

BEFORE THE ECONOMIC CRISES

1. Politics and Economics

Thailand had recorded spectacular economic growth rates since it implemented export-led industrialisation policies in the mid-1970s. Annual growth rates had been over 8 per cent and new buildings had changed the skyline of Bangkok (Table 1). In the early 1990s, the Anand and the first Chuan Governments had pushed on deregulation and liberalisation in order to attract more foreign investment. In 1996, however, an economic slowdown was expected and the Bank of Thailand revised its estimation of GDP growth rates from 8 per cent at the end of 1995 to 6.7 per cent. Exports were inactive and the current deficit was rising (Table 2). The Banharn Government in 1995 and the new Chavalit Government in 1996 could not handle the situation appropriately. Deregulation and financial liberalisation, along with political reforms, had weakened these governments' discretion and power. The fixed exchange rate system could not respond swiftly to the fast-growing trade deficit.

The Thai economy started to show signs of fading in 1996, and by early 1997 GDP growth rates were not as robust as previously. The GDP growth was sluggish in the third quarter of 1996, and recorded a minus growth rate in the first quarter of 1997. While inflation had been modest (between 4.2 per cent and 7.4 per cent) (www.nso.go.kr/cgi-bin/sws_999.cgi 2001),[3] external debt reached at the end of 1996 was US$108.7 billion (about 60 per cent of GDP) where short-term debts accounted for US$47.7 billion (43.9 per cent of the total external debt) (www.bot.or.th/bothomepage/databank/EconData 2001). In 1997, Thai external debt increased further, and so did the proportion of private debt.

---

[3] Developing economies usually have higher rates of inflation than those in developed economies.

Table 1. Gross Domestic Product, Q1 1996 - Q3 2000

Year and Quarter	Thailand (mil. of baht)	Indonesia (bil. of Rp)	S. Korea (bil. of won)
1996			
Q1	1,120,089	122,530	94,533
Q2	1,151,915	128,846	102,169
Q3	1,154,597	136,940	104,870
Q4	1,196,231	144,253	116,907
1997			
Q1	1,159,123	145,801	101,061
Q2	1,168,765	149,406	110,337
Q3	1,181,739	163,252	113,227
Q4	1,230,622	169,252	112,865
1998			
Q1	1,211,955	217,654	107,674
Q2	1,118,301	232,387	107,992
Q3	1,112,595	273,463	108,357
Q4	1,185,580	266,108	120,344
1999			
Q1	1,162,112	281,052	107,797
Q2	1,095,676	279,712	116,412
Q3	1,144,423	277,583	121,847
Q4	1,213,177	281,095	137,722
2000			
Q1	1,229,472	301,929	121,240
Q2	1,197,668	317,604	126,123
Q3	1,226,205	329,279	130,426

Data: Indonesia - www.bi.go.id/bank_indonesia2 (2001);
Thailand – www.bot.or.th /bothomepage/databank/EconData (2001);
S. Korea – www.nso.go.kr/cgi-bin/sws_999.cgi (2001).

The government and the central bank failed to control the excessive borrowings of private financial institutions (Punyaratabandhu 1998, 162).[4] In July, the Thai government adopted a floating exchange system, but foreign investors competed to withdraw their money from the Thai market. The popularity of the Chavalit Government had dropped considerably. In the same month the cornered government asked for a Stand-by Credit Arrangement from IMF.

Until mid-1997, Indonesia under Suharto had healthier macroeconomic indicators than Thailand and Korea. GDP had grown steadily (Table 1) and inflation had been contained under 10 per cent (www.nso.go.kr/cgi-bin/sws_999.cgi 2001). Although current account was in deficit, the trade balance was positive (Table 2). Also, Indonesian external debt had been slightly decreasing in 1996 and in early 1997, from US$64 billion to US$56 billion (about 25 per cent of GDP) (www.bi.go.id/bank_indonesia2 2001). However, the New Order had been

---

[4] The Bangkok International Banking Facility, established in 1993 by the central bank, played an intermediary role between foreign lenders and private Thai corporations (Punyaratabandhu 1998, 163).

eroding the soundness of the Indonesian economy. Mostly Chinese private banks had been spawned by the 1988 deregulation, and many of them had connections with Suharto's family and friends. Foreign investments were wasted in support of prestige national projects such as the construction of a bridge to Malaysia and the tallest building in Jakarta (Bird 1998, 172).

Before the crisis, Bank Indonesia had set the rupiah's exchange rates to be depreciated 4-5 per cent annually. This 'managed' floating foreign exchange system was doomed to collapse when international funds massively flowed out, as occurred in Thailand, and the rupiah was depreciated by 9 per cent in August. The government further eased the 49 per cent limitation of foreign investors' stakes in corporations for holding foreign capital, but even this could not compensate for the short-term borrowings amounting to US$33 billion. In November, the Indonesian government and the IMF agreed on a US$38 billion package loan.

Korea was economically different from Indonesia and Thailand.[5] It was a member of the OECD and the eleventh largest economy in the world, and its per capita income was US$13,269 in 1995.[6] The history of Korea's economic development also had been considerably more seasoned than those of Thailand and Indonesia.

Table 2. National Account Balance / Trade Balance (millions of US$), Q1 1996 - Q2 2000

Year/Quarter	Thailand	Indonesia	S. Korea
1996			
Q1	-3,420 / -2,741	-2,034 / 1,166	-4,358 / -2,383
Q2	-4,888 / -3,032	-2,564 / 910	-5,127 / -3,125
Q3	-3,628 / -2,154	-2,111 / 1,343	-7,249 / -5,528
Q4	-2,756 / -1,561	-954 / 2,529	-6,272 / -3,931
1997			
Q1	-2,098 / -1,492	-2,192 / 1,438	-7,353 / -5,402
Q2	-3,134 / -1,413	-1,103 / 3,482	-2,723 / -806
Q3	-696 / 705	-1,393 / 2,176	-2,053 / -27
Q4	2,907 / 3,773	-201 / 2,979	3,962 / 3,055
1998			
Q1	4,183 / 4,100	1,001 / 4,821	10,712 / 9,717
Q2	2,799 / 3,633	669 / 4,971	11,007 / 11,458
Q3	3,406 / 4,148	1,682 / 5,100	9,745 / 10,596
Q4	3,854 / 4,357	744 / 3,537	8,901 / 9,856
1999			
Q1	3,954 / 3,671	1,512 / 4,039	6,057 / 6,770
Q2	2,220 / 3,274	852 / 4,457	6,146 / 7,902
Q3	3,003 / 3,597	1,886 / 6,344	6,597 / 6,923
Q4	3,251 / 3,471	1,535 / 5,804	5,676 / 6,776
2000			
Q1	3,188 / 3,350	1,898 / 6,264	-
Q2	1,484 / 2,408	-	-

Data: www.nso.go.kr/cgi-bin/sws_999.cgi (2001).

---

[5] Korea was a creditor and an investor in Southeast Asia.

[6] When the IMF prepared the draft of its conditionality, the IMF, the US Treasury, Wall Street and major European bankers, as well as the American Chamber of Commerce in Korea, acted in coordination. The IMF introduced a new loan system for Korea, the Supplemental Reserve Facility, in order to circumvent the quarter option. Korea received a rescue loan that was 20-fold larger than its quarter (Focus on the Global South and CAFOD 1998, 54-56).

Moreover, the country's development was mainly owing to the internal savings gained from export, although foreign capital had had its share. Korean GDP growth was set back in early 1997 (Table 1), but not many seriously worried about it because macroeconomic indicators such as inflation, the unemployment rate, and fiscal balance appeared to be sound.[7] The foreign currency market had maintained stability until October 1997, despite the Southeast Asian countries' foreign currency crises.

However, several interrelated factors had eroded the robustness of the Korean economy. First of all, trade had been under continuous stress in the 1990s. The US, suspecting Korea to be another Japan, had pressed heavily on the Korean government to reduce its trade surplus. In 1992, Korea started to record a trade deficit with the US.[8] Meanwhile, other East Asian countries, notably China, had emerged as competitors in international markets. Thanks to the democratisation in the latter half of the 1980s, labour unions and strikes had appeared, and wages had increased at unprecedented levels. In the presence of deteriorating businesses, Korean corporate owners tried in 1996 to trim their sizes by legalising lay-offs. However, the relevant bill could not pass the legislature because of strong opposition from both the unions and the opposition party. Korean companies were obliged to rely on borrowing to cope with decreasing profits.[9] Taking advantage of the recently introduced liberalisation and deregulation,[10] financial institutions, especially the newly established secondary (non-bank) financial institutions, competitively invited short-term loans from foreign financial institutions.[11] The result was growing national debt; external debt had increased from US$127.5 billion in 1995 to US$163.5 billion (about 32 per cent of GDP) in 1996.

Making things worse, the ratio of short-term borrowing in total foreign debt had been increasing and rose to 59 per cent at the end of 1997, while the foreign exchange reserves usable during this period had been reduced to approximately US$33 billion (www.nso.go.kr/cgi-bin/sws_999.cgi 2001). In addition to this, business accounts of major firms and banks were deteriorating due both to the bankruptcies of some big companies like Hanbo and to the foreign exchange crises in Southeast Asian countries.[12] Foreign creditors refused to roll over their loans, and the lame duck of the Kim Young Sam Government prevented Korea from steering clear of economic instability. In December 1997, the won

---

[7] The issue of currencies seems tricky because there is no agreed standard for judging a currency's overvaluation. According to Park (2000), exchange rates of the three countries before the crises were not seriously overvalued if the currency value is analysed based on the evaluation of their purchasing powers. However, if the currency value is tested based on the equilibrium of real exchange rates considered in terms of trade, the difference of productivity between domestic and international industries, capital accounts, and the ratios of governmental expenditure on national product, all three countries had had considerably overvalued currencies for one or two years before the crises.

[8] The US asked for voluntary restrictions on exports such as cars and steel, and strongly protested along with the EU at the Korean government's boycott campaigns against importation of luxury goods.

[9] In early 1997, chaebols like Hanbo, Sammi, and Kia were on the verge of bankruptcy. It is also true that chaebols, the long-served engines of Korean economic development, had sunk into moral hazards; they had neglected efforts in RandD when their businesses were doing well. Many of them, instead, sought to make profits in real estate and portfolio investments.

[10] Korea was not prepared for the opening of its financial market. Without appropriate regulatory, supervisory, and legal provisions, Korea hastily permitted financial liberalisation in order to acquire OECD membership, which was encouraged by the US Treasury Department, on the basis that Korean financial liberalisation would serve US financial interests (Joongang Ilbo 1997).

[11] Korean financial institutions played a dangerous game; they borrowed short-term loans for long-term lending.

[12] In 1997 Korea had lent a total of US$173 million to Thailand, and 34 per cent of export was destined to Southeast Asian countries (Digital Chosunilbo 1997; 1998b).

slumped and foreign currency reserves dropped from US$22.5 billion in October to the value of US$3.9 billion. The Korean government, afraid of a moratorium, urgently requested help from the IMF, and a relief loan of US$55 billion was agreed between the IMF and Korean government on 3 December.

To summarise, macroeconomic statistics reveal that the Thai economy was the worst among the three countries before their crises. Its production looked worse than that of Korea, and, above all, its debt was too heavy compared to its GDP. If we look at just macroeconomic data, it is not easy to understand why Indonesia had fallen into an economic crisis.[13] Above all, the political leaderships of Indonesia and Korea had been without serious threats, although Thai governments had been short-term as usual. However, all three countries' governments could not effectively control their economies because of recent deregulation and liberalisation.

2. International Perspectives

It is not difficult to explain an event after it took place; more illuminating is an examination of what the international society had in mind when the crisis was in progress. The IMF claimed that it had given the Thai government continuous warnings for the 18 months preceding the foreign exchange crisis. However, according to Gohama (1999, 128), it was nothing but an *ex post facto* excuse. Although the Thai financial industry had shown signs of unhealthiness, there is little evidence indicating that the IMF as well as individual governments did in fact realise the formidable seriousness of the problem. On the contrary, the IMF and the World Bank reports continuously praised Thailand as a model country of sound macroeconomic management and open economy. Even foreign debt, the lion's share of which belonged in private hands instead of being the direct responsibility of the government, was regarded as a sign of Thailand's favorable business environment for foreign investors (Focus on the Global South and CAFOD 1998, 12-16). Thailand's 1996 economic inactivity was regarded by the other East Asian governments and international institutions as a sign of tuning up its overheated growth (*Joongang Ilbo* 1997). It is not surprising that Thai governments and financial institutions failed to respond accordingly. Like Thailand, Indonesia was also praised by international financial institutions as a country of successful macroeconomic management, deregulation and liberalisation, as was Korea. Korean president Kim Young Sam argued just several days before his country's asking for rescue that Korea was different from Southeast Asian countries.

In short, it would be reasonable to say that Asian countries and international agents, with the exception of speculative investors, did not take the situation seriously before the crises became apparent.

---

[13] However, this judgement should be weighed against the consideration that there are no clear or agreed standards to judge a country's economic conditions based on statistical figures.

CAUSES OF THE ECONOMIC CRISES

There are many analyses that address the causes of the Asian crises (see Goldstein 1998; Delhaise 1998, 11-32; Yoo and Moon 1999; Warne 1998; Demetriades and Fattough 1999). The causes presented range widely from a simple liquidity bottleneck, a US conspiracy, and so on, to the defects of Confucian state and corporate governances.[14] Now there seems a general agreement that all of these factors are interwoven.

1. Internal Factors

Among the explanations focusing on internal factors, the negativity (or out-of-datedness) of the East Asian development model or Confucian capitalism are prominent. The so-called East Asian development model[15] is characterised by the close formal and informal relationship between government, business and finance sectors. It sometimes means the patriarchal character of governmental leadership and the protection of domestic industries, and, in an extreme expression, crony capitalism where human networks play a much more important role than institutional provisions. Of the three countries, Korea seems to fit the first type, and Suharto's Indonesia can be labelled as the last type. Thailand is located somewhere between the two.

According to critics, the East Asian model of development has produced moral hazards and market inefficiency, and eventually hurt the soundness of the market economy, resulting in the crises (Delhaise 1998, 33-35). The crony relations among governments, banks and corporations have developed weaknesses in financial institutions and inadequacies in bank regulation and supervision (Fischer 1998). Large corporations had relied on lending to fuel their expansions. It is also true that capital for investments had been inefficiently used in real estate and money games leading to bubble economies (Corsetti, et al. 1999; Bird and Milne 1999). However, there is evidence that modifies this argument. First, it is not clear why the problem bulged out at that time. The government-led development strategy had been long embedded in East Asia, and many developmentalists had praised it when the regional economy looked good.[16] Also, the argument *per se* cannot explain why China, where the government was heavily involved in economic management, was immune from crisis when the others were not.

It is not clear, moreover, what proportion of bankers' and businessmen's moral hazards can be explained by the East Asian development model. Their moral hazards may simply be the result of protracted economic growth and generous investment. East Asian business and

---

[14] If we talk about the cause of the 'exchange rate' crises, this can be understood simply as the combined force of the withdrawal of foreign funds and the shortages of an individual country's liquidity. According to a report of the McKinsey consulting company, the Thai exchange rate crisis was initiated by the loan collecting of Japanese, French, and German banks, not by either stock or foreign exchange withdrawing (Digital Chosunilbo 1998a). However, when we say the Asian 'economic' crises, we comprehend them in a broader conceptual framework comprising major macroeconomic instabilities.

[15] For discussion of the Asian model, see Chun (2000).

[16] Many developmentalists recommend developing countries appropriate governmental interventions for their economic development. They argue that it is necessary in the presence of, among other elements, capital shortage (Rosenstein-Rodan 1989).

financial actors with limited experience could be too optimistic about their futures to respect risks. In fact, most East Asian countries except Hong Kong and, controversially, Singapore, have adopted state-led developmental strategies, and the countries devastated by the crises were ironically the model students of deregulation and liberalisation.[17] As we will see later, especially in the case of Indonesia, the negativity of politico-economic coalitions is prominent in the process of coping with the crises, not in the introductory phase of the crises.

Another explanation focusing on internal factors is the argument of governmental failure. It cannot be denied that Thailand, Indonesia and Korea had liberalised and deregulated their financial industries without adequate provision of supervisory and auditing institutions.[18] Although contemporary international financial transactions are very speedy and grow at rates well over those of objective economies, the governments can not avoid being blamed for their negligence. However, as mentioned before, the exchange rate crises and the economic crises should be distinguished from each other. Governmental agents were surely responsible for the occurrences of the exchange rate crises, but the ensuing economic crises included many other factors beyond that.

2. International Factors

If we turn to the explanations focusing on external causes, a series of factors can be named. Firstly, the conspiracy hypothesis claims that the crises were intended by Western economic powers that were feeling threats from the rising Asian economies. According to this argument, the Western interests concerned had agreed to discipline Asian countries to follow 'international' market principles. It is true that the essence of the so-called Washington consensus in the early 1990s was liberalisation and deregulation. Accordingly, one of the major objectives of IMF programs is the realisation of transparent and freer business activities. It is in a sense a compulsory program for making recipient countries assimilate into the US-led global market system. Although this argument seems persuasive, it might be implying a more complicated reasoning than is actually the case.

According to Sachs (1998, 17), the IMF's imposing of conditionality on troubled economies had made the international financial market aware of the looming crises. The IMF had encouraged rather than subdued the crises in East Asia. To normalise the foreign exchange crisis, investors' confidence needed to be restored as soon as possible. However, the investors equipped with electronic transaction instruments respected uncertainty above other indicators. Hedge funds and credit rating companies have also been blamed for contributing to the situation. Although hedge funds did not account for great volumes, they could have played the role of pilot in the international financial market. In Thailand, hedge funds sold baht in May and strengthened the confidence of those concerned about the Thai economic

---

[17] Some may argue that the East Asian developmental state is out of date because corporations now can access the global capital market. However, the Asian crises have shown that states still can exert their wills to tame corporations. Moreover, the crises had stemmed from the lack of governmental regulation, not from regulation. Thus, East Asian states require changes in regulation not the removal of regulation itself.

[18] In Korea the policy confusion had been partly due to the reorganisation of government. In December 1994 the Korean government had merged the Economic Planning Board and the Ministry of Finance into the Board of Finance and Economy, which later in February 1998 changed its name to the Department of Finance and Economy, transferring some rights to other governmental agencies.

crisis (*Economist* 1998a). In a similar vein, the downgrading of country and corporation credits by such international credit rating companies as Moody's Investor's Service and Standard and Poor had driven foreign investors to retreat from risky businesses. Although the empirical causality between the prophecy effect and the economic crisis is not easy to trace, this argument seems logically robust.

Thirdly, some argue that the Asian crises were rooted in the changed international politico-business environment. In the post-Cold War era the US was not sufficiently concerned with protecting its strategic partners. Its hegemony had more interest in maintaining system-level stability than in helping individual needs. When the shocks shattered Asian economies, the victims were individual countries, not the international financial system itself.[19] Since the 1980s, China, with plenty of cheap labour, has risen as a competitor of the other Asian countries in export markets. The growth rates of Chinese exports of goods and services in GDP were 17.5 per cent in 1990 and 24.0 per cent in 1995 respectively, while its GDP growth rates during the equivalent years were each 4.0 per cent and 10.5 per cent (World Bank 2001). What these statistics show is that Chinese exports had grown at a very fast rate. Behind this development lay the 40 per cent depreciation of Chinese currency in 1994. Thai and Indonesian goods, therefore, lost their competitiveness in the presence of cheap Chinese products. Moreover, wages in manufacturing had risen rapidly in Thailand and Indonesia because of an insufficient pool of experienced workers.

The Japanese economic slump has been also blamed. When real estate and stock prices fell after the bursting of the bubble, Japanese financial institutions began to look for new international markets. They had increased their investments in Southeast Asia to a great degree; in 1994, Japan's investment in that region was US$40 billion, but by 1996 it was US$260 billion (*Businesshankyung* 1998, 52). The massive inflow of capital into Southeast Asian countries had raised real estate prices, encouraging speculative investment in real estate that eventually led to the bubble economies. Moreover, the low yen since the mid-1990s had weakened the competitive powers of the other East Asian countries, especially Korea, which had entered a technological upgrading process.[20] In addition to this, the Japanese trade surplus could not efficiently provide liquidity to East Asian countries because of the troubles and backwardness of its own financial institutions. Most trade surplus had been either kept inside Japan or invested in US Treasury bonds.

The boom of the US economy has also been named as a cause of the Asian economic crises. When the exchange rate crises took place, opportunistic international investors were not obliged to remain on risky East Asian capital markets. They regarded the US capital market that had prospered for nearly 10 years as a safe refuge. The economic boom of the US in the latter 1990s has sucked in considerable foreign direct investment (FDI), providing a shelter for the capital flowing from Asia. The total amount of the world FDI had been US$320.4 billion in 1995, and increased to US$884.5 billion in 1999, but during this period the FDI flowing into the US amounted to US$57.8 billion and US$275.5 billion, respectively

---

[19] The socially disadvantaged in the victim countries were hurt most and the international capital investors fared best.

[20] Some argue that Japan should increase its imports from the troubled countries; the US already has trade deficits with East Asian countries, and Europe is busy both preparing for further economic integration and supporting former communist neighbours. Thus Japan, which has close production networks with Southeast Asia, should play a leading role as export market. However, we have to admit that Japan's economy itself has long been in recess.

(World Bank 2001). While the world FDI grew 2.8 times, the US equivalent increased 4.8 times, accounting for 31.1 per cent of the total world FDI in 1999. These international factors can partially, although not completely, explain the occurrence of the crises.

Lastly, the 'contagion effect' needs to be mentioned. When the Thai crisis had become apparent, international investors suspected the soundness of the other East Asian countries' economies. A country's vulnerability to the contagion of economic crisis is conditioned by both the visible similarities of economic behaviour and the proximity of geographical location between the country under crisis and the other countries (Pavan 2000). The strategic behaviour of foreign investors is understandable in two senses. One is rooted in the nature of money games. When selling is the common strategy of players, the faster player is less damaged in stock markets. Even banks competitively collect their lendings to make sure they receive their money back. The other driving factor is uncertainty and risk. If a country's business operations lack transparency, foreign investors cannot secure sufficient information in making decisions and generally choose safety over risk (as was claimed to be the case in East Asia). However, this argument refers to a catalyst factor and cannot explain the crises *per se*.

In brief, there were numerous factors in the Asian economic crises. If we concentrate on actors for the convenience of discussion, three groups seem prominent. The first is the group of international investors who made speculative or strategic choices of withdrawal. The second is the IMF that amplified the exchange crises. The third is the group of Asian governmental officials who neglected their roles in supervising dangerous financial games, and businessmen who engage in them. It was possible to cope with some changes in the international business environment in advance, but not all. The crisis-hit countries could have prepared for the intensification of international competition, but a shock like the sudden depreciation of the Chinese currency was purely, at least in the short run, external. Above all, it is noteworthy that the contemporary international financial market is not a perfect market in that, while demand exists everywhere, supply rests with the limited number of wealthy countries' financial institutions and funds (see Radelet and Sachs 1998, 70-71). This oligopolistic supplier market can be unstable in the short run and the occasional instability can hurt individual economies seriously, although it may seek an equilibrium in the long run.

COPING WITH THE ECONOMIC CRISES

1. IMF Conditionalities

IMF conditionality prescribes in general fiscal balance, price stability, restructuring of corporate governance, and free trade and capital/foreign exchange transactions. While these neoliberal prescriptions have positive effects in augmenting the transparency of economic activities and market efficiency, they may bring about unemployment, tax increases, and high interest rates (Choi 1999). However, the recipient countries that desperately need IMF money usually cannot make their own voices heard in arranging the loan conditions.

In Thailand, the Chavalit Government was replaced in early November 1997 by the Chuan-led coalition government on the excuse of its failure to handle economic disturbances. Although the new cabinet was not a cohesive body, Thai economic ministers could devote themselves to implementing IMF-recommended programs. Indonesia under Suharto admitted the IMF's assistance reluctantly, unlike Thailand and Korea. To this old dictator, Indonesia was a regional hegemony and a big country in terms of population and natural resources. The conflict between the IMF and Suharto, however, had caused enormous pain to the Indonesian people. Post-IMF Indonesia had fallen into confusion; Suharto's health was in doubt; his family and ministers had continued their old-style practices; and the IMF was embarrassed in the presence of the discrepancies between governmental announcements and actions. Later on, Indonesia had to negotiate with the IMF twice to gain the relief loans.

Although President Kim Dae Jung's party was not the first major party in the National Assembly, he could concentrate on rebuilding Korea's economy thanks to his coalition with the third party. The opposition party, the former government party responsible for the economic crisis, could not influence the new government at its disposal. Kim, who was elected just before the occurrence of the crisis, managed to implement the IMF package consistently.

The total amount of the rescue loans agreed to be given to Thailand was US$17.2 billion, and the equivalents to Indonesia and Korea were US$42.3 and US$58.4 billion, respectively (Gohama 1999, 122). Although the IMF was the main donor, the World Bank, the Asian Development Bank, and individual countries also contributed to these funds. Despite the IMF's announcements of rescue, there had been a continuous exodus of foreign investment from all three countries. As the Fund later painfully admitted, Thai, Indonesian and Korean markets failed to regain foreign investors' confidence.

It has been said that the IMF committed some critical mistakes in the early phase of the crises (Madrick 1998). The first was tight monetary policy, that is, maintaining high interest rates in the framework of a floating exchange system. In the three countries, the sharp increases in interest rates were associated with the flight, not holding or invitation, of foreign investments. Investors suspected that higher levels of interest rates would bring about the bankruptcy of companies. As a result, risk levels in these countries had increased, and speculative investors had turned their faces away (Basurto and Ghosh 2000).[21] Moreover, even if interest rates were set at high levels, they could not invite foreign investments if the levels were not high enough to compensate the decrease in exchange rate.[22]

It is conventionally believed that an external impact or shock is absorbed in the exchange rate regime under a floating exchange system. However, it did not happen in any of these three countries.[23] The depreciation of their currencies had failed not only to restore market confidence, but also to boost exports. The economies of the three countries, especially Thailand and Korea, are heavily dependent on their exports (about 30 per cent). In the presence of the contracted domestic markets, exports should have led their economic recoveries. Exports, however, were sluggish, at least in the early phase of the crises. The Thai

---

[21] Although there were other factors that conditioned country risk, it cannot be said that this tight monetary policy was irrelevant to the decreasing country risk ratings of Thailand and Indonesia. The Thai foreign currency rating could not recover until early 1999, and that of Indonesia, in late 2000 (www.standardandpoors.com/ratings/sovereigns/index.htm 2001). Korea, however, has increased its equivalent rating ever since the occurrence of the foreign exchange crisis.

[22] If an interest rate increases by 10 per cent and an exchange rate decreases by 10 per cent, there are no offsetting effects from which foreign investors benefit.

[23] Indonesia and Korea had had floating foreign exchange systems before their crises, although the former had 'managed' the system. Thailand changed its foreign exchange system just before the crisis from a managed floating to a floating system.

baht, Indonesian rupiah, and Korean won dropped by about half their value after the crises, but these countries' exports had recorded only one digit rates of increase, unlike that of Mexico in the mid-1990s that recorded over 30 per cent. The currency values of the other competing exporters also dropped, while the prices of imported raw materials and parts increased. Moreover, following the IMF guidelines, the banks of these countries sharply raised interest rates (about 20-30 per cent) and became more prudent in their lending activities in order to meet the international Bank for International Settlements (BIS) standard.[24] One of the main outcomes was a kind of liquidity trap and severe credit crunch. The three Asian countries could not secure the raw materials and parts necessary for their exports because of their foreign currency shortage and domestic credit crunch. What made things worse was that the Asian market had shrunk[25] because of the member countries' tight fiscal policies and high interest rates, and Japan's economic stagnation. The IMF's prescription for recovering trade balance worked in the end, but it owed more to import contraction than to export growth, and above all it led to the costly extension of the economic disaster.

The IMF also made strong requests for the restructuring of corporate governance and bank activities. Many of the Thai, Indonesian and Korean business and financial sectors had high levels of moral hazard from their long associations with the financial and business conglomerates, *chaebols*,[26] which had dominated markets. As mentioned earlier, the IMF imposed the BIS capital ratio on banks, and, in order to maintain their reserve and capital adequacy ratios, banks were very prudential in their lending. As governments guaranteed deposits and investors did not have other viable alternatives, banks could accumulate deposits. However, the high interest rates resulted in a credit crunch, which in turn led to the contraction of business and to the increase in non-performing loans. Although the IMF programs have positively contributed to the transparency of business activities and to the decrease in moral hazards, they had led to business contraction and a tightening of liquidity. After this early post-IMF period, the East Asian governments lowered interest rates but their economies already had deep scars.

What were urgently needed in troubled Thailand, Indonesia and Korea were not austerity programs but agreeable expansionist policies that would have made up for the decreases in foreign investment. The government finances of the three countries had been healthy before the crises. The tight fiscal policies 'recommended' by the IMF in the early stage of the foreign exchange crises had driven these countries near to a state of economic depression. The fiscal adjustment requested by the IMF was 3 per cent of GDP for Thailand, 1 per cent for Indonesia, and 1.5 per cent for Korea, reflecting the sizes of their current account deficits (Fischer 1998). The IMF later agreed to ease the tightness of the targets but they had badly hurt the economies already.

---

[24] The Bank of International Settlements is located in Switzerland. Established after the First World War to take care of German reparation, the bank now mainly deals with European central banks' foreign currency exchanges. The bank proposed in 1988 an international standard of banks' capital ratio (the BIS standard) in order to cope with risk.

[25] The Asian market explains about 30-40 per cent of the total exports of Indonesia, Thailand and Korea (Lee 1998).

[26] The US and other developed countries worried about the Korean chaebols' aggressive building of semi-conductors, steel, and car producing facilities.

2. Post-IMF Intervention Development

Since the first half of 1999 the three East Asian countries have shown healthier economic indicators than right after the crises. However, the improvements of these indicators are mainly due to such Keynesian credit creations as the expansion of fiscal expenditure, generous monetary policies, and international rescue funds. Their real economies have not recovered fully to the pre-crises level. Although the trade balances of the three countries have been positive (Table 2), such surpluses were, as previously mentioned, owed more to the decrease in imports than to the increases in export.

The Thai GDP has recovered since the latter half of 1999 (Table 1). Inflation also has been reduced from the mid-1998 double digits to lower one-digit levels since early 1999. The exchange rate, which plunged by 77 per cent in December 1997, has become stable in the range of around Bt40 per US$1 since the latter half of 1998. As the Thai economy has become healthy, so has its stock market. The Stock Market Exchange of Thailand (SET) increased by 29.8 per cent in mid-June 1999 (*Hanguk Ilbo* 1999). In 1999, the Bank of Thailand, the Ministry of Finance, the National Economic and Social Development Board, and international agencies such as the World Bank and the IMF agreed that the Thai economy has recovered steadily, although slowly (Bowornwathana 2000, 88-89). Although Thai businesses have shown clear signs of recovery since the latter half of 1999, thanks to the improvements in consumption, manufacturing output, export (cars and electronics), and construction, the country still has a huge sum of bad loans. The ratio of non-performing loans to the total bank loans was over 46 per cent in the first half of 1999 (*Far Eastern Economic Review* 1999, 63). Thus, the clearance of bank debts has become an urgent agenda for the Thai government.

Unlike the situation in Thailand, the Indonesian economy has taken a jagged way. It was only since late 1999 that Indonesia has shown signs of the restoration of economic stability. Indonesia was hit worse by the crisis than Korea or Thailand. Right after the crisis of 1997, the Indonesian rupiah plunged to Rp5,000 per US$1; the stock market index dropped from 734 to 335; inflation recorded double digits; and numerous small companies in Java closed their doors (Bird 1998, 175). In November 1997, Indonesia closed 16 private banks by the direction of the IMF,[27] but the closure of banks made people rush to withdraw their deposits, and Chinese capital started flying out to Singapore and Hong Kong looking for safe refuge. The Indonesian financial crisis had deepened, and the internal and international confidence in the Indonesian economy had weakened. Thus, in January 1998, the value of the rupiah dropped further to Rp11,200 per US$1. Of the 282 companies listed in the stock market, 260 were put into a state of default. The inconsistent attitudes of Suharto towards reform had made things worse. Sometimes he cooperated with, but sometimes resisted, the IMF. The Fund detailed the dismantling of the cartel, monopoly, and preferential treatment, and the cancellation of national projects where Suharto and his family had their vested interests (*Economist* 1998b).

In early 1998, unlike its Thai and Korean equivalents, the Indonesian financial system had not yet restored stability. As living expenses went up (inflation had increased by 250-500

---

[27] Also, four national banks were merged into one.

per cent since July 1997),[28] attacks on ethnic Chinese and other social disturbances proliferated. In May, riots and violent demonstrations by not only students, but also by the middle class, took place. The sudden rise in food prices further led to the paralysis of food trading because many decided to secure foodstuffs at home. Importers could not fulfil their jobs because foreign banks refused to issue letters of credit, and the prices of importing goods were doubled or trebled. The exchange rate plunged beyond Rp10,000 per US$1, even lower than that of the foreign exchange crisis period in 1997. The central bank raised interest rates by 58 per cent making it impossible for many borrowers to pay back their interest. The number of unemployed reached around 8 million in May. Eventually the government dispatched soldiers to control the social disturbances. The then president Habibi and the IMF, realising the seriousness of the Indonesian economic situation, agreed with the third revision of the original IMF program. As a result, fiscal tightness was eased and macroeconomic targets were rearranged.[29]

The Indonesian GDP has shown signs of recovery since the end of 1999 (Table 1). From that time on, official inflation also declined considerably to less than 2 per cent, but it has increased again to more than 5 per cent since August 2000 (www.nso.go.kr/cgi-bin/sws_999.cgi 2001). The exchange rate had become stable since October 1998 at less than Rp9,000 per US$1, but has slightly increased again since May 2000 (www.nso.go.kr/cgi-bin/sws-999.cgi 2001). Also, the Indonesian composite stock price index rebounded in the latter half of 1999 but has dropped again since May 2000 (www.bi.go.id/bank_indonesia2 2001). Indonesian macroeconomic indicators such as inflation, exchange rate, and stock index, have deteriorated since the latter half of 2000, albeit not as seriously as before. The leadership crisis of Wahid is named as one of the main reasons.[30]

The recovery of the Korean economy has been relatively smooth compared to those of Thailand and Indonesia. The foreign currency reserve increased to US$30 billion in May 1998, US$64.3 billion in October 1999, and to over US$90 billion in 2000. International investors have started to reinvest in Korea since 1998. Exchange rates have been stable from the end of 1998 at under 1,300 won per US$1. GDP, National Account and the Balance of Trade all have shown robust signs of improvement (Tables 1 and 2). In 1999, some even worried about the possibility of business overheating. The recovery was owed largely to the increase in exports, thanks to the robust US economy and to the government's pump-priming policies. Consumption and major internal businesses like construction, however, were not yet so active. In 1999, the investments in manufacturing machines and equipment reached only 77 per cent of the pre-crisis level. Korea then encountered, in the latter half of 2000, another, although less serious, economic setback when the stock market deteriorated and the Daewoo, the then third greatest *chaebol*, became insolvent. As a result, the exchange rate increased to

---

[28] The IMF asked for the dismantling of the Bulog, a monopolistic importing organisation aided by the government and responsible for providing food such as rice, sugar, cooking oil, and the like at lower prices than international levels. This led to an abrupt rise in cost of basic necessities.

[29] They agreed to lower their expectations as follows: GDP growth rate, from -5 per cent to over -10 per cent; inflation, from 45 per cent to 80 per cent; and the end-year exchange rate, from Rp6,000 to Rp10,000 per US$1 (Ko 1998, 119).

[30] On Wahid's announcement in spring 2000 of the legalisation of the communist party, Islamic parties threatened to leave the coalition government. In spring, Indonesia also suffered from the independence movements of Sulawesi and Aceh.

about 1,300 won per US$1 in early 2001 but there have been no apparent signs of serious economic setback.

Although Thailand and Korea have suffered from the crises, Indonesia has been most damaged of the three. In Indonesia, politics and economics have amplified each other's negativities. Political leadership has been unstable, and Indonesian business activities, which have long been explained by human networks rather than market principles, have been in turmoil. The Indonesian government also traditionally has been involved in the country's resource allocation to a greater degree than Thai and Korean governments. Indonesian society experienced much greater social disintegration than the other two countries. These factors together have aggravated the country's efforts to restore economic stability, and distorted the effects of reform programs (*Far Eastern Economic Review* 1999).

CONSEQUENCES OF THE ECONOMIC CRISES

1. Political Aspects

Thai, Indonesian and Korean governments all launched campaigns against corruption, clientism and cronyism in order to enhance efficiency and invite foreign investment. It has been said that their crises in part had stemmed from the opaque relationship between political and business sectors. As a byproduct of the economic crises, these countries could in some degree promote political development.

However, behind this façade, the political developments of individual countries show divergent paths. While the Korean political situation has been relatively stable compared to Thailand and Indonesia, the latter two countries' political situations have not settled down. The Thai general election of 6 January 2001, the first small-district election in Thai history, and the re-election of 26 January (held because 109 of those elected were nullified on the accusation of dishonest campaigns by the newly established Election Commission), showed enormous evidence of electoral irregularities, as did the 1998 Senate election. Apparent vote-buying and even bloody shootings contaminated the elections. The leader of the Thai Rak Thai (TRT, Thai Love Thai) party and a telecommunications tycoon, Thaksin Shinawatra, could secure the support of more than half of the 500-member Lower House. However, Thaksin himself is still under the investigation of the National Anti-Corruption Commission because of his intentional omission of millions of US dollars worth of stocks when he was inaugurated as deputy Prime Minister in 1997. His commitment to writing off farmers' and banks' debts would also be a political burden in the future. Further, one major reason for the defeat of the Chuan-led Democratic Party was the popular criticism of his government's selling-off of national banks and companies to foreigners. In order to perform economic reform successfully, Thaksin needs to convert the Thai people's nationalism to positive means of economic recovery. If he fails to handle it (and returns to protectionism), Thailand may invite further trouble.

Indonesia has experienced political instability ever since the crisis. Because of this political, and thus social, instability, Indonesia could not attract its previous levels of tourism, despite its depreciation of currency, although traditionally it has been a famous sightseeing country. In 1997, the number of tourists to Indonesia was 5.2 million, but it dropped to 4.6

million in 1998 and to 4.7 million in 1999 (www.bps.go.is/statbysector/tourism 2001). Suharto, whose 32 years' dictatorship[31] had been blamed for the economic crisis, stepped down on 21 May 1998, leaving his country near a state of default. Habibi, the then Vice-President, replaced Suharto, but gave his position to Wahid in October 1999. Wahid's democratisation programs (such as the legalisation of the communist party) have provoked internal disputes in his government. As a coalition, Wahid's government could not exert its power effectively, and, as a byproduct of democratisation, some Indonesian provinces have asked for their independence. Moreover, Wahid himself has been suspected of embezzlement, and the powerful military and students still have strong voices in Indonesian politics. In early 2001, street demonstrations both for and against Wahid have covered the front pages of the press, and Wahid's cabinet has continued to experience internal disputes.

Korea has been under the leadership of President Kim Dae Jung from the crisis until now. Although there was a general election in 2000, the political landscape of Korea has changed little. What has been lucky for Korea is its relative political stability compared to the other two countries after their crises.

In brief, the crisis has changed government in Thailand, and a more nationalistic and, in a sense, populist Thaksin and his party replaced the old coalition government. Indonesian politics has been beleaguered by government change and instability, troubling its economics and shaking its role as the leader of ASEAN. The present Korean government that took its power right after the crisis has managed to get along with economic difficulty.

2. Economic Aspects

The three countries have partially trimmed their economies. In Thailand, 56 of the total of 89 financial companies closed permanently because of bad loans. In Indonesia and Korea, 16 and 5 commercial banks were closed, respectively. In Thailand and Korea, corporate restructuring has proceeded in some degree, and parts of non-core businesses have been sold off through asset auctions aimed at lowering debt. Also, many Chinese family business networks in Thailand have disintegrated.

In Korea, many *chaebols*, such as Daewoo, Kia, Donga and Hanla, have disappeared. Although some bigger *chaebols* regarded their groups as too big (and thus too important to the economy) to be discarded, the Daewoo Group, the then third biggest conglomerate, could not continue its existence. The Daewoo case appeared to show that, if *chaebols* refuse to change their old-style business practices, they would, without exception, be restructured.[32] In August 1999 President Kim reconfirmed his government's will to reform corporate governance in order to enhance transparency. Regulations imposed on *chaebols* include the prohibition of cross-share holding, unfair internal transactions, and mutual assurance of payment. Mandatory framing of combined (consolidated) balance sheets has been codified also. As a result, the transparency of business has been enhanced considerably, and the financial soundness of the *chaebols* has become robust at the level of an approximately 200

---

[31] Suharto had made political parties powerless by the forcible merging of opposite parties and by organising a de facto ruling party, Golkar (a coalition of vocational representatives). Moreover, all parties had to adopt Pancasila (nationalism, democracy, internationalism, socialism, and monotheism) as their party ideology.

per cent debt-equity ratio. However, this record of Korean restructuring should not be exaggerated. Many corporations had been marginal before their bankruptcy, and restructuring has been more successful in promise than in action.

The ratio of short-term loans in the total debt has significantly fallen in all three countries. In Thailand, it dropped from US$44.1 billion in 1995 to US$23.4 billion in 1999 (World Bank 2001). The equivalent figures for Indonesia and Korea are each from US$26.0 billion to US$20.0 billion, and from US$46.6 billion to US$34.7 billion (World Bank 2001). All countries have introduced safeguard systems and early warning systems. For example, in Korea, the Fair Trade Commission and the Financial Supervisory Service were established in 1999 for the supervision, examination and enforcement of the business activities of financial institutions.

Among the three East Asian countries, the Thai FDI had fallen from US$2.4 billion in 1990 to US$2.1 billion in 1995, but recovered to US$6.2 billion in 1999 (World Bank 2001). Korea has shown a continuous increase in inviting FDI after its foreign exchange crisis; from US$0.8 billion in 1990, to US$1.8 billion in 1995, and to US$9.3 billion in 1999 (World Bank 2001). Unlike these two countries, Indonesian FDI has dropped from US$4.3 billion in 1995 to US$2.8 billion in 1999 (World Bank 2001). This difference in inviting FDI is the reflection of the country's difference in economic recovery.

Certainly there have been negative effects of the crises. Public debt has increased in the East Asian countries because their governments have pursued expansionist fiscal policies during the last two or so years for the purpose of stimulating their economies. While tax collection, which may contract business again, cannot be activated, governmental expenditures either for bailing out troubled major corporations (Korea) or for supporting public corporations and activities (Thailand and Indonesia) have increased considerably.

In addition to this, the Thai external debt recorded in 1999 was US$94.3 billion, and it still cast a murky prospect on Thai economic recovery considering its GDP (US$124.4 billion in 1999) (World Bank 2001). The external debt is also too great considering its GDP. As of 1999, the external debt is US$149.7 billion, whereas that of GDP is US$142.5 billion (World Bank 2001). Korean external debt in 1999 was US$124.3 billion, a little over one fourth of its GDP (US$406.9 billion) (World Bank 2001). This external debt is a considerable amount, even if it indicates a much better performance than exists in Thailand and Indonesia, and the country can avoid foreign exchange crisis thanks to its provision of over US$90 billion foreign reserve.

There have been growing numbers of foreign investors in the economies of these countries, especially in their stock markets. After the crises foreign investors could increase their shares in many business and financial institutions when entry restrictions were lifted. Foreign hands took over some of the major banking and finance industries.[33] Also, much real estate has been sold to foreign investors.

The ratios of trade in national production have increased in all three countries, helping the recovery of their economies (World Bank 2001). The world averages of the trade ratio to GDP have been 19.4 per cent in 1990, 21.4 per cent in 1995, and 26.0 per cent in 1999 (World Bank 2001). However, the equivalent ratios of Thailand's trade are 37.9 per cent in

---

[32] However, the relief of the near bankrupt Hyundai construction company in spring 2001 shows that there can be an exception.

[33] For the Thai case, see Bowornwathana (2000, 18).

1990, 45.2 per cent in 1995, and 51.1 per cent in 1999, and those of Korea, 29.7 per cent in 1990, 31.0 per cent in 1995, and 38.7 per cent in 1999, respectively (World Bank 2001). Indonesian trade ratios in GDP have shown relatively sluggish growth rates (24.5 per cent in 1990, 27.0 per cent in 1995, and 30.9 per cent in 1999) compared to those of Thailand and Korea, reflecting its economic instability. Although trade *per se* can not be assumed to have negative effects on the economy, and it is true that trade growth is an international phenomenon, these figures imply that the three countries' economies have become increasingly sensitive to outside influences, and other outer shocks could interfere with policy efforts to revive their troubled economies. For firm economic restoration, domestic consumption needs to be revived.

There have been resistances and delays in reforming as well.[34] In Thailand, where many cabinet members are former businessmen, politicians and other vested interests have slowed the pace of restructuring (*Far Eastern Economic Review* 2000, 76-79). One typical example is Siam Cement, the largest Thai business group which is also partially owned by the royal family. The company was funded in the early crisis period by international investors who believed the announcement of restructuring. Many believed that the group could play a role as the model for Thailand's corporate restructuring. However, the group's selling-off of non-core branch companies and slashing of debt seem to have failed to show any progress (*Far Eastern Economic Review* 2000, 81). According to a foreign entrepreneur in Bangkok, Thai companies do not yet quite understand why they should change their managerial practices, which traditionally have stressed total assets and gross outputs, into those emphasising net assets and profits (*Far Eastern Economic Review* 2000, 82). Lack of legal provisions, as well as political interventions, mean that punishment of economic criminals has not been very visible. Moreover, the estimated non-performing loans as of July 1999 are still 46.1 per cent of the total loans (Limskull 2000).

In Indonesia, financial scandals have been more frequent than restructuring stories. The Bank Indonesia, the Ministry of Finance, and even the Indonesian Bank Restructuring Agency (IBRA), which was established after the 1998 banking collapse to assume the function of financial restructuring, have been riddled with scandals (Liddle 2000, 40-41). Also, populist styles of policy have continued, for example, bus fares were frozen and the rice and sugar industries have been protected. Politicians have resumed their interventions in market functioning, too. President Wahid claimed that four large, but financially troubled, Indonesian business groups, the Texmaco Group, Barito Pacific, the Gajah Tungal Group, and the Slaim Group, must be saved in order to keep up their exports (*Far Eastern Economic Review* 2000, 76).[35] Many major companies are still under the influence of a small group of Chinese families who have intimate relationships with politicians. Moreover, Indonesian restructuring has been focused on debt-to-equity swaps, loan extensions, and debt discounts rather than the introduction of new accounting and management systems and corporate culture. In Indonesia corporate restructuring has failed to show visible outcomes.

In Korea, lay-off has turned out to be the first and highest hurdle in the restructuring process. While the cosmetic accounting practice of corporations is finally being wiped out

---

[34] For detail, see Sikorski (1999); Economist (1999).

[35] These groups have accounted about 41.6 per cent of the total amount owed to the Indonesian Bank Restructuring Agency (IBRA). Of major concern, however, is that, rather than being punished, the owners are still controlling their groups without inviting new management partners.

thanks to strengthened auditing, many public corporations are still believed to have excess labour (*Digital Chosunilbo* 2001). The resistance of workers and labour unions against layoff have intensified also. As the term of President Kim Dae Jung will end in 2002, the government will encounter increasingly difficult obstacles.

In brief, the signs of economic recovery vary across countries. While Korea has shown the most robust outcomes of recovery, Indonesia has fared worst, reflecting its political and social instability. What the restructuring efforts in the three countries have revealed in common is that old practices stubbornly remain in place. Moreover, as economic liberalisation proceeds, governments are losing their policy leverages *vis-à-vis* private financial institutions and corporations. Restructuring has a trade-off nature; while the benefit may be given to the society in general, the immediate cost is likely to be borne by certain social groups, especially workers and small investors; and the government enthusiasm for driving restructuring may hurt either democratic or market values. Although restructuring is a worthy pursuit, its structural complexity requires strenuous policy efforts and time.

3. Social Aspects

The crises have yielded enormous impacts on Thai, Indonesian and Korean societies. Because of restructuring and bankruptcy many people had fallen into a state of poverty. In all three countries a considerable proportion of the middle classes has disappeared. In the absence of social safety nets for the unemployed, and of flexible labour markets, lay-offs have brought serious social problems.[36]

The unemployment rates of these countries, however, have shown different patterns. In Thailand, the official unemployment rate at one time reached 10 per cent (3 million), and many unemployed had to go to the countryside where the situation was by no means better than in the cities. However, the unemployment rate has fallen from 4.6 per cent in February 1998 to 3.7 per cent in November 2000 (www.bot.or.th/bothomepage/databank/EconData 2001). In Indonesia, the unemployment rate increased to 10 per cent (20 million) and over 40 per cent of 220 million had been put into a state of absolute poverty (*Chosun Ilbo* 1998a). Even after the initial stage of the crisis, the situation has not improved significantly; even the official data reveals the rise of unemployment from 4.7 per cent in 1997, 5.5 per cent in 1998, to 6.4 per cent in 1999 (www.bps.go.id/statbysector/employ 2001). Thailand and Indonesia have numerous unofficial and provisional labourers, and the official statistics may not represent adequately their abject situations.

In Korea, the income of the middle class (those between the upper 20 per cent and lower 20 per cent) decreased on average by 5.5-5.8 per cent in 1998, and, as of June 1998, 64.9 per cent of Koreans thought they belonged to the lower class while only 34.8 per cent responded that they belong to the middle class (*Chosun Ilbo* 1998b).[37] A year ago those figures were 44.5 per cent and 53.1 per cent, respectively. The unemployment rate reached 6.8 per cent in 1998, and, moreover, among the unemployed, the ratio of the structural unemployed had increased to 20 per cent. In 1998, the real wage considering inflation dropped by 9.3 per cent,

---

[36] Thailand and Indonesia still have traditional sectors. Fortunately, the effects of the crises in the modern sector did not reach into the more remote areas, which consequently avoided significant economic hardship.

[37] For the detailed discussion of the Korean unemployment issue, see Yoon (1998).

while the upper 10 per cent of urban households raised their annual income by 4 per cent thanks to their increased banking and portfolio incomes. But, in the same year, the lower 20 per cent, mainly relying on wage income, had experienced a 17.2 per cent decrease in their incomes.[38] However, the recent data shows an improvement; the unemployment rate has dropped to 6.3 per cent in 1999 and to 4.1 per cent in 2000 (www.nso.go.kr/eindex 2001).

The resistance of the workers in these three countries has been stronger and more effective than before thanks to the rise of their union powers and activities. Korean trade unions, which have developed through the democratisation movements in the 1980s, seem to be much stronger than their Thai and Indonesian counterparts. In Thailand two factors have suppressed labour union movements; one is the segregation of labour by region, gender, age, skill, and the like, and the other, submissive attitudes owing to the Buddhist culture (Yoon 1997, 83-84). Thai civil organisations have initiated many protests and demonstrations for the poor, and union strikes also have increased since the crisis. In Indonesia, thanks to the democratisation pursued by Wahid, trade unions have been spawned and labour movements have expanded since early 1998. Before that, Indonesian trade union movements had been heavily suppressed by the strong authoritarian state. According to a foreign businessman in Indonesia, the lack of experience with labour movements has encouraged the unorganised labour campaigns by workers (*Digital Chosunilbo* 1998b).

Another social issue stemming from the crises is racial conflict. Although Chinese hold economic power both in Thailand and Indonesia, Thai Chinese have had good relationships with the indigenous Thai. Their immigration history can be traced farther than that of Indonesian Chinese, and many of them have been incorporated into the Thai nation. In Indonesia, however, the indigenous Indonesians often have attacked Chinese in the presence of economic difficulties.

Since the economic crises, all three countries have curtailed expenditure on health, education, social development and welfare. Social vices gain secondary consideration in relation to economic recovery in these countries. Poverty, disease, crime and child abuse, all of which have long-term negative effects, have increased enormously. The neglect of these issues may cost them dearly in the future.

4. International Aspects

The East Asian crises reminded the international society of the predominance of the US in the region. Although Japan contributed significant funds to help the three Asian countries, its role has not been so conspicuous.[39] The United States sponsored, either directly or via international organisations, the post-crisis economic management.

While the crises have proceeded, the need for regional cooperation has gained attention. The Asian Monetary Fund (AMF) was proposed by Japan at the annual meeting of the IMF,

---

[38] Although the Korean job market recently has been generous, many of the jobs offered are part-time. It is not surprising that many workers, who have witnessed their discharged colleagues' tragedies, stubbornly resist being dismissed.

[39] Japan provided US$44 billion to help the three troubled Asian countries (Gohama 1999). Kim (1998) argues that Japan's role has been neither enough nor appropriate. Because of its lack of initiative, Japan seemed to fail to gain international respect. However, considering that the total amount given to the three countries was US$117.9 billion, Japan's monetary contribution should be appreciated.

in September 1997, to prevent another crisis and to enhance the region's financial stability.[40] At first the US and China, afraid of lowering their voices and concerned by the rise of Japan's influence,[41] opposed the proposal; later, at the APEC Conference in November 1998, they indicated positive attitudes towards its institutionalisation. In a separate arrangement, Korea, China, Japan and ten ASEAN countries agreed in May 1998 to establish a collective foreign exchange swap system. Already Korea-Japan and Japan-Malaysia had organised reciprocal foreign currency swap systems after the crises.

CONCLUSION - SUMMARY AND POLICY IMPLICATIONS

The East Asian crises, originating in Thailand, spread quickly to other countries. Not many predicted the occurrence of the crises. Among those countries affected by the crises, Thailand, Indonesia and Korea requested IMF rescue loans. These countries had open economic systems heavily reliant on export and foreign investment, and all three countries had weak, underdeveloped financial sectors. Numerous factors, which are to some degree or another inter-related, explain the crises. Although the three countries' foreign exchange crises are unlikely to be repeated (except, perhaps, in Indonesia), the economic crises are not over yet, especially if one considers consumption, investment, and the normalisation of the banking system.

From a theoretical perspective, the development of the Asian crises strongly supports the argument of structuralism rather than liberal or realism traditions. US hegemony fails to provide regional stability, or, at best, it could contain the spread of economic instability beyond the region. Mutual transactions between Western investors and East Asian countries turn out to be structured for the interests of the former. The deeply vulnerable position of the borrowers casts doubt on the universal application of the interdependence thesis. The economic philosophy of neoliberalism and its practical program of globalism appear to downplay the difference in size and strength of transaction partners. Moreover, the beneficiaries of the crises have not been national entities, as the argument of neomercantilism would have it. Although the US Treasury and the IMF have initiated the post-crisis treatments, capital interests, not the states in general, have benefited most. Such structural approaches as Wallerstein's world-system argument (Wallerstein 1974; 1989) and Galtung's international structuralism (Galtung 1971) provide robust explanations of the Asian economic crises.[42] While Western investors, who had long enjoyed lucrative businesses in Asia, were exempted from paying the cost, the socially disadvantaged in the victim countries encountered most of the backwash. Foreign investors could successfully collect their shares from the crises, while many East Asian citizens paid the prices and donor countries' citizens contributed to the funds through their taxes.[43]

---

[40] For a discussion of new international rescue systems, see Wesley (1999); Kumar et al. (2000).

[41] See Feng and Choo (1998).

[42] Although both macrohistoric approaches pay attention to the inequality of international and internal structures, Wallerstein emphasises the exchange structure, while Galtung stresses the actors.

[43] Unlike Latin American foreign currency crises in the early 1980s, foreign investors were exempted from accountability in the East Asian crises.

The conditionality of the IMF propelled the damaged economies into a vicious chain reaction of economic troubles that eventually led to economic contraction. In order to be flexible, the IMF should consider both the particular conditions of individual countries and the long-term stability of the regional economy. Thanks to the effects of the crises themselves as well as the policy prescriptions of the IMF, the three countries could somehow or other tune up their economies to varying degrees. However, the old practices have strongly resisted reform. The crises have had great impact on political and social fields, too. While democratisation has been enhanced to some extent, social problems have been generated by the crises. The most conspicuous costs of reform and restructuring have been the sharp increase in the number of the unemployed and the poor, and the contraction of the middle class. Along with economic difficulties, both class and ethnic conflicts have intensified. The shadow of the crises will long linger in the three countries.

The policy prescriptions of the IMF have centred on securing investment and institutionalising neoliberal economic order, rather than promoting healthy and smooth economic development. The general feature of the Asian economic crises clearly shows that the present international financial system is of advantage to investors rather than to investment recipients.

International financial institutions should take responsibility for their imprudent investments. The amount of international money transacted overnight is known to be more than US$1 trillion. If financial big hands play a game of 'casino' capitalism, small open countries are easily exposed to economic turmoil. Although individual investors and traders are rational, the contemporary international economic system is neither perfect nor rational in nature, considering both the imbalance of power between participants and the high mobility of information and transaction. Foreign exchange crisis can take place in any weak economy, especially in fast developing countries where capital is short, generating serious negative externalities that are very likely to develop into serious financial and economic crises. In order to prevent this inhumane misfortune, both national and international safeguarding arrangements should be introduced.

REFERENCES

Basurto, Gabriela and Atish Ghosh (2000) 'The Interest Rate-Exchange Rate Nexus in the Asian Crisis Countries'. *IMF Working Paper WP/00/19.*

Bird, Judith (1998) 'Indonesia in 1997: The Tinderbox Year'. *Asian Survey* 38: 2.

Bird, Graham and Alistair Milne (1999) 'Miracle to Meltdown: A Pathology of the East Asian Financial Crisis'. *Third World Quarterly* 20: 2.

Bowornwathana, Bidhya (2000) 'Thailand in 1999: A Royal Jubilee, Economic Recovery, and Political Reform'. *Asian Survey* 40: 1.

Businesshankyung (1998) 'Special Report: Asian Economic Crisis (Korean)'. March 3. *Chosun Ilbo* (Korean Newspaper) (1998a) August 14.—— (1998b) September 26.

Choi, Kwang (1999) 'Korean Financial Crisis and Fiscal Policy'. *International Area Review* 2: 2.

Chun, Jin-Hwan (2000) 'East Asian Economic Development and Confucian Tradition'. A Paper at the 8th International Regional Cooperation in Northeast Asia, Cheju, Korea.

Corsetti, Giancarlo, Paolo Pesenti and Nouriel Roubini (1999) 'Paper Tigers? A Model of the Asian Crisis'. *European Economic Review* 43.

Delhaise, Philippe F. (1998) *Asia in Crisis: The Implication of the Banking and Finance Systems*. Singapore: John Wiley and Sons.

Demetriades, O. Panicos, and Bassam A. Fattough (1999) 'The Korean Financial Crisis: Competing Explanations and Policy Lessons for Financial Liberalization'. *International Affairs* 75: 4.

Digital Chosunilbo (Korean Newspaper) (1997) October 1.

—— (1998a) April 3.

—— (1998b) April 10.

—— (2001) March 6.

Economist (1998a) June 13-19. 'A Hitchhiker's Guide to Hedge Funds'.

—— (1998b) January 17-23. 'And Now the Political Fall Out'.

—— (1999) August 21-27. 'On their Feet Again?'

Far Eastern Economic Review (1998) October 15.

—— (1999) August 19.

—— (2000) October 19.

Feng, Zhu and Jaewoo Choo (1998) 'Asian Financial Crisis and East Asian Economic Cooperation: A Chinese View'. *Global Economic Review* 27: 4.

Fischer, Stanley (1998) 'The Asian Crisis, the IMF, and the Japanese Economy'. *www.imf.org/external/np/speeches/1998/040898.htm*. April 8.

Focus on the Global South and CAFOD (1998) *IMF's Taming of Asian Tigers: The Economic Crises of Korea, Thailand, and Indonesia* (Korean). Seoul: Munhwagwagaksa.

Galtung, Johan (1971) 'A Structural Theory of Imperialism'. *Journal of Peace Research* 8: 1.

Gohama, Hirohisa (1999) 'The East Asian Economic Crises and Japan's Cooperation (Korean)'. *Wolganataejiyukdinghyang* 88.

Goldstein, Morris (1998) *International Policy Brief*. Washington, D.C.: Institute for International Economics.

Hanguk Ilbo (Korean Newspaper) (1999) June 9.*Joongang Ilbo* (Korean Newspaper) (1997) March 10.

Kim, Gyu-ryun (1998) 'Financial Crises and Asian International Relations (Korean)'. *Sinasea* 5: 1.

Ko, Woo-sung (1998) 'The Influence of Southeast Asian Politico-Economic Instability on Korea (Korean)'. *Ataefocus* 9.

Kumar, Manmohan S., Paul Masson and Marcus Miller (2000) 'Global Financial Crises: Institutions and Incentives'. *IMF Working Paper WP/00/105*.

Lee, Kyung-Sook (1998) 'The Three Countries' Exports are Less Lively than Expected (Korean)'. *KIET Silmukyngje*.

Liddle, R. William (2000) 'Indonesia: Democracy Restored'. *Asian Survey* 40: 1.

Limskull, Kitti (2000) 'The Financial and Economic Crisis in Thailand: Dynamics of the Crisis-Root and Process'. *Economic Crisis in Southeast Asia and Korea: Its Economic, Social, Political and Cultural Impacts*. Seoul: Tradition and Modernity.

Madrick, Jeff (1998) 'The IMF Approach: The Half-Learned Lessons of History'. *World Policy Journal* 15: 3.

Park, Dae-Geun (2000) 'Looking for the Indicators of Overestimated Exchange Rate during the Asian Foreign Exchange Crisis (Korean)'. *Daedoekyungjejongchaekyongu* 4: 1.

Pavan, Ahluwalia (2000) 'Discriminating Contagion: An Alternative Explanation of Contagious Currency Crisis in Emerging Markets'. *IMF Working Paper WP/00/14.*

Punyaratabandhu, Suchitra (1998) 'Thailand in 1997: Financial Crisis and Constitutional Reform'. *Asian Survey* 38: 2.

Radelet, Steven and Jeffrey D. Sachs (1998) 'The East Asian Financial Crisis: Diagnosis, Remedies, Prospects'. *Brookings Papers on Economic Activity* 1.

Rosenstein-Rodan, Paul N. (1989) 'External Economies and Industrialization'. In Gerald M. Meier, ed., *Leading Issues in Economic Development.* New York: Oxford University Press.

Sachs, Jeffrey (1998) 'The IMF and the Asian Flu'. *The American Prospect* March-April.

Sikorski, Douglas (1999) 'The Financial Crisis in Southeast Asia and Korea: Issues of Political Economy. *Global Economic Review* 28: 1.

Wallerstein, Immanuel M. (1974) *The Modern World System I: Capitalist Agriculture and the Origin of the European World-Economy in the Sixteenth Century.* New York: Academy Press.—— (1989) *The Modern World System III: The Second Era of Great Expansion of the Capitalist World-Economy, 1730-1840s.* New York: Academy Press.

Warne, W. Robert (1998) 'Washington's Perceptions on Korea's Financial Crisis'. *Korea Observer* 29: 3.

Wesley, Michael (1999) 'The Asian Crisis and the Adequacy of Regional Institutions'. *Contemporary Southeast Asia* 21: 1.

World Bank (2001) May 3. 'Country Data'. *www.worldbank.org/data/countrydata.*

Yoo, Jang-Hee and Chul Woo Moon. 'Korean Financial Crisis during the 1997-1998: Causes and Challenges'. *Journal of Asian Economics* 10: 2.

Yoon, Jin-ho (1998) 'IMF Regime and the Unemployment Crisis'. *Korea Focus* 6: 2.

Yoon, Jin-Pyo (1997) 'Changing State-Market Relations: The Case of Thailand (Korean)'. *Dongnamasiayongu* 5.

www.bi.go.id/bank_indonesia2 (2001) February 4.

www.bot.or.th/bothomepage/databank/EconData (2001) Feburuary 4.

www.bps.go.id/statbysector/employ (2001) May 3.

www.bps.go.is/statbysector/tourism (2001) May 3.

www.nso.go.kr/cgi-bin/sws_999.cgi (2001) February 7.

www.nso.go.kr/eindex (2001) May 5.

www.standardand poors.com/ratings/sovereigns/index.htm (2001) January 25.

In: Development Economics Research Trends
Editor: Gustavo T. Rocha, pp. 197-238

ISBN 978-1-60456-172-2
© 2008 Nova Science Publishers, Inc.

Chapter 8

EQUITY MARKETS AND ECONOMIC DEVELOPMENT: WHAT DO WE KNOW?

Thomas Lagoarde-Segot[*,1] *and Brian M. Lucey* [2]

[1]Euromed Marseille Ecole de Management and DEFI, Université de la Méditerranée
[2]School of Business Studies and Institute for International Integration Studies, Trinity College Dublin.

ABSTRACT

The objective of this chapter is to review the transmission mechanisms uniting equity market development and economic growth in developing countries. Overall, conclusions suggest that domestic development and international integration of equity markets have dissociated effects on economic welfare. At the domestic level, equity markets foster the mobilization and allocation of financial resources, and improve corporate governance subject to a satisfactory level of informational efficiency. However, equity market integration lowers the cost of capital, but increases financial vulnerability and exerts a non linear impact on capital flows. We summarize these ambiguous mechanisms in an *'equity market development triangle'* and suggest a few directions for future research.

JEL classification: G11;G12;G15
Keywords: *Equity Markets, Economic Development.*

1. INTRODUCTION

Sixty years after Keynes' demise, the relationship uniting equity markets and economic development is still highly controversial. Countries embarking on financial reforms usually bear two objectives in mind: (a) to raise the level of saving and investment; and (b) to improve the allocation of investment resources in consistency with certain economic and social objectives. Nevertheless, equity market development constitutes a separate component of financial liberalization policies, and its economic impact remains ambiguous.

* Corresponding Author: thomas.lagoarde-segot@euromed-marseille.com. Telephone: +33 (0) 491 827 390.

On the one hand, standard transmission mechanisms include increased resource mobilization, better allocation of capital, and improved corporate governance (Cho, 1986; Stulz, 1999). However, not only are these theoretical arguments under-investigated at the empirical level, but a number of arguments also suggest that policy makers should remain cautious with equity market development. First, equity markets fail to allocate resources to the most desirable uses in the presence of information asymmetries (Stiglitz, 1989; Mayer, 1990). Second, shareholder dominance may disturb the implementation of long-run objectives and the necessary balance between stakeholders, both within the firm and the economy (Jeffers, 2005). Third, capital flow volatility and international financial contagion to emerging markets have underlined the risks associated to equity market integration (Calvo and Mendoza, 2000). These observations have led some economists to argue that equity markets constitute *"costly irrelevances which (developing countries) can ill afford"* (Singh, 1999; Singh & Weiss, 1998). Taken together with certain dissatisfaction with the Washington Consensus policies, this lack of empirical evidence has made criticism of equity markets a cornerstone of the *alter-globalisation* movement[1].

This chapter thus aims to survey a large body of theoretical and empirical literature on equity markets and development in an effort to identify potential lessons for policy making, and to suggest areas for future research. It is structured as follows. The first section reviews the internal effects of capital market reforms in emerging countries. The second section focuses on equity market integration and its associated effects. The third section summarizes our findings by considering the intersection of these analyzes, and the fourth section identifies promising research ideas.

2. Review of Internal Implications

2.1. Mobilization and Allocation of Financial Resources

The pioneering work of Goldsmith (1969), Shaw (1973) and McKinnon (1973) underlined the role of finance in economic development. These authors argued that domestic financial liberalization would lead to higher savings, improved resource allocation and economic growth. However, in their work the emphasis was on the liberalization of the commercial banking system, as opposed to equity markets. Their reasoning was based on the neoclassical assumption of an identity relationship between aggregate investment and aggregate savings, which in turn are positively correlated to interest rates.

To illustrate this point one can suppose a 'financial repression' situation in which interest rates ceilings prevail, so that the interest rate is $r1$ such as $r1 < r^*$, where r^* is the natural equilibrium rate. This interest rate corresponds to a savings rate $S1 < S^*$, which ultimately leads to an investment rate $I1 < I^*$; where I^* and S^* are the equilibrium investment and savings rate, respectively. The direct consequence is that a fraction (I^*-I1) of investment projects cannot be financed. Moreover, credit rationing may also lead banks to minimize risk and allocate savings to projects carrying a lower level of risk. As a consequence, the unsatisfied

---

[1] Over the past ten years, many non-governmental organizations have attempted to provide a 'citizen expertise' on the social and economic consequences financial globalisation. See, for instance, www.attac.org or www.macroscan.com.

investment demand segment (*I*-II*) tends to gather projects with the highest potential returns, i.e. the most socially useful projects. This magnifies the aggregate welfare loss for the economy. By contrast, the increase in interest rates that result from financial liberalization may lead to an improved mobilization and allocation of domestic resources.

However, these initial models of 'financial repression' have been criticized for overlooking the possibility that endogenous constraints in the credit market may constitute obstacles to the allocative efficiency of investment (Stiglitz and Weiss, 1981). In a seminal model, Cho (1986) assumed that banks and equity investors have the same level of information about firms. In addition, information asymmetries in the credit market imply that although individual borrowers can be sorted according to their expected productivities, their degrees of risk are unknown, so that banks cannot identify the individual risk characteristics of firms. As a consequence, lenders aggregate borrowers into groups, and base their decisions on the expected variance in the distribution of risk for each group of borrowers.

In this context, the banking sector's expected return is a function of a fixed interest rate $r*$ and of the default risk. The model further supposes that a group of firms j are innovative and highly productive while a group of firms i are less productive, but have established customer relations with banks. Other things equal, the bank's subjective expected variance in the distribution of the risk of group j should be larger than the other group i. As a consequence, the banks' expected return from lending to group i may be higher than that of lending to group j (i.e., $E\Pi i*\rangle E\Pi j*$), although the expected productivity of the latter is higher than that of the former (i.e., $Ri\langle Rj$). This results in a suboptimal allocation of savings.

However, equity market investors do not take default risk into account, as their expected returns $E\Pi j*$ are equivalent to the project's expected return, i.e. $E\Pi j* = Rj$. In other words, shareholders make their investment decisions based on the comparison of expected productivities, which are known. This allows groups with more risk (such as group j) to obtain financing. Overall, the model suggests that equity market development is a necessary complement to reforms in the banking sector, as it contributes to better resource mobilization in the presence of information assymetries in the credit market (Cho, 1986).

Recent contributions in institutional economics have also highlighted a number of intuitive mechanisms through which market development may positively impact on the allocation of mobilized resources in developing countries. One argument is that banking systems in such countries are often characterized by a high ownership structure resulting in oligopolistic practices. As a consequence, the selection of investment projects based on expected operating results can be disturbed by strategic political interactions between agents, which ultimately results in suboptimal investment decisions and in a weak corporate sector. The poor allocative performance of the bank-based financial structure magnifies the relative advantages of equity markets (Henry and Springborg, 2004).

Other studies have underlined the liquidity–enhancing function of equity markets. For instance, the creation of a domestic stock market in developing countries may provide households with an additional instrument which may better meet their risk preferences and liquidity needs (Dailami and Atkin, 1990). Domestic stock investment may thus constitute an alternative to consumption, the purchase of land and real estate, or the seeking of more profitable investment abroad, and ultimately results in a better mobilization and allocation of savings (Oshikoya and Ogbu, 2003). Similarly, other authors have underlined the role of a large and active secondary market in mitigating the problem of the availability of long-term funds: investors and corporations tend to have conflicting concerns over the optimal degree of liquidity of financial transactions. Investors may indeed prefer high liquidity, whereas corporations need to be assured of long-term credits to match their long term assets. Transactions in the secondary markets may permit the reconciliation of these conflicting concerns and allow new equity issues in the primary markets to be successful. In other words, equity market development may ease the tension between savers' preference for liquidity and entrepreneurs' need for long-term finance (Ndikumana, 2001).

2.2. Corporate Governance

It should also be noted that foreign equity participation may promote further development of the domestic securities market. For instance, Errunza (1999) argued that foreign portfolio investment fosters managerial efficiency. There are five main mechanisms through which stricter governance rules are implemented following foreign equity investment (Stulz, 1999). *First*, firms tapping into foreign capital markets need to minimize agency problems and therefore tend to have an active board of directors that are independent of management. *Second*, international stock issuance requires managers to hire investment bankers. Such bankers have certain responsibilities within global capital markets, and thus play a key certification role in monitoring management. *Third*, globalization allows foreign shareholders to participate significantly in local firms. The introduction of foreign standards may be assimilated to a knowledge transfer from the foreign shareholder to the developing country corporation, which may then spill over to the rest of the economy through job turnover. *Fourth*, opening up to foreign capital creates a market for corporate control, in which fear of takeover or effective takeover fosters managerial discipline and increases efficiency. *Fifth*, local firms cross-listed in countries that better protect minority shareholders may face legal action from foreign shareholders. This constitutes an incentive for the convergence of domestic legal systems towards the highest international standards.

Overall, it is expected that improved institutions, shareholder protection, disclosure standards, along with the active participation of foreign investors,- i.e., the emergence of a local 'equity culture'- would instil confidence among local investors and contribute to further market development and greater managerial efficiency, ultimately resulting in higher economic growth.

2.3. Pervasive Effects

Nevertheless, there are also downsides to equity market development. More specifically, one problem with financial markets is that they tend to be biased towards the short run. This is magnified by the growing importance of institutional investors. Mutual funds managers who benchmark portfolio performance indeed tend to focus on market momentum rather than long-term prospects. In doing so, analysts prioritize quarterly as opposed to annual company reports (a situation described as a *"quarterly report dictatorship"* (Albert, 1995)). This short-term bias is magnified by portfolio diversification: managers can easily cancel some of their positions when their other holdings are well balanced.

By contrast, the identification of sound investment opportunities by a company's management requires a longer time horizon. The design and implementation of sound economic policy also requires a significantly slower pace. Overall, equity market development may favour shorter temporal horizons, in the economy, which may conflict with governmental and managerial timelines. Such a dynamic can be particularly harmful in developing countries, where economic challenges are extremely demanding.

Concurrently, while a lack of market liquidity is generally perceived as a fundamental cause of brutal variations in price, an informal view suggests that in some circumstances, too much liquidity can prove destabilizing. In the context of an underdeveloped financial market, additional liquidity may positively affect price variation by fostering market participants' ability to accommodate order flows. This positively impacts on the adjustment of prices to new information, and may generate a multiplier effect on volatility transmission in times of turmoil. Increased liquidity may induce a reciprocal loop between prices and orders, thereby amplifying market responses. This results in bubble-like booms in asset prices, and in magnified distress when the market plummets (Kenny and Moss, 1998). By contrast, the transmission of market effects is negligible where there are low levels of liquidity (Piesse and Hearn, 2001).

Besides, certain authors have questioned the impact of shareholder dominance on corporate governance. In a world of perfect capital mobility, the dominance of foreign shareholders may lead managers to focus on *one-dimensional* corporate performance measures (e.g. stock prices, return on equity). This tends to bias companies toward adaptive rather than innovative strategies. According to Lazonick and O'Sullivan (1996), shareholder dominance implies the pursuit of liquidity, which is incompatible with the financial commitment required by innovation. These authors do not recognize shareholders as 'principals' who benefit from residual revenue because *'given their quest for liquidity, of all the stakeholders in the modern industrial corporation, shareholders are the ones with the least stake in a particular company as an ongoing entity because, via the stock market, shareholders have the easiest conditions for exit of any stakeholders'* (p.58). Rejecting projects whose returns fail to satisfy investor demand for rapid payoffs may result in a shift of research away from projects with longer-term payoffs. This impacts on innovation and weakens technological development. For example, according to a survey of US companies, the average length of research projects decreased from 21.6 months in 1991 to 16.7 months in 1996 (OECD, 1999).

The pressure to generate returns for shareholders may also be detrimental to other stakeholders, and tends to reduce corporate governance to the sole relationship between shareholders and management (Jeffers, 2005). Other groups, such as employees, customers and suppliers, the state and society in general, are not properly taken into consideration. Environmental issues constitute a good example. Environmental economics theory states that social and environmental sustainability requires companies to internalize all types of costs into their decision function. However, lenders' portfolio decisions are solely based on the expected risk-return characteristics associated with borrowers' projects. Therefore, unless the existing regulatory regime causes product market capital-seekers to fully internalize all types of costs, the non-internalized costs and benefits of prospective investments will not figure into the capital suppliers' decision function. This may result in a sub-optimal resource allocation and in negative social and environmental externalities (Goldstein, 2001). Some authors have also suggested that this problem might be aggravated by the dynamic of financial globalization. For instance, Kim and Wilson (1997) developed a theoretical model in which independent welfare-maximizing governments may regulate pollution emissions from production activities, and tax residential labour and mobile capital in order to finance public good expenditures. Their results suggested that intergovernmental competition for mobile capital may lead to inefficiently lax environmental and social standards. They concluded that financial globalization may lead to a social and environmental 'race to the bottom'. Overall, these observations have led some economists to argue that equity markets constitute *'costly irrelevances which (developing countries) can ill afford'* (Singh, 1997).

2.4. Informationnal Efficiency

However, the mechanisms uniting equity market development and the allocation of investment appear more complex when one incorporates information costs and the informational requirements they impose on the individual equity investor. In line with the financial repression paradigm, proponents of *market efficiency* argue that financial markets collect and allocate savings to the most socially desirable economic projects. Nevertheless, the hypotheses underlying this reasoning are still the object of considerable debate.

2.4.1 Definition

In the broadest sense, market efficiency requires the simultaneous presence of three types of efficiency: *risk-diversification efficiency*, which states that markets fully diversify risks in line with the predictions of the Arrow-Debreu theorem; *valuation efficiency*, which refers to the market's capacity to reflect the fundamental value of financial assets; and *informational efficiency*, which states that active portfolio management strategies are ineffective. Within this framework, there is a direct causality link between informational efficiency, valuation efficiency and allocative efficiency (Aglietta, 2001). This has placed the notion of informational efficiency at the forefront of finance research over the last three decades. In a general sense, informational efficiency implies that the pricing of securities reflects all available information that is relevant to their valuation. However, Fama (1970) identified three types of market information and subsequently suggested three forms of market efficiency: strong, semi-strong, and weak.

'Strong form' efficiency states that all public and private historical information is entirely reflected in asset prices. This implies first, that private information (inside information) is difficult to obtain due to the competition among active investors in the market; and second, that even investors that manage to access private information are unable to achieve abnormal rates of returns. This, however, is unlikely to happen in reality, so that the strong form of efficiency is unlikely to hold.

The semi-strong form of efficiency states that current market prices reflect all publicly available information, including both macroeconomic information (money supply, exchange rate, interest rates...) and corporate information (announcement of dividends, annual earnings, stock splits). In this form of market efficiency, market prices instantaneously adjust to any good or bad news contained in such information as they are revealed. As a consequence, market participants cannot make consistently superior returns by analyzing publicly available information: only insiders may achieve abnormal profits.

Finally, the weak form of efficiency constitutes the most restrictive definition of the concept. It implies that asset prices reflect all past available information relevant to their valuation, so that the analysis of past prices cannot help predicting future patterns. Therefore, it is not possible for a trader to make abnormal returns based on technical analysis. Rejecting the weak-form of efficiency automatically implies rejecting the 'semi strong' and 'strong' forms. As a consequence, the weak-form definition of market efficiency constitutes the main operational definition for efficiency studies (Mobarek & Keasey, 2000). At the theoretical level, weak-form efficiency can be related to the 'random walk model' developed by Fama (1970).

2.4.2 Consequences of Informational Efficiency

The idea that a lack of informational efficiency may disturb the market-based system of incentives and affect the investment allocation process was originally popularized by J.M Keynes (1883-1946) in his description of the 'beauty contest'. Over the last decade however, a set of additional transmission mechanisms has been put forward to account for this phenomenon.

First, a firm may not be able to raise the outside funds necessary to undertake a worthy investment project if a manager cannot fully and credibly reveal information to outside investors and lenders (Myers and Majluf, 1984). *Second*, asymmetries of information between managers and outsiders may lead to diverging perceptions of asset pricing. For instance, given the alternative of financial leverage, managers may then issue new equity only if they assume that stock prices are overvalued. As a consequence, risk-averse investors may be reluctant to invest in new equity issues (Stiglitz, 1989; Franks and Mayer, 1990; Hubbard, 2000). Similarly, entrepreneurs may also hesitate to implement public offerings as a result of high transaction costs or the uncertainty of getting a fair price (Bekaert and Harvey, 1997). *Third*, inefficient markets are often characterized by the absence of reliable accounting standards and usually lack a regular, adequate and reliable disclosure of information. This magnifies the informational advantage of insiders, who are able to manipulate stock prices in order to make extra profits. For instance, better-informed investors may gain inside information about firm productivity. This advantage may be used to retain the high-productivity firms and to sell the low-productivity ones to partially informed savers, resulting in a misallocation of domestic savings (Razin, Sadka and Yuen, 1999). *Fourth*, market efficiency constrains the impact of stock market development on corporate governance. Tying the managers' income to biased market prices would result in a set of wrong managerial incentives, and would ultimately introduce disturbances in the corporate governance mechanism (Pollin, 2002). *Fifth*, market cycles tend to be particularly pronounced in inefficient markets. A lack of reliable information favours noise and herding behaviour among investors, increasing the probability of sudden opinion reversals (Singh, 1997). The negative consequences of market volatility are well known. The cost of capital for corporations may increase due to market fluctuations, which discourages risk-averse investors (Caporale, Howells and Soliman, 2004). Major booms and busts in the secondary market may also undermine the confidence of investors and affect the ability of companies to raise additional funds in the primary market. *Sixth*, speculative bubbles and crashes in the equity market may undermine the whole financial system and generate financial crises with very large economic and social costs (Agénor, 2003). It should also be noted that general equilibrium models have also underlined the positive relationship between informational efficiency and economic development (Capasso, 2004). Taken together, these intuitions constitute considerable backing for the idea that the market efficiency hypothesis largely conditions the economic impact of equity market liberalization policies.

2.4.3 Efficiency in Emerging Markets

In the context of developing markets, it should be noted that a number of specific factors may hinder the flow of information and imply departure from efficiency. Structural and institutional specificities, such as the fragmentation of capital markets, or the presence of political and economic uncertainties, may account for low efficiency (El-Erian and Kumar, 1995). Nonetheless, 'de jure' financial liberalization may not be a sufficient condition for informational efficiency. For instance, Kawakatsu and Morey (1999) investigated market efficiency before and after financial liberalization. They used two sets of dates and data from nine different countries, and found that market efficiency levels were unaffected by the selected events. However, 'de facto' levels of market development may exert a more significant impact on informational efficiency. The low degree of competition in thinly traded markets may indeed result in the presence of dominant players who can cause stock prices to deviate from their intrinsic value (Mobarek and Keasey, 2000). Such a phenomenon is likely to be accompanied by a lack of market transparency, as reflected by corporate information scarcity, low auditing experience, lax disclosure requirements, and overall weak regulations, which together result in truncated fundamental information and favour insider strategies (Blavy, 2002). By contrast, an increase in market capitalization and in the number of listed firms generally results in an enlarged investor base, whose informational needs may foster the development of an individual stock and market-wide research industry.

Insufficient liquidity levels may also affect the market's ability to accommodate orders, and hence weaken the link between prices and information. For instance, Brown and Zhang (1997) discussed the impact of liquidity on informational efficiency by comparing a dealer market and a limit-order book. In their theoretical model, dealers may be better informed than other traders, but the introduction of a limit-order book lowers the execution-price risk faced by speculators, and allows them to react more aggressively to information flows. The introduction of the limit order book thus simultaneously diminishes dealers' profits and increases informational efficiency. More generally, the development of an 'equity culture' in emerging countries societies appears to be an overarching requirement for establishing the conditions of market efficiency (Aloui, 2003).

2.5 Empirical Evidence

Empirical studies related to the theoretical processes discussed above can be divided into two main components: (i) financial development studies, and (ii) informational efficiency studies.

2.5.1 Financial Development Studies

As underlined in Demirgüc-Kunt and Levine (1996), the scarcity of data on stock markets in developing countries has led most research on the ties between financial development and economic growth to focus on the impact of the banking sector. For instance, King and Levine (1993) examined the relationship between financial intermediation and long-run economic growth in eighty countries from 1960 to 1989. They found that the level of financial intermediary development was strongly linked to long-run growth, even after controlling for many other factors associated with long run growth.

Turning to capital market development, Haber (1991), using a historical analysis, documented the positive impact of capital market reforms on competition and industrialization using evidence from Brazil, Mexico, and the United States during the nineteenth and early twentieth centuries. Atje and Jovanovic (1993) were the first to formally investigate the impact of stock market development on economic growth. Using a sample of forty countries over the 1980-1988 period, they reported a strong relationship between a stock market development indicator (value traded as a percent of GDP) and economic growth. Levine and Zervos (1998) constructed aggregated indexes of overall stock market development and found that stock markets remained positively and significantly correlated to long-run growth over the 1976-1993 period for a wide number of developing countries, even after controlling for development level and economic policy variables. More recent empirical work has also suggested that equity market liberalization is associated with higher real growth, in the range of one percent per annum for the average emerging nation (Bekaert, Harvey and Lundblad, 2001).

Other studies have attempted to compare the respective impact of banks and equity markets. For instance, Demirgüc-Kunt (1992) highlighted a positive and significant relationship between firm leverage and stock market development, suggesting that equity finance may increase the borrowing capacity of firms through risk sharing and raise the quality and quantity of bank lending through timely and systematic information flows. Demirgüc-Kunt and Levine (1995) underlined that the level of stock market development is highly correlated to the development of banks, nonbanks, insurance companies and private pension funds. Their results indicated that, as an economy develops, its aggregate debt-to-equity ratio tends to diminish.

Along similar lines, Demirgüc-Kunt and Maksimovic (1998) explored the effect of stock market development on firms' financing choices. Looking at a sample of thirty industrial and developing economies, they observed that the effect of stock market development on firm debt-to-equity ratios depends on the initial level of stock market development. These empirical studies echo Boyd and Smith's (1996) theoretical model, which showed that the negative association between financial leverage and economic growth can be explained by rising aggregate investment monitoring costs. These are due to the adoption of more complex technology. In other words, the adoption of monitoring costs minimization strategies, as firms move up the value chain, may skew the economy's aggregate financial structure towards equity rather than debt. Recently, a few microeconomic investigations have also suggested that equity market liberalization leads to a modification of the pattern of corporate financing in emerging countries. For instance, Bekaert and Harvey (2000) investigated the impact of financial liberalization on asset pricing in a sample of 20 emerging countries and found that the cost of capital - as measured by dividend yields - always decreased after liberalization but that the effect was relatively weak (0.15%). Errunza and Miller (1998) used a sample of 126 firms from 32 countries and documented a reduction of 42.2 % in long run returns as well as significant positive returns around the announcement of ADR offerings. More recently, Patro and Wald (2005) investigated a panel of 18 emerging markets and found an average decrease in returns of 2.88% per month during the 36 month period starting three and a half year afters the liberalisation date, suggesting a significant decrease in the cost of capital. This result echoes that of Chari and Henry (2004), who used a similar dataset and an international asset pricing modelling framework to obtain similar results, while also underlining the role of firm-specific risk sharing characteristics in corporate valuation. This set of studies hence suggests that equity market development slackens the financial constraint in developing countries by inducing a significant decrease in the cost of capital[2].

Overall, financial development studies have underlined that equity markets have a role to play in financial liberalization policies, as a necessary complement to the banking sector.

2.5.2 Informational Efficiency

Informational efficiency studies have used various datasets and methodologies and can be divided into three main components. One first group of papers tested for the random walk hypothesis based on variance ratio and seasonality tests. A second group of papers directly examined the performance of technical trading rules in predicting price changes. Finally, a third group of papers investigated microstructures in emerging markets.

2.5.2.1 Variance Ratio and Seasonality Tests

Market efficiency tests through the random walk constitute a voluminous amount of literature, which can be chronologically described as follows. In a seminal paper, Urrutia (1995) implemented variance ratio and run tests using monthly data for market indexes in Argentina, Brazil, Chile and Mexico during the 1975-1991 period and yielded contrasting results. Fawson (1996) implemented a wide battery of tests including autocorrelation tests, run tests and unit root analysis to test for the random walk hypothesis in the Taiwan Stock Exchange using monthly stock market returns for the 1967-1993 periods. He was unable to reject the weak form efficiency hypothesis. Similarly, Dockery and Vergari (1997) were unable to reject the weak form efficiency hypothesis in the case of the Budapest Stock Exchange, using weekly stock market indexes covering the 1991-1995 period.

By contrast, Grieb and Reyes (1999) implemented variance ratio tests in the Brazilian and Mexican stock exchanges during the 1988-1995 periods, and significantly rejected the weak form efficiency hypothesis for all market indexes and most individual stocks. Mobarek and Keasey (2000) also attempted to assess the behaviour of stock price movement in the Dhaka Stock Exchange in Bangladesh for the 1988-1997 period and reported market inefficiency based on a runs test, an autocorrelation test, an auto-regression test and an auto-regressive integrated moving average model. However, Chang and Ting (2000) implemented a variance ratio analysis using weekly, monthly, quarterly and yearly returns for the Taiwanese market index for the period from 1971 to 1996. They were unable to reject the random walk hypothesis for all series, except weekly series. Cheung and Coutts (2001) also investigated weak form efficiency in the Hong Kong stock exchange based on variance ratio analysis, using daily data over the 1985-1997 period. They were unable to reject the random walk hypothesis. However, Groenewold et.al (2003) implemented autocorrelation and unit root tests using daily return series for seven indices of the Shangai and Shenzen Chinese stock exchanges and significantly rejected the random walk hypothesis. Lima and Tabak (2004) also applied a variance ratio analysis to daily stock price indexes for Shangai, Shenzen, Hong

---

[2] The underlying theoretical mechanisms have been described by Stulz (1999).

Kong, and Singapore stock exchanges from 1992 to 2000 and rejected the null hypothesis of efficiency in the case of Singapore. Finally, Seddighi and Nian (2004) used autocorrelation, unit root and auto regressive conditional heteroskedasticity models and were unable to reject the null of a random walk in the Shangai stock exchange using daily data from the market index and eight individual shares for the year 2000.

Concurrently, a few authors have tested for day-of-the-week effects in emerging markets. Aggarwal and Rivoli (1989) examined seasonal and daily patterns in equity returns in Hong Kong, Singapore, Malaysia and the Philippines using daily data for the 1976-1988 period. Their results suggested the presence of a robust January effect (higher returns) and Monday effects (lower returns) in all markets except the Philippines. Nath and Dalvi (2004) examined the anomaly in the Indian equity market for the period from 1999 to 2003 using high frequency and end of the day data, and found significant Monday and Friday effects. Finally, Basher and Sodorsky (2006) investigated the day-of-the-week effect in 21 emerging stock markets using daily data for the 1992-2003 period, and found significant support for such effects in the Philippines, Pakistan and Taiwan, Argentina, Malaysia, Thailand and Turkey. Overall, it appears that variance ratio and seasonality tests have raised very mixed results.

2.5.2.2 Technical Trading Rules

An alternative way to check for the random walk hypothesis is to examine the outcomes of technical analysis. The latter can be defined as the deliberate study of market price history, with a view to predicting price changes and enhancing trade profitability. In a seminal paper, Brock et al. (1992) demonstrated profitable moving average trading rules using the Dow Jones Industrials Average from 1897 to 1986. Bessembinder and Chan (1998) assessed whether technical analysis can predict stock price movement in Malaysia, Thailand, Taiwan, Hong Kong and Japan. They found that trading rules are successful in the least developed markets (Malaysia, Thailand and Taiwan), but have less explanatory power in the more developed markets (Hong Kong and Japan). Ratner and Leal (1999) applied technical trading rules to ten emerging equity markets in Latin America and Asia from January 1982 through April 1995. Their results suggested that trading strategies may be profitable in Taiwan, Thailand and Mexico, but not in other markets. Similarly, Parisi and Vasquez (2000) adopted a similar methodology using daily closing prices for the 1987–1998 periods in the Chilean stock market and provided strong support for the technical strategies. Finally, Chang et.al (2004) implemented a comprehensive technical trading analysis, testing for different sub-samples and analyzing returns in bear and bull markets in 11 emerging markets for the 1991-2004 periods. Their results suggested that emerging equity indices do not resemble a random walk, as opposed to more developed markets such as the USA and Japan.

2.5.2.3 Institutions and Efficiency

In light of current theory, authors have attempted to measure the impact of institutions on price patterns. For instance, one first group of studies documented a mutually reinforcing relationship between market efficiency and liquidity levels. Demirgüc-Kunt and Levine (1996) suggested a positive correlation between liquidity, institutional development and market efficiency using data for 41 emerging countries from 1986 to 1993. In developed markets, Jones (2001) assembled an annual time series of bid-ask spreads on Dow Jones stocks from 1900 to 2000, and showed that time varying spreads and turnovers are important determinants of conditional expected stock market returns.

It should also be noted that liquidity levels also have legal and political origins. Using a price-based measurement of liquidity, Lesmond (2005) underlined that countries with weak political and legal institutions have significantly higher liquidity costs than countries with strong political and legal systems: higher incremental political risk tends to be associated with a 10 basis point increase in transaction costs. In a similar vein, Khwaja and Mian (2005) investigated the relationship between poor regulatory environments and the presence of abnormal returns among brokers in Pakistan using trade level data. Their results highlighted a possible manipulation of stock prices by collusive brokers: when prices are low, brokers tend to trade amongst themselves in order to artificially raise prices and attract positive-feedback traders. Once prices have risen, the former exit and leave the latter to suffer the ensuing price fall. These authors underlined that brokers may earn annual rates of return that are 50-90 percentage points higher than those earned by outside investors. These large rents may explain why market reforms are hard to implement, and why emerging equity markets often remain marginal with few outsiders investing and little capital raised.

Another group of papers studied the bid-ask spread price patterns. Cajueiro and Tabak (2005) investigated the causes of long-range dependence in bid–ask prices for all stocks traded in the Brazilian financial market from January 1998 through November 2003. Their findings suggested that price patterns are not solely driven by fundamentals but also by other market characteristics such as capitalization measures (a proxy for liquidity), dividends payments, return on equity (ROE) and financial leverage. Speculative behavior (for example, technical analysis) and speculative bubbles in stock markets have important roles in the determination of prices. Finally, Gorkittisunthorn et.al (2006) examined 104 stock splits that occurred in the Stock Exchange of Thailand during the 2000–2004 period and documented a negative and statistically significant relationship between insider ownership level and change in the percentage bid–ask spread. This further highlights the link between corporate governance structure and equity market efficiency in emerging countries. Overall, empirical investigations of efficiency have yielded mixed results.

Taken together, theoretical and empirical studies suggest that the economic impact of internal equity market development is ambiguous. On the one hand, standard transmission mechanisms include better mobilization and allocation of domestic financial resources, as well as improved corporate governance. Recent empirical macroeconomic and microeconomic models seem to confirm these theoretical intuitions. On the other hand, informational efficiency should be considered as a *relative* rather than *absolute* phenomenon, and is linked to institutional developments.

Overall, the material reviewed in this section suggests that equity market development is an appropriate strategy to foster the mobilization and allocation of domestic financial resources in developing countries. However, such policies must simultaneously tackle insufficient levels of informational efficiency by setting up adequate institutions.

Nonetheless, the trend towards financial globalization generates a number of additional effects with powerful impact on domestic financial systems. These are discussed in the next section.

3. REVIEW OF EXTERNAL IMPLICATIONS

The globalization of financial services has, over the last decade, given rise to a voluminous amount of academic work analyzing both the extent and the consequences of international market integration for financial systems in developing countries. The objective of this section is to discuss the main conclusions from this literature. It is structured as follows. The first sub-section defines equity market integration. The second sub-section derives its main theoretical consequences. The third sub-section reviews the associated empirical literature.

3.1 Equity Market Integration: Definition

Although mostly used by empiricists, the concept of 'equity market integration' is embedded in asset pricing theory. Asset pricing models have highlighted three possible situations: full segmentation, mild segmentation and full integration of equity markets (Bekaert and Harvey, 1995).

3.1.1 Full market segmentation

Full equity market segmentation can be described based on the standard Capital Asset Pricing Model (CAPM), as developed by Sharpe (1964) and Lintner (1965). In this framework, the relevant risk faced by investors is the asset's contribution to the variance of a diversified portfolio within the domestic country. For any individual stock in the segmented stock market we have:

$$
\begin{cases}
E(R_i) = r_f + \beta_{im}\left[E(R_m) - r_f\right] \\
\left[E(R_m) - r_f\right] = \gamma(W)\sigma_m^2 \\
E(R_i) = r_f + \gamma(W)COV(R_i, R_m)
\end{cases}
\tag{1}
$$

Where $E(R_i)$ is the required rate of return on firm i's stock, r_f is the risk-free rate in the domestic market, β_{im} is the beta coefficient of firm i with the domestic market portfolio, and $E(R_m)$ is the expected return on the domestic market. The aggregate risk premium can be established as the product of the coefficient of relative risk-aversion $\gamma(W)$ by the variance of the domestic market portfolio σ_m^2. $COV(R_i, R_m)$ is the covariance between the individual stock and the domestic portfolio.

3.1.2 Mild Segmentation

Mild segmentation constitutes an intermediary situation which was initially described by Errunza and Losq (1985). In their analysis, under mild segmentation governments maintain one restriction on financial liberalization: while domestic investors are allowed to invest in the world market portfolio, foreign investors can only hold a subset of domestic equities. This corresponds to a hybrid CAPM in which assets are divided into freely tradable and restricted assets. Freely tradable assets are priced according to the world factor, which is the relevant source of systematic risk for foreign investors. The pricing of investible securities under mild segmentation is thus given by: $E(R_i) = r_f + \beta_{iw}[E(R_w) - r_f]$. However, the pricing of non-investible securities includes a 'super risk premium', which compensates domestic investors for bearing the risk associated with holding all of the non investible stocks. For any individual restricted stock, we have:

$$E(R_i) = r_f + \gamma_u(W)COV(R_i, R_w) + \gamma(W)COV(R_i, R_n | R_I) \qquad (2)$$

In equation (2), R_n and R_I are the returns on the portfolio non-investible and investible securities, respectively. The variable $COV(R_i, R_n | R_I)$ represents the covariance of firm i's return with the return on the portfolio of non-investible stocks, taking the return on the investible securities as given. γ and γ_u are risk aversion coefficients for restricted international investors and unrestricted domestic investors, respectively.

3.1.3 Market Integration
Finally, full integration means that the domestic equity market becomes a part of the global equity market. As a consequence, domestic assets are rewarded according to their covariance with the world portfolio, as the risk premium on any asset is proportional to its world beta. In other words, risk is measured through asset contribution to the world portfolio. The international version of the CAPM was proposed by Solnik (1974). For any local firm, we have:

$$\begin{cases} E(R_{i*}) = r_{f*} + \beta_{iw}[E(R_w) - r_{f*}] \\ [E(R_w) - r_{f*}] = \gamma(W)\sigma^2 w \\ E(R_{i*}) = r_{f*} + \gamma(W)COV(R_{i*}, R_w) \end{cases} \qquad (3)$$

Where β_{iw} denotes firm i's beta with the world market, $E(R_w)$ denotes the required rate of return on the world equity market portfolio, $\sigma^2 w$ denotes the variance of the return of the world portfolio and r_{f*} is the world risk-free rate. In other words, expected local returns $E(R_i)$ in a fully integrated market depend solely on non-diversifiable international factors.

3.2 Main Theoretical Implications

From a theoretical point of view, equity market integration affects (i) the dynamics of international diversification opportunities, and (ii) the domestic market's sensitivity to international shocks.

3.2.1 International Diversification Opportunities

Modern finance theory shows that including weakly correlated assets in a domestic portfolio reduces risk and maximizes long run yields (Markowitz, 1952, 1959). In this context, two main factors explain the attractiveness of international diversification for portfolio managers. First, the correlations between the returns of the securities that make up a portfolio are crucial in determining the associated level of risk. Generally, the lower the correlation between securities, the lower the portfolio risk, and risk-averse investors tend to select securities with low correlation (Markowitz, 1959). Second, the correlation between domestic and foreign returns is expected to be lower than that between purely domestic securities. This is due to the monetary, fiscal, and industrial policies varying from country to country, which add up to differing industrial compositions of stock market and countries and result in significant differentials in country returns dynamics. International diversification is thus beneficial to both value stability and long run yields because it facilitates the selection of foreign investment projects that exhibit very low correlation with the domestic portfolio.

The relationship uniting market integration, correlation and diversification has been recently formalized by Arouri (2003). The model proceeds from a dynamic representation of the International Asset Pricing Model risk premium (Solnik, 1974). and shows that the gains from international diversification are a negative function of the conditional correlation coefficient between the domestic portfolio and the global portfolio:

$$E\left(R_I - R_i / \Omega_{t-1}\right) = \delta_{t-1} * \left(1 - p_{i,w,t-1}\right) * VAR\left(R_{i,t} \Omega_{t-1}\right) \tag{1}$$

In (1), I represents the international portfolio and i is the local portfolio. The left-hand side term thus represents the gain from international diversification. In addition, δ represents the price of market covariance risk and p_i represents the correlation coefficient between the domestic and the global portfolio. t denotes time and Ω represents the set of available information. This equation shows that the power of portfolio diversification is magnified in segmented markets where $p_{i,w,t-1}$ tends towards 0. The CAPM indeed shows that in such markets, returns tend to be predominantly determined by the systematic risk of each security in the context of the national portfolio, as opposed to the world beta. By contrast, the gains from international diversification are equal to zero under perfect integration; i.e. when the domestic portfolio is perfectly positively correlated to the global portfolio ($p_{i,w,t-1}=1$). This suggests that the gains from international diversification to emerging markets can considerable in the aftermath of liberalisation episodes. However, these gains may disappear in the middle-run as international cross-market correlations increase. This phenomenon may lead to nonlinearities in the dynamics of capital flows.

3.2.2 Financial Contagion

The concept of 'financial contagion' is another important consequence of market integration and refers to the tendency of bear markets to move downwards in a synchronized fashion. The linkage between market integration and contagion has been formally described by Bekaert, Harvey and Ng (2005) within an empirical model. Their approach was to extend the traditional CAPM from a one-factor to a two-factor setting. To do so, they divided the world market into the United States (US) and a particular region (reg), and allowed for local factors to be priced. Letting i and j be two individual countries, and assuming that the idiosyncratic shocks to the US, regional and individual markets are non correlated, these authors have derived the following dynamic relation between covariances h, betas β and variances σ:

$$\begin{cases} h(i,us,t) = \beta_{i,US,t-1} \times \sigma^2_{US,t} \\ h(i,reg,t) = \left(\beta_{i,reg,t-1} \times \beta_{US,reg,t-1} \times \sigma^2_{US,t}\right) + \left(\beta_{i,reg,t-1} \times \sigma^2_{reg,t}\right) \\ h(i,j,t) = \left(\beta_{i,US,t-1} \times \beta_{j,US,t-1} \times \sigma^2_{US,t}\right) + \left(\beta_{i,reg,t-1} \times \beta_{j,reg,t-1} \times \sigma^2_{reg,t}\right) \end{cases} \quad (1)$$

Equation (1) has three several important implications. *First*, a market's covariance with the U.S. (regional) market return is positively related to its country-specific beta with the U.S. (or region). *Second*, provided that the country specific beta parameter is positive, higher volatility in the U.S. market induces higher return covariance between the U.S. and market i. *Third*, the covariance with the regional market or any other national market j within the same region increases in times of high return volatility in the U.S. and/or the regional market. According to these authors, the direct implication of these relationships is the appearance of 'contagious bear markets' in times of financial turmoil.

3.2.3 Empirical Evidence

Related empirical studies have addressed the three following themes: (i) measuring equity market integration, (ii) analyzing portfolio allocations and the dynamics capital flows and (iii) investigating the issue of financial contagion.

3.2.3.1 Equity Market Integration

The existing empirical literature on equity market integration may be divided into two components. The first component gathers studies that test for static equity market integration. The second component gathers studies that account for the time-varying nature of equity market integration.

3.2.3.1.1 Static Estimates of Integration

One standard way to measure market integration is to derive a set of static measures based on time-series empirical models. Within this branch of the literature, a first type of study looked at integration through asset pricing models. For instance, one set of models directly tested for the hypothesis of perfect world equity market integration. Wheatley (1988) used an asset-pricing model in which a country level asset pricing line related a representative individual's expected real return on each asset to the covariance of this return with growth in the individual's real consumption. Using monthly data from January 1960 to December 1985, he was unable to reject the null hypothesis of equity market integration. Ferson and Harvey (1992) examined multifactor asset pricing models for real and expected returns on 18 national equity markets, in which multiple betas were chosen to represent global economic risks. Their results showed that multiple betas, as opposed to world market betas, are able to better explain cross-sectional differences in average returns. Bekaert and Hodrick (1992) followed a slightly different approach. They first estimated the predictable component in excess rates of returns for the equity markets of the US, Japan, the UK and Germany, using lagged excess returns, dividend yields, and forward premiums as instruments. They then implemented vector autoregressive regressions in which constraints were derived from dynamic asset pricing theory. Their estimates suggested mixed evidence in favour of financial integration. However, the main weakness of these studies is that they identify the source of asset risk purely with the covariance of the local returns with the world market portfolio. By doing so, these studies directly test for the hypothesis of perfect world integration by implementing a binary framework in which local markets are either perfectly segmented from the world market, or represent an adequate proxy to the world market. Neither of these assumptions is inherently plausible. Not surprisingly, these studies have performed unspectacularly overall in empirical tests (Kearney and Lucey, 2004).

An alternative approach is to consider the competing hypotheses of integration, mild segmentation and segmentation, in line with the theoretical model of Errunza and Losq (1985). Directly testing this hypothesis for a group of emerging markets, Errunza, Losq and Padmanabhan (1992) provided evidence in favour of a non-polar structure, showing that equity markets are neither fully integrated nor completely segmented. More recently, Akdogan (1997) investigated different degrees of market segmentation across twenty-six large countries for two sub-sample periods (1970's and 1980's) based on an international risk decomposition model. The originality of his approach was to provide a precise segmentation/integration score. The latter also constitutes an operational tool for portfolio managers, who may then identify portfolio diversification opportunities by ranking countries according to their level of international integration.

Checking for co-integration relationships is another way to assess the degree of international integration in equity markets. The Johansen and Juselius (1988) co-integration analysis constitutes the most common approach. Integrated stock markets are expected to have a common stochastic trend with stationary error terms when the data are examined by applying multivariate co-integration analysis to a system of nonstationary stock prices. According to Bernard (1991), the necessary condition for complete integration is that there be n-1 cointegrating vectors in a system of n indices. A voluminous number of studies are based on this approach.

For instance, Kasa (1992) found a single co-integrating vector between the US, Japanese, UK, German and Canadian equity markets over the 1974-1990 period. Chou, Ng and Pi (1994) found evidence of integration among G7 countries over the 1976-1987 period. De Fusco, Geppert and Tsetsekos (1996) suggested that emerging markets were not co-integrated with the US over the 1989-1993 period. Sheng and Tu (2000) examined the interrelationship of Asia-pacific markets around the Asian financial crisis and found evidence of pair-wise co-integration for South East Asia 'tiger' countries. Gallagher (1995) found no evidence of co-integration between Irish and either German or UK equity markets. Kanas (1988) examined the relationship between the U.S. and six large European equity markets pre and post October 1987, and found no evidence of co-integration. Serletis and King (1997) found that European markets did demonstrate integration over the 1971-1992 periods. Using the same methodology, Phylaktis (1999) found that the Pacific Basin countries are closely linked with world financial markets and more so with Japan than with the US. Finally, Arbelaez, Urrutia and Abbas (2001) found evidence of global integration in the Colombian equity market from the period ranging from January 2, 1988 through August 9, 1994.

3.2.3.1.2 Dynamic Estimates of Integration

However, one important line of criticism against static approaches is that they implicitly assume that the degree of integration remains constant over time (Kearney and Lucey, 2004). In doing so, they miss the important element of time variation in equity risk premiums. Taking this into account, a number of alternative approaches have been deployed over time.

In a seminal paper, Harvey (1989) presented strong evidence that conditional co-variances do change over time based on tests of asset pricing models that allow for time variation. Estimates of the expected excess return highlighted the standard Sharpe-Lintner CAPM's inability to capture the dynamic behaviour of asset returns. In an effort to improve existing results, Bekaert and Harvey (1995) investigated expected returns in countries that were segmented from world capital markets in one part of the sample and become integrated later in the sample. Using a measure of capital market integration arising from a conditional regime-switching model, they found that a number of emerging markets exhibited time-varying integration. In turn, Hardouvelis, Malliaroupoulos and Priestley (1999) examined the speed of integration among the EU equity markets by developing an explicit equilibrium asset-pricing model with a time-varying measure of integration. They found that the process of intra European equity market integration seems to have been completed by mid 1998. Along the same lines, Flood and Rose (2003) used an inter-temporal asset-pricing model, in which expected risk-free rates were allowed to vary freely over time, constrained only by the fact that they were equal across assets. Estimating and comparing expected risk-free rates across assets, they found that the S&P 500 and NASDAQ markets seemed to be well integrated, while the NASDAQ was poorly integrated with the S&P 500. Finally, Barari (2004) proposed a recursive version the Akdogan (1997) equity market integration score, thus providing a time-varying measure of equity market integration. Applying this extended methodology to a sample of six Latin American countries for the period of 1988-2001, she observed a trend towards increased regional integration relative to global integration until the mid-1990's, followed by a significant increase in global integration during the second half of the 1990's.

Parallel to these contributions is a branch of literature that examined the international integration of equity markets from the perspective of dynamic correlations between returns. The null hypothesis of no integration was rejected if the correlation matrix of international asset returns demonstrated instability over time. Early papers, such as Panton, Lessig, and Joy (1976) and Watson (1980) found stability. More recent work, however, indicated instability in the relationship. Koch and Koch (1991) estimated a simultaneous equation model over a number of contiguous sub-periods and found significant and increased linkages among world equity markets. Wahab and Lashgari (1993) implemented intertemporal stationarity tests of the variance-covariance matrix of monthly returns on seven international equity indices. Historical analysis revealed that pairwise covariances were invariably highly nonstationary over forecast intervals that varied in length between one month and five years, suggesting increasing integration. Longin and Solnik (1995) refined the analysis by estimating a multivariate general autoregressive conditional heteroskedasticity model with constant conditional correlation in order to capture the evolution in the conditional covariance structure. They studied the correlation of monthly excess returns for seven major countries over the period 1960-90 and also found that the international covariance and correlation matrices were unstable over time, indicating increasing integration. More recently, Steeley (2006) plugged the system of bi-variate equity market correlations into a smooth transition logistic trend model in order to establish how rapidly the countries of Eastern Europe were moving away from market segmentation. She found that Hungary was the most rapidly integrating country.

Recursive co-integration constitutes an alternative to the analysis of correlation coefficients. The idea is to plot the λ_{trace} statistic (which is a general test to determine whether there is one or more co-integrating vectors) and the λ_{max} statistic (which is a test to determine the precise number of co-integrating vectors) in order to examine how the nature of market integration changes over time. Rangvid (2001) used this approach, focusing on quarterly share indices for France, Germany and the UK over the 1960–1999 period. He found evidence of increasing convergence since 1982. Aggarwal, Lucey and Muckley (2004) also investigated the time-varying integration process within the EMU countries based on a recursive co-integration approach and highlighted increased integration through time with specific breaks around selected events. Another possibility is to use an alternative co-integration methodology that takes into account the dynamic component of the integration process. For instance, Voronkova (2004) investigated the existence of long-run relations between emerging Central European stock markets and the mature stock markets of Europe and the United States for the period ranging from September 7, 1993 through April 30, 2002. She implemented the Gregory and Hansen (1996) co-integration approach in an effort to consider the possibility of instability in long-run relations between time-series. She obtained evidence of increasing linkages and structural breaks between the Central European markets and between Central European and developed markets' indices.

In turn, Davies (2006) followed suggestions detailed in Gabriel et al. (2002) and considered the possibility of multiple switches in the long run co-integrating relationship by implementing a co-integration model based on Markov-switching residuals. He documented significant evidence to support a two-regime long-run equilibrium for the MSCI total return index data during the period ranging from 1969 to 2005. In the same spirit, Lucey and Voronkova (2006) used an extensive set of co-integration techniques including a stochastic co-integration test by Harris, McCabe and Leybourne (2002) and the non-parametric co-integration method of Breitung (2002). They focused on the Russian market and documented an increasing degree of co-movements of the Russian market with other developed markets in the aftermath of the Russian crisis of 1998, but not with Central European developing markets.

Finally, other dynamic studies were based on GARCH methodologies. For instance, Fratzscher (2001) used a multivariate GARCH framework to examine financial market integration in Europe and found that the move towards EMU contributed to an increasing integration of financial markets. However, he found that the degree of financial market integration in Europe has been very unstable and volatile over time. Gérard, Thanyalakpark and Batten (2003) modelled second moments and risk exposures using a bi-diagonal multivariate GARCH process and tested a conditional international asset pricing model with both world market and domestic risk included as independent pricing factors for five East Asian markets, the US and world markets. They found little evidence of market segmentation in East Asia over the 1985–1998 period. Kearney and Poti (2006) extended the multivariate dynamic conditional correlation (DCC-MV) GARCH model of Engle (2001) with the inclusion of a deterministic time trend. Their results confirmed a significant rise in the correlations amongst national stock market indexes, which they explained by a structural break shortly before the official adoption of the Euro.

Overall, there are a plethora of empirical studies investigating integration across international equity markets. This, in itself, is a good indicator of the importance of the phenomenon.

3.2.3.2 Portfolio Allocations and Capital Flows

Empirical studies analyzing portfolio allocations and the dynamics of capital flows can be divided into three main components. One type of studies attempted to measure the gains from diversification. Other studies emphasized the presence of specific risks when diversifying into emerging markets. Finally, macroeconomic investigations highlighted nonlinearities in the allocation of portfolio flows to emerging countries in the aftermath of equity market liberalization.

3.2.3.2.1 The Gains from Diversification

As discussed above, financial theory suggests that the net impact of equity market integration on portfolio flows is proportional to changes in time-varying international co-variances. This has given rise to many empirical studies. Investigating developed markets, Sinquefield (1996) argued that the integration of world markets has led to a significant decrease in diversification gains when mixing U.S. domestic portfolios with the MSCI World Index. Arouri (2003) investigated ex ante benefits from world market diversification in 8 markets: the world market, 4 developed markets and 3 emerging markets over the 1973 to 2003 period. His results confirmed the presence of significant benefits from international diversification; however, gains appeared considerably larger for investors from segmented markets. More recently, Timmermann and Blake (2005) analyzed international equity holdings of a large panel of U.K. pension funds over the 1991-1997 period and found that conditional co-variances were not quite as important as own-market volatility in Japan North America, and Europe. The evidence thus appears in line with theoretical models in the case of developed markets.

A considerable body of literature has also underlined the role of emerging market diversification as a return-enhancing strategy for private investors. In a seminal paper, Errunza (1977) investigated the mean-variance implications of including developing countries in a panel of 29 countries for the 1957-1971 period and found that the small correlation of the least developed markets justified their inclusion into the optimal portfolio. Divecha, Drach and Sefek (1992) carried out a similar analysis using a dataset of 23 emerging markets over the 1986-1991 period. Their results suggested that including emerging markets in a global portfolio (up to a 20% threshold) would significantly improve the ex post risk-to-return ratio. Sappenfield and Speidell (1992) used data for 18 emerging markets and 18 developed markets over the 1986-1991 period and suggested that emerging market diversification could be useful during periods of global turmoil such as the 1987 krach, or the 1990 Kuwait invasion. Along the same lines, Diwan, Errunza and Senbet (1994) divided world markets into three components: a developed portfolio, an emerging portfolio and a mixed emerging/developed portfolio. Their simulations were based on the 1989-1991 period and suggested that optimal strategies were, in increasing order, the developed portfolio, the emerging portfolio, and the combined portfolio. Harvey (1995), investigating the 1986-1992 period, showed that adding an emerging market component to a diversified developed portfolio would result in a reduction of six percentage points in the portfolio's total volatility while the expected returns would remain unchanged. More recently, Gilmore et.al (2005) constructed Eastern European portfolios for both US and German investors using various optimization models and several risk measures over the 1995-2003 period. Their results showed that diversification benefits were statistically significant for US investors, but not for German investors.

3.2.3.2.2 Specific Risks in Emerging Markets

There are, however, five specific risks associated with emerging market investment. Exchange risk constitutes the first category. It is related to the variability of cash flow generated in risky currencies. While studies have shown that the exchange risk decreases with firm size and export revenues (Kim and Sung, 2005), it is generally agreed that hedging strategies have partial results, so that conclusions drawn from an international capital asset pricing model that omits currency risk would be misguided (Madura, 1992; Phylaktis and Ravazzolo, 2002). In a seminal paper, Bailey and Chung (1995) suggested that currency fluctuations were a priced factor in cross-sections of emerging stock indexes converted in US dollars over the 1986-1994 period. Investigating the nature of the exchange risk premium in a sample of seven emerging markets for the 1976-2000 period, Carrieri, Errunza et.al (2006a) found that while exchange rate and domestic market risks were priced separately, the local currency risk was, on average, smaller than the domestic market risk but increased substantially during crisis periods, when it could be almost as large as the market risk. Exchange risk stemming from emerging market currencies also seems to be significantly priced in global equity returns, so that information about emerging market crisis episodes affects the prices of global risk factors (Carrieri, Errunza et.al, 2006b).

Political risk is another significant downside to emerging market investment. It includes various dimensions such as expropriation risk, firm nationalization, property seizing etc… There is growing consensus that political risk is a priced factor in emerging markets. For instance, Bilson et.al (2002) investigated the relation between political risk and stock returns within the context of 17 emerging markets and 18 developed markets over the 1984-1997 period. They highlighted the importance of political risk in explaining return variation in individual emerging markets, but not in developed markets. More particularly, they presented evidence to support a positive relation between political risk and ex-post returns in emerging markets. This echoes the conclusions of Perottu and Van Oijen (2001), who noted that political risk tends to have an effect on excess returns in emerging economies. Progress in privatization, however, is significantly correlated to improvements in perceived political risk. Finally, one important characteristic of political risk is that it can be considered 'binary': if it materializes, investors lose most of their expected gains. As a consequence, political risk is significantly associated with capital flights. Recently, Vu Le and Zaq (2006) estimated the equilibrium capital flight equation for a panel of 45 developing countries over 16 years. Their results highlighted that political instability, rather than economic risk, is the most important factor associated with capital flight from emerging markets.

Information asymmetries constitute another specific risk in emerging markets. This risk refers to potential difficulties in monitoring local managers due to cultural differences and inefficiencies in information systems (Lee and Kwok, 1988). Using a market microstructure framework, Krishnamurti et.al (2005) investigated whether there are cross-sectional differences in effective spread, depth and the adverse selection component of spread in a sample of 55 firms originating from 15 emerging markets over the January-June 2000 period. Their results suggested the existence of an information premium for firms with an inferior quality of disclosure. Al-Khouri (2005) also explored the identity and concentration of different block holders and firm value for 89 industrial and service firms listed at the Amman Stock Exchange (ASE) over the 1998–2001 period. His findings indicated a positive and significant relationship between ownership concentration and firm value. Existing studies also suggest that corporate governance and stock market development are associated with lower informational asymmetries. For instance, Bunkanwincha et.al (2006) used firm-level panel data from listed companies from Thailand and Indonesia to analyze the firm's corporate financing behaviours in connection with its corporate governance arrangements, and underlined that weaker corporate governance firms tend to have a higher debt level. Similarly, Black et.al (2006) found a strong correlation between governance and market value in Russia for the 1999-2006 period.

The global finance risk is another category of risk which refers to the transmission of financial crises into emerging markets. The period of financial turmoil that began with the Mexican 'tequila' crisis in January 1995, the Asian 'flu' crisis in August 1997 and the Russian default in 1998 have contributed both to an increase in return volatility and negative returns on the S&P/IFCI Composite Index over the 1994-2003 period (AIMR, 2005).

Finally, the 'self-fulfilling' risk refers to behavioural patterns among investors: by demanding higher returns from emerging markets investment, investors tend to automatically select projects with a higher degree of risk (Bancel and Perrotin, 2005). There are hence several risks associated with emerging market investment. However, the extent to which such risks may deter investors from entering emerging markets is difficult to measure. These risks may indeed be compensated by higher than average returns due to a faster rate of capital accumulation and faster economic growth than in developed countries (Bartram and Dunfey, 2001). They also need to be assessed on a case-by-case basis and depend on the country-context and on the investor's psychology. The 2005 AIMR report summarized the residual uncertainties associated with emerging market investment by arguing that in the last resort, investing in a particular market comes down to *'a bet on emergence'*.

3.2.3.2.3 Portfolio Allocations and Capital Flows

In line with theoretical models, empirical studies have shown that equity market liberalisation tends to be followed by a short-lived surge in capital flows. For instance, Bacchetta and Wincoop (1998) showed that aggregate portfolio flows rose from 0% to about 4% of emerging countries' GDPs during the 1980 to 1996 period. In a similar way, Bekaert and Harvey (2000) investigated a sample of 16 emerging markets and observed that American holdings increased on average from 6.2% to 9.4% of market capitalization from five years before liberalisation to five years after liberalisation. Empirical evidence also suggests that these capital flows are subject to sudden reversals. For instance, Bekaert and Harvey (2001) showed that equity capital flows to emerging markets increased by 1.4% of market capitalization on an annual basis after liberalisation, but were usually levelled out three years later.

The relationship between returns and capital flows can be traced back to Bohn and Tesar's (1995) empirical study. These authors indeed examined whether the expansion of US investment in foreign equities and the change in portfolio composition over time was consistent with models of international portfolio choice. Using monthly data on US equities and those of 22 countries over the 1980-1994 period, they found that foreign investors were mostly 'return chasers', i.e. that portfolio weights appeared to be mainly triggered by changing portfolio returns. Along the same lines, Froot, O'Connell and Seasholes (2001) explored the behavior of daily international portfolio flows into and out of 46 countries from 1994 through 1998. They found that flows increased following unexpectedly high returns in the host market. Turning to emerging markets, Nardari, Griffin and Stulz (2002), used daily data on net equity flows for nine emerging market countries over the 1996-2001 period, and confirmed the fact that a market experiences net equity inflow when its stocks earn unexpectedly high returns.

It has also been observed that capital flows simultaneously lead to higher returns by exerting pressure on local prices. For instance, Clark and Berko (1997) investigated the correlation between monthly foreign purchases of Mexican stocks and Mexican stock returns and found that a surprise foreign inflow equivalent to 1% of domestic market capitalization was associated with a 13% increase in Mexican stock prices. Along the same lines, L'Her and Suret (1997) defined the hyper-return period as a calendar year during which a cumulative geometric return in excess of 70% is observed. Analyzing hyper-return periods from 1976 to 1994 for 20 emerging stock markets, their results also suggested a positive impact of financial liberalization episodes on returns. Finally, Calvo, Leiderman and Reinhart (1996) also documented a significant increase in emerging markets share prices in the period following equity market liberalization: the Argentinean index posted an annual return of 400% in 1991, while Chile and Mexico offered returns of about 100%.

This phenomenon results in a mutually reinforcing dynamic between portfolio adjustment and price pressure within the context of a portfolio-optimizing framework. However, the inevitable opinion reversal among investors often leads to sudden capital outflows and a sharp adjustment in returns. The re-adjustment can be destabilizing for the recipient economy. For instance, Calvo and Mendoza (2000) attempted to measure the consequences of capital account liberalization in the context of informational inefficiencies and multiple equilibriums. They developed a theoretical model in which investors acquire country-specific expertise at a fixed cost and incur variable reputation costs, in a context where information asymmetries give rise to herding behaviour and sudden opinion reversals. They also implemented numerical simulations in the case of Mexico. According to their estimations, a rumour that reduced the expected return on Mexican equity from the equity market forecast (22.4 %) back to the level of the OECD mean return (15.3%) implied an outflow of about $20 billion, or a reduction in the share of the world portfolio invested in Mexico of 40%. The associated economic destabilization costs can be substantial in emerging countries which are often characterized by limited central bank foreign reserves. For instance, using a panel data set over 1975–1997 and covering 24 emerging-market economies, Hutchison and Noy (2006) found that the cumulative output loss of a sudden stop in capital flows amounts to around 13–15% of GDP over a 3-year period.

In line with this type of studies, Tobin (2000) underlined the speculative nature of financial globalization: according to his data, capital flows to emerging countries only represent US$150 billion a year, as opposed to US$1.5 trillion of overall foreign exchange transaction per business day, of which 90% are reversed within a week. The resulting international financial instability has led some authors to cast doubts on the usefulness of capital account liberalization for developing countries. Rodrik's (1998) empirical study is also widely cited. For a cross-section of East Asia, Latin America, and East Asian developing countries, and after controlling for per-capita income, education, institutional quality and regional dummies, he found no correlation between capital account liberalization and growth over the 1975-1989 period. In a recent paper, Jeanne and Gourinchas (2005) also put forward an 'allocation puzzle' in international capital flows: as opposed to neoclassical model assumptions, their theoretical model and estimates suggest that foreign investment has a tendency to flow 'upstream' from capital scarce to capital abundant countries.

3.2.3.3 Financial Contagion

The issue of financial contagion was placed at the forefront of academic debate following the repeated episodes of financial crises that hit emerging markets. These crises include the 1997-1998 Asian crisis, the 1998 Russian crisis, the 1999 Brazilian crisis, the 2001 Turkish crisis, and the 2002 Argentinean crisis. The particularity of these crises is that turmoil originating in a particular market tended to extend to other markets. As a consequence, the term 'contagion' became popular, both in the press and in academic literature, to refer to this phenomenon.

A myriad of studies have empirically tested for financial contagion by modelling shock spillovers among international equity markets. Three salient facts emerge from an investigation of this literature. *First*, financial contagion is common to a vast geographical area and many crisis episodes. *Second*, the nature of the findings cannot be separated from an ongoing methodological debate among empiricists. *Third*, financial contagion interacts with the dynamics international portfolio flows, and destabilizes domestic economies.

3.2.3.3.1 Fundamental or Shift-contagion?

Edwards (2000) underlined that, in the tradition of epidemiological studies, contagion reflects a situation where the effect of an external shock is larger that which was expected by experts and analysts. However, according to Marais and Bates (2006), two types of contagion may be distinguished. *Fundamental contagion* is a mechanic phenomenon resulting from normal interdependencies among economies, both in tranquil and crisis periods. Within this framework, 'monsoonal effects' refer to the cross-country transmission of aggregate shocks that hit different countries and lead to simultaneous negative co-movements. These shocks can be real or financial, and include an increase in international interest rates, a decrease in international demand, or sudden variations in the exchange rates of major currencies (Glick and Rose, 1999). Masson (1998) also argued that emerging market crises were triggered by major economic shifts in industrial countries, while Kaminsky and Reinhardt (2000) emphasized the role of real economic linkages, international bank lending, potential for cross-market hedging, and bilateral and third-party trade in the propagation of international financial shocks.

By contrast, *shift-contagion* is mainly a psychological phenomenon, which appears strongly related to behavioural patterns among investors in specific times of turmoil[3]. This phenomenon is usually explained by sudden opinion reversals among international investors in a situation characterized by informational asymmetries and the presence of multiple equilibriums (Chang and Velasco, 2001). The resulting *shift* in market expectations leads to a significant increase in cross-market linkages after a shock to an individual country or to a group of countries (Forbes and Rigobon, 2001). In other words, shift-contagion refers to the influence of excess returns in one country on the excess returns in another country *after* controlling for the effects of fundamentals. Shocks thus spread through a channel that does not exist during tranquil periods. Shift-contagion is thus a structural break producing both an intensification of relationships and discontinuities in the shock transmission mechanism during a period of turmoil.

This second definition has the advantage of emphasizing the important role played by indiscriminating investors and speculators during a crisis. It is thus a more restrictive definition than the "monsoonal effect", fundamental definition. The concept of shift contagion is also particularly appropriate for statistical analysis, as the structural break can be modelled as a shift in international linkages (AIMR, 2005). Finally, within this definition, *financial vulnerability* refers to the probability that a country will be affected by shift-contagion. Whereas shift-contagion deals with country-to-country crisis transmission within the framework of a specific crisis, vulnerability considers the broader financial interactions within a longer time period (Serwa and Bohl, 2005).

3.2.3.3.2 A Wide Geographical Coverage

Many empirical studies have revealed the wide spread nature of the contagion phenomenon. In developed markets, King and Wadhani (1990) modelled volatility spillovers between the US, the UK and Japan by estimating time-varying correlations between equity returns. They found a significant increase in correlations following the October 1987 stock market crash. Using a similar approach, Lee and Kim (1993) extended the analysis to 12 developed markets and documented further evidence of financial contagion.

Turning to Asian and Latin American emerging markets, Calvo and Reinhart (1995) indicated that the degree of co-movement across weekly equity and Brady bond returns for emerging markets in 11 Latin American countries increased in the wake of the Mexican crisis. Baig and Goldfajn (1998) also presented evidence of an increase in cross-market correlation after the 1997 Asian crisis among the financial markets of Thailand, Malaysia, Indonesia, Korea and the Philippines.

The debate surrounding the integration of Central and European Economies into the European Union has also drawn attention to the question of contagion in those countries. For instance, Serwa and Bohl (2005) investigated contagion in 17 Eastern and Western European stock markets in the wake of 7 big financial shocks between 1997 and 2002. Their results documented stronger evidence of structural breaks in cross-market linkages in Eastern Europe than in Western Europe. Darvas and Szapary (2000) examined the spillover effects of the global financial crises of 1997-1999 on the Czech Republic, Greece, Hungary, Israel and Poland. They found significant evidence of contagious spill-over. Likewise, Gelos and Sahay (2001) examined financial market co-movements across European transition economies and compared their experience to that of other regions using high-frequency data. Their results suggested that the pattern of high-frequency spillovers during the Russian crisis was similar to that observed in other regions during turbulent times.

Turning to Africa, Collins and Biekpe (2003) investigated financial contagion in eight frontier African equity markets during the Asian crisis and found evidence of contagion in the case of Egypt and South Africa. Finally, Alper and Yilmaz (2005) presented an empirical

---

[3] For instance, Eichengreen, Rose, and Wyplosz (1995) highlighted that the countries that came under speculative attack during the ERM crisis had heterogeneous macroeconomic fundamentals: only in some cases could the attack be justified by the degradation of fundamentals.

analysis of real stock return volatility transmission from emerging markets to the Turkish market since 1992, and documented clear evidence of volatility contagion in the aftermath of the Asian Crisis.

3.2.3.3.3 An Ongoing Methodological Debate

The analysis of financial contagion is also indissociable from the ongoing methodological debate on the appropriate means to estimate contagion spillovers. For instance, Forbes and Rigobon (2002) used daily data for stock indices of 28 developed and emerging countries to test for evidence of contagion during the 1987 U.S. stock market crash, the 1994 Mexican peso crisis, and the 1997 Asian crisis and found that most shocks were transmitted through non-crisis-contingent channels after addressing the problem of heteroscedasticity in correlation coefficients.

However, Favero and Giavazzi (2002) extended the measure to a full information framework capturing all nonlinearities in shock transmission and rejected the null of normal interdependency among seven European countries over the 1988-1992 periods. In a similar way, Pesaran and Pick (2002) developed a canonical model of contagion that allowed them to overcome the crisis identification bias inherent to correlation-based analysis. Their results suggested contagion in the European markets during the 1988–1992 period.

Using different assumptions for the variance of country-specific shocks, Corsetti et.al (2005) found contagion in five emerging markets out of a sample of 17 following the 1997 Hong Kong stock market crisis. Using an endogenous method based on a panel approach, Baur and Fry (2005) were able to identify contagion in 11 Asian equity markets during four distinct periods of the same crisis. Finally, modelling Australian equity prices in a structural VAR framework that distinguished between common shocks in international equity markets and domestic shocks in local financial and goods markets, Dungey, Fry and Martin (2004) uncovered additional contagion effects in Australian equity markets during the Asian financial crisis of 1997–1998 and the World Com crisis of 2000.

3.2.3.3.4. Contagion and International Portfolio Investment

The fundamental rationale for international portfolio diversification is that it expands investment opportunities beyond those available through domestic securities. However, the impact of financial contagion on international correlations could lead to a paradox: diversification works the least efficiently when it is most needed.

For instance, Gerlach et.al (2006) analyzed diversification benefits in four East Asian markets using weekly price returns from the 1993-2001 period. Their results showed the existence of significant linkages among these markets and highlighted that fund managers diversifying in East Asia should not ignore the impact of short-term turmoil on portfolio performance when examining the impact of globalization. Similarly, Butler and Joaqui (2002) assessed the benefits of international portfolio diversification by investigating correlations between US, UK, Japanese, Australian and European stock market indices and the corresponding MSCI world-ex-domestic index (that is, world market return excluding the domestic return) over the 372 months from January 1970 through December 2000. Their results suggested that equally weighted portfolio returns in the most extreme bear markets average about 2% less than predicted by a normal distribution. Finally, Schwebach et.el (2002) examined the correlations and volatility of 11 developed and emerging markets and revealed that potential diversification benefits changed dramatically following the devaluation of the baht in Thailand in July of 1997, causing the efficient portfolio set to shift downward and to the right in the Markowitz mean–standard deviation space. Overall, these empirical results echo Das and Uppal's (2004) theoretical model, which suggested that systemic risk reduces the gains from diversification and penalizes investors for holding levered positions.

In turn, the portfolio rebalancing process might also aggravate the contagion wave. Many authors have indeed sought to explain international financial contagion based on portfolio choice mechanisms. In a seminal paper, Schinasi and Smith (2000) argued that elementary portfolio theory offers key insights into financial contagion. They presented a model in which portfolio diversification explains why an investor would find it optimal to significantly reduce all risky asset positions when an adverse shock impacts on just one asset, thereby creating contagious spillovers through the 'contagious selling' of financial assets.

Kodres and Pritsker (2001) also showed how investors may respond to shocks in one market by optimally readjusting their international portfolios, thereby transmitting shocks and generating contagion. In this model, the extent of contagion is worsened in the presence of information asymmetries, which exaggerate price movements due to a bias in the information underlying the order flow.

In a similar vein, Lagunoff and Shreft (2001) developed a model in which agents hold diversified portfolios that link their financial positions to those of other agents in tranquil periods. Shocks at the initial crisis date cause some portfolio losses, to which agents who incur losses respond by reallocating their portfolios. Two related types of financial crisis occur in response: a gradual crisis, occurring as losses spread, and an instantaneous crisis, occurring when forward-looking agents pre-emptively shift to safer portfolios to avoid future losses resulting from contagion.

From an empirical point of view, Ang and Bekaert (2002) investigated the portfolio allocation consequences of increasing correlations and volatilities in bear markets. They modelled the time-varying investment opportunity set using a regime-switching process in which correlations and volatilities increased in bad times. Their results highlighted the significant impact of changing regimes on portfolio weights. More recently, Broner et.al (2006) argued that the impact of past gains and losses on international investors' risk aversion is an important factor in the propagation of financial shocks throughout countries. They examined the behaviour of international mutual funds by monitoring the geographic asset allocation of hundreds of equity funds with a focus on emerging markets, for the 1996-2000 period. Their results suggested that the tendency of mutual funds to respond to relative losses by moving closer to the average portfolio may exacerbate the effect of crises by creating both financial contagion and momentum trading at the country level. Overall, there appears to be a reciprocal relationship between portfolio rebalancing and waves of international contagion.

3.2.3.3.5 Contagion and Economic Instability

Finally, it should be underlined that the recent episodes of financial crisis have highlighted the economic costs associated with financial contagion: during the 1995-2003 periods, the return on the S&P/IFCI Composite Index (a widely used benchmark of emerging market returns) was negative and volatility increased (AIMR, 2005). Adelman and Yeldan (2000) investigated the impact of the East Asian contagion cycle on economic output in the developing world within the framework of an inter-temporal computable general equilibrium model. Their experiments suggested that the affected area's fixed investment declined by 7.9% while its GDP declined by 7.8% upon contagion impact, while the long term effects of the crisis were also felt severely as a consequence of deceleration in the rate of capital accumulation.

Not surprisingly, the issue of contagion vulnerability has become of particular concern for policy making in emerging countries. Some have wondered whether an optimum point between market segmentation and integration might exist, where countries could reap the benefits of financial integration without enduring the costs of contagion (Collins and Biekpe, 2002).

4. THE 'EQUITY MARKET DEVELOPMENT TRIANGLE'

Overall, this survey of the literature reveals that internal and external equity market developments exert separate economic effects. On the one hand, internal market development fosters the mobilization of financial resources and improves corporate governance, subject to satisfactory levels of informational efficiency. On the other hand, evidence highlights the ambiguous economic outcomes of equity market integration. The latter may indeed facilitate corporate financing, but impacts ambiguously on the dynamics of portfolio allocations, and increases the volatility of domestic financial systems. Overall, the optimal degree of international integration seems to depend on a trade-off between cheaper capital and financial stability

Two conclusions arise. *First*, policies seeking to maximize the growth-enhancing impact of equity markets should in priority reach and maintain adequate levels of institutional transparency. *Second*, the external equity market development process should be monitored very carefully. Potential nonlinearities in capital flows and the introduction of an external systemic risk component in domestic markets may indeed induce significant destabilization costs. In the worst possible configuration, premature financial integration would result in increased economic volatility, in a context where additional financial resources would be misallocated due to informational inefficiencies, thereby further increasing economic fragility. In other words, emerging countries may endure the costs of the market integration process without reaping its economic benefits. Taking this into account, policy makers should view institutional and corporate governance reforms as prerequisites for further market integration.

This conclusion appears in line with conventional wisdom. For instance, Aizenman and Powell (2003) suggested that legal and information-related problems explain why volatility has profound effects on emerging market economies. Similarly, Mishkin (1999) claimed that policy makers must put in place the proper institutional structures before liberalizing their financial systems. More generally, the importance of quality institutions for economic development has emerged as a central theme in economic thought. For instance, Rodrik et.al. (2002) have shown that institutional development tends to outperform geography and openness as explanations of real income per capita.

These mechanisms are summarized below using a simple heuristic device. From each side of this *'equity market development triangle'* runs a different axis representing a different facet of equity market development. The origins of these three axes are linked together to form a single triangle. This reflects the existing correlation between the different facets of equity market development.

From the top of this triangle runs a 'resource allocation' axis, which varies from 'institutional underdevelopment' to 'informational efficiency'. This axis represents the impact of market development and informational transparency levels on the allocation of internally and externally mobilized resources. From the right side of this triangle runs a 'resource mobilization' axis, which varies from 'market segmentation' to 'market integration'. This axis represents the impact of market development on the domestic financial sector, in which financing conditions vary from scarce and expensive capital to easier access to finance as equity markets develop and become integrated into global finance. Finally, from the left side runs a 'financial vulnerability' axis, which varies from 'financial repression' to 'financial vulnerability'. This axis represents the pervasive effects of international market integration, which may result in greater shock sensitivity, nonlinearities in capital inflows and a short-term bias in corporate governance. We suggest that the objective of market development policies is to approach the equilibrium point, which is represented by the intersection of these three axes. At this point, market development and market integration result in a slackening of financial constraint at the cost of a reasonable level of financial vulnerability, while the economic efficiency of the additional investments is ensured by an adequate level of market efficiency.

5. SUGGESTIONS FOR FUTURE RESEARCH

This analysis allows us to identify at least three promising research ideas. *First*, the exact factors driving market efficiency are yet to be identified. Such an investigation would help policy makers to design an optimal sequencing of market development reforms. A possible research strategy could be to develop *de facto* and *de jure* institutional indicators reflecting market organizations, by-laws and market size, as well as composite indexes of market efficiency encompassing the various definitions of the concept. It could then be possible to assess the nature of the time-varying relationship between institutions and efficiency within a large panel of frontier, emerging and developed markets.

Second, theoretical models and empirical evidence suggest that equity market integration lowers the cost of capital, but increases financial volatility. Clarifying the relationship uniting market integration, financial vulnerability and the cost of capital, and identifying the main characteristics of firms affected by financial contagion would help policy makers to design appropriate responses. One possibility would be to measure the variations of the firm-level cost of capital within periods of externally induced financial stress and.

Third, the impact of financial integration and shareholder dominance on corporate governance and social, economic and environmental externalities in emerging countries could also be investigated. One possible approach might be to develop proxies for social, environmental and corporate governance, before assessing the impact of equity market development and international integration on these. Ethical funds and Islamic funds also constitute a burgeoning industry providing a new dataset for the traditional finance research agenda (efficiency studies, asset pricing, etc…).

To conclude, one might note that the complexity of the equity market development process may call for an interdisciplinary approach. Financial liberalization has implications for various social sciences including development economics, political science and law.

Increasing data availability and advances in econometric theory also permit researchers to obtain a very high degree of precision in empirical investigations. Taken together, these possible research angles seem to create the conditions for a vast research agenda.

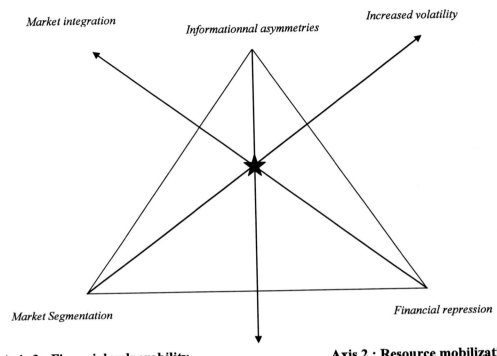

Figure 1. The equity market development triangle.

REFERENCES

Abraham, A., Seyyed, F.J, Alsakran, S.A, 2002. Testing the random walk behaviour and efficiency of Gulf Stock Market. *The Financial Review*, 37, 469-480.

Adelman, I., Yeldan, E., 2000. The minimal conditions for a financial crisis: A multiregional intertemporal CGE model of the Asian crisis. *World Development*, 28, 1087-1100.

Agenor, P.-R. 2003. Benefits and costs of international financial integration: theory and facts. *World Economy* 26, 1089-1118.

Aggarwal, R., B., Lucey, C., Muckley, 2004. Dynamics of equity market integration in Europe: evidence of changes over time and with events. *Institute of International Integration Studies Discussion paper*, DP 19.

Aggarwal, R., Rivoli, P., 1989. Seasonal and day of the week effects in four emerging stock markets. *Financial Review*, 24, 541-50.

Aglietta, M., 2001. Macroéconomie Financière 1. Repères, Editions La Découverte.

Aizenmann, J., Powell, A., 2003. Volatility and financial intermediation. *Journal of International Money and Finance* 22, 657-679.

Akdogan, H, 1997. International security selection under segmentation: theory and application. *Journal of Portfolio* 21, 33-40.

Akyüz Y., Boratav K., 2005. The making of the Turkish financial crisis. in *Financialization and the World Economy*, edited by Gerald Epstein of the Political Economy Research Institute.

Al-Khouri, R., 2005. Corporate governance and firms' value in emerging markets: the case of Jordan. *Advances in Financial Economics* 11, 31-50.

Al-Loughani, N., Chappell, D. Modelling the day-of-the-week effect in the Kuwait stock exchange. *Applied Financial Economics* 11, 353-359.

Al-Loughani, N.E, 1995. Random walk in thinly traded stock markets: the case of Kuwait. *Arab Journal of Administrative Science* 3, 198-209.

Aloui, C., 2003. Long-range dependence in daily volatility on Tunisian stock market. *Economic Research Forum*, Working Paper 40.

Alper, C. E., Yılmaz, K., 2004. Volatility and contagion: evidence from the Istanbul stock exchange. *Economic Systems* 28, 353-367.

Alper, C.E., 2001. The liquidity crisis of 2000: what went wrong? *Russian East Europe Finance Trade* 37, 54–75.

Al-Saad, K., Moosa, I.A., 2005. Seasonality in stock returns: evidence from an emerging market. *Applied Financial Economics* 15, 63-71.

American Institute for Management Research, 2005. Investing in Emerging Markets, *CFA Publications*.

Andrews, D.W.K., 1993. Tests for parameter instability and structural change with unknown change point. *Econometrica* 61, 821-856.

Ang, A., Bekaert, G., 2002. International asset allocation with regime shifts. *Review of Financial Studies*, Oxford University Press for Society for Financial Studies 15, 1137-1187.

Arbelaez H., Urrutia J., Abbas N., 2001. Short-term and long-term linkages among the Colombian capital market indexes. *International Review of Financial Analysis* 10, 237-273.

Arouri, M.E.H, 2003. Intégration financière et diversification internationale de portefeuilles : une analyse multivariée. *Working Paper, MODEM-CNRS*, Université Paris X-Nanterre.

Atje, R., Jovanovic, B., 1993. Stock markets and development. *European Economic Review*, 37, 632-640.

Bacchetta P., Wincoop, E.V., 2000. Capital flows to emerging markets. Liberalization, overshooting and volatility., in Edwards S.(Ed.) *Capital Inflows and the Emerging Economies*, University of Chicago Press and NBER, Cambridge, MA. 61-98.

Bae, K.-H., Karolyi, G.A., Stulz, R.M., 2003. A new approach to measuring financial contagion. *Review of Financial Studies* 16, 717–763.

Baig, T., Goldfajn, I., 1998. Financial market contagion in the Asian crisis. *IMF Staff Paper* 98-155.

Bailey, W., Chung, Y.P., 1995. Exchange rate fluctuations, political risk and stock returns: some evidence from an emerging market, *Journal of Financial and Quantitative Analysis* 30, 541–560.

Balaban, E., 1995. Day of the week effects: new evidence from an emerging stock market, *Applied Economics Letters* 2, 139-43.

Bancel, N., Perrotin, T., 2005. Le cout du capital dans les pays émergents. *ESCP-EAP Working Paper.*

Barari, M. 2004. Equity market integration in Latin America: A time-varying integration score analysis. *International Review of Financial Analysis* 13, 649-668.

Bartram, S. M., Dunfey, G., 2001. International portfolio investment: theory, evidence, and institutional framework. *Financial Markets, Institutions and Instruments* 10, 85-155.

Basher, S.A., Sadorsky, P. 2006. Day-of-the-week effects in emerging stock markets. *Applied Economics Letters* 13, 621-628.

Baur, D., Fry, R. 2005 Endogenous contagion – A panel analysis . *CAMA and EC Working Paper.*

Bekaert, G., Harvey C., 1998. Capital markets: an engine for economic growth. *Brown Journal of World Affairs* (Winter/Spring),.33-53.

Bekaert, G., Harvey, C. 1995. Time-varying world market integration. *Journal of Finance,* 50, 403-444.

Bekaert, G., Harvey, C., 1997. Emerging equity market volatility. *Journal of Financial Economics* 43, 29-78.

Bekaert, G., Harvey, C., 1998. Capital flows and the behavior of emerging market equity returns. *NBER Working Paper No. W6669.*

Bekaert, G., Harvey, C., 1998. Foreign speculators and emerging markets. *The Davidson Institute Working Paper Series*, Number 79.

Bekaert, G., Harvey, C., 2000. Foreign speculators and emerging equity markets. *Journal of Finance,* 55, 565-613.

Bekaert, G., Harvey, C., 2002. Research in emerging markets finance: looking to the future. *Emerging Markets Review* 3, 429–448.

Bekaert, G., Harvey, C., 2003. Emerging markets finance. *Journal of Empirical Finance* 10, 3–55.

Bekaert, G., Harvey, C., Lumsdaine, C., 2002. Dating the integration of world capital markets. *Journal of Financial Economics* 65, 203-249.

Bekaert, G., Harvey, C., Lundblad, C., 2001. *Does financial liberalization spur growth. Working Paper,* Columbia University and Duke University.

Bekaert, G., Harvey, C., Lundblad, C., 2001. Emerging equity markets and economic development. *Journal of Development Economics* 66, 465-504.

Bekaert, G., Harvey, C., Lundblad, C.T., 2000. Emerging Equity Markets and Economic Development. *NBER Working Paper No. W7763.*

Bekaert, G., Harvey, C., Ng, A., 2005. Market integration and contagion. *Journal of Business* 78, 39–70.

Bekaert, G., Hodrick, H., 1992. Characterizing predictable components in excess return on equity and foreign exchange markets. *Journal of Finance* 47, 467-509.

Bernard, A., 1991. Empirical implications of the convergence hypothesis. *CEPR Working Papers.* London.

Bessembinder, H., Chan, K., 1995. The profitability of technical trading rules in the Asian stock markets, *Pacific-Basin Finance Journal* 3, 257-284.

Bessembinder, H., Chan, K., 1998. Market efficiency and the returns to technical analysis. *Financial Management* 27, 5–17.

Bilson, C.M., Brailsford, T.J., Hooper, V.C., 2002. The explanatory power of political risk in emerging markets. *International Review of Financial Analysis* 11, 1-27.

Black F., 1972. Capital market equilibrium with restricted borrowing. *Journal of Business* 45, 444-454.

Black, B.S., Love, I., Rachinsky, A., 2006. Corporate governance indices and firms' market values: Time series evidence from Russia. *Emerging Markets Review* 7, 361-379.

Blavy, R. 2002. Changing volatility in emerging markets: a case study of two Middle Estern stock exchanges. *Revue Entente Cordiale* 02.

Bohn H., Tesar, L. 1996. US equity investment in foreign markets: portfolio rebalancing or return chasing? *American Economic Review* 86, 77-81.

Boubakri, N., Cosset, J.C., Guedhami, O., 2005. Liberalization, corporate governance and the performance of privatized firms in developing countries. *Journal of Corporate Finance* 11, 767–790.

Boyd, J. , Smith, B., 1996. The coevolution of the real and financial sectors in the growth process. *World Bank Economic Review*, Oxford University Press 10, 371-96.

Brock, W., Lakonishok, J., LeBaron, B., 1992. Simple technical trading rules and the stochastic properties of stock returns. *Journal of Finance* 47, 1731–1764.

Broner, F.A, Gelos, G., Reinhart, C.M, 2006. When in peril, retrench: Testing the portfolio channel of contagion. *Journal of International Economics* 69, 203-230.

Brown, D. P., Zhang, Z.M., 1997. Market orders and market efficiency. *Journal of Finance* 52, 277-308.

Bunkanwicha, P., Gupta, J., Rofikoh, R., 2006. Debt and entrenchment: Evidence from Thailand and Indonesia. *European Journal of Operational Research*, In Press, Corrected Proof, Available online 20 October 2006.

Butler, K.C., Joaqui, D.C., 2002. Are the gains from international portfolio diversification exaggerated? The influence of downside risk in bear markets. *Journal of International Money and Finance* 21, 981-1011. Cajueiro, D.O., Tabak, B.M., 2005. Possible causes of long-range dependence in the Brazilian stock market Physica A 345, 635-645.

Calvo, G. A, Leiderman, L., Reinhart, C.M., 1996. Inflows of capital to developing countries in the 1990s. *Journal of Economic Perspectives* 10, 123-139.

Calvo, G.A.,Mendoza, E. G., 1998. Rational herd behavior and the globalization of securities markets. *Duke Economics Working Paper* No. 97-26.

Calvo, G., Mendoza, E., 2000. Rational contagion and the globalization of securities markets. *Journal of International Economics* 51, 79-113.

Calvo, S., Reinhart, C., 1996. Capital flows to Latin America: Is there evidence of contagion effects? In G. Calvo, M. Goldstein, & E. Hochreiter (Eds.), Private capital flows to emerging markets after the Mexican crisis. Washington, D.C.: *Institute for International Economics*.

Capasso, S., 2004. Stock market development and economic growth: A matter of information dynamics. *CNR-ISSM Working Paper*, University of Salerno.

Caporale, G.M., Howells, P.G, Soliman, A.M, 2004. Stock market development and economic growth: the causal linkage. *Journal of Economic Development* 29, 156-178.

Carrieri, F., Errunza, V., Majerbi, B., 2006a. Does emerging market exchange risk affect global equity prices? *Journal of Financial and Quantitative Analysis*, in press.

Carrieri, F., Errunza, V., Majerbi, B., 2006b. Local risk factors in emerging markets: Are they separately priced? *Journal of Empirical Finance* 13, 444-461.

Cartapanis, A., 2004. Les marchés financiers internationaux. *Repères, Editions La Découverte.*

Chang R., Velasco, A., 2001. A model of financial crises in emerging markets: a canonical model. *Quarterly Journal of Economics* 116, 489-517.

Chang, E.J., Lima, E.J.A., Tabak, B.M., 2004. Testing for predictability in emerging equity markets. *Emerging Markets Review* 5, 295-316.

Chang, K.P., Ting, K.S., 2000. A variance ratio test of the random walk hypotheses for Taiwan's stock market. *Applied Financial Economics* 10, 525-532.

Chari, A., Henry, P.B., 2004. Risk sharing and asset prices: evidence from a natural experiment. *Journal of Finance* 59, 1295-1324.

Chelley-Steeley, P., 2004. Equity market integration in the Asia-Pacific region: A smooth transition analysis. *International Review of Financial Analysis* 13, 621-632.

Cheung K-C., Coutts J.A., 2001. A note on weak form market efficiency in security prices: evidence from the Hong Kong stock exchange. *Applied Economics Letters* 8, 407-410.

Cho Y.J., 1986. Inefficiencies from financial liberalization in the absence of well-functioning equity markets. *Journal of Money, Credit, and Banking* 18, 559-580.

Chordia, T., Roll, R., Subrahmanyam, A., 2005. Evidence on the speed of convergence to market efficiency. *Journal of Financial Economics* 76, 271-292.

Chou, R., Ng., V., Pi. L., 1994. Cointegration of international stock market indices. *IMF Working Papers.*

Chuah, H.L., 2004. Are international equity market co-movements driven by real or financial integration? *Duke University Durham Working Paper*, 2004.

Chuhan, P., 1992. Sources of portfolio investment in emerging markets. *Working Paper, International Economics Department, World Bank.*

Clark, J., Berko, E., 1997. Foreign investment fluctuations and emerging stock returns: the case of Mexico. Staff Report, 24, *Federal Reserve Bank of New-York*, New York, NY.

Collins, D., Biekpe, N. 2002. Contagion: A fear for African equity markets? *Journal of Economics and Business* 55, 285-297.

Corsetti, G., Pericoli, M., Sbracia, M., 2005. Some contagion, some interdependence: More pitfalls in tests of financial contagion. *Journal of International Money and Finance* 24, 1177-1199.

Dailami, M., Atkin, M., 1990. Stock markets in developing countries: key issues and a research agenda. PRE Working Paper Series, WPS 515. Washington D.C.: *International Finance Corporation & The World Bank.*

Darvas, Z., Szapáry, G., 2000. Financial contagion in five small open economies: does the exchange rate regime really matter? *International Finance* 3, 25–51.

Das, S. Uppal, R., 2004. Systemic Risk and International Portfolio Choice. *Journal of. Finance* 59, 2809-2834.

Davies, A., 2006. Testing for international equity market integration using regime switching cointegration techniques. *Review of Financial Economics* 15, 305-321.

De Fusco, R., Geppert, J., Tsetsekos, G., 1996. Long run diversification potential in emerging stock markets. *The Financial Review* 31, 343-363.

De Santis, G., Imrohoroglu, S., 1997. Stock returns and volatility in emerging financial markets, *Journal of International Money and Finance* 16, 561–579.

Dellas H., Hess M., 2005. Financial development and stock returns: A cross-country analysis. *Journal of International Money and Finance* 24, 891-912.

Demirguc-Kunt, A. Levine, R., 1996. Stock markets, corporate finance, and economic growth: an overview. *World Bank Economic Review* 10, 223-239.

Demirguc-Kunt, A., 1992. Developing country capital structures and emerging stock markets. Policy Research Working Paper Series 933, *The World Bank.*

Demirguc-Kunt, A., Levine, R. 1996. Stock market development and financial intermediaries: stylized facts. *World Bank Economic Review*,10, 291-321.

Demirguc-Kunt, A., Levine, R., 1995. Stock market development and financial intermediaries: stylized facts, Policy Research Working Paper Series 1462, *The World Bank.*

Demirgüç-Kunt, A., Maksimovic, V., 1998. Law, finance, and firm growth. *Journal of Finance* 53, 2107-2137.

Divecha, A.B., Drach, J., Sefek, D., 1992. Emerging markets. A quantitative perspective. *Journal of Portfolio Management.* Fall: 41-50.

Diwan, I., Errunza, V., Senbet, L., 1994. Diversification benefits of country funds. Investing in Emerging Markets, *Euromoney Books and the World Bank Working Paper.*

Dockery, E., Vergari, F., 1997. Testing the random walk hypothesis: evidence for the Budapest stock exchange. *Applied Economic Letters* 4, 627-629.

Dungey, M., Fry, R., Martin, V., González-Hermosillo, B., 2004. Empirical Modeling of Contagion: A Review of Methodologies. IMF Working Papers 04/78, *International Monetary Fund.*

Dyck, A., 2001. Privatization and corporate governance principles, evidence, and future challenges. *The World Bank Research Observer* 16, 59–84.

Edison, H.,Warnock, F., 2003. A simple measure of the intensity of capital controls. *Journal of Empirical Finance,* 10, 81-103.

Edwards, S., 2000 Contagion. *World Economy*, 23, pp. 873–900.

Ehling, P., Ramos, S.,B., 2005. Geographic Versus Industry Diversification: Constraints Matter. FAME Research Paper Series rp113, *International Center for Financial Asset Management and Engineering.*

Eichengreen B., Pempel T.J., 2002. Why has there been less financial integration in East Asia than in Europe? *Institute of East Asian Studies and the Institute of European Studies,* Working Paper.

Eichengreen, B., Rose, A.K., Wyplosz, C., 1996. Contagious currency crises. *NBER Working Paper No. 5681.*

El-Erian, M.A, Kumar M.S, 1995. Emerging equity markets in Middle Eastern countries, *IMF Staff Paper* 42, 313-343.

Engle, R., 2001. Financial econometrics – A new discipline with new methods. *Journal of Econometrics* 100, 53-56.

Erdal F., Gunduz L., 2001. An empirical investigation of the interdependence of Istanbul Stock Exchange with selected stock markets. An International Conference: *Economies and Business In Transition, Global Business and Technology Association,* Istanbul.

Errunza, V., 1977. Gains from portfolio diversification into less developed countries' securities. *Journal of International Business Studies* 8, 83-99.

Errunza, V., 1999. Foreign portfolio equity investments in economic development. Working paper available at SSRN: *http://ssrn.com/abstract=176939.*

Errunza, V., Losq, E., 1985. International asset pricing under mild segmentation: Theory and test. *Journal of Finance* 40, 105-124.

Errunza, V., Losq, E., Padmanabhan., P., 1992. Tests of integration, mild integration and segmentation hypotheses. *Journal of Banking and Finance* 16, 949-972.

Errunza, V., Miller, D., 1998, Market segmentation and the cost of capital in international equity markets, *McGill University Working Paper*.

Estrada, J., 2000. The cost of equity in emerging markets: a downside risk approach. *Emerging Market Quarterly* 56, 19–30.

Estrada, J., 2002. Systematic risk in emerging markets: the D-CAPM. *Emerging Markets Review* 3, 365–379.

Eun, C.S., Resnick, B.G., 1994. International Diversification of Investment Portfolios: U.S. and Japanese Perspectives, *Management Science* 40, p. 140-160.

Fama, E., 1970. Efficient capital markets: A review of theory and empirical work. *Journal of Finance* 25, 383–417.

Favero, C.A., Giavazzi, F., 2002. Is the international propagation of shocks non linear? Evidence from the ERM. *Journal of Financial Economics* 57, 231-246.

Fawson, R., 1996. The weak-form efficiency of the Taiwan share market. *Applied Economics Letters* 3, 663-67.

Fernandez-Arias, E., 1996. The new wave of private capital inflows: Push or pull?, *Journal of Development Economics* 48, 389–418.

Ferson, W.E., Harvey, C., 1992. Seasonality and consumption-based asset pricing. *Journal of Finance* 47, 511-552.

Fishburn, P.C., 1977. Mean-risk analysis with risk associated with below-target returns. *American Economic Review* 67, 116–126.

Flood, R.P.,Rose, A.K., 2005. Estimating the expected marginal rate of substitution: A systematic exploitation of idiosyncratic risk. *Journal of Monetary Economics* 52, 951-969.

Forbes, K.J., Rigobon, R., 2001. Measuring contagion: conceptual and empirical issues. In: Claessens, Stijn, Forbes, Kristin J. (Eds.), International Financial Contagion: How it Spreads and How it Can be Stopped. *Kluwer Academic Publishers*, Dordrecht, pp. 43–66.

Forbes, K.J., Rigobon, R., 2002. No contagion, only interdependence: measuring stock market co-movements. *Journal of Finance* 57, 2223–2261.

Franks, J., Mayer, C., 1990. Takeovers: capital markets and corporate control: a study of France, Germany and the UK. Economic Policy: *A European Forum* 10, 189-231.

Fratzscher, M. 2001. Financial market integration in Europe: on the effects of EMU on stock markets. Working Paper Series 48, *European Central Bank*.

Froot K.A., O'Connell, P.G.J., Seashole, M.S., 2001. The portfolio flows of international. investors. *Journal of Financial Economics* 59, 151-193.

Frost, P.A., Savarino, J.E., 1988. For better performance: constrain portfolio weights. *Journal of Portfolio Management*, 15, 29-34.

Füss, R., 2002. The financial characteristics between emerging and developed equity markets. Paper presented at the *ECOMOD conference*, 2002.

Gabriel, V.J., Sola, M., Psaradakis, Z., 2002. A simple method for testing for cointegration subject to multiple regime changes. *Economics Letters* 76, 213–221.

Gallagher, L. 1995. Interdependancies among the Irish, British and German Stock Markets. *Economic and Social Review* 26, 131-147.

Gębka, B., Serwa, D., 2006. Intra- and inter-regional spillovers between emerging capital markets around the world. Research in International Business and Finance, forthcoming.

Gelos, G., Sahay, R., 2001. Financial spillovers in transition economies. *Economics of Transition* 9, 53–86.

Gérard, B., Thanyalakpark, K., Batten, J.A., 2003. Are the East Asian markets integrated? Evidence from the ICAPM. *Journal of Economics and Business*, Volume 55, 585-607 .

Gerlach, R., Wilson, P., Zurbruegg, R., 2006. Structural breaks and diversification: The impact of the 1997 Asian financial crisis on the integration of Asia-Pacific real estate markets. On line Working Paper.

Gilmore, C.G., McManus, G.M., Tezel, A., 2005. Portfolio allocations and the emerging equity markets of Central Europe. *Journal of Multinational Financial Management* 15, 2887-3000.

Glick, R., Rose, A.K., 1999. Contagion and trade: Why are currency crises regional? *Journal of International Money and Finance*, 18, 603-617.

Goldsmith, R. 1969. *Financial Structure and Development*, New Haven, CT, Yale University Press.

Gorkittisunthorn, M., Jumreornvong, S., Limpaphayom, P., 2006. Insider ownership, bid–ask spread, and stock splits: Evidence from the Stock Exchange of Thailand. *International Review of Financial Analysis* 15, 450-461.

Grieb, T., Reyes, M., 1999. Random walk tests for Latin American equity indexes and individual firms, *Journal of Financial Research* 22, 371-383.

Groenewold, N., Tang, S.H.K., Wu, Y., 2003. The efficiency of the Chinese stock market and the role of the banks. *Journal of Asian Economics* 14, 593-609.

Haber, S., 1991. Industrial concentration and the capital markets: A comparative study of Brazil, Mexico, and the United States, 1830-1930. *The Journal of Economic History* 19, 57-67.

Hardouvelis, G. A., Malliaropoulos, D., Priestley, R., 1999. EMU and European Stock Market Integration. *CEPR Discussion Papers* 2124, C.E.P.R. Discussion Papers.

Harvey, C., 1989. Time-varying conditional covariances in tests of asset pricing models. *Journal of Financial Economics* 24, 289-317.

Harvey, C., 1995. Predictable risk and returns in emerging markets. *Review of Financial Studies* 8, 773-816.

Harvey, C., 2000. Drivers of expected returns in international markets. *Emerging Market Quarterly* 4, 32–49.

Henry, C., Springborg, R., 2004. Globalization and the Politics of Development in the Middle-East. Cambridge, Mass, *Cambridge University Press.*

Hubbard, M., 2000. Money, the Financial System, and the Economy. Reading, MA: In Glenn Hubbard (Ed.) *Asymmetric Information, Corporate Finance and International Development* 11, 343-365.

Hutchison, M., Noy, I., 2006. Sudden stops and the Mexican wave: currency crises, capital flow reversals and output loss in emerging markets. *Journal of Development Economics*, 79, 225-248.

Ickes, B.W., Seabright, P., Yudaeva, K, 2004. Book Reviews. *Economics of Transition* 12, 801-809.

Jeanne, O., Gourinchas, P.O., 2005. Capital flows to developing countries: the allocation puzzle. Meeting Papers 240, *Society for Economic Dynamics.*

Jeffers, E., 2005. Corporate governance: towards converging models? *Global Finance Journal* 16, 221-232.

Jefferson, G. H., 2002. China's evolving (implicit) economic constitution *China Economic Review* 13, 394-401.

Jensen, M., Meckling, W., 1976.Theory of the firm: managerial behavior, agency costs, and capital structure. *Journal of Financial Economics* 3, 305-360.

Johansen, S., Juselius, K., 1990. Maximum likelihood estimation and inference on cointegration - with applications to the demand for money. *Oxford Bulletin of Economics and Statistics,* 52, 2.

Jones, C., 2001. A century of stock market liquidity and trading costs. Working paper, Columbia University. Available at: *www.columbia.edu/~cj88/papers/century.pdf.*

Kaminsky, G.L., Reinhart, C.M., 2000. On crises, contagion, and confusion. *Journal of International Economics,* Vol. 51, Issue 1, pp. 145-168.

Kanas, A., 1988. Linkages between the US and European equity markets: further evidence from cointegration tests. *Applied Financial Economics* 8, 607-614.

Karolyi, G.A., Stulz, R., 1996. Why do markets move together? An investigation of the US-Japan stock return comovements. *The Journal of Finance* 2, 951-986.

Kasa, K., 1992. Common stochastic trends in international stock markets. *Journal of Monetary Economics* 29, 95-124.

Kawakatsu, H., Morey, M., 1999. Financial liberalization and stock market efficiency: an empirical examination of nine emerging market countries. *Journal of Multinational Financial Management* 9, 353-371.

Kearney, C., Lucey, B. 2004. International equity market integration, *International Review of Financial Analysis Special Issue* 13-5 (eds).

Kearney, C., Poti, V., 2006. Correlation dynamics in European equity markets. *Research in International Business and Finance* 20, 305-321.

Kenny, C., Moss, T., 1998. Stock markets in Africa: emerging lions or white elephants? *World Development,* 26, 829-843.

Khwaja, A.I., Mian, A., 2005. Unchecked intermediaries: Price manipulation in an emerging stock market. *Journal of Financial Economics* 78, 203-241.

Kim, J., Wilson, J. 1997. Capital mobility and environmental standards: racing to the bottom with multiple tax instruments. *Japan and the World Economy* 9, 537-551.

Kim, W., Sung, T. What makes firms manage FX risk? *Emerging Markets Review* 6, 263-288.

King R., Levine, R., 1993. Finance, entrepreneurship, and growth. Paper presented at *World Bank Conference* on "How Do National Policies Affect Long-term Growth",Washington D.C., February, 1993.

King, M.A., Wadhwani, S., 1990. Transmission of volatility between stock markets, *Review of Financial Studies* 3, 5–33.

Koch, P.D., Koch, T.W., 1991. Evolution in Dynamic Linkages across National Stock Indexes. *Journal of International Money and Finance* 10, 231-251.

Kodres L.E., Pritsker M., 2001. A rational expectations model of financial contagion. *International Monetary Fund and the Board of Governors of the Federal Reserve System*, Working Paper.

Krishnamurti, C., Šević, A., Šević, Z., 2005. Voluntary disclosure, transparency, and market quality: Evidence from emerging market ADRs. *Journal of Multinational Financial Management* 15, 435-454.

Kumar, P. C., Tsetsekos, G.P., 1999. The differentiation of 'emerging' equity markets. *Applied Financial Economics* 9, 443-453.

L'Her, J.M., Suret, J.F., 1997. Liberalization, political risk and stock market returns in emerging markets. *CIRANO Working Paper*, 97s-15.

Lagunoff, R., Schreft, S., 2001. A model of financial fragility. *Journal of Economic Theory* 99, 220-264.

Lazonick, W., O'Sullivan, M., 1996. *Organisation, Finance and International Competition; Industrial and Corporate Change*, 5, 1.

Lee, S.B., Kim, K.J., 1993. Does the October 1987 crash strengthen the co-movements among national stock markets? *Review of Financial Economics* 3, 89–102.

Lee., K.C., Kwok., C.V., 1988. Multinational corporations versus domestic corporations: International environment factors and determinants of capital structure. *Journal of International Business Studies* 19, 195-217.

Lesmond, D.A., 2005. Liquidity of emerging markets. *Journal of Financial Economics* 77, 411-452.

Lesmond, D.A., Ogden, J., Trzcinka, C., 1999. A new estimate of transaction costs. *Review of Financial Studies* 12, 1113–1141.

Levine, R., Zervos, S., 1998. Stock markets, banks, and economic growth. *The American Economic Review* 88, 537-558.

Li, K., Sarkar, A., Wang, Z., 1999. Diversification benefits of emerging markets subject to portfolio constraints. Working Paper No. UBCFIN99-5

Lima, E.J.A, Tabak, B.M., 2004. Tests of the random walk hypothesis for equity markets: evidence from China, Hong Kong and Singapore, *Applied Economics Letters* 11, 255-258.

Lintner, J., 1965. The valuation of risk assets and the selection of risky investments in stock portfolios and capital budgets. *Review of Economics and Statistics* 47, 13-37.

Lo, A. W., Mackinlay, A.C, 1988. Stock market prices do not follow random walks. Evidence from a simple specification test. *Review of Financial Studies* 1, 41-66.

Lo, A. W., MacKinlay, A.C., 1989. The size and power of the variance ratio test in finite samples. *Journal of Econometrics* 40, 203-238.

Longin, F., Solnik, B., 1995. Is the correlation of international equity returns constant: 1960-1990? *Journal of International Money and Finance* 14, 3-26.

Lucey B., Voronkova, S., 2006. Linkages and relationships between emerging European and developed stock markets before and after the Russian crisis of 1997-1998. In *Emerging European Financial Markets: Independence and Integration Post-Enlargement*, Routledge.

Lucey, B., Voronkova, S., 2006. The relations between emerging european and developed stock markets before and after the Russian crisis of 1997–1998. *International Finance Review* 6, 383-413.

Madura, J., 1992. *International Financial Management*. New York : West Publishing Company.

Madura, J., Abernathy, G., 1985. Playing the international stock diversification game with an unmarked deck. *Journal of Business Research* 13, 465-71.

Marais, E., Bates, S., 2006. An empirical study to identify shift contagion during the Asian crisis. *Journal of International Financial Markets*, Institutions and Money 16, 468-479.

Markowitz, H., 1952. *Portfolio Selection :* Efficient Diversification of Investment, Yale University Press.

Markowitz, H., 1959. *Portfolio Selection*. John Wiley & Sons, New York.

Masson, P., 1998. Contagion-Monsoonal Effects, Spillovers, and Jumps Between Multiple Equilibria," IMF Working Papers 98/142, *International Monetary Fund.*

McKinnon, R., 1973. *Money and Capital in Economic Development.* Washington D.C., Brookings Institution.

Mishkin, F.S, White, E.N., 2003. U.S. Stock Market Crashes and Their Aftermath: Implications for Monetary Policy in William B. Hunter, George G. Kaufman and

Michael Pormerleano, eds., Asset Price Bubbles: The Implications for Monetary, Regulatory and International Policies, *MIT Press*, 53-79.

Mishkin, F.S., 1999. Lessons from the Tequila Crisis. *Journal of Banking and Finance* 23,1521-1533.

Mobarek, A., Keasey, K., 2000. Weak- form market efficiency of an emerging market: evidence from Dhaka stock market of Bangladesh. Presented at *ENBS Conference*, Oslo, 2000. Available online at: *http://www.bath.ac.uk/cds/enbs-papers-pdfs/mobarek-new.pdf*

Moosa, A., Al-Loughani, A., 2003. The role of fundamentalists and technicians in the foreign exchange market when the domestic currency is pegged to a basket. *Applied Financial Economics* 13, 79-84.

Myers, S., Majluf, N., 1984. Corporate financing and investment decisions when firms have information that investors do not have. *Journal of Financial Economics* 13, 187-221.

Nardai, F., Griffin, J.M., Stulz, R., 2002. Do Investors Trade More when Stocks have Performed Well? Evidence from 46 Countries. *Dice Center Working Paper* 13. Available at *SSRN: http://ssrn.com/abstract=567082.*

Nath, G.C., Dalvi, M., 2004. Day of the week effect and market efficiency – evidence from Indian equity market using high frequency data of national stock exchange. Working paper, CCIL, India.

Ndikumana, L., 2001. A study of capital account regimes in Africa. Paper prepared for the *UNCTAD workshop on "Management of capital flows: comparative experiences and implications for Africa"* held in Cairo on March 20- 21, 2001.

Oshikoya T.W., Osita O., 2003. Financial liberalization, emerging stock markets and economic developments in Africa. *In African Voices on Structural Adjustment*, Edited by Thandika Mkandawire and Charles C. Soludo, International Development Research Center.

Panton, D.B., Lessig, V.P., Joy, O.M., 1976. Comovement of international equity markets : a taxonomic approach. *The Journal of Financial and Quantitative Analysis* 11, 415-432.

Parisi, F., Vasquez, A., 2000. Simple technical trading rules of stock returns: evidence from 1987 to 1998 in Chile. *Emerging Markets Review* 1, 152–164.

Park Y.C., 2002. Financial liberalization and economic integration in East Asia. Unpublished manuscript, Korea University.

Patro, D.K., Wald, J.K., 2005. Firm characteristics and the impact of emerging market liberalizations. *Journal of Banking and Finance* 29, 1671-95.

Perotti, E., van Oijen, P., 2001. Privatization, market development and political risk in emerging economies. *Journal of International Money and Finance* 20, 43-69.

Pesaran H., Pick A., 2004. Econometric Issues in the Analysis of Contagion. *Cambridge Working Papers in Economics* 0402, Faculty of Economics, University of Cambridge.

Phylaktis, K., 1999. Capital market integration in the Pacific Basin region. An impulse response analysis. *Journal of International Money and Finance* 18, 287-91.

Phylaktis, K., Ravazzolo, F., 2002. Currency risk in emerging equity markets. *City University Business School, Finance Working Paper.*

Phylaktis, K., Xia, L., 2006. Sources of firms' industry and country effects in emerging markets. *Journal of International Money and Finance* 25, 459-475.

Piesse, J., Hearn, B., 2001. Integration and the asymmetric transmission of volatility: a study of equity market in sub-Saharan Africa. Paper presented at the *Financial Empowerment for Africa conference,* Cape Town, RSA.

Pollin, J.P, 2002. L'excessive volatilité des marchés financiers : quelles explications, quelles conséquences, quelles régulations ? *Chroniques Economiques, Le Cercle des Economistes.*

Rangvid, J., 2001. Increasing convergence among European stock markets? A recursive common stochastic trends analysis. *Economics Letters* 71, 383–389.

Ratner, M., Leal, R.P.C., 1999. Tests of technical trading strategies in the emerging equity markets of Latin America and Asia. *Journal of Banking and Finance* 23, 1887–1905.

Razin, S.E., Yuen, C.W., 1999. An information-based model of foreign direct investment: the gains from trade revisited. *NBER WP 6884.*

Rodrik, D. 1998. Who needs capital-account convertibility? In Should the IMF Pursue Capital Account Convertibility? *Essays in International Finance* no. 207, Department of Economics, Princeton University.

Rodrik, D., Subramanian, A., Trebbi, F., 2002. Institutions rule: the primacy of institutions over geography and integration in economic development. *CEPR Discussion Paper*, no. 3643. London: CEPR.

Santiso, J., 1997. Wall Street face à la crise mexicaine : Une analyse temporelle des marchés émergents. *Les Etudes du CERI,* 34. 12/97.

Sappenfield, R., Speidell, L., 1992. Global diversification in a shrinking world. *Journal of Portfolio Management* 19, 57-67.

Schinasi, G., Smith, T., 2000. Portfolio diversification, leverage, and financial contagion, *IMF Staff Papers* 47, 159–176.

Schwebach, R.G., Olienyk, J.P, Zumwalt, J.K., 2002. The impact of financial crises on international diversification. *Global Finance Journal* 13, 147-161.

Seddighi, H.R., Nian, W., 2004. The Chinese stock exchange market: operations and efficiency. *Applied Financial Economics* 14, 785-797.

Serletis, A., King, M., 1997. Common stochastic trends and convergence of European Union stock markets. *Manchester Business School Working Paper 65.*

Serwa, D., Bohl, M., 2005. Financial contagion vulnerability and resistance: a comparison of European capital markets. *Economic Systems* 29, 344-362.

Sharpe, W.F., 1964. Capital asset prices - A theory of market equilibrium under conditions of risk. *Journal of Finance* 1964, 425-442.

Shaw, E.S., 1973. Financial Deepening in Economic Development. New York, *Oxford University Press.*

Sheng, H.-C., Tu, A.H., 2000. A study of cointegration and variance decomposition among national equity indices before and during the period of the Asian financial crisis. *Journal of Multinational Financial Management* 10, 345-365.

Singh, A., 1997. Financial liberalization, stock markets and economic development. *The Economic Journal* 107, 771-782.

Sinquefield, R.A., 1996. *Where are the Gains from International Diversification?* On line working paper.

Smith, G., Jefferis, K., 2005. The changing efficiency of African stock markets. *South African Journal of Economics* 73, 54-67.

Solnik, B., 1974. An equilibrium model of the international capital market. *Journal of Economic Theory* 8, 500-524.

Steeley, J.M., 2006. Volatility transmission between stock and bond markets. *Journal of International Financial Markets, Institutions and Money* 16, 71-86.

Stein, C., 1955. Inadmissibility of the usual estimator for the mean of a multivariate normal distribution. Proceedings of the 3rd Berkeley Symposium on Probability and Statistics. Berkeley, *University of California Press*, 197-206.

Stevenson, S., 2000. Emerging markets, downside risk and the asset allocation decision. *Emerging Markets Review* 2, 50–66.

Stiglitz J.E., 1989. Financial markets and development. *Oxford Review of Economic Studies.*, 85, 156-79.

Stiglitz J.E., Weiss, A., 1981. Credit rationing in markets with imperfect information. *American Economic view* 71, 393-410.

Stulz, R.M., 1999. Globalization, corporate finance, and the cost of capital, Journal of *Applied Corporate Finance* 12, 8-25.

Taylor, M., Sarno, L., 1997. Capital flows to developing countries: Long- and short-term determinants. *The World Bank Economic Review* 11, 451–470.

Timmermann, A., Blake, D, 2005. International Asset Allocation with Time-Varying Investment Opportunities. *The Journal of Business* 78, 71–98.

Tobin, J. 2000. Financial globalization. *World Development* 28, 1100-1104.

Urrutia, J.L., 1995. Test of random walk and market efficiency for Latin American emerging equity markets, *The Journal of Financial Research* 18, 299-309.

Vinh Vo, X., 2005. Determinants of international financial integration. Australasian Financial Research Group - *University of Western Sydney Working Paper.*

Voronkova, S., 2004. Equity market integration in Central European emerging markets: A cointegration analysis with shifting regimes, *International Review of Financial Analysis, Special Issue,* 13-5.

Vu Le, Q., Zal, P.J., 2006. Political risk and capital flight. *Journal of International Money and Finance* 25, 308-329.

Wahab, M., Lashgari, M., 1993. Covariance stationarity of international equity markets returns: recent evidence. *Financial Review* 28, 239-260.

Wheatley, S. 1988. Some tests of international equity integration. *Journal of Financial Economics* 21, 177-212.

Yeldan, E., 2002. Behind the 2000/2001 Turkish crisis: stability, credibility, and governance for whom? Paper presented at the `1.

In: Development Economics Research Trends
Editor: Gustavo T. Rocha, pp. 239-246

ISBN 978-1-60456-172-2
© 2008 Nova Science Publishers, Inc

Chapter 9

GOVERNANCE AND DEVELOPMENT IN DEVELOPING COUNTRIES: AN OVERVIEW OF ISSUES

Kartick C. Roy[1] and Biman C. Prasad[2]
[1]School of Economics, University of Queensland, Brisbane, Australia
[2]School of Economics, University of South Pacific, Suva, Fiji

1. INTRODUCTION

As the number of newly independent countries continues to rise, the need for the World Community to assist the leaders of these countries with finance, technology and other goods and services to enable them to implement development programs to eliminate poverty and to achieve better quality of life for their citizens continues to rise in the world. This kind of help is provided by individual governments and by multilateral agencies. But during the last few decades, the countries, which gained independence, and received substantial amount of international finance and other assistance, have not been able to improve the economic and social conditions of the population. The economic and social condition of the people living in newly independent former breakaway provinces of some sovereign states has become worse than when they were citizens of their former states, although the leaders of these newly independent states immediately sought and received international aid to help rebuild their countries. So where has all the aid money gone? One can then argue that the real reasons for the leaders of a community to seek independence from their former rulers is, perhaps to obtain aid money, a large part of which disappears into their pockets as their personal wealth and to capture the state powers to further their own benefit at the expense of the benefits of the country as a whole.

Many former Soviet Union Republics, Russia, Papua New Guinea, East Timor and many African states are examples of countries in which economic and social conditions of the people at large have significantly worsened after these countries became independent, although these countries received significant amounts of international aid.

If the aid money is misused in this way, then one may legitimately argue that it should be channeled to the newly independent countries only on the condition that this assistance is used productively.

Amongst the developing countries, the more developed ones have achieved progress in economic and human development. While the gap between the potential and actual achievements in growth and development outcomes in these countries is narrowing, the gap still persists and for some of these countries, it is quite large. In terms of economic theory, we can say, that the persistence of a gap between a country's potential output and actual output means that the country is currently at a point inside its production possibility frontier (PPP) and not on the PPP. The reasons are misallocation of resources resulting from inappropriate policy formulation and ineffective policy implementation. These in turn result from inefficient governance of the economy.

Governance failure which results from institutional failure can be blamed for hunger, starvation and poverty malnutrition which contribute to deaths of thousands of adults and children in several African countries, such as Sierra Leone, Rwanda and Ethiopia every year. International organizations (World Bank 2002 and donor governments), accordingly, in recent years have been insisting on the need to improve governance in the economic and political sphere as a pre-condition for the granting and eventual disbursement of any financial assistance to the developing countries. With these comments we now turn to the discussion of the crucial role that "governance" plays in growth and development outcomes of any country.

2. DEVELOPMENT AND GOVERNANCE

While the term "economic development" seems to refer to the rise in economic indicators such as increase in per capita income, employment, increase in the total output, and in the value of the output of manufactured goods, and of exports, increase in the supply of consumer goods to the population and so on, it also implies the improvement in social indicators such as education, health, environment and social freedom of women as well as the improvement in political indicators such as freedom of speech, freedom of the press, freedom of movement and in the representation of the minority and economically weaker members of the community in the political decision making bodies. Apart from the area of social freedom of women, where any improvement requires the action by the society and the state, in all other areas, improvement in social, economic and political well being of people requires effective state action in formulating and implementing appropriate policies to ensure that the outcome is consistent with the goals of the policies.

The state's "governance regime" consists of:

1. formulation of policies;
2. rules and regulations to implement those policies;
3. implementation of those policies and;
4. ensuring that the rules of the game have been followed in implementing any development program.

However, if state institutions are inefficient, appropriate policies to realize the pre-determined development outcomes may not be formulated. Alternatively, even if the policies are appropriate, the goals may not be realized if the state institutions fail to enforce on the players the rules of the game. Hence, divergence appears between the stated goals and the actual results. In our hypothetical case suppose that the government of Pakistan makes a policy decision to improve the infrastructure of all primary schools in the country by renovating existing school buildings, providing each school with tables, chairs, desks, benches, blackboards, text books, and so on with an allocated budget of RS100 million. The government officials in-charge of overseeing the implementation of the program, selects through tender, a private sector company with lowest service delivery charge (10% of the budgeted expenditure, i.e. RS10 million) for improving infrastructure in schools. Hence the private sector contractor is required to spend RS90 million on infrastructure improvement within 6 months from the date of official acceptance of the contract. After 6 months, the contractor submits to the government officer in-charge of the project, a statement of expenditure of RS90 million duly certified by a chartered accountant for the acquittal of the expenditure. However, an investigative journalist after 6 months of investigation reported in a leading national daily that only 40 per cent of RS90 million was actually spent on infrastructure improvement and the other 60 per cent was distributed among the minister in-charge of education who was related to the contractor, the contractor, and the officials in-charge of the project. In this hypothetical case, one can assume that the actual result achieved in infrastructure improvement in primary schools was 60 per cent less than the expected result because of the corruption among the state officials.

In Kenya, "questionable" public expenditures noted by the controller and Auditor General in 1994 amounted to 7.6 per cent of GDP. In Tanzania, service delivery data suggests that bribes paid to officials in the police force, courts, tax services and land offices amounted to 62 per cent of official public expenditures in these areas. In the Philippines, the commission on Audit estimates that $4 billion is diverted annually because of public sector corruption. (Shah and Schacter, 2004). In China hundreds of billions of dollars of national income disappear underground as bribes or due to acts of private predation. A recent World Bank (2004) study shows that corruption hurts growth, impairs capital accumulation, reduces the effectiveness of development aid, and increases income inequality and poverty.

What we can infer from this discussion is that there is an inverse relationship between good governance and corruption; an inverse relationship between corruption and development outcomes; and a positive relationship between good governance and development outcomes; i.e. the higher the quality of governance, the lower the level of corruption and the higher the level of development outcome.

3. GOVERNANCE

Governance can be defined as traditions and institutions by which the authority in a country is exercised for a common good. This includes the process by which those in authority are selected, monitored and replaced (political dimension); the government's capacity to manage its resources effectively and implement sound policies (economic dimension) and the respect of citizens and the state's agents for the country's institutions (Kauffmann 2005).

A sound governance system in accordance with the definition outlined above requires the government of a country to focus on a number of issues. N'Diaye (2001) lists the following four main issues:

1. Transparency of government
    This can be achieved if citizens are kept informed of the decisions of the state and their justification.
2. Simplicity of procedures
    This can be achieved if administrative procedures in all economic, political and social matters are kept as simple as possible, and the numbers of participants are reduced to a minimum.
3. Responsibility
    It can be ensured, if public officials can be held accountable and, if necessary, can be penalized for offences.
4. Fight against corruption
    Without the eradication of corruption, healthy competition cannot be promoted, rent-seeking behaviour cannot be eliminated, and efficiency of economic management cannot be strengthened.

However, the State cannot achieve satisfactory results in all these areas, if the State power is captured by the vested interest groups (North, 1987) within the executive branch of the government and by the agents of these groups
The governance failure therefore occurs due to

1. the lack of information (meaning transparency)
2. the diversion of government's power from pursuing the general welfare to promoting the welfare of some at the expense of others. North's (1987) concern was also echoed by Romer (1998) who commented that the members of a government with powers over economic affairs can easily divert that power from its public purpose and put it to private use.

Thus, while institutions must not be vulnerable to capture by narrow interests, Romer (1988) is quite concerned that a government with extraordinary powers, enhanced by a police force and an army, often damages human welfare intentionally.

4. CORRUPTION

One has to note that the government is made up of people who, like those in any other organization, are welfare maximizing rational individuals but they examine the alternative courses of action available to them and the constraints within which they operate. Therefore, if, with the help of the power of the state, they can enhance their welfare by depriving some people of their legitimate income and wealth and transferring that to others, they will try to bring about such a transfer. This line of argument has also been strongly supported by Olson (1996).

However, the rent seeking behaviour is not confined to government officials alone. The members of the entire executive branch starting from the head of the executive can join hands with members of the bureaucracy to collect rents from the society. The members of the legislature can also engage in corrupt practices and a highly corrupt executive branch of the state can greatly undermine the independence of the judiciary, although it cannot terminate the employment of judges. Even where the judiciary is enforcing rules, the state's credibility can be limited if the public has little reason to believe that the rules will be stable over time (Pradhan, 1997).

5. Causes and Forms of Consumption

Following from this discussion, it can be argued that corruption, which is simply the abuse of public power for private gain, is symptomatic of the more general problem of perverse underlying incentives. Therefore the principal causes of corruption in a country would be the presence of distortions in the policy and regulatory mechanisms, which provide incentives for corruption to flourish and also the presence of weak institutions of restraint. Institutions of restraint will be weak because restrictions on trade and government interventions in the economy are designed in the first place to prevent open trade regime and transparency in economic activities from taking hold in the country.

Empirical Studies (VanRijckghem and Weder, 1997; Mauro, 1998) support the hypothesis that corruption is less where there are fewer restrictions; where governments do not engage in favouritist industrial policies; and perhaps where natural resources are more abundant.

Furthermore, corruption tends to be less in a country where civil servants are paid better compared with similarly qualified workers in the private sector. We do not entirely support the view that lower wages received by bureaucrats relative to those received by private sector employees performing comparable tasks is an important reason for corruption. In fact bureaucrats are sometimes forced to engage in rent seeking activities by their political masters.

Undoubtedly regulations that are complex and hence costly for people and firms to follow can induce bribes or the lobbying activities to bring about changes in regulations or alternatively to get the transactions completed within the shortest possible time by complying with the regulations as well as cutting the red tape with the help of "regulation busters". In Brazil and Russia many groups of people earn their living by organising permits and authorization for the people to adopt unfair means to avoid tax payment. If the tax rates are low and the tax structure is simple, then most people would pay tax and the whole tax avoidance industry will disappear. Similarly public transfers and subsidies generate rent-seeking activities. An IMF study (Tanzi and Davoodi, 1997) found that in cases of extreme corruption, expenditure on the maintenance of the physical infrastructure of a country is intentionally neglected so that some infrastructure will need to be rebuilt, thus allowing corrupt officials the opportunity to extract additional commissions from new investment projects.

However, since the existing institutions (rules and regulations) contribute greatly to the bureaucratic corruption, it cannot be completely eliminated unless the rules and regulations are changed. But who is going to change the rules and regulations? These rules and regulations can be changed if those who manage these rules are properly constrained by a rule of law and a press, free of corruption. But Mbaku (1998), referring to the African situation, comments that many of the police officers and judges who are called upon to clean up corruption are themselves beneficiaries of the system of resource allocation.

6. Forms of Corruption

Corruption generally takes the following forms (Shah and Schacter, 2004):

1. Bureaucracy or administrative corruption.
    This type of corruption occurs when public officials who abuse their office by demanding bribes and kickbacks diverting public funds or awarding favours in return for personal considerations.,
2. Massive Corruption
    This occurs when massive amounts of public resources are misused by state officials associated with political or administrative elites.
3. State Capture
    This occurs when private citizens, in any capacity (entrepreneurs, company executives etc) collude with state officials and political leaders to capture executive and judicial apparatus for their own purposes. After the state power is captured by private sector individuals, public officials still may extort private sector individuals and business for their private gains.

All these forms of corruption usually gather strength in highly corrupt countries where:

1. the community at large has lost its faith in the capacity of the state to rise above the private interest to protect the broader public interests
2. the law is enforced for furthering one person's private interest at the expense of another person's private interest or at the expense of public interest;
3. judiciary cannot enforce the rule of law through the police force, which itself acts as a law breaker rather than law enforcers, and
4. the institutions of accountability are ineffective.

7. Consequence of Corruption

Corruption undoubtedly reduces economic growth by lowering incentives for both domestic and foreign entrepreneurs to invest in a country.

A sizeable portion of the country's GDP is produced underground i.e. in the black economy. The black economy operates in most countries. In a country, the size of the GDP produced in the underground economy and its official GDP together would represent the GDP that the country actually produces, but corruption prevents the country from making use of this GDP produced in its black economy for improving the quality of life of the population.

In a country where corruption is rampant, the cost of most transactions rises because it includes the normal cost of compliance with the rules and bribe cost. Hence the bribe cost acts as a tax on all activities.

Thus it can be said that corruption reduces growth and development outcomes by lowering the quality of public infrastructure and services, decreasing tax revenue, causing talented people to engage in rent seeking rather than productive activities and distorting the composition of government expenditure to the extent that a part of the income generated in the underground economy goes out of circulation. It represents a leakage in the transformation process of the country's savings into investment and thereby lowering the country's GDP. With a lower amount of money in circulation, the velocity of circulation of money and consequently the price level and inflation rate rise.

The corrupt politicians may spend more public resources on those items, which create opportunities for them to collect substantial bribes and at the same time may seek bribes undercover i.e. away from the watchful eyes of the media. The details of contracts for the purchase of national defense related equipments are usually kept secret by the government.

Mauro's (1998) study based on country comparisons reveals that corruption alters the composition of government expenditure probably more in favour of public investment and less in favour of social sector development such as in education, health, housing, sanitation etc. There is also increasing evidence that education and better health foster economic growth.

One can undoubtedly argue that since corruption along with some form of institutional inefficiency causes a low level of economic growth and development, every developing country must pay greater attention than before to the application of effective measures to substantially curtail the level of corruption.

REFERENCES

Kauffmann, D. (2005) "10 Myths About Governance and Corruption", *Finance and Development*, 42(3) pp.41-43.

Mauro, P. (1998) "Corruption: Causes, Consequences, and Agenda for Further Research", *Finance and Development*, 35(1), pp.11-14.

Mbaku, J.M. (1998) "Bureaucratic Corruption in Africa: The Futility of Cleanups", *Cato Journal*, 16(1), pp.98-118.

N'Diaye, S. (2001) "The Role of Institutional Reforms", *Finance and Development*, 38(4) pp.18-21

North, D. (1987) "Institutions, Transactions and Economic Growth", *Economic Enquiry*, 25, pp.419-425.

Olson, M. (1996) "Big Bills Left on the Sidewalk: Why some Nations are Rich and Others Poor", *Journal of Economic Perspectives*, 10(2), pp.3-24.

Pradhan, S. (1997) "Improving the State's Institutional Capability", *Finance and Development*, 34(3) pp.24-27.

Romer, P.M. (1998) "Economic Growth" in D.R. Henderson, Ed; *The Fortune Encyclopedia of Economics,* New York: Warner Books

Shah, A and M. Schacter (2004) "Combating Corruption: Look Before You Leap", *Finance and Development*, 41(4), pp.40-43.

Tanzi, V and H. Davoodi (1997) "Corruption, Public Investment and Growth", *IMF Working Paper* 97/139, Washington: IMF

Van Rijckeghem and B. Weder (1997) "Corruption and the Rate of Temptation: Do Low Wages in the Civil Service Cause Corruption?" *IMF Working Paper*, 97/73, Washington: IMF.

World Bank, (2002) *World Development Report* 2002, New York: Oxford University Press.

World Bank, (2004) *Mainstreaming Anti-Corruption Activities in World Bank Assistance – A Review of Progress Since 1997*, Washington: World Bank.

INDEX

D

E

H

J

K

S